Child Support Handbook

23rd edition

Updated by Mark Brough

CPAG promotes action for the prevention and relief of poverty among children and families with children. To achieve this, CPAG aims to: raise awareness of the causes, extent, nature and impact of poverty, and strategies for its eradication and prevention; bring about positive policy changes for families with children in poverty; and enable those eligible for income maintenance to have access to their full entitlement. If you are not already supporting us, please consider making a donation, or ask for details of our membership schemes, training courses and publications.

Published by Child Poverty Action Group
30 Micawber Street, London N1 7TB
Tel: 020 7837 7979
staff@cpag.org.uk
www.cpag.org.uk

A CIP record for this book is available from the British Library

ISBN: 978 1 910715 01 7

Child Povery Action Group is a charity registered in England and Wales (registration number 294841) and in Scotland (registration number SC039339), and is a company limited by guarantee, registered in England (registration number 1993854). VAT number: 690 808117

Cover design by Colorido Studios
Internal design by Devious Designs
Content management system by Konnect Soft
Typeset by David Lewis XML Associates Ltd
Printed in the UK by CPI Group (UK) Ltd, Croydon CR0 4YY

The author

Mark Brough is a freelance writer. He previously worked for many years as a welfare rights adviser for people with learning disabilities.

Acknowledgements

A huge debt is owed to Nick Turnill for checking the text of this edition, Edward Jacobs, and to all the authors of previous editions, in particular, Will Hadwen.

Thanks are also due to Alison Key for editing and managing the production of the book, Anne Ketley for compiling the index, and Kathleen Armstrong for proofreading the text.

Finally, thanks are due to Robin van den Hende and colleagues at the Department for Work and Pensions for patiently answering queries and providing helpful information, particularly about the '2012 rules' scheme.

The law described in this book was correct at 1 June 2015.

Contents

Appendices

Abbreviations

CMEC	Child Maintenance and Enforcement Commission
CMED	Child Maintenance and Enforcement Division for Northern Ireland
CMS	Child Maintenance Service
CSA	Child Support Agency
DEO	deduction from earnings order
DLA	disability living allowance
DSDNI	Department for Social Development Northern Ireland
DWP	Department for Work and Pensions
ECJ	European Court of Justice
ECHR	European Convention on Human Rights
ESA	employment and support allowance
EU	European Union
HMCTS	HM Courts and Tribunals Service
HMRC	HM Revenue and Customs
IB	incapacity benefit
ICE	Independent Case Examiner
IMA	interim maintenance assessment
IMD	interim maintenance decision
IS	income support
JSA	jobseeker's allowance
NI	national insurance
PAYE	Pay As You Earn
PC	pension credit
PIP	personal independence payment
RPC	regular payment condition
SAYE	Save As You Earn
UC	universal credit
WTC	working tax credit

Part 1

Introduction

Chapter 1

. . . .

Introduction

This chapter covers:
1. What is child support (below)
2. Calculating child support: the different statutory schemes (p4)
3. Responsibility for the statutory child support system (p5)
4. Arrangements in Northern Ireland (p7)
5. Using this *Handbook* (p8)

1. What is child support

Child maintenance paid by parents who do not live with their children is intended to reflect their legal responsibility to provide financial support for their children. Some people make voluntary arrangements to pay maintenance, others have arrangements made by a court order, and some people have maintenance calculated and enforced under the statutory schemes run by the Department for Work and Pensions. Some people may pay or receive child maintenance in more than one of these ways.

Throughout this *Handbook*, the term **'child support'** is used to refer to maintenance calculated and enforced under the statutory schemes. **'Child maintenance'** is used as a generic term for all types of child maintenance, including child support, voluntary agreements and payments made under a court order.

Responsibility for child maintenance

Both parents of a child have a legal duty to contribute to the maintenance of that child.[1] This duty is fulfilled when a parent who does not have the main care of a child makes payments of child support.[2]

This duty applies whether or not:
- the child is living with the other parent or with someone else who is not legally her/his parent; *or*
- the child is living with a lone parent or with a couple; *or*
- the child's parents are on benefit.

2. **Calculating child support: the different statutory schemes**

The statutory child support system has been in operation since 1993. This calculates the amount of child support people have to pay in different situations. There are three different statutory schemes.

- **The '1993 rules'.** The original scheme introduced in 1993 uses a complex formula for calculating child support (the '1993 rules' formula) with several steps to work out how much child support should be paid. An application can be made for departure from the formula in certain circumstances. For a summary of the '1993 rules', see Chapter 10. For full details, see previous editions of this *Handbook*.
- **The '2003 rules'.** The original scheme was replaced by a simpler calculation from 3 March 2003. The '2003 rules' use one of four rates of child support for each non-resident parent, based on her/his net income (see Chapter 8). The calculation can be varied in certain circumstances (see Chapter 9). These rules mostly apply to applications made on or after 3 March 2003. Many applications made before this date are still dealt with under the '1993 rules', but some cases may have been converted to the '2003 rules'. See Chapter 10 of the 2013/14 edition of this *Handbook* for details.
- **The '2012 rules'.** A new system of calculating child support began to be introduced on 10 December 2012, and since 25 November 2013 all new applications (and some existing cases linked to new applications) have been dealt with under this system (see Chapter 5). The '2012 rules' calculation is similar to the '2003 rules' calculation, but is based on gross income and has other significant differences. The calculation can be varied in certain circumstances (see Chapter 7). Fees now apply to cases dealt with under the '2012 rules' (see Chapter 5).

Which set of rules a case comes under is important, not only because it determines how much child support should be paid, but also because there are some differences in how other aspects of child support apply – eg, enforcement. In addition, the legislative references are often different. All three schemes have been amended since they were introduced.

Note: all child support cases will eventually be dealt with under the '2012 rules'. All existing '1993 rules' and '2003 rules' cases will be closed over the period up to 2017, and parents will be invited to make their own arrangements for child maintenance or make a new application to the statutory system under the '2012 rules' (see Chapter 5).

3. **Responsibility for the statutory child support system**

The Department for Work and Pensions (DWP) is responsible for operating the statutory child support system in Great Britain. The DWP's aim is to maximise the number of effective maintenance arrangements that are in place.[3] The DWP took on this responsibility directly on 1 August 2012, when the Child Maintenance and Enforcement Commission (CMEC) was abolished.[4] CMEC was responsible for the statutory child support system in Great Britain from 1 November 2008 until 31 July 2012.

The change in responsibility for the system from CMEC to the DWP has not changed the way cases are dealt with. Anything done by CMEC before it was abolished remains valid. Any decisions that were in the process of being made, or actions being done, by CMEC when it was abolished are now made/done by the DWP.[5]

The child support schemes operate through two child maintenance services staffed by the DWP:

- the **Child Maintenance Service** (CMS), dealing with applications under the '2012 rules'; *and*
- the **Child Support Agency** (CSA), continuing to deal with cases under the '1993 rules' and the '2003 rules', and collecting and enforcing child support calculated under these rules.

The DWP is also responsible for the **Child Maintenance Options** service (see p6), which provides information and support.

The Child Maintenance Service and the Child Support Agency

The CMS and CSA are responsible for calculating child support payments and, in some cases, their collection and enforcement. This includes tracing non-resident parents and investigating parents' means.

All new applications are dealt with by the CMS under the '2012 rules'. If an existing application to the statutory child support system is still covered by the '1993 rules' or '2003 rules', parents continue to deal with, and receive letters from, the CSA. CMS and CSA staff work in the same offices. However, CSA staff work only on '1993 rules' and '2003 rules' cases, and CMS staff only on '2012 rules' cases. Each service operates with a separate computer system. When the process of closing '1993 rules' and '2003 rules' cases is completed (expected to be in 2017), all cases will be dealt with by the CMS.

The staff are divided into six regional business units (see Appendix 1). Each business unit has a regional office, which assesses child support.

There are also local offices, called local service bases or field offices. These may be used to conduct face-to-face interviews with parents, although most contact is done by telephone.

The CMS and CSA have wide powers to gather information. These are covered in Chapter 4. If a parent is unhappy with a child support decision, s/he may be able to challenge it (see Chapter 12) or appeal against it (see Chapter 13). A complaint about the service provided by the CMS or CSA can also be made (see Chapter 15).

The CMS and CSA work closely with Jobcentre Plus, which is responsible for identifying when a parent with care claims benefit. Jobcentre Plus staff pass the parent with care's details to the Child Maintenance Options service, which then contacts her/him to discuss the different options for pursuing child maintenance.

Child Maintenance Options

The DWP is responsible for the Child Maintenance Options service, which provides information and support.

Child Maintenance Options offers free, impartial information and support to help parents make informed choices about child maintenance arrangements. It can be used by separating and separated parents, as well as by family, friends, guardians and anyone with an interest in child maintenance.

Child Maintenance Options is intended to be the first port of call for anyone seeking information on child maintenance. Parents are required to contact the service before making a new application to the statutory schemes (see p42).

Child Maintenance Options can provide information and assistance with:[6]

- setting up a child maintenance arrangement following separation;
- establishing child maintenance arrangements for parents who are not in a relationship;
- switching from a private arrangement to an application under the statutory schemes, or vice versa;
- situations in which an existing child maintenance agreement has broken down or is not working well.

The service is delivered by telephone, via a website and through a face-to-face service if required. See Appendix 1 for contact details. It seeks to encourage voluntary maintenance arrangements by offering estimated calculations based on the statutory schemes, and other guidance to help parents decide on maintenance arrangements and amounts. It also provides information on other related areas, such as housing, employment and money, and can put people in touch with specialist advice agencies.

Child Maintenance Options can be used anonymously and records are not linked, so if two parties contact the service independently in relation to the same child(ren), no information about one party will be divulged to the other. The website includes leaflets explaining how personal information will be used[7] and how to complain about the service (see Chapter 15).[8]

4. **Arrangements in Northern Ireland**

The child support system is largely the same throughout the UK, but Great Britain and Northern Ireland are treated as two separate territories for child support purposes.

There is a separate Child Maintenance and Enforcement Division (CMED) for Northern Ireland, now also known as the Child Maintenance Service. It is part of the Department for Social Development (DSDNI). There is also an information and support service, known as Child Maintenance Choices, providing impartial information and support in a similar way to Child Maintenance Options. CMED's powers are the same as those of the Child Maintenance Service and Child Support Agency in England, Scotland and Wales. Also part of DSDNI is the Social Security Agency, the Northern Ireland equivalent of Jobcentre Plus.

If this *Handbook* is being used in Northern Ireland, references to the Department for Work and Pensions should be read as references to the DSDNI, and references to Jobcentre Plus should be read as references to the Social Security Agency. **Note:** some legislative references are different in Northern Ireland.

If an application is made to the statutory child support schemes and the person with care, non-resident parent and qualifying child do not all reside in the same territory, there are special rules to determine how the application is dealt with.

Applications under the '2012 rules' are generally dealt with by the territory where the non-resident parent named in the application lives. They are dealt with by the territory in which the applicant lives until the address of the non-resident parent is verified and, if the applicant lives in Great Britain, any application fee due is paid. If the same non-resident parent is also named in an existing '1993 rules' or '2003 rules' case, the '2012 rules' case is transferred to the territory in which the non-resident parent lives once the existing case has closed. If a '2012 rules' application is being made as part of the case closure process (see p83), the new application is transferred to the territory in which the non-resident parent lives once the existing case has closed.[9]

Cases under the '1993 rules' and '2003 rules' are dealt with by the agency of the territory where the person with care lives.[10]

Any calculation made must take into account the rules of the other territory.[11] Because the rules for calculating child support in the two territories are very similar, this should not, in practice, make any difference.

5. **Using this** *Handbook*

This *Handbook* deals mainly with the rules of the statutory child support schemes and how they are operated by the Child Maintenance Service (CMS) and Child Support Agency (CSA). It is intended to help parents who use these schemes and their advisers. It covers the child support scheme in England, Wales and Scotland as at 1 May 2015. Separate chapters detail how child support is worked out under the '2012 rules' and the '2003 rules', and provide a summary of the '1993 rules' formula. All other chapters relate to all three sets of rules.

Structure of the book

Part 1 is an introduction to child support. It explains how to use this *Handbook* and provides definitions of some of the main terms used in the child support schemes. **Part 2** explains how applications are made and how the CMS and CSA seek information. Once all the information is available, the amount of child support can be worked out. **Part 3** explains how this is done under the '2012 rules'. The closure of existing cases and full transition to the '2012 rules' is also covered. **Part 4** explains how the amount of child support is worked out under the '2003 rules', and **Part 5** summarises the '1993 rules' formula. For full details and examples that show how the various elements of the '1993 rules' formula are worked out, and for how '1993 rules' cases may have converted to the '2003 rules', see previous editions of this *Handbook*. **Part 6** covers decisions and how to change, query or challenge them, the collection and enforcement of child support, and how to complain.

The **appendices** contain useful addresses and information about reference materials.

The best way to find the information you need is to use the **index** at the back of the book.

Footnotes

Footnotes at the end of each chapter contain the legal authorities, relevant caselaw, other sources of information that support the text, and any further information. These can be quoted to the CMS/CSA if the statement in the text is disputed. Appendix 5 explains the abbreviations used in the footnotes, with information on how to obtain the sources.

The Department for Work and Pensions (DWP) does not publish the guidance used in making child support decisions. As the guidance is not readily available, this *Handbook* generally avoids using it as a source. The guidance can, however, be obtained by making a request to the DWP under the Freedom of Information Act 2000. Anyone concerned about the application of a particular aspect of the law may wish to ask the CMS/CSA to provide a copy of any guidance it has taken into account when making the decision.

Notes

1. **What is child support**
   1 s1(1) CSA 1991
   2 s1(2) and (3) CSA 1991

3. **Responsibility for the statutory child support system**
   3 *Government Response to Consultation on the Abolition of CMEC*, DWP, March 2012
   4 Arts 2 and 3 PB(CMEC)O
   5 Art 5 PB(CMEC)O
   6 *Information for Parents Living Apart From Their Child*, CMO, March 2014
   7 *How Child Maintenance Options Uses Your Personal Information*, CMO, November 2013
   8 *How to Complain about Child Maintenance Options*, CMO, November 2013

4. **Arrangements in Northern Ireland**
   9   Sch 1 Art 5(8)-(8D) CS(NIRA) Regs, inserted by Sch 1 CS(NIRA)(A) Regs 2014
   10 Sch 1 Art 5(5) CS(NIRA) Regs
   11 Sch 1 Art 5(4) and (7) CS(NIRA) Regs

Chapter 2

Child support terminology

This chapter covers:
1. Parent (p11)
2. Qualifying child (p13)
3. Person with care (p14)
4. Non-resident parent (p17)
5. Shared care (p21)
6. Relevant person or 'party' (p23)
7. Relevant child and stepchild (p23)
8. Family and second family (p24)
9. Relevant week (p25)
10. Maintenance period (p26)
11. Welfare of the child (p27)

This chapter explains some of the main terms that are used most frequently throughout this *Handbook*. Where terms are used in different ways for '2012 rules', '2003 rules' and '1993 rules' cases, this is explained.

Throughout this *Handbook*, the term 'child support' is used for maintenance calculated under the statutory schemes administered by the Child Maintenance Service and the Child Support Agency. 'Child maintenance' is used as a generic term for all types of child maintenance, including child support, voluntary agreements and payments made under a court order. Where the statutory scheme uses the word 'maintenance' (eg, 'default maintenance decisions'), an explanation is provided if necessary to make clear what relates to child support and what relates to maintenance in general.

Around 95 per cent of people with the care of a qualifying child are women. However, the rules apply in the same way whatever the gender of the person with care or non-resident parent, or if both parents are men or both are women. The various parties are, therefore, referred to in a gender-neutral way in this *Handbook* wherever possible.

1. **Parent**

A 'parent' is a person who is legally the mother or father of the child.[1] This includes:
- a biological parent;
- a parent by adoption;[2]
- a parent under a parental order (used in surrogacy cases).[3]

If a child was conceived by artificial insemination or *in vitro* fertilisation:
- the mother is the woman who gave birth to the child (wherever in the world the insemination or fertilisation took place),[4] unless an adoption order or parental order is made;[5]
- the father is the man who provided the sperm (but see below).

If the insemination or *in vitro* fertilisation took place on or after 1 August 1991 but before 6 April 2010, the father is:
- the mother's husband, unless he did not consent to[6] or died before insemination;[7] *or*
- if the insemination was during licensed treatment services provided for the mother and a man, that man.[8] The man and woman must have received treatment services together.[9] This rule does not apply to a woman inseminated or fertilised outside the UK.[10]

From 6 April 2009, in the case of assisted reproduction:[11]
- a man who is married to the mother is the father unless he did not consent;
- if a man and woman are not married and the woman has a child as a result of licensed treatment, the man is the father if there is a notice of consent between them.

Two women who are married or are civil partners are treated in the same way as a man and woman who are married – ie, if one partner gives birth to a child as a result of donor insemination (anywhere in the world), she is the mother of the child and her partner is automatically the other parent, unless she did not consent to the mother's treatment.[12]

An **adoption order** means the child is, in law, the child of the adopter(s).[13] The liability of a biological parent to maintain her/his child ends on adoption, and the parent(s) by adoption become the only people liable to maintain the child.

A person who has legal parental responsibility[14] is not necessarily a parent for child support purposes.[15] For example, a step-parent who has acquired parental responsibility (except one assumed to be a parent under the rules below) cannot be required to pay child support.[16] The courts could, however, order her/him to pay maintenance.

A **foster parent** is not a parent for child support purposes because the child has been placed with her/him by a local authority (see p14).

When someone is assumed to be a parent

If a person denies being the parent of a child, the Child Maintenance Service (CMS) or Child Support Agency (CSA) must assume that the person is a parent of the child (unless the child has subsequently been adopted by someone else) if:[17]

- in England, Wales or Northern Ireland, a declaration of parentage or, in Scotland, a declarator of parentage, is in force for that person. This includes situations where the person with care or the CMS/CSA has applied to court for a declaration on whether the person is a parent of the child;[18]
- in Scotland,[19] England and Wales,[20] the person is a man who:
  - was married to the mother at any time between the child's conception and birth; *or*
  - acknowledged his paternity *and* was acknowledged by the mother *and* was named as the father on the birth certificate issued in the UK;
- the person is a man who was found to be the father by a court in England or Wales in proceedings under certain legal provisions (see Appendix 2). The court decision usually states the legal provision under which it was made;[21]
- the person is a man who was found by a court in Northern Ireland to be a father in proceedings under similar legal provisions to those in Appendix 2;[22]
- the person is a man who was found by a court in Scotland to be the father in any action for affiliation or aliment;[23]
- the person is a man who refuses to take a DNA test, or if the results of the test show that he is the father (even if he refuses to accept it);[24]
- a parental order has been made in favour of that person following an application made within six months of a birth which is the result of a surrogacy arrangement;[25]
- certain types of fertility treatment have been carried out by a licensed clinic and the person is treated as a parent of the child under the Human Fertilisation and Embryology Acts 1990 and 2008.[26]

If none of the above applies, the CMS/CSA cannot make a calculation until parentage is admitted by a person or decided by a court.

The rules above apply even if parentage was not disputed in the proceedings.[27] If the alleged non-resident parent disputes that the rules apply (eg, s/he says the person named in a court order is someone else), s/he can appeal against the CMS/CSA decision. This appeal is dealt with by a magistrates'/sheriff court rather than by the First-tier Tribunal (see also p63).[28]

If the alleged non-resident parent accepts that the rules apply, but disputes the correctness of the court order referred to by the CMS/CSA (eg, the court declaration/declarator of parentage was wrong), s/he should consider applying to the court to set aside its order and/or making a late appeal against it. Parentage cannot be disputed through the revision and appeals process for challenging CMS/CSA decisions.

If no one is assumed to be the other parent under these rules, the CMS/CSA usually attempts to arrange voluntary DNA testing or applies to court for a declaration/declarator of parentage. See p63 for further details on parentage investigations.

2. **Qualifying child**

Child support is only payable for a 'qualifying child'. A child is only a **'qualifying child'** if one or both of her/his parents are non-resident parents (see p17).[29]

A **'child'** is defined as a person who is:[30]

- under 16 years of age; *or*
- a young person aged 16–19 inclusive, who meets certain qualifying conditions (see below).

Even if a person falls into one of these groups, s/he is not a child if s/he is, or has been, married or in a civil partnership. This applies even if the marriage or civil partnership has been annulled or was never valid – eg, because s/he was under 16.[31]

The qualifying conditions are that:[32]

- child benefit is payable in respect of the young person; *or*
- the young person is receiving full-time, non-advanced education.

Since 10 December 2012, the upper age limit for a young person to be a qualifying child for child support purposes has been her/his 20th birthday. This aligns the definition of qualifying child with child benefit rules.

Note: child benefit just has to be 'payable' for the young person, not actually paid. If a person has elected not to receive payments of child benefit for a young person because s/he would be liable to the 'high income child benefit charge' in income tax, child benefit is still treated as payable in respect of her/him. 'Payable' means properly and lawfully payable, so a young person may not be a qualifying child if child benefit is being paid for her/him in error.[33]

See CPAG's *Welfare Benefits and Tax Credits Handbook* for full details of the rules for child benefit.

Full-time, non-advanced education

A course is **non-advanced** if it is up to A level or higher level Scottish Certificate of Education (this includes Scottish advanced higher level and a national diploma or certificate). Courses of degree level and above (and DipHE, higher national diploma or certificate, or a higher diploma or certificate) count as advanced education.[34]

The child must attend a recognised educational establishment (such as a school, college or university) *or* the education must be recognised by the Child Maintenance Service (CMS) or Child Support Agency (CSA). The CMS/CSA can only recognise such education if it was being provided for the young person immediately before s/he reached 16.[35]

The CMS/CSA must treat a child as receiving **full-time** education if s/he attends a course with more than 12 hours of weekly contact time. Contact time includes teaching, supervised study, exams and practical or project work which are parts of the course. It does not include meal times or unsupervised study, whether on or off school premises. It is the hours of education received that count, not the hours of attendance.[36]

If a child is not attending such a course (eg, if the contact time is less than 12 hours), the CMS/CSA must look at all the facts and decide whether the education is full time.[37]

After leaving school or college, a child still counts as being in full-time education until child benefit stops being paid. This is known as the '**terminal date**'.[38]

Breaks in full-time education

If a young person is no longer treated as a qualifying child, s/he can regain this status in certain circumstances. Someone at school or college still counts as a child if there is a temporary break in full-time education.[39] It does not matter whether s/he is under or over 16 when education is interrupted. A break of up to six months can be allowed. The CMS/CSA can allow longer if the break is due to an illness or disability of the young person.

For someone to continue to count as a child, any breaks in full-time education must not be followed by a period during which child benefit stops being payable.[40]

3. **Person with care**

A '**person with care**' is the person with whom a child has her/his home (see below) and who usually provides day-to-day care (see p15) for the child.[41] This means a person who actually and usually provides day-to-day care in practice, and may not necessarily be someone who has parental responsibility for the child. What is 'usual' is a question of fact and takes time to evolve.[42] There may be more than one person with care of a particular child.[43]

A person with care is usually a parent of the child or another individual who provides day-to-day care for the child, but could also be, for example, an organisation such as a children's home. However, a local authority, or someone looking after a child who has been placed with her/him by the local authority, *cannot* be a person with care.[44] The only exception to this rule is if someone in England and Wales is the child's parent and the local authority has allowed a child it looks after to live with her/him.[45]

Note: for '2012 rules' cases, the Child Maintenance Service (CMS) uses the term 'receiving parent' instead of 'person with care' in its leaflets and letters. 'Person with care' is, however, still the term used in the legislation.

Home

The person with care must have a home with the child. A **'home'** is the physical place where the child lives. It is different from a household (see p18). Where a child has her/his home is usually clear. A child may have more than one home – in which case, the CMS or Child Support Agency (CSA) decides which is the principal home.[46]

Day-to-day care

For the purpose of deciding who is a 'person with care' and, therefore, who can receive child support, **'day-to-day-care'** is not formally defined. The ordinary definition of the phrase should be used for this purpose. In many cases, who has day-to-day care of a qualifying child will be clear.

Where care is shared, however, it may be less clear. All three schemes have rules for dealing with the situation in which two or more people living in different households each provide day-to-day care for the same child and at least one of those people is the child's parent. If a parent provides day-to-day care to a lesser extent than another person, s/he is treated as a non-resident parent (see p19).

For a person to count as providing day-to-day care **under the '2003 rules' and '1993 rules'**, s/he must provide care, on average, for at least 104 nights a year.[47] In some cases, this means that there may be no one providing day-to-day care for a particular child. **Under the '2012 rules'**, 'day-to-day care' is not defined.

In deciding whether a person provides 'day-to-day care', the CMS/CSA should consider the overall care arrangements for the child. A person who is responsible for a child's daily routine may be providing day-to-day care, even if some things are done by another person – eg, a childminder. For the '2003 rules' and '1993 rules', it may not be necessary for a person to be *with* the child for at least 104 nights a year if s/he is nevertheless the person responsible for overall care during that time. What matters is the degree to which a person continues to exercise control over the child and to be responsible for the child's behaviour and protection.[48] Changes in the pattern of care may be grounds for a supersession.

In some cases, care may be shared according to its everyday meaning, but both parents are not providing day-to-day care according to the definition. For example, if a mother provides care during the day but her children sleep at their father's home, each may care for the children an equal number of hours a week, but because they are not both providing day-to-day care according to the definition for the '2003 rules' and '1993 rules', the rules cannot be used to treat one of them as a non-resident parent. No calculation or assessment should be carried out. In a case like this, the CSA may argue that the father is the parent with care and the mother is the non-resident parent, because she does not have day-to-day care. If this happens, she should challenge the decision on the basis that the definition of day-to-day care based on overnight care is not intended to be used to decide whether someone is a person with care, but just for the special cases where two or more people each have day-to-day care (which is not the case in this example, using the 104-night definition).[49]

Example 2.1

A mother on night shifts leaves her son in the care of grandparents for 22 nights a month. She decides what he eats and when he goes to bed, and each morning she dresses him and takes him to school. Using the ordinary meaning of these words, she is the principal provider of day-to-day care (even though she does not provide overnight care for at least 104 nights a year).

If a change in the pattern of care occurs, the CMS/CSA should be informed, as this may be grounds for a supersession.

Example 2.2

John and Aneela are separated. John only looks after their children for six weeks in the school holidays. He is not accepted as a person with care. However, he could request a supersession during the summer holidays on the grounds that he is now a parent with care and a shorter period should then be used to calculate who has day-to-day care to reflect the current arrangement. It is unlikely that this would be grounds for supersession if the six-week period had already been taken into account. However, if the arrangement for the holiday had not been known at the time, this may be successful. If day-to-day care were to be reassessed over the summer holidays, John would become the parent with care and Aneela the non-resident parent. (John may also be able to apply for child support from Aneela.) **Note:** the relevant week in this case is the seven days preceding the request for a supersession. In a '2003 rules' or '1993 rules' case, the request, therefore, should not be made right at the beginning of the summer holiday.

If a supersession cannot be carried out, John remains the non-resident parent over the holiday when he has the children full time. He is liable to continue paying Aneela the full level of child support, even for those weeks the children spend with him. John and Aneela may be able to come to a voluntary arrangement to reflect John's level of care over this time, but this may not be financially viable.

For all three sets of rules, in certain situations the care actually being provided does not matter. If a child is placed with her/his parent by a local authority in England and Wales, even though the local authority is legally responsible, the parent is treated as providing day-to-day care.[50] If a child is a boarding-school boarder or a hospital inpatient, the person who would otherwise provide day-to-day care is treated as providing day-to-day care.[51] In the case of boarding school, the person who is treated as having day-to-day care for such periods need not be the person who pays the school fees.[52]

In '2003 rules' cases only, if a child is temporarily in someone else's care, whoever would otherwise have day-to-day care is treated as providing care.[53]

Parent with care

A 'parent with care' is a person with care who is also a parent (see p11) of a qualifying child (see p13).[54]

However, if there is a shared care situation, someone who might otherwise be a parent with care may be treated as a non-resident parent (see p19).

4. Non-resident parent

A 'non-resident parent' is a parent (see p11) who is not living in the same household (see p18) as her/his child, and the child has her/his home with a person with care (see p14) – eg, where the parents of a child have separated.[55] Both parents of a 'qualifying child' (see p13) are responsible for maintaining her/him,[56] but the Child Maintenance Service (CMS) or Child Support Agency (CSA) can only require a non-resident parent to pay child support. In cases where people share the care of a child, a person who would otherwise be classed as a parent with care may be treated as a non-resident parent (see p19).[57] If a parent thinks that a decision that s/he is a non-resident parent is wrong, s/he should seek advice.

Both parents can be non-resident parents, in which case they can both be required to pay child support to a person with care – eg, to a grandparent who provides day-to-day care for a child.[58]

If a step-parent adopts a child and, therefore, legally replaces a biological parent, there may be no non-resident parent.[59]

In '2012 rules' and '2003 rules' cases, a calculation may cease to have effect because of a reconciliation during which the parent with care and non-resident parent are living together, since this means that the non-resident parent is no longer non-resident. How soon this happens depends on the circumstances – eg, the nature of the reconciliation and the intentions of the parties. It may mean that the calculation ceases to have effect immediately.

In '1993 rules' cases, an assessment ceases to have effect if the parent with care and non-resident parent have been living together for a continuous period of

2

six months. A shorter period of cohabitation may not result in the assessment being cancelled, even though there may technically be no parent who is non-resident for this period.[60]

Note: 'absent parent' is the term used in '1993 rules' cases. The CMS uses the term 'paying parent' in its leaflets and letters for '2012 rules' cases, although 'non-resident parent' is still the term used in the legislation for the '2012 rules'. 'Non-resident parent' is used throughout this *Handbook* for simplicity.

Household

'**Household**' is not defined in child support legislation. A household is something abstract, not something physical like a home (see p15). It is either a single person or a group of people held together by social ties.[61] In many cases, whether or not people are members of the same household is obvious. If it is not obvious, the CMS/CSA considers other factors. No one factor on its own should be conclusive. There does not need to be any settled intention about future arrangements for a household to exist.[62]

The meaning of household has been considered in family law and social security cases as well as child support cases, and this caselaw may be used to help make child support decisions. For some of the social security caselaw, see CPAG's *Welfare Benefits and Tax Credits Handbook*.

Guidelines from the caselaw include the following.
- There can be two or more separate households in one house.[63]
- One or more members of a household can be temporarily absent from the home without ending their membership of the household.[64]
- There does not need to be a relationship like marriage for people to share a household – eg, two sisters can form a household.[65]

If there is a polygamous marriage, the CMS/CSA decides whether the qualifying child lives in a different household from at least one of the parents when establishing whether there is a non-resident parent. There can only ever be two legal parents, regardless of the number of partners either parent may have.

A couple may become members of the same household even if they get back together only briefly, assuming that they are hoping the relationship and their domestic arrangements will be indefinite.[66] In this case, a new household could be formed immediately, whether or not it then ceases to exist a few weeks or months later. A household can be formed as soon as people live together intending to form a household, and before they have arranged joint domestic and financial matters.

Advisers should be careful when arguing that a supposed non-resident parent shares a household with a parent with care on benefit. A decision by the CMS/CSA or First-tier Tribunal that the couple share a household for child support purposes is likely to mean that the couple share a household for benefit or tax credit purposes. For more information about cohabitation decisions for benefits and tax credits, see CPAG's *Welfare Benefits and Tax Credits Handbook*.

When a parent with care is treated as a non-resident parent

If parents share the care of a child for whom an application has been made and the CMS/CSA accepts that both parents have 'day-to-day care' (see p15), one of the parents with care must be treated as a non-resident parent in order for there to be a liability to pay child support.[67]

If one of these parents with care is treated as non-resident, the amount of child support s/he must pay to the other parent is worked out as normal. The remaining parent with care does not have to pay child support. See p21 for how the amount of care provided by the parent treated as non-resident affects her/his liability for child support.

Who is treated as the non-resident parent

The parent who provides day-to-day care to a 'lesser extent' is treated as the non-resident parent.[68] A 'lesser extent' could be interpreted as meaning either for fewer *nights* per week on average or fewer *hours* per week on average.

In '2012 rules' cases, overall care arrangements should be considered.

In '1993 rules' and '2003 rules' cases, the number of nights is considered first by the CSA, but it should be argued on the basis of hours if this would give a fairer result. For example, if one parent has a school-age child from 4pm Friday to 8.30am Monday (three nights), it could be argued to be as much care as the other parent who is with the child from 4pm Monday to 8.30am Friday (four nights). It might be possible to argue that the degree of responsibility, as well as the amount of time, is relevant to determining the extent of the care – eg, who buys the child's clothes, who attends school functions or arranges visits to the dentist. These issues need not be raised if both parents agree that the number of nights of care fairly determines the question.

For a parent to count as providing day-to-day care under the '2003 rules' or '1993 rules', s/he must be providing care for at least 104 nights a year, on average. The amount of care can be averaged over a different period than a year if this would be more representative of actual arrangements. The number of nights of care in that period must be in the same ratio as 104 nights is to 12 months – ie, 52 nights in six months, 26 nights in three months, 17 nights in two months or nine nights in a month. A different period may be used – eg, if there is a recent relationship breakdown, a court ruling on residence or contact, or the person now providing day-to-day care has been abroad, in prison, in hospital, away from home or otherwise unable to provide care. If the arrangement has simply been renegotiated between the two parents, written acceptance of this should be provided so that the CSA knows this is now the current arrangement and not a temporary change.

The usual assumption is that the parent who does *not* receive child benefit is providing the lesser amount of care and is, therefore, treated as the non-resident parent. This assumption should only be made if the parents are sharing care equally.[69] This may lead to competing claims for child benefit. If more than one person who is entitled makes a claim for child benefit, an order of priority is used to decide who receives it.[70] For example, the person with whom the child is living has priority over other claimants. If the priority rules do not decide the matter and the entitled claimants cannot come to an agreement, HM Revenue and Customs makes the decision. Priority can be conceded by a higher priority claimant to someone else, in writing.

Note: if a person has elected not to receive payments of child benefit because s/he would be liable to the 'high income child benefit charge' in income tax, child benefit is still treated as payable in respect of the child.[71] See CPAG's *Welfare Benefits and Tax Credits Handbook* for full details of the rules for child benefit.

In '2012 rules' cases, if there is evidence to challenge the assumption that the parent who does *not* receive child benefit is providing the lesser amount of care, the CMS considers whether this shows that one parent is the principal provider of care. If the evidence shows that day-to-day care is shared exactly equally, neither parent is treated as non-resident and so there is no liability for child support. This is the case regardless of the fact that the two parents may have significantly different levels of income. A parent who provides some care can only be treated as a non-resident parent if s/he provides care to a lesser extent than the other parent.[72] In deciding whether care is shared equally, the CMS considers the care arrangements as a whole. Whether or not the number of nights of care is equal is not decisive.

In '1993 rules' and '2003 rules' cases, if care is shared equally, one parent is still treated as the non-resident parent. If care is shared equally and neither parent receives child benefit, the CSA decides who is the principal provider of day-to-day care.[73] The parent who is not the principal provider is treated as non-resident. This situation can result in one parent paying child support to another, even though both provide what appears to be an equal amount of care for the child. This conclusion may be hard for parents to accept, but caselaw has established that it is not irrational or discriminatory.[74]

It is helpful if parents keep a record of the time the children spend in each household, especially if there are changes to the usual pattern of care. The extent of care is measured over the period explained on p15, usually the last year or since a change in the arrangements was made.

Example 2.3

Marcia and Nathan are divorced. They have two children, Oscar (7) and Patrick (5). Every fortnight the children spend five nights with Nathan. The rest of the time they live with Marcia.

Marcia has the children nine out of every 14 nights = approximately 234 nights a year.

Nathan has the children five out of every 14 nights = approximately 130 nights a year.

Do both parents have day-to-day care? Yes (both in terms of an ordinary meaning of day-to-day care for '2012 rules' cases and in terms of the number of nights for '1993 rules' and '2003 rules' cases).

Because Nathan looks after the boys to a lesser extent, he is treated as a non-resident parent and a calculation is carried out to decide how much child support he should pay to Marcia.

Marcia remains a parent with care and has no liability to pay child support.

A year later, Nathan has moved onto shift work. One week he has the children four nights, the second week three nights. Marcia cares for the children the rest of the time. They now share care equally. As Marcia receives child benefit, Nathan is still treated as the non-resident parent.

(If the case came under the '2012 rules', the CMS may accept that care was now shared exactly equally. If so, the calculation would be cancelled.)

There may be cases where each child of a family spends a different amount of time with the two parents – ie, the mother may be treated as the non-resident parent for one child, and the father for the other. If this is the case, the situation is similar to that of a divided family in which different children live full time with different parents (also known as 'split care' – see p270 for '2003 rules' and '2012 rules' cases, and see previous editions of this *Handbook* for details of the '1993 rules'). Two separate calculations are carried out: if the mother cares for the daughter for the greater amount of time, the daughter's child support is worked out with the father treated as the non-resident parent; child support for the son, who spends more time with the father, is worked out with the mother treated as the non-resident parent.

How care provided by a non-resident parent affects child support

As well as being used to decide whether one parent with care can be treated as a non-resident parent, the amount of care provided by a non-resident parent (or a parent who is treated as a non-resident parent) is also used to decide whether the amount of child support the non-resident parent is required to pay can be adjusted (see below for details).

5. **Shared care**

A number of people may be involved in caring for a qualifying child. The term **'shared care'** is used in this *Handbook* to describe a situation where there is more than one person looking after a particular child and those people live in different households. If the people providing care live in the same household (see p18), this is not shared care.[75]

If the non-resident parent provides sufficient care for a qualifying child, this may affect the amount of child support s/he has to pay. To be classed as sharing care under the '2012 rules' or the '2003 rules', a non-resident parent must look after the qualifying child for at least 52 nights a year on average. Under the '1993 rules', s/he must look after the qualifying child for at least 104 nights a year. See p106 and p145 for details of shared care in '2012' rules and '2003 rules' cases respectively. For details of shared care in '1993 rules' cases, see previous editions of this *Handbook*.

The Child Maintenance Service (CMS) or Child Support Agency (CSA) makes a decision on shared care by looking at all the evidence. Oral or written evidence may be accepted. Normally, this information is obtained at the time of the application – ie, from telephone contact with the person with care and non-resident parent or from written material provided by them. The CMS/CSA calculates the amount of shared care by looking at the pattern of care provided or that is expected. Contact arrangements ordered by a court or agreed in writing are only evidence and not decisive proof of the care situation.[76] If the evidence of the person with care and non-resident parent conflicts, further evidence may be required to resolve the issue.

Parents should keep a note of the nights the child spends with them and, in case of dispute, be willing to supply further evidence – eg, a diary. The CMS/CSA (and, in any subsequent appeal, the First-tier Tribunal) must then determine the number of nights spent in each person's care over the period.[77]

For the '2012 rules', the CMS considers the number of nights the non-resident parent is expected to provide care for the 12 months after the effective date (see p106).[78] When considering whether a person provides shared care under the '2003 rules' or '1993 rules', the CSA generally considers the pattern of care over the 12-month period ending with the relevant week, but does not have to.[79] A future period cannot be used but, in '2003 rules' cases only, if there is an intended change, a period before the relevant week may include a care pattern that is closer to the intended new arrangement, and the CSA can use this period rather than the 12 months.[80] If there is a pattern of care over a 12-month period, even if it is occasionally disrupted, a shorter period cannot be used unless there is an intended change in the pattern.[81]

A court should determine contact arrangements and the amount of shared care without regard to the effects on child support liability.[82] Therefore, neither parent can argue that a court should vary an order because of the amount of child support payable.

Note: if a non-resident parent is providing some care but not enough for it to count as 'shared care', there is no adjustment to take account of the level of care s/he provides and s/he is expected to pay the same amount of child support as if s/he were not looking after the child at all. This means, for example, that a parent who provides some regular care for her/his children may pay the same level of child support as one who does not. However, anon-resident parent who provides some care, but not enough for it to qualify as shared care, can apply for a variation or departure on the grounds that the contact costs are 'special expenses'. Under the '2012 rules', a variation for contact costs may be considered even if the contact is also being counted as part of a shared care arrangement. See Chapters 7 and 9 respectively for details on variations under the '2012 rules' and '2003 rules'. See previous editions of this *Handbook* for details of departures under the '1993 rules'.

Note also: under the '2012 rules', if care is shared exactly equally, there is no liability for child support (see p20).

6. **Relevant person or 'party'**

The term **'relevant person'** is used in many of the child support rules to refer to a person who has a direct interest in a particular case – eg, someone who the Child Support Agency must notify that a departure or variation application has been made.[83] It has the same meaning **for both '1993 rules' and '2003 rules' cases.** The relevant persons are:

- the person with care;
- the non-resident parent;
- a parent who is treated as a non-resident parent (see p19);
- a child applicant in Scotland.

In the '2012 rules', the term 'party' is used rather than 'relevant person', but it has the same meaning.[84]

7. **Relevant child and stepchild**

A **'relevant child'** (or 'relevant other child') is the term used by the Child Maintenance Service (CMS) in '2012 rules' cases and the Child Support Agency (CSA) in '2003 rules' cases for a child, other than a qualifying child, for whom the non-resident parent or her/his partner receives child benefit.[85] This can include a child who does not live with the parent all the time – eg, because s/he is at boarding school or there is a shared care arrangement for her/him. This can also include a child for whom the non-resident parent or her/his partner would get child benefit, but for:[86]

- the rules about presence in Great Britain not being met; *or*
- the non-resident parent or her/his partner having elected not to receive child benefit because s/he would be liable to the 'high income child benefit charge' in income tax.

If a relevant child is cared for by a local authority for either some or all of the time, s/he continues to count as a relevant child if the non-resident parent or her/his partner receives child benefit for her/him.[87]

See CPAG's *Welfare Benefits and Tax Credits Handbook* for full details of the rules for child benefit.

The number of relevant children is important because it affects the calculation of child support. In '1993 rules' cases, the term is not used, but children who live with the non-resident parent may affect the assessment in different ways.

The term **'stepchild'** is used in this *Handbook* to describe the child of a person's partner, whether or not they are a married couple or in a civil partnership.

Relevant non-resident child

'Relevant non-resident child' is a term used by the CMS/CSA **in '2012 rules' and '2003 rules' cases** to refer to a child of the non-resident parent for whom an application for child support cannot be made because the non-resident parent is liable to pay maintenance for her/him under a maintenance order (or, in Scotland, registered maintenance agreement), an order of a non-British court, or under the legislation of a country outside the UK.[88] This is a child who would be considered a qualifying child if an application for child support could be made for her/him. It could be a child who does not live with the non-resident parent, or a child whose care is shared between the non-resident parent and someone else in a situation in which the child would be regarded as a qualifying child but for the court order. See p37 for more information about when a court order prevents an application for child support being made.

For the '2012 rules', a child who is not a qualifying child but the non-resident parent is paying maintenance under another maintenance arrangement (eg, a family-based arrangement) for her/him can also count as a relevant non-resident child. The child must be habitually resident in the UK. There is a wide definition of the other arrangements that can qualify, including verbal agreements. The arrangement must be between the non-resident parent and person with care of the relevant child, and must be for regular payments for the benefit of the child. Payments made to third parties can count, as well as those made to the parent with care.[89]

The number of relevant non-resident children is important because it also affects the calculation of child support. Although the term 'relevant non-resident child' is not used in '1993 rules' cases, child maintenance paid under a court order may affect the calculation.

---

8. **Family and second family**

For the purposes of the **'2003 rules'** and **'1993 rules'**, **'family'** is defined as a couple or a single person and any children in the same household for whom the single person, or at least one member of the couple, is responsible.[90] 'Family' is not defined for the **'2012 rules'**.

A **'couple'** is:[91]

- two people who are married to, or civil partners of, each other and are members of the same household; *or*
- two people who are not married to, or civil partners of, each other but are living together as a married couple.

For information on when two people are living together as a married couple, see CPAG's *Welfare Benefits and Tax CreditsHandbook*. The children living with a couple or lone parent do not have to be biological or adopted children to count as family members, but foster children are not included. A person under 16 cannot be a member of a couple.[92]

The term **'second family'** is used loosely in this *Handbook* to describe the situation where a parent of a qualifying child (usually the non-resident parent) also has children who live with her/him. This could be a third or fourth family, or even a first family – eg, if a couple remain together despite one of them having had a child with another person.

Partners

A **'partner'** in the context of this *Handbook* means a married partner living with her/his spouse, a man or woman living with his/her civil partner, or someone living with a partner 'as a married couple' or 'as if they were civil partners'. The definition of partner includes those living in polygamous marriages.[93]

Child support rules were amended from 5 December 2005 to take account of same-sex couples being able to register as civil partners.[94] From this date, civil partners who are parents (including those who have adopted a child) are treated for most child support purposes in the same way as married partners. Parents who are living with a same-sex partner but have not formed a civil partnership are treated in the same way as couples of the opposite sex who are living together but have not married. Before 5 December 2005, same-sex couples were *not* treated as partners.[95] From 13 March 2014 in England and Wales, and from 16 December 2014 in Scotland, child support rules were amended to take account of same-sex couples being able to marry.[96]

9. **Relevant week**

The concept of the **'relevant week'** is important in child support calculations under the '2003 rules' (and assessments under the '1993 rules'), particularly when assessing income. The definitions of 'relevant week' are similar for both '1993 rules' and '2003 rules' cases.[97]

The concept of 'relevant week' is not used in the '2012 rules'. **In '2012 rules' cases**, the 'relevant week' is replaced by the principle that the information taken into account by the Child Maintenance Service when making a decision is the information that applied at the date that decision would have effect.[98]

For '2003 rules' cases:

- on application by the non-resident parent, the relevant week is the seven days immediately before the application is made;
- on application in any other case, the relevant week is the seven days immediately before the date the non-resident parent was first given notice that an application for child support had been made;
- if the original decision is revised (or superseded because of ignorance, a mistake in a material fact or an error in law), the relevant week for the new decision is the same as the original decision;
- if the original decision is superseded because of a change of circumstances, the relevant week is the seven days immediately before the date on which the application to supersede was made;
- if the original decision is superseded by the Child Support Agency (CSA) on its own initiative (except for ignorance, a mistake about a fact or error), the relevant week is the seven days immediately before the date of notification of that intention.

In some cases, the CSA may make separate calculations for different periods in a particular case.[99] If this is because of a change of circumstances, the relevant week for each separate calculation made to take account of the change is the seven days immediately before the date of notification of the change. See Chapter 12 for more information on revisions and supersessions of decisions.

10. **Maintenance period**

Child support is calculated on a weekly basis, although it is not always paid weekly (see p272). It is payable in respect of successive seven-day periods, known as **'maintenance periods'**. The first maintenance period begins on the effective date (see p206).[100]

The date on which many child support decisions take effect is the first day of the maintenance period in which a particular event happens. For example, a supersession generally takes effect on the first day of the maintenance period in which the decision is made (see p228).

The concept of a maintenance period is not used for the '2012 rules'. **In '2012 rules' cases**, decisions generally take effect from the day on which an event happens or a decision is made rather than by referring to the 'maintenance period'.

11. **Welfare of the child**

Whenever the Child Maintenance Service (CMS) or Child Support Agency (CSA) makes a discretionary decision about a case, it must take into account the welfare of any child likely to be affected by the decision.[101] This also applies to discretionary decisions made by the First-tier Tribunal and Upper Tribunal.

Many child support decisions involve choosing between alternatives, such as whether a person is habitually resident or not, but these are not usually discretionary decisions. A person has discretion only if, after deciding on the facts of a case and what the law requires, s/he still has a choice about what decision to make. An example is how to collect or enforce payments, including whether to make a deduction from earnings order.

Because there is usually no discretion about whether or not to make a calculation (or '1993 rules' assessment), or about the amount due, there are only a limited number of cases in which the welfare of a child can make a difference. It is important to give the CMS/CSA full details at the earliest stage about the effect a discretionary decision may have on a child's welfare.

Only the welfare of a child has to be taken into account (see definition of a child on p13), not that of any adults involved. However, it is not just qualifying children or those named in the application who must be considered. The situation of any child likely to be affected by the decision must be looked at – eg, a child of the non-resident parent's new family, known under the '2012 rules' and '2003 rules' as a 'relevant other child', or another child of the non-resident parent who does not live with her/him.[102]

The duty to consider the welfare of children is 'a general principle' in child support law.[103] The legislation does not make it the paramount consideration, or impose a duty on the CMS/CSA or First-tier Tribunal/Upper Tribunal to promote the welfare of any children.[104] However, considerable weight should be given to this.[105] In general, the principle should be considered along with the other principles of child support.[106]

'**Welfare**' includes the child's physical, mental and social welfare. For example, if a deduction from earnings order (see p293) would prevent a non-resident parent from visiting a child, that child's emotional welfare may be affected. However, an order may mean the parent with care has more money coming in, which may improve the child's physical and social welfare.

Generally, the welfare of a child must be balanced with the benefits of child support being paid for that child or other children. It is likely to be rare that the welfare of a child will be deemed to justify a decision or action that is contrary to the principle that parents should support their children. For example, if the non-resident parent has a child in her/his household who is disabled and who would be adversely affected if there were less money to spend on her/his living costs, or adversely affected by the implications of enforcement action, this might mean that certain enforcement action should not be taken. However, when deciding on enforcement action, the CMS/CSA must not use the welfare of the child principle to avoid full use of its powers, unless it is genuinely appropriate.[107]

Reasoning on the welfare of all children who could be affected has to be fully documented, and it may be useful to ask to see these records. If a decision has been made in ignorance of its effect on a child, the information should be supplied and the CMS/CSA asked to reconsider. Some decisions that should involve the welfare of the child principle can be challenged (see Chapters 12 and 13). If the decision cannot be appealed (eg, if it is about enforcement), a CMS/CSA client could consider making a complaint or applying for a judicial review (see p215).

In addition to the general principle of the welfare of children in child support law, the UK is also bound to comply with international obligations, including a commitment to the welfare of children under the United Nations Convention on the Rights of the Child. This means that in instances where more than one interpretation of the law is possible, the one chosen should be that which more closely complies with protecting the welfare of children.[108]

Notes

1. Parent
1 s54 CSA 1991
2 s39 AA 1976; s39 A(S)A 1978; s26(2) CSA 1991 Case A
3 s30 HF&EA 1990; s26(2) CSA 1991 Case B
4 s27(3) HF&EA 1990
5 ss27(2) and 29(1) HF&EA 1990
6 s28(2) HF&EA 1990; *Re CH (Contact: Parentage)* [1996] 1 FCR 768, [1996] 1 FLR 569, [1996] Fam Law 274
7 s28(6) HF&EA 1990
8 s28(3) HF&EA 1990
9 See *Re D (A Child Appearing by her Guardian Ad Litem)* [2005] UKHL 33
10 Because such a clinic would not have a UK licence: *U v W (A-G intervening)* [1997] 3 WLR 739, [1997] 2 CMLR 431 [1997] 2 FLR 282
11 ss35-37 HF&EA 2008
12 s42 HF&EA 2008
13 **EW** s67 A&CA 2002
    S s40 A&C(S)A 2007
    Both s54 CSA 1991, definition of 'parent'
14 **EW** CA 1989
    S C(S)A 1995
15 **EW** s3(4) CA 1989
    S s3(3) C(S)A 1995
16 R(CS) 6/03
17 s26 CSA 1991
18 Under ss55A or 56 Family Law Act 1986, Art 32 Matrimonial and Family Proceedings (Northern Ireland) Order 1989 or s7 LR(PC)(S)A 1986
19 s26(2) CSA 1991 Case E; s5(1) LR(PC)(S)A 1986
20 s26(2) CSA 1991 Cases A1 and A2
21 s26(2) CSA 1991 Case F(a)(i) in 'relevant proceedings' under s12(5) Civil Evidence Act 1968 or affiliation proceedings

22 s26(2) CSA 1991 Case F(a)(i) in 'relevant proceedings' under s8(5) Civil Evidence Act (Northern Ireland) 1971 or affiliation proceedings
23 s26(2) CSA 1991 Case F(a)(ii) in affiliation proceedings
24 s26(2) CSA 1991 Case A3
25 s26(2) CSA 1991 Case B
26 s26(2) CSA 1991 Case B1
27 *R v Secretary of State for Social Security ex parte Shirley West*, CO/568/1998, 30 April 1999, unreported
28 Arts 3 and 4 CSA(JC)O ('1993 rules') and Arts 3 and 4 CSA(JC)O 2002 ('2003 rules'); Art 3(1)(s) and (t) C(AP)O

2. Qualifying child
29 s3(1) CSA 1991
30 s55(1) CSA 1991
31 s55(2) and (3) CSA 1991
32 **2012 rules** Reg 76 CSMC Regs; s142(2) SSCBA 1992; regs 2-7 CB Regs
2003 rules Sch 1 CS(MCP) Regs
1993 rules Sch 1 CS(MAP) Regs
33 *JF v SSWP and DB (CSM)* [2013] UKUT 209 (AAC)
34 Sch 1 para 2 CS(MCP) Regs; CCS/12604/1996
35 **2012 rules** Reg 76 CSMC Regs; s142(2) SSCBA 1992; reg 3 CB Regs
2003 rules Sch 1 para 7 CS(MCP) Regs
1993 rules Sch 1 para 7 CS(MAP) Regs
36 CCS/1181/2005
37 Sch 1 para 3 CS(MCP) Regs; *CF v CMEC (CSM)* [2010] UKUT 39 (AAC); CCS/1181/2005
38 See CPAG's *Welfare Benefits and Tax Credits Handbook* for more details.
39 Sch 1 para 4(1) CS(MCP) Regs
40 Sch 1 para 4(2) CS(MCP) Regs

3. Person with care
41 s3(3) CSA 1991
42 *GR v CMEC (CSM)* [2011] UKUT 101 (AAC)
43 s3(5) CSA 1991
44 s3(3)(c) CSA 1991
2012 rules Reg 78(1)(a) CSMC Regs
2003 rules Reg 21(1)(a) CS(MCP) Regs
1993 rules Reg 51(1)(a) CS(MAP) Regs
45 **2012 rules** Reg 78(1)(b) CSMC Regs
2003 rules Reg 21(1)(b) CS(MCP) Regs
1993 rules Reg 51(1)(b) CS(MAP) Regs
s23(5) CA 1989
46 **2003 rules** Reg 1(2) CS(MCSC) Regs, definition of 'home'. There is no specific definition of this for the '2012 rules'.

47 **2003 rules** Reg 1(2) CS(MCSC) Regs, definition of 'day-to-day care'
1993 rules Reg 1(2) CS(MASC) Regs
48 R(CS) 11/02; *GR v CMEC (CSM)* [2011] UKUT 101 (AAC)
49 *GR v CMEC (CSM)* [2011] UKUT 101 (AAC)
50 **2012 rules** Reg 51 CSMC Regs. This applies where a child is placed under ss22C(2) or 23(5) CA 1989.
2003 rules Reg 13 CS(MCSC) Regs. This applies where a child is placed under s23(5) CA 1989.
1993 rules Reg 27A CS(MASC) Regs
51 **2012 rules** Reg 55 CSMC Regs
2003 rules Reg 12 CS(MCSC) Regs
1993 rules Reg 27 CS(MASC) Regs
52 R(CS) 8/98
53 Reg 1(2)(b)(i) CS(MCSC) Regs, definition of 'day-to-day care'
54 s54 CSA 1991

4. Non-resident parent
55 s3 CSA 1991
56 s1(1) CSA 1991
57 **2003 rules** Reg 8 CS(MCSC) Regs
1993 rules Reg 20 CS(MASC) Regs
58 s1(3) CSA 1991
59 *RW v SSWP (CSM)* [2013] UKUT 576 (AAC)
60 *Brough v Law* [2011] EWCA Civ 1183; *SM v CMEC (CSM)* [2010] UKUT 435 (AAC); *SL v CMEC* [2009] UKUT 270 (AAC). These decisions disagreed with R(CS) 8/99, which held that even a short period of cohabitation would mean that the child ceased to be a qualifying child, leading to the assessment ceasing to have effect.
61 *Santos v Santos* [1972] 2 WLR 889, [1972] All ER 246, CA
62 CCS/2318/1997
63 CSB/463/1986
64 R(SB) 4/83
65 R(SB) 35/85
66 CCS/2332/2006
67 **2003 rules** Reg 8(2) CS(MCSC) Regs
1993 rules Reg 20(2) CS(MASC) Regs
68 **2012 rules** Reg 50(2) CSMC Regs
2003 rules Reg 8(2)(a) CS(MCSC) Regs
1993 rules Reg 20(2)(a) CS(MASC) Regs
69 **2012 rules** Reg 50(3) CSMC Regs
2003 rules Reg 8(2)(b)(i) CS(MCSC) Regs
1993 rules Reg 20(2)(b)(i) CS(MASC) Regs
70 s144(3) and Sch 10 SSCBA 1992

71 **2012 rules** Reg 50(4) CSMC Regs
   2003 rules Reg 8(3)(b) CS(MCSC)
   Regs
   1993 rules Reg 1(2B) CS(MASC) Regs
72 Reg 50(2) CSMC Regs
73 **2003 rules** Reg 8(2)(b)(ii) CS(MCSC)
   Regs
   1993 rules Reg 20(2)(b)(ii) CS(MASC)
   Regs
74 R(CS) 1/09, following R(CS) 14/98

5. Shared care
75 **2012 rules** Reg 50(1)(b) CSMC Regs
   2003 rules Reg 8(1) CS(MCSC) Regs
   1993 rules Reg 20(1) CS(MASC) Regs
76 CCS/2885/2005
77 CCS/11728/1996
78 Reg 46(2) CSMC Regs
79 CCS/128/2001
80 Reg 7(4) CS(MCSC) Regs
81 *SO v CMEC (CSM)* [2011] UKUT 149
   (AAC)
82 *Re B (A Child)* [2006] EWCA Civ 1574

6. Relevant person or 'party'
83 **2003 rules** Reg 9(1)(a) CS(V) Regs
   1993 rules Reg 8(1)(a) CSDDCA Regs
84 Reg 2 CSMC Regs

7. Relevant child and stepchild
85 Sch 1 para 10C CSA 1991
86 Sch 1 para 10C(2)(b) CSA 1991
   2012 rules Reg 77 CSMC Regs
   2003 rules Reg 1(3) CS(MCSC) Regs
87 **2012 rules** Reg 54 CSMC Regs
   2003 rules Reg 10 CS(MCSC) Regs
88 **2012 rules** Reg 52 CSMC Regs
   2003 rules Reg 11 CS(MCSC) Regs
89 Sch 1 para 5A(6)(b) CSA 1991; reg 48
   CSMC Regs

8. Family and second family
90 **2003 rules** Reg 1(2) CS(MCSC) Regs;
   the '1993 rules' definition in Reg 1(2)
   CS(MASC) Regs is equivalent, but
   specifies children for whom the single
   person, or at least one member of the
   couple, has day-to-day care.
91 **2012 rules** Reg 2 CSMC Regs; Sch 1
   para 10C(5) and (6) CSA 1991
   2003 rules Reg 1(2) CS(MCSC) Regs
   1993 rules Reg 1(2) CS(MASC) Regs
92 CFC/7/1992
93 **2012 rules** Reg 2 CSMC Regs; Sch para
   10C(4)(b) CSA 1991
   2003 rules Reg 1(2) CS(MCSC) Regs
   1993 rules Reg 1(2) CS(MASC) Regs

94 CPA 2004; CP(PSS&CS)(CP)O; CPA
   2004 (RACP)O
95 *SSWP v M* [2006] UKHL 11
96 Marriage (Same Sex Couples) Act 2013;
   Marriage (Same Sex Couples) Act 2013
   (Consequential Provisions) Order 2014,
   No.107; Marriage (Same Sex Couples)
   Act 2013 (Consequential and Contrary
   Provisions and Scotland) Order 2014,
   No.560; Marriage and Civil Partnership
   (Scotland) Act 2014 and Civil
   Partnership Act 2004 (Consequential
   Provisions and Modifications) Order
   2014, No.3229

9. Relevant week
97 **2003 rules** Reg 1(2) CS(MCSC) Regs
   1993 rules Reg 1(2) CS(MASC) Regs
98 Reg 5 CSMC Regs
99 Sch 1 Part II para 15 CSA 1991

10. Maintenance period
100 s17(4A) CSA 1991

11. Welfare of the child
101 s2 CSA 1991
102 CCS/1037/1995
103 s2 CSA 1991
104 *Brookes v SSWP* [2010] EWCA 420
105 *R v Secretary of State for Social Security ex
    parte Biggin* [1995] 2 FCR 595, [1995] 1
    FLR 851
106 *Brookes v SSWP* [2010] EWCA 420
107 *Brookes v SSWP* [2010] EWCA 420
108 *Smith v SSWP* [2006] UKHL 35

Part 2

Applications for child support

Chapter 3

Applications

This chapter covers:
1. Who can apply for child support (below)
2. When an application can be accepted (p34)
3. How to apply (p42)
4. Withdrawing or cancelling an application (p47)
5. Multiple applications (p48)
6. Communicating with the Child Maintenance Service and Child Support Agency (p49)

From 25 November 2013, all new child support applications are dealt with by the Child Maintenance Service under the '2012 rules'. This chapter, therefore, mainly covers the process for applications under the '2012 rules'. However, some sections are also relevant to existing cases dealt with under the '2003 rules' or the '1993 rules'.

See Chapter 5 for details of how existing '2003 rules' and '1993 rules' cases are being closed and the parties invited to consider applying under the '2012 rules'.

There may be rare cases where applications under the '2003 rules' or '1993 rules' made some time ago have not yet been fully determined. For full details of the process for dealing with such applications, see previous editions of this *Handbook*.

1. Who can apply for child support

Any person with care (see p14) or non-resident parent (see p17) can apply to the Child Maintenance Service (CMS) for child support – but see p34 for when the CMS can accept an application and make a calculation.[1] In Scotland, children aged 12 or over can apply to the CMS for child support, provided no application has been made, or is treated as having been made, by the person with care or the non-resident parent.[2]

If there are two or more people in different households who each have day-to-day care of a qualifying child and at least one, but not all, of them has parental responsibility for the child, only those with parental responsibility can apply for child support.[3] For example, if a child is cared for partly by her/his mother who has parental responsibility and partly by her/his grandmother who does not have parental responsibility, only the mother can apply. This means that if the person with parental responsibility decides not to apply, another person with care could lose out on child support.

'Parental responsibility' has the same meaning as in other areas of law.[4] Parents who were married to each other when the child was born automatically have parental responsibility, which continues even if they divorce.[5] If the parents are not married, the mother can make a formal agreement giving the father parental responsibility.[6] In addition, in England and Wales, if a child's parent is married to (or in a civil partnership with) someone who is not the child's other parent (ie, a step-parent), the parent (or if both biological parents have parental responsibility, both parents) can make a parental responsibility agreement with the step-parent, giving her/him parental responsibility for the child.[7] The courts can also give parental responsibility to a person (including a non-parent or step-parent) who applies for it.[8]

In England and Wales, if an unmarried father's name appears on a birth certificate on or after 1 December 2003, he has parental responsibility.[9] In Scotland, this applies if an unmarried father jointly registers a birth on or after 4 May 2006.[10] Unmarried fathers who signed a birth certificate before these dates cannot acquire parental responsibility without going through one of the other routes – ie, arranging a formal agreement with the mother or applying for a court order.

A female partner of the mother of a child conceived on or after 6 April 2009 automatically has parental responsibility if her details are included in the birth registration on or after 1 September 2009.[11] If they are not civil partners, the non-birth parent must be present at the registration.

If a birth certificate was issued before these dates, a female partner can only acquire parental reponsibility through one of the other routes.

2. **When an application can be accepted**

There is no obligation to apply to the Child Maintenance Service (CMS) for child support. The government aims to encourage parents to consider other arrangements first and intends the statutory child support scheme to be the option that parents will choose only if other arrangements cannot be agreed. The parties can make an informal arrangement or draw up a written maintenance agreement that may be formalised. However, there are certain circumstances in which the CMS does not have jurisdiction or cannot accept an application.

The CMS cannot make a child support calculation unless the person with care, non-resident parent and qualifying child are all 'habitually resident' in the UK (see p35). If the CMS (or the Child Support Agency (CSA) for an existing '2003 rules' or '1993 rules' case) decides that it no longer has jurisdiction because one of the parties is no longer habitually resident in the UK, the calculation or assessment is cancelled (see p209).

The CMS also cannot accept an application for child support if there are certain maintenance orders made by a court or certain written maintenance agreements for the child(ren) concerned (see p37). If the CMS has jurisdiction to make a calculation, the child support scheme has priority over the court system and there are limits on the role of the courts in relation to child maintenance.

A CMS decision on whether it has jurisdiction (eg, a decision refusing to make a calculation) can be revised (see Chapter 12) and subsequently appealed to the First-tier Tribunal (see Chapter 13).[12] A court ruling that the court has no jurisdiction can be appealed or judicially reviewed (see p215).[13] No case should be outside the jurisdiction of both the CMS and the courts.

Habitual residence

The CMS cannot make a child support calculation unless the person with care, non-resident parent and qualifying child are all 'habitually resident' in the UK.[14]

Relevant other children do not have to be habitually resident in the UK.[15] The person with care does not have to be habitually resident if that 'person' is an organisation.[16]

The UK means England, Scotland, Wales and Northern Ireland (including coastal islands like the Isle of Wight). It does not include the Isle of Man or the Channel Islands.[17]

The government has indicated that, since 18 June 2011, the CMS/CSA has some ability to enforce certain arrears that accrued while both parents were resident in the UK if the non-resident parent now resides in another European Union (EU) country. For the purposes of enforcing child support arrears owed in the UK, the CMS/CSA may also make enquiries about assets a non-resident parent may own in another EU state. The CMS/CSA can also assist parents with care to obtain a court order for ongoing maintenance, which can then be enforced by applying to the Reciprocal Enforcement of Maintenance Orders (REMO) Unit at the Office of the Official Solicitor and Public Trustee in England and Wales, or an equivalent legal mechanism in Scotland.[18]

If a person is not habitually resident in the UK, see p42.

For more information on habitual residence, see CPAG's *Welfare Benefits and Tax Credits Handbook*.

Meaning of habitual residence

A person is habitually resident if s/he is ordinarily resident in the UK and has been so for an appreciable period of time.[19] For child support purposes, habitual residence is considered bearing in mind that the purpose of child support is to require non-resident parents to contribute to the costs of supporting their children.[20] 'Ordinary residence' means 'residence for a settled purpose'.[21]

Each case is different and a decision on habitual residence must take into account all the person's circumstances and intentions. Some of the most important factors that are considered include:

- the person's normal centre of interest or connections to a particular place;
- the length, continuity and purpose of residence in the UK;
- the length and purpose of any absence from the UK; *and*
- the nature of the person's work.

The following principles are some of those that have been established by caselaw. Cases that do not relate directly to child support are 'persuasive', but may not be followed.

- A person can habitually reside in more than one country or in none.[22]
- Habitual residence can continue during an absence from the UK.[23]
- A person cannot be habitually resident in the UK if s/he has never been here.
- A person who leaves the UK intending never to return to reside stops being habitually resident in the UK on the day s/he leaves.[24] The intention never to return must be a settled intention and not to see how things will work out in another country.[25]
- A person held in a country against her/his will may not be habitually resident there, even after long residence (but see below).[26]
- A person unlawfully in the UK may be habitually resident.

If a non-resident parent is not habitually resident in the UK, the CMS still has jurisdiction to make a calculation if s/he is employed by the civil service, the armed forces, a UK-based company, a local authority or the NHS (including trusts).[27]

A person returning to the UK after an absence may have remained habitually resident in the UK during her/his absence.[28] When deciding whether a person has ceased to be habitually resident in the UK for child support purposes, the emphasis should be on the nature and degree of past and continuing connections with the UK, and any future intentions.[29] If the non-resident parent requests a supersession of the calculation because s/he is no longer habitually resident in the UK, the onus is on her/him to prove that this is the case.[30]

Children

For a child, habitual residence depends on where the parent or person with parental responsibility lives. If there are two such people who live apart, one person should get the consent of the other to a change in the residence of the child, otherwise the child may be considered to have been abducted. If there is only one parent or person with parental responsibility, the child's residence changes with that person's.[31]

If a child has been abducted, s/he is considered still to be resident with the person with whom s/he was lawfully living, unless that person later agrees to the move.[32] Agreement might be assumed if that person does not act.[33] However, if a child is of sufficient maturity, her/his views may prevail in a child abduction case.[34]

Written maintenance agreements and court orders

Note: it is advisable to seek legal advice about any court proceedings. The following is not intended to be a comprehensive guide to the law.

Written maintenance agreements

Even if an application could be made to the CMS for child support under the statutory scheme, the parties can choose to make a maintenance agreement.[35] Anyone who considers that s/he would get a better deal from an agreement than under the child support calculation may wish to try to make one. A maintenance agreement made on or after 5 April 1993 cannot prevent any of the parties, or any other person, applying to the CMS for a child who is the subject of the agreement, except if the agreement has been endorsed by a court (see below). Any clause included in the agreement that claims to prevent anyone from applying to the CMS is void.[36]

Certain written maintenance agreements, when endorsed by a court, *do* affect whether an application can be made for child support.

If a maintenance agreement was endorsed by a court in a consent order (or a registered minute of agreement in Scotland) before 3 March 2003, it prevents an application being made to the CMS. Such a consent order or registered minute of agreement made on or after 3 March 2003 prevents a party to the agreement from applying to the CMS for one year from the date it was made (see p38).[37]

- -

Maintenance agreement and consent order

'**Maintenance agreement**' means an agreement for making (or securing the making of) periodic payments of maintenance (or aliment in Scotland) to, or for the benefit of, a qualifying child.[38] This does not include any agreement to make a lump-sum payment (a 'capitalised payment'), even if this is intended to be the equivalent of regular child maintenance payments for a future period.[39]

A '**consent order**' is an order made by the court with the written consent of both parties. It is legally binding and can be enforced like any other court order and cannot be changed by one party without the court's permission.

- -

Parents who want a consent order should seek assistance from a family law solicitor to turn their agreement into a draft order to be submitted to the court. This is because a consent order must be made as part of a formal application to the court and must refer to the family law provisions under which it is made. The wording of the order is important – eg, a consent order containing an order to provide maintenance for the parent with care, and undertakings to provide maintenance for the children, may not prevent a calculation by the CMS.[40] However, in some circumstances, both undertakings and orders can be interpreted as a whole without any distinction.[41]

The court can also use its powers to vary an existing agreement(whenever made) by *increasing* periodic child maintenance due under that agreement,[42] but not by *adding* a requirement to pay periodic child maintenance, unless the parties give their written consent.[43] A person who does not want to apply to the CMS, or who is waiting for a CMS decision, can go back to court to increase (or reduce) maintenance. This is especially important if it is unclear whether the CMS has jurisdiction (eg, if the non-resident parent may no longer be habitually resident in the UK), as it allows the level of child maintenance to be reconsidered quickly by the court and not left unchanged until any CMS decision is finally made.

Note: a written maintenance agreement for a child made before 5 April 1993 prevented an application for child support under the statutory schemes being made for that child.[44] There are now no child support applications where such an agreement is relevant. For further details on agreements that prevent an application being made, see previous editions of this *Handbook*.

Maintenance orders by the courts

A maintenance order made by a court before 3 March 2003 prevents an application for any child to whom it relates – ie, the CMS will refuse to make a calculation.[45] If the order was made on or after 3 March 2003 and has been in force for less than one year, it also prevents an application.[46] If an application is made within a year of an order made after 3 March 2003, the CMS may hold it until after the period expires and then treat it as an application rather than insisting that a new one be made.[47]

A **'court order'** only counts for these purposes if:

- it requires the making (or securing the making) of periodic payments of maintenance (or aliment in Scotland) to, or for the benefit of, a qualifying child.[48] Orders for payment of costs in connection with the education or training of the child, or because the child is disabled, or to 'top up' maintenance where child support has been calculated on the basis that the non-resident parent's income is above the maximum amount (gross income of £3,000 a week for '2012 rules' cases and net income of £2,000 a week for '2003 rules' cases) all count as maintenance orders, but do not prevent an application being made (it can still be made even if the CMS/CSA has jurisdiction and a child support calculation or assessment is in force – see p39).[49] Such top-up orders may be made in addition to any liability worked out by the CMS. Because an order only prevents an *application* to the CMS, an order made *after* the application does not stop the CMS making a calculation, or prevent the CMS/CSA revising or enforcing an existing calculation or assessment. A court order directing capital payments (ie, not periodic payments) does not count as an order for these purposes.[50] The wording of the order is important (see p37);

- it is in force. The meaning of 'in force' is not defined in the legislation, and applicants may wish to seek advice as this can be a complex issue. The fact that parties may have waived their rights under an order, or agreed to make different arrangements, does not affect the status of the order itself.[51] It may be arguable that an order is 'in force' only if it is still relevant – eg, the non-resident parent against whom the order was made is still a non-resident parent.[52] An order is in force if some undertakings or arrangements, such as for residence of the child, are still in effect, even though there is no further liability for maintenance payments[53] or the liability for child maintenance under the order has not yet begun.[54] If a court decides that it has no power to vary or enforce an order, an application can be made to the CMS;[55]
- it is made under one of certain legal provisions (see Appendix 2).[56] The order usually states the legal provision under which it was made.

These rules also apply to consent orders (see above) and to a registered minute of agreement (a form of enforceable legal agreement in Scotland) in relation to child maintenance in the same way as to maintenance orders made by a court.[57]

An application to the CMS is not prevented by the existence of a type of order known as a 'Segal order'. This is one that makes specific provision for an award of maintenance to reduce at a later date because a child support calculation is made.[58]

A person who cannot apply to the CMS because of an order can ask the court to:

- vary or enforce the amount of maintenance under the order;
- revoke it so that a CMS application can be made (but see p42).

Although the courts can revoke child maintenance orders, this is not usually done simply to allow an application to be made to the CMS.[59] If revocation is being considered, advice should be sought on the likely child support calculation.

People with court orders can use the CMS/CSA's collection and enforcement service for amounts due under these orders, but this facility is currently only available if child support is also being collected (see p278).

The role of the courts if the Child Maintenance Service has jurisdication

In general, the courts cannot make, vary or revive an order for periodic payments of child maintenance if the CMS has jurisdiction to make a calculation. The courts can still, however, revoke a maintenance order.[60] The CMS has jurisdiction if a child is a qualifying child and all the relevant parties (child, person with care and non-resident parent) are habitually resident in the UK, even if the CMS *would not* in fact make a calculation.[61]

However, the courts do have the power to make certain orders in relation to maintenance (eg, consent orders, orders on special expenses and maintenance orders) for a young person who is no longer considered a child by the CMS. Courts can also vary orders in situations where an application to the CMS cannot be accepted (see p42).

Even if the CMS has jurisdiction, the courts may still be able to make orders for children who are no longer qualifying children, and can still make orders for:[62]

- maintenance of stepchildren of the non-resident parent – ie, children who were accepted by that parent as members of her/his family when they used to live with her/him, but who are not qualifying children;[63]
- maintenance for the expenses of a child's education or training for a trade, profession or vocation;[64]
- maintenance to meet the expenses of a child's disability. A child counts as disabled if s/he is getting disability living allowance (DLA) or personal independence payment (PIP), or does not get DLA/PIP but is blind, deaf, without speech, or is substantially and permanently handicapped by illness, injury, mental disorder or congenital deformity.[65] The courts may even extend payments beyond the age at which the child may no longer be a qualifying child for child support purposes;[66]
- maintenance for a spouse or civil partner;
- maintenance from the person with care;[67] *and*
- child maintenance in excess of the maximum worked out under child support rules.[68]

The courts can backdate these maintenance orders to the effective date (see p206) of a child support calculation, if the application is made within six months of that date.[69] Backdating is at the court's discretion and can ensure that other maintenance is in step with child support.

The court's power to make a lump-sum award for a child is not used to provide regular support for the child, but only to meet a need for a particular item of capital expenditure – eg, acquiring a home.[70]

The child support scheme does not change the court's powers in relation to other aspects of relationship breakdown (eg, contact and residence orders, maintenance for a spouse or civil partner and property division) or the court's jurisdiction to deal with parentage disputes (see p12).

If a court order is cancelled because it was made by mistake when a CMS calculation was in force, any payments made under the order are treated as payments of child support.[71]

If a court order ceases to have effect because of a child support calculation (see p207), but the CMS revises the decision and decides no child support is payable as the previous decision was made in error, the court order revives and any child support already paid counts as maintenance paid under that order.[72]

The effect of a calculation on existing court orders and agreements

When a child support calculation is made, any existing court order or maintenance agreement either ceases to have effect or has effect in a modified form in relation to periodic payments.[73]

These rules apply even to 'clean break' orders or agreements. There are conflicting court decisions on whether the child support scheme (or changes made to it) allows the court to reopen the capital or property part of such an order.[74] The arrangement may be self-adjusting to address the effect of any calculation which may be made. This could mean, for example, a legal charge on the transferred home so that the non-resident parent could recover any sums paid under the child support scheme from the transferred asset.[75] It could also mean an order that the non-resident parent top up any future calculation to a certain total amount of maintenance.[76]

If a child support calculation is made for all of the children still covered by a court order, that order ceases to have effect on the effective date of the calculation (see p207).[77]

If the order includes provisions for additional maintenance, such as a child's education or training expenses or for a disabled child's special needs, only the elements for periodical maintenance for a qualifying child should cease to be in force. If the order is made solely for these additional expenses, it remains in force.[78] Parts of the order for matters other than periodic maintenance for the children named in the calculation (eg, other children or spousal maintenance) remain in force.[79]

In Scotland, if the CMS/CSA ceases to have the power to make a calculation in respect of a child, the original order revives from the date it ceases to have that power.[80] The same is not explicitly stated for England and Wales, which means that the original order does not revive when CMS/CSA involvement ceases. However, it could be argued that it should apply, since the court order has not been revoked but simply ceased to have effect for the duration of a child support calculation. If the original order does not revive, a new agreement or consent order needs to be negotiated. If this is no longer possible, a parent may have no other option but to use the CMS/CSA to calculate and enforce child support.

Maintenance agreements are unenforceable from the effective date (see p207) of the calculation.[81] Again, this only affects the part of the agreement to pay periodic maintenance for the children named in the calculation. The agreement remains unenforceable until the CMS/CSA no longer has the power to make a calculation.[82]

If the CMS/CSA is aware that an order is in force, it must notify the parties and the relevant court about the calculation.[83] Similarly, if a court makes an order which affects, or is likely to affect, a child support calculation, the relevant officer of the court (see p56) must notify the CMS/CSA of this if s/he knows a calculation is in force.[84]

The role of the courts if the Child Maintenance Service has no jurisdiction

If the CMS does not have jurisdiction (eg, because one parent or the qualifying child is not habitually resident in the UK), the courts may make, vary or revive a maintenance order. If there is a pre-3 March 2003 court order for child maintenance, or an order made on or after 3 March 2003 which has been in force for less than a year, the courts have the power to vary such orders.[85]

In the past, many courts used calculations under the '1993 rules' formula as a guide when setting levels of child maintenance. This was intended to avoid child support applications being made as soon as the order had been in force for a year. So courts may now decide to use the '2003 rules' calculation (or the '2012 rules' calculation in appropriate cases) as a guide. Parents seeking a variation of an order can ask their solicitors to prepare a calculation. An online calculator is available on the gov.uk website. The '2003 rules' or '2012 rules' calculation is likely to be seen as 'highly persuasive', but not legally binding on courts (as the '1993 rules' formula was in the past).[86] This principle has been emphasised in Scotland.[87] The courts also have the power to enforce orders and agreements, including those made by courts in other countries.[88]

In England and Wales, applications for maintenance are made to the family proceedings (magistrates') court, the county court or High Court. In Scotland, they are made to the sheriff court or Court of Session.

If a child support calculation is cancelled because one of the parties moves abroad (see p209), an application for maintenance can be made to the court. If the application is made within six months, the order can begin from the date that child support ended.[89]

3. How to apply

From 25 November 2013, all new applications are dealt with by the Child Maintenance Service (CMS) under the '2012 rules'. Before applying to the CMS, a parent must contact the Child Maintenance Options service (see p6) and take part in what is known as a 'gateway' conversation. Child Maintenance Options is normally contacted by telephone or an online chat service, or face-to-face if required.

The 'gateway' conversation is intended to encourage parents to consider the range of child maintenance options available before applying to the statutory scheme and, in particular, to consider making a private family-based arrangement. It is also intended to provide details of other support and information services.

An applicant who states that s/he is a victim of domestic violence is fast-tracked through the gateway process to apply to the statutory scheme rather than being encouraged to consider an unsuitable family-based arrangement.

Application fees

From 30 June 2014, there is a fee of £20 for making an application to the CMS under the '2012 rules'.[90] The fee is payable whether or not a child support calculation is actually made as a result of the application. An application is not treated as properly made until the fee is paid or is waived by the CMS.

The application fee can be waived if:[91]

- the applicant is aged 18 or under on the date of the application; *or*
- the CMS accepts that the applicant is a victim of domestic violence or abuse.

The CMS accepts that an applicant is a victim of domestic abuse or violence if s/he:

- has reported the violence or abuse to an 'appropriate person' (see below); *and*
- informed the CMS that s/he is a victim of domestic violence or abuse and that s/he has reported this to an appropriate person. The CMS must be informed at the time of making the application or in a written declaration that the CMS may ask the applicant to complete (provided the application fee has not already been paid before the declaration has been returned).

Definitions

The CMS has published guidance on how it decides whether a person is the victim of domestic violence or abuse.[92] **'Domestic violence'** is defined as 'any incident or pattern of incidents of controlling, coercive or threatening behaviour, violence or abuse towards the applicant which is between persons aged 16 or over who are or have been intimate partners or family members, regardless of gender or sexuality. This can encompass but is not limited to the following types of abuse: psychological, physical, sexual, financial, emotional.'

The CMS has also published guidance on who is accepted as an **'appropriate person'** for these purposes.[93] These are:

– a court;
– the police;
– a medical professional;
– social services;
– a multi-agency risk assessment conference;
– a specialist domestic violence organisation or service, including a refuge;
– an employer;
– educational services;
– a local authority;
– a legal professional;
– specialist support services.

If an application does not proceed because a qualifying child has died before the calculation is made, the fee must be refunded.[94]

Note: an application fee is not expected to be introduced in Northern Ireland.[95]

Making the application

After the gateway conversation with Child Maintenance Options, if a parent wishes to apply to the statutory scheme, s/he is given a unique 12-digit reference number that allows an application to be made. Child Maintenance Options does not deal with applications for the statutory scheme, but transfers a parent to the CMS at the end of the gateway conversation or provides a contact number for making an application to the CMS at a later date. If a parent contacting the CMS does not have a reference number or has forgotten it, s/he is usually told to contact Child Maintenance Options first before the CMS proceeds with an application.

The CMS can determine how an application under the '2012 rules' should be made and what information must be provided to process it.[96] In practice, this means that applications usually begin by contacting the CMS by telephone following the gateway conversation with Child Maintenance Options. Applications can also be made in writing. Contact details for the CMS can be found on the gov.uk website and in Appendix 1.

The CMS can require the applicant to provide any evidence or information reasonably needed to process the application (including, if the applicant is the person with care, sufficient information to allow the non-resident parent to be identified).[97] The application is treated as having been properly made when any information required to process it has been provided to the CMS.[98] In most cases, the CMS expects to gather information by telephone and paper application forms are not routinely issued, but an application can be made in writing. An application by a child in Scotland is always dealt with by telephone.

The reference number given to the applicant by Child Maintenance Options is used to verify identity and personal details when contacting the CMS about the application. Once an application is made, applicants can register with the 'government gateway' to manage their case through an online 'self-service' account.[99] This is intended to allow applicants to check the progress of an application, opt in or out of a text messaging service, report changes of circumstances, make one-off payments and view calculation details and payment history.

Information required for an application

An applicant is likely to have to provide the following kinds of information in order for the CMS to process an application:

- personal details – eg, name, address, national insurance (NI) number, date of birth, phone numbers and the best time to ring, and armed forces service number;
- child(ren) being applied for – eg, name, date of birth, NI number if 16 or over, who gets child benefit for the child, maintenance arrangements and shared care arrangements (or local authority care);
- if the parent/person with care is applying, whether the non-resident parent knows that s/he is named as the parent and whether s/he knows where the applicant lives;
- the child's education (if aged 16–19) – eg, school/college, course, type of course and hours;
- local authority details (if the child is being cared for);
- the non-resident parent's details – eg, name (other names), address or last known address and when s/he lived there, NI number, date of birth, employment details, phone numbers and whether the parent is the father or mother of the child;
- payment details – eg, whether child support is to be collected by the CMS, the preferred method and frequency of payment to the person with care and bank/ building society details;
- details of any representative – eg, name, address, phone numbers and the best time to ring. If the representative is a solicitor, an attorney under a power of attorney, Scottish mental health guardian, mental health appointee or receiver, the representative can apply on behalf of the applicant.

The CMS may wish to see original documents to confirm certain details – eg, any relevant court order and the representative's authority – eg, power of attorney document.

There are penalties for knowingly providing false information (see p58).

Applications with more than one non-resident parent

An applicant can choose from which non-resident parent s/he wishes to apply for child support. So, if someone is a person with care of qualifying children of more than one non-resident parent, s/he could apply for child support from one (or more), but not necessarily all, of them.

When to apply

There are no time limits for applying to the CMS. It can be done as soon as someone becomes a person with care or a non-resident parent, or at any later date.[100] Liability to pay child support usually runs from two days after the date notification of the application was sent to the non-resident parent, and the CMS cannot do this until it receives an effective application (see p46). This means that delaying the application may delay the start of liability. The parent with care should be aware that this is the case even if the reason for the delay is that s/he has been in touch with the Child Maintenance Options service and is considering alternatives, such as setting up voluntary maintenance arrangements. There is no provision for applying in advance – eg, before the birth of a baby.

Refusal to accept an application

The CMS may refuse to accept an application – eg, because it believes an existing maintenance order prevents an application or because it does not have jurisdiction. If this happens, the would-be applicant should explain to the CMS why s/he believes s/he is entitled to apply and ask for a written CMS decision. If a written decision is issued, s/he can try to challenge this decision by seeking a revision (see Chapter 12) and then appealing to the First-tier Tribunal (see Chapter 13). If this is not successful or if the CMS refuses to respond in writing, a complaint (see p324) and/or judicial review (see p215) should be considered.

Effective applications

The CMS can only make a child support calculation if the application is 'effective'.[101] All applicants must provide information to enable the non-resident parent to be identified and traced and the amount of child support payable to be calculated and recovered (see Chapter 4).[102] If an applicant does not supply the information, the CMS may refuse to process the application (see p47).

Once an effective application has been made, the address of the non-resident parent has been verified and any application fee due has been paid, the non-resident parent must be notified in writing as soon as possible and asked for any information required to make the calculation. (This applies even if the non-resident parent is the applicant.) S/he is informed of the effective date of the application, that the CMS can estimate income in certain circumstances and of the rules on 'default maintenance decisions'.[103]

The CMS cannot refuse to deal with an effective application, even if it considers that processing it would be against the welfare of the children concerned.[104] If it refuses to accept an application, see above.

For delays in dealing with applications, including if the non-resident parent is not co-operating, see p202.

Amending the application

An application can be amended at any time before a calculation is made, but not to take into account a change which occurs after the effective date. For details of this and of changes after the effective date, see p202.

4. **Withdrawing or cancelling an application**

The applicant no longer wants the Child Maintenance Service/Child Support Agency to act

An applicant may request that the Child Maintenance Service (CMS)/Child Support Agency (CSA) cease to act on her/his application for child support. The request can be made at any time, whether or not a calculation (or '1993 rules' assessment) has been made. The CMS/CSA cannot refuse this request.[105] For more information on cancelling calculations, see p208. Requests to cease acting can be made by telephone or in writing to the CMS/CSA office processing the application, or to the regional centre if it is not clear which office has responsibility.

The Child Maintenance Service/Child Support Agency withdraws or cancels an application

The CMS/CSA may withdraw or cancel an application before a calculation is made if the applicant does not provide information (see below).

The rules are different if the qualifying child dies before the calculation decision is made (see below).

An applicant does not provide information

If a person with care does not provide sufficient information, the CMS/CSA can close the case and s/he will not receive child support.

Cases can only be cancelled if no effective application has been made (see p46). If there is an effective application, a decision must be made and notified, even if it is a decision not to make a calculation (see p203). If an effective application is cancelled against the wishes of the applicant, s/he should seek advice.

The qualifying child dies

If a qualifying child dies before a calculation has been made for an application **under the '2012 rules'**, a decision on liability is still made for the period from the effective date to the date of death. If the child was the only child named in the application, the decision is then cancelled with effect from the date of death; otherwise, it is superseded with effect from that date.[106]

For an existing '2003 rules' or '1993 rules' case, if a qualifying child dies, any calculation or assessment is superseded because of a change of circumstances (see p224). If the child was the only child named in the calculation or assessment, the case will be cancelled.

5. **Multiple applications**

This section covers the rules for multiple '2012 rules' applications. Multiple applications under the '2003 rules' and '1993 rules' are dealt with differently. See previous editions of this *Handbook* for details.

If more than one application for child support is made in respect of the same qualifying child, only one can go ahead.[107]

The decision on whose application goes ahead does not affect the outcome of any calculation or have any effect on who is liable to pay any resulting child support. It only determines which applicant can withdraw an application or request a cancellation of any resulting calculation. If one application is given priority, information provided in another application that the Child Maintenance Service (CMS) will not proceed with may still be taken into account to help decide the application.

Note: once a '2003 rules' calculation or '1993 rules' assessment is in force, any subsequent application for child support made in the same circumstances in respect of the same person with care, non-resident parent and qualifying child(ren) is not dealt with.[108] This is not explicitly stated for the '2012 rules', but the same principle should apply. The subsequent application may, however, be treated as a request for a supersession (see p224) or, depending on the circumstances and information contained in the application, as a request for a variation (see Chapter 7 for '2012 rules' and Chapter 9 for '2003 rules') or departure (see previous editions of this *Handbook*).[109]

Note also: new applications under the '2012 rules' may also trigger the closure of related '1993 rules' or '2003 rules' cases. If this does not apply, existing '2003 rules' and '1993 rules' cases continue to be dealt with under those rules until they end or are closed as part of the case closure process. See Chapter 5 for details.

Multiple '2012 rules' applications

There are simplified rules for deciding on the priority between applications under the '2012 rules'. If more than one application is made in respect of the same qualifying child before the calculation decision is made, the CMS can decide which application goes ahead. When deciding this, the CMS must take into account the following order of priority.[110]

- In Scotland, an application by a person with care or a non-resident parent has priority over an application by a child.
- In other circumstances, an earlier application has priority over a later one.

If:
- an application is made and both parents of a qualifying child are non-resident
  – eg, an application made by a person with care who is not a parent of the

qualifying child, or by a child in Scotland whose parents are both non-resident; *or*

- both parents of a qualifying child are non-resident and both apply,

the CMS must treat this as a single application in relation to the qualifying child.[111]

Although the '2012 rules' do not state this explicitly, if more than one application is made by the same person in the same circumstances, they are likely to be treated as if they were a single application if the calculation decision has not been made.

If a calculation is in force, depending on the circumstances and information contained in the application, a further application may be treated as a request for a supersession (see p223) or as a request for a variation (see Chapter 7).

Applications for additional children

If there is an existing '2012 rules' or '2003 rules' calculation, or an existing '1993 rules' assessment, and there is an application for an additional child of the same non-resident parent cared for by the same person with care, this is a relevant change of circumstances and a new calculation/assessment is made which supersedes the existing one.

---

6. **Communicating with the Child Maintenance Service and Child Support Agency**

The first point of contact with the Child Maintenance Service (CMS) or Child Support Agency (CSA) is usually by telephone to make an application.

Most contact with the CMS/CSA is likely to be by telephone. This is the preferred method of communication of the CMS/CSA. Parents must make a request if they wish to be contacted by letter instead. Details of the relevant office handling the case is on any letters received from the CMS/CSA.

The CMS/CSA should answer telephone calls promptly. It should reply to letters, resolving the issue or agreeing what will happen next, within three weeks. Anyone who has difficulty in contacting the CMS/CSA, or obtaining a response within a reasonable time, should complain (see Chapter 15). The government intended the establishment of the CMS to deal with '2012 rules' cases to improve the level of service provided to clients.

Face-to-face interviews may be requested by a party to a case, or the CMS/CSA may decide on its own initiative to arrange an interview. A parent's request should be considered seriously if the CMS/CSA agrees that it is the most effective way to make contact or if all other ways of progressing the case have been exhausted. The CMS does not normally offer face-to-face interviews in '2012 cases', but these may be arranged if the CMS considers that the case involves complex issues and an interview may help to resolve them more quickly. An interview may also be considered if a party has difficulty with communication that would make other methods problematic.

The CMS/CSA should also meet any accessibility or language needs of the applicant – eg, if English is not her/his first language or if s/he has difficulty using the telephone.

Once an application is made, applicants can register with the 'government gateway' to manage their case through an online 'self-service' account.[112] This is intended to allow applicants to check the progress of an application, opt in or out of a text messaging service, report changes of circumstances, make one-off payments and view calculation details and payment history.

It is advisable to keep copies of letters and make a note of the date, time and content of telephone calls.

Dates of postage

Under the '2012 rules', a document sent to the CMS is treated as being sent on the day the CMS receives it.[113] If the CMS posts a document to a person's last known address (or the address the person last notified to the CMS), it is treated as being received on the second day after the day it was posted.[114] It is understood that this is intended to exclude Sundays and bank holidays. **Note:** where no statutory timescale applies for a particular action to be done or for information to be provided, the CMS generally allows a person 14 days to provide information, and extends this to 16 days to allow for the time taken for information to reach the CMS by post.

Under the '2003 rules', if the CSA posts a document, it is usually treated as sent on the day of posting.[115] A document sent to the CSA is treated as being sent on the day the CSA receives it. A document is treated as having been 'sent' by the CSA if it was properly addressed, pre-paid and posted. Evidence that it was not received does not show that it was not sent.[116]

Under the '1993 rules', documents are treated as having been sent by the CSA on the second day after the day of posting (unless this day is a Sunday or bank holiday).[117] If more than one document is required to be sent and they are posted on different days, or they need to be sent to different people and this is done on different days, they are treated as having been posted on the latest of the dates concerned (and so sent on the second day after this).[118] A document sent to the CSA is treated as having been sent on the day the CSA receives it, but in some cases the CSA can treat documents as having been sent earlier if there was unavoidable delay.[119]

It is important to bear these rules in mind, especially where time limits are concerned.

Representatives

Anyone dealing with the CMS/CSA can appoint a representative to act on her/his behalf.[120] If the person is not legally qualified, authorisation for her/him to act needs to be confirmed in writing, although if the client is with the representative during a telephone call, s/he can authorise the representative verbally for the duration of the call. An authorised or legally qualified representative can complete forms, receive documents and supply information. A person with care may also choose to have payments of child support made to a representative.

A representative who understands the law and/or is experienced in dealing with the CMS/CSA may find it easier to get a quick response and clearer information from the CMS/CSA, and can advise about rights and options. For information about how to find independent advice, see Appendix 3.

Representatives with legal authority to act for a CMS/CSA client (eg, someone with power of attorney, a receiver or a mental health appointee or Scottish mental health guardian) can act for the client in every respect, as if they were the client.

The legal advice and assistance scheme in Scotland can cover child support cases.

Notes

1. **Who can apply for child support**
   1 ss4(1) and 6(1) CSA 1991
   2 s7(1) CSA 1991
   3 ss5(1) and 54 CSA 1991
   4 As in CA 1989 and C(S)A 1995
   5 s3(1) CA 1989; s3(1) C(S)A 1995
   6 s4(1)(b) CA 1989; s4(1) C(S)A 1995
   7 s4A CA 1989, as amended by s75 CPA 2004
   8 ss4(1)(a), 4A(1)(b) and 5(6) CA 1989; s11 C(S)A 1995
   9 s4(1) CA 1989
   10 s3(1)(b)(ii) C(S)A 1995
   11 s4ZA CA 1989; s3 C(S)A 1995

2. **When an application can be accepted**
   12 R(CS) 3/97
   13 rr8.1(2)-(6), 10.24 and 10.25 Family Proceedings Rules

14 s44(1) CSA 1991
15 CCS/2314/2008; *AF v SSWP* [2009] UKUT 3 (AAC)
16 s44(2) CSA 1991
17 Sch 1 Interpretation Act 1978
18 House of Commons, *Hansard*, Written Answers, 20 July 2011, col 1063W
19 *Nessa v Chief Adjudication Officer* [1998] 2 All ER 728, [1998] 2 FCR 461, [1998] 1 FLR 879, [1998] Fam Law 329, CA applying *Re J (A Minor) (Abduction: Custody Rights)* [1990] 2 AC 562, [1990] 3 WLR 492, [1990] 2 All ER 961, [1991] FCR 129, [1990] 2 FLR 442, [1991] Fam Law 57, HL; *Cruse v Chittum* [1974] 2 All ER 940; *Brokelmann v Barr* [1971] 3 All ER 29; *Langford Property Co v Athanassoglou* [1948] 2 All ER 722

20 R(CS) 5/96; CCS/7207/1995
21 *Shah v Barnet LBC* [1983] 2 AC 309, [1983] 2 WLR 16, [1983] 1 All ER 226, HL
22 CCS/2314/2008; [2009] UKUT 3 (AAC)
23 *Lewis v Lewis* [1956] 1 WLR 200, [1956] 1 All ER 375
24 *Re J (A Minor) (Abduction: Custody Rights)* [1990] 2 AC 562, [1990] 3 WLR 492, [1990] 2 All ER 961, [1991] FCR 129, [1990] 2 FLR 442, [1991] Fam Law 57, HL
25 CCS/3574/2008; *H v CMEC* [2009] UKUT 84 (AAC)
26 *Shah v Barnet LBC* [1983] 2 AC 309, [1983] 2 WLR 16, [1983] 1 All ER 226, HL; *Re Mackenzie* [1940] 4 All ER 310
27 s44(2A) CSA 1991; reg 7A CS(MAJ) Regs
28 R(CS) 5/96
29 R(CS) 5/96
30 CSCS/6/2006
31 *Re J (A Minor) (Abduction: Custody Rights)* [1990] 2 AC 562, [1990] 3 WLR 492, [1990] 2 All ER 961, [1991] FCR 129, [1990] 2 FLR 442, [1991] Fam Law 57, HL
32 *Re M (Minors: Residence Order: Jurisdiction)* [1993] 1 FCR 718, [1993] 1 FLR 495, [1993] Fam Law 285, CA
33 *Re A (Minors: Abduction: Acquiescence)* [1992] 2 WLR 536, [1992] 1 All ER 929, [1992] 2 FCR 97, [1992] 2 FLR 14, [1992] Fam Law 381, CA
34 *Re M (A Minor) (Abduction: Child's Objections)* [1995] 1 FCR 170, [1994] 2 FLR 126, [1994] Fam Law 366, CA
35 s9(2) CSA 1991
36 s9(4) CSA 1991
37 ss4(10) and 7(10) CSA 1991; reg 2 CS(APD) Regs
38 s9(1) CSA 1991
39 *SJ v SSWP (CSM)* [2014] UKUT 82 (AAC)
40 CCS/316/1998; CCS/8328/1995
41 CCS/316/1998
42 s9(6) CSA 1991
43 ss8(5) and 9(5) CSA 1991
44 ss4(1) and 6(1) CSA 1991
45 ss4(10)(a) and 7(10)(a) CSA 1991; reg 2 CS(APD) Regs
46 ss4(10)(aa) and 7(10)(b) CSA 1991; reg 2 CS(APD) Regs
47 *YW v CMEC (CSM)* [2011] UKUT 176 (AAC)
48 s8(11) CSA 1991
49 s8(6)-(8) CSA 1991; s18(6) CSA 1995; *MR v SSWP and CR (CSM)* [2014] UKUT 198 (AAC)

50 CCS/4741/1995, upheld by the Court of Appeal in *AMS v CSO* [1998] 1 FLR 955
51 CCS/4049/2007
52 CCS/4049/2007. This and other cases have disagreed with the conclusions reached in R(CS) 4/96. The Court of Appeal in *Kirkley v Secretary of State for Social Security* ruling on an application for leave to appeal against R(CS) 4/96 also disagreed with the reasoning. Authorities differ as to whether changes in child(ren)'s residence (eg, from the parent with care to the non-resident parent) mean that an order ceases to have effect (CCS/3127/1995) or not (CCS/2567/1998). In the latter case, the commissioner suggested that it would instead be grounds to seek to vary the court order.
53 CCS/4741/1995
54 CCS/11364/1995
55 Reg 9 CS(MAJ) Regs
56 s8(11) CSA 1991; reg 2 CS(MAJ) Regs. Provisions repealed before 1 April 1980 are not listed.
57 Reg 26(1)(c) CS(MCP) Regs
58 CCS/4047/2007, citing *Dorney-Kingdom v Dorney-Kingdom* [2000] 2 FLR 855
59 s8(4) CSA 1991; *B v M (Child Support: Revocation of Order)* [1994] 1 FLR 342, [1994] 1 FCR 769, [1994] Fam Law 370
60 s8(1), (3) and (4) CSA 1991. It has been decided that this lack of access to the courts is not inconsistent with Art 6(1) European Convention on Human Rights. See *R v SSWP ex parte Kehoe* [2005] UKHL 48.
61 s8(2) CSA 1991
62 s8 CSA 1991
63 **EW** MCA 1973
S FL(S)A 1985
64 s8(7) CSA 1991
65 s8(8) and (9) CSA 1991
66 Sch 1 para 3(2)(b) CA 1989. In *C v F* [1997] 3 FCR 405 the court held that where s8(1) CSA 1991 applies, s8(8) CSA 1991 limits this power to children aged under 19. However, this seems to be wrong because the fact that the CSA 1991 only applied at the time of the judgment to those aged under 19 can hardly prevent an order being made under the CA 1989 for a person aged 19 or over.
67 s8(10) CSA 1991
68 s8(6) CSA 1991

69 s29(7) MCA 1973; s5(7) DPMCA 1978;
Sch 1 para 3(7) CA 1989 as amended
by Sch 3 paras 3, 5, and 10 CSPSSA
2000 respectively
70 Sch 1 CA 1989; *Phillips v Pearce* [1996] 2
FLR 230
71 Reg 8(2) CS(MAJ) Regs
72 Reg 8(1) CS(MAJ) Regs
73 s10(1) and (2) CSA 1991
74 *Crozier v Crozier* [1994] 1 FLR 126;
Mawson v Mawson [1994] 2 FLR 985
75 *Smith v McInerney* [1994] 2 FLR 1077.
However, an arrangement like this
might be void under s9(4) CSA 1991
because it would 'restrict the right to
apply for a maintenance assessment',
though the commissioner in CCS/2318/
1997 thought not.
76 See the arrangement in CCS/2318/
1997
77 Reg 3(2) CS(MAJ) Regs
78 Reg 3(3) CS(MAJ) Regs
79 Reg 3(2) CS(MAJ) Regs
80 Reg 3(4) CS(MAJ) Regs
81 Reg 4 CS(MAJ) Regs
82 Reg 4(3) CS(MAJ) Regs
83 Reg 5(1) CS(MAJ) Regs
84 Reg 6 CS(MAJ) Regs
85 ss8(3A) and 9(6) CSA 1991; *McGilchrist v
McGilchrist* [1997] SCLR 800
86 *E v C* [1996] 1 FLR 472; *GW v RW* [2003]
EWHC 611 (Fam), [2003] 2 FLR 108
87 *Sutherland v Sutherland* [2004] GWD 20-
436
88 MO(RE)A 1992
89 s29(7) MCA 1973; s5(7) DPMCA 1978;
Sch 1 para 3(7) CA 1989

3. **How to apply**
90 s6 CMOPA 2008; reg 3 CSF Regs 2014
91 Reg 4(1)-(3) CSF Regs 2014
92 *Guidance on Regulation 4(3) of the Child
Support Fees Regulations 2014: how the
Secretary of State will determine if an
applicant is a victim of domestic violence
or abuse*, DWP, 2 December 2013,
available online at www.gov.uk
93 *Guidance on Regulation 4(3) of the Child
Support Fees Regulations 2014: list of
persons to whom an applicant must have
reported domestic violence or abuse*,
DWP, 2 December 2013, available
online at www.gov.uk
94 Reg 5 CSF Regs 2014
95 DSDNI news release, 20 September
2013
96 Reg 9(1) CSMC Regs
97 Reg 9(1) CSMC Regs

98 Reg 9(2) CSMC Regs
99 www.gateway.gov.uk
100 R(CS) 10/02
101 Reg 9(2) CSMC Regs
102 ss4(4), 6(7) and 7(5) CSA 1991
103 Reg 11 CSMC Regs
104 R(CS) 4/96; CCS/14/1994; CCS/17/
1994; CCS/16535/1996

4. **Withdrawing or cancelling an
application**
105 ss4(6) and 6(5) CSA 1991
106 Reg 18(3) CSMC Regs

5. **Multiple applications**
107 s5(2) CSA 1991
108 **2003 rules** Sch 2 para 4 CS(MCP) Regs
1993 rules Sch 2 para 4 CS(MAP) Regs
109 *DB v CMEC* [2010] UKUT 356 (AAC)
110 Reg 10(2) CSMC Regs
111 Reg 10(3) CSMC Regs

6. **Communicating with the Child
Maintenance Service and Child Support
Agency**
112 www.gateway.gov.uk
113 Reg 7(1) CSMC Regs
114 Reg 7(2) CSMC Regs
115 Reg 2 CS(MCP) Regs
116 R(CS) 1/99
117 Reg 1(6) CS(MAP) Regs
118 Reg 1(8) CS(MAP) Regs
119 Reg 1(7) CS(MAP) Regs
120 **2012 rules** Reg 8 CSMC Regs
2003 rules Reg 22 CS(MCP) Regs
1993 rules Reg 53 CS(MAP) Regs

Chapter 4

Information

This chapter covers:
1. Information-seeking powers (below)
2. Contacting the non-resident parent (p59)
3. Parentage investigations (p63)
4. Further investigations (p70)
5. Change of circumstances (p73)
6. Disclosure of information (p74)

This chapter covers the rules for '2012 rules' cases, and deals with only these rules when describing information relating to new applications. It also includes information that is relevant for existing '2003 rules' cases, and describes any differences between the two sets of rules. In most respects, the information in this chapter relating to existing '2003 rules' cases also applies to '1993 rules' cases.

1. Information-seeking powers

The Child Maintenance Service (CMS) and Child Support Agency (CSA) have wide powers to obtain information from (among others) parents, employers, local authorities and HM Revenue and Customs (HMRC).[1] The CMS/CSA can require information to be provided in order to make any child support decision.[2]

In addition, the CMS/CSA can appoint inspectors who have extensive powers to obtain information (see p72). In general, CMS/CSA staff seek information by telephone, but may also conduct face-to-face enquiries.

When the Child Maintenance Service/Child Support Agency can request information

All applicants are under a duty to provide information to:[3]
- identify and trace a non-resident parent;
- calculate, collect or recover child support;
- verify information already gathered.

After an application has been made under the '2012 rules', the non-resident parent is formally notified of the application in writing (see p59). The date this notice is issued sets the effective date for the calculation (see p206). This notice is followed up by a telephone call to gather and confirm information. There is no standard enquiry form.

Information can be requested in order to:[4]

- determine an application for child support and any issues which arise under that application – eg, to establish which parent receives child benefit and so who is the parent with care in shared care cases;
- make any other decisions under child support law – eg, to contact an employer in order to determine the income of the non-resident parent;
- enable the calculation, collection and enforcement of child support.

See p56 for who can be required to give information, and p58 for the effects of failing to provide it.

Information the Child Maintenance Service/Child Support Agency can ask for

Issues on which the CMS/CSA can request information include:

- the habitual residence of the person with care, the non-resident parent and any child covered by the application to determine jurisdiction (including if the individual works abroad);
- the name and address of the person with care and non-resident parent, their marital or civil partnership status, and the relationship of the person with care to any child covered by the application;
- the name, address and date of birth of any child covered by the application, the child's marital or civil partnership status and any education the child is undergoing;
- if there is more than one person with care:
  - who has parental responsibility (or parental rights in Scotland) for any qualifying child; *and*
  - how much time is spent by that child with each person with care;
- if parentage is disputed, whether someone can be assumed to be a parent (see p11) and, if not, who is the parent of a child;
- the name and address of any current or recent employer of a non-resident parent and the gross earnings from any such employment;
- if the non-resident parent is self-employed, the address, trading name, gross receipts and expenses, other outgoings and taxable profits of the trade or business;
- any other income of the non-resident parent;
- how much is paid or payable under a court maintenance order or maintenance agreement;
- details of anyone who lives in the same household as the non-resident parent, their relationship to her/him and to each other, and the date of birth of any child of those people;

- details and statements of any account in the name of the non-resident parent, including bank and building society accounts;
- whether a person counts as a qualifying child for the purposes of child support (see p13);
- information needed to decide whether a calculation should end (see p210).

Who must give information to the Child Maintenance Service/Child Support Agency

Information can be required from the people listed below. It can only be required from a person who has that information or evidence in her/his possession or can reasonably be expected to acquire and provide it.[5] Information or evidence can also be given to the CMS/CSA when there is no obligation to provide it – eg, from a relative, neighbour, GP or landlord. For information on disclosure by the CMS/CSA, see p74.

A relevant person

The person with care and non-resident parent (or a parent treated as non-resident for the purposes of the calculation) must provide the information listed on p55, if requested.[6] A child applicant in Scotland must provide the same information, except information enabling the non-resident parent to be identified.[7]

If information is not provided by a person with care (or child applicant in Scotland), an application may be treated as withdrawn (see p47). If a non-resident parent does not supply requested information, a 'default maintenance decision' may be made (see p204). In '1993 rules' cases, an 'interim maintenance assessment' may have been made. See previous editions of this *Handbook* for details.

Someone who denies parentage of a child

Someone who denies parentage of a child named in an application is required to give information:[8]

- to decide whether or not all the relevant persons are habitually resident in the UK and, therefore, whether the CMS/CSA has jurisdiction to make a calculation; *or*
- to identify a non-resident parent.

This means, for example, that if the CMS/CSA only wants to identify a person as the non-resident parent, employment details would not normally be necessary and so should not be requested until parentage is established.

Court officials

The following court officials can be required to give information.[9] **In England and Wales:**

- the senior district judge of the High Court Family Division or, at a district registry, the district judge;
- the district judge of a county court, or the chief clerk or other officer who may be acting on her/his behalf;[10]
- the justice's chief executive for a magistrates' court.

In Scotland:
- the deputy principal clerk of the Court of Session;
- the sheriff clerk of a sheriff court.

Court officials can be required to give information for the purposes listed on p55 to:
- identify how much is payable under a court maintenance order;
- collect child support or maintenance under a court order;
- identify any proceedings about a court maintenance order;
- decide whether a maintenance order is in force that may affect whether an application can be made (see p37); *or*
- decide who has parental responsibility for the qualifying child if there is more than one person with care.

Government benefit departments

Any Department for Work and Pensions (DWP) agency or anyone providing services to the DWP may give information held for benefits purposes to the CMS/CSA.[11]

HM Revenue and Customs

Under the '2012 rules', there are specific arrangements for information about the non-resident parent's gross income to be passed from HMRC to the CMS (see Chapter 6).

Apart from these specific arrangements, HMRC can be required to disclose information or evidence for the purposes listed on p55.[12] Information provided can be used for any function related to child support. If the parent is self-employed, this also includes details of the taxable profits, gross receipts and expenses. Any information disclosed must not go any further than authorised CMS/CSA staff, unless it is about civil or criminal proceedings under the Child Support Act 1991. However, if information is obtained under the Social Security Administration Act 1992, no such restriction applies. Information may also be obtained under the Tax Credits Act 2002.[13] It is unlawful for HMRC to give the CMS/CSA any other information.[14]

Others

The CMS/CSA can also require the following to provide information for the purposes listed on p55:

- current or previous employers of the non-resident parent (including if the employer is the 'Crown' – eg, a government department).[15] In '1993 rules' cases, the parent with care's employer may also be required to provide information needed to make, or revise or supersede an assessment;
- a person (including a company or partnership, and including the Crown – eg, a government department) for whom the non-resident parent provides, or has provided, goods or services under a contract.[16] This means, for example, that a self-employed IT consultant could be traced and have her/his income investigated through companies for which s/he has provided services;
- a person who acts, or has acted, as the non-resident parent's accountant;[17]
- credit reference agencies;[18]
- the local authority in whose area either the non-resident parent or person with care lives or has lived.[19] The CMS/CSA may require the authority to provide information such as address and bank account details relating to, for example, rent, council tax or housing benefit claims;[20]
- the Driver and Vehicle Licensing Agency. In particular, it may be asked for information needed to trace the non-resident parent, and to collect and enforce payments;[21]
- prison authorities;[22]
- 'deposit takers'– eg, banks and building societies;[23]
- gas and electricity suppliers.[24]

When information must be supplied

A person who has been requested to provide information must do so if that information or evidence is in her/his possession or s/he can reasonably be expected to acquire and provide it.[25]

The information must be supplied as soon as it is reasonably practicable.[26] The CMS/CSA can allow information to be provided by a later date if it is satisfied that the delay was unavoidable.

See p50 for when documents are treated as having been sent and received.

Failing to provide information and providing false information

It is a criminal offence for a person to fail to provide information, to provide false information or to allow false information to be provided. If this happens, the CMS/CSA may decide not to process the application (see p47).

If the person is a non-resident parent, a default maintenance decision may be made. For '2012 rules' cases, a decision based on estimated income could be made in certain circumstances instead of a default maintenance decision.

The CMS/CSA may also go to court and a criminal fine (currently up to a level of £1,000) can be imposed.[27] This is paid to the court, not to the CMS/CSA.

A person charged with an offence of failing to provide information may be able to avoid conviction if there is a good reason why the information cannot be provided.[28] However, a non-resident parent who fails to provide information may have both a default maintenance decision and a fine imposed. If a non-resident parent makes an application and the parent with care fails to provide information, the parent with care can be fined, though this would be extremely rare.

All requests for information issued by the CMS/CSA must state that it is a criminal offence to refuse to supply information, or knowingly supply false information.[29]

If a parent does not give the required information, the CMS/CSA may ask another person for it – eg, a parent's employer or accountant. As certain other people also have a duty to give information, the criminal sanctions also apply to them.

Change of address

The non-resident parent must notify the CMS/CSA within seven days if s/he changes address.[30] If s/he does not do so, s/he may have committed a criminal offence and a fine (currently up to a level of £1,000) may be imposed.[31]

Disputing the information required

A request for information could be queried and challenged (see p215) if:
- it is not relevant to the reason for the request;
- it is of a very different kind from the examples given in the regulations;
- it is made to a person who cannot be required to give it; *or*
- the CMS/CSA has sufficient information to make a full calculation.

If a person in this situation refuses to give information, s/he should explain this, preferably in writing, in order to avoid a penalty. A complaint could also be made (see Chapter 15).

2. **Contacting the non-resident parent**

Note: the information in this section covers the procedures used for applications under the '2012 rules'. For full details of procedures relating to existing '2003 rules' and '1993 rules' applications, see previous editions of this *Handbook*.

When an application under the '2012 rules' is made, the address of the non-resident parent has been verified and any application fee due has been paid, the Child Maintenance Service (CMS) must notify the non-resident parent in writing as soon as reasonably practical. The notification enquires about any information needed to make the calculation, and it is at this point that the non-resident parent may dispute any of the facts relating to the application. The date liability for child support usually starts (this is known as the 'initial effective date' – see p206) is specified in the notice issued to the non-resident parent. The CMS may telephone the non-resident parent on or before the initial effective date and then confirm this in writing to the parent's last known address. If the CMS does not telephone the parent, it must send written notice to the parent's last known address at least two days before the initial effective date.[32] The initial effective date is normally expected to be two days after the written notice is issued.

If there is a long delay in setting the effective date, the person with care should consider complaining and seeking compensation (see Chapter 15).

Tracing the non-resident parent

The CMS can use its information-seeking powers (including contact with the people and agencies on pp56–57) to identify and trace the non-resident parent.[33]

Finding a reliable address

The CMS seeks to confirm the identity and address of the non-resident parent from information given by the person with care, DWP computer records and other methods. The fact that an address is her/his current address does not have to be established beyond all reasonable doubt for the CMS to decide that it is sufficiently reliable for it to use.[34] If the DWP computer gives the non-resident parent's address and it is the same as that of the person with care, this is not considered reliable.

Information from the person with care

The person with care is asked for the address of the non-resident parent, or for any information that could help trace her/him. This could include:
- middle name(s) and any other names by which s/he may be known;
- other addresses at which s/he may have lived;
- her/his place of work and any previous employers;
- the name and address of her/his accountant;
- any benefit claims made; *and*
- if s/he has a car, the registration or make, model, colour and other details.

The CMS may contact the person with care again if additional information is required – eg, where parentage is disputed. A parent may be asked to give a recent photograph of the non-resident parent where DNA testing may be involved, and to provide any relevant documents, such as a marriage certificate or expired passport. A person with care could also be asked other detailed questions – eg, whether the non-resident parent has ever lived with her/him. The CMS may contact friends and relatives with whom the non-resident parent may be living. If it does this, it must preserve confidentiality and should not disclose its interest.

The CMS does not normally offer face-to-face interviews (see p49), but these may be arranged if the CMS considers that the case involves complex issues and an interview may help to resolve them more quickly.

Initial contact with the non-resident parent

Once an effective '2012 rules' application (see p46) has been made, the address of the non-resident parent has been verified and any application fee due has been paid or waived, the CMS must notify the non-resident parent in writing to her/his last known address as soon as reasonably practical.[35]

This notice includes a provisional calculation, based on details provided by the applicant and information received by the CMS from HM Revenue and Customs (HMRC) or other parts of the Department for Work and Pensions (DWP).[36] The provisional calculation is not a decision, but an illustration of the non-resident parent's child support liability if the calculation is done on the basis of the information the CMS currently has.

The notification advises the non-resident parent of any information that s/he is required to provide for the formal child support calculation decision to be made. Information on the income of the non-resident parent is normally provided to the CMS automatically by HMRC (see Chapter 6), unless HMRC has no income data or is unable to supply it, in which case the non-resident parent is asked for this information. The provisional calculation also takes account of any information about shared care provided by the applicant.

A few days after issuing the notification, the CMS then attempts to phone the non-resident parent to gather information for the calculation decision. If the CMS is unable to contact the non-resident parent by telephone, a reminder notice is issued in writing. If there is no response from the parent after 14 days, the CMS may proceed to make a default maintenance decision.

The CMS intends that all (or most) of the information needed to work out child support will usually be provided or collected by phone. There is no standard enquiry form used in '2012 rules' cases. If s/he prefers to be contacted in writing, the non-resident parent must request this.

If the parent is unaware of the child or is not named on the birth certificate, the CMS may try to arrange a face-to-face interview, although this is not expected to be done often.

There are special rules for young non-resident parents (see p62).

During the initial phone call, the non-resident parent may be asked questions to gather or confirm any information needed to make a calculation. This information can also be provided by the parent in writing if s/he wishes.

The non-resident parent may be asked to confirm details such as:

- personal details – name, address, other names used, phone number (work and mobile), national insurance (NI) number, date of birth, best contact times;
- details required to confirm whether the CMS has jurisdiction;
- whether s/he accepts parentage for all, or some, of the qualifying children named;
- any income-related benefits being claimed by, or for, her/him;

- student details, if appropriate – ie, college, course, qualification, full- or part-time status (evidence is requested);
- children who live with her/him – ie, date of birth, NI number (if appropriate), who gets child benefit for the child (evidence is requested);
- details of any shared care, average per week and any other special arrangements;
- employment details – title, employer (name, address and phone number), start and end dates (if appropriate);
- income details – frequency of pay, gross pay, bonus, expenses (pay slips are requested);
- self-assessment form or tax calculation notice if the parent is self-employed;
- other income – eg, pension;
- other payments made to a personal or private pension;
- collection details – when the CMS will be collecting the child support, bank details such as account number and sort code;
- representative details, name address, phone number and best contact times (signed authorisation is needed in certain circumstances).

The non-resident parent should be warned that a default maintenance decision (or, in certain circumstances in '2012 rules' cases, a calculation based on an estimate of income) may be made if s/he fails to provide sufficient information to make a calculation. At various stages, s/he is given the opportunity to provide more information and a time limit of at least seven days in which to provide it.

Parents must also be informed that failure to provide the information requested, or knowingly to provide false information, is a criminal offence (see p58).

Information given can be amended at any time before a calculation is made. However, information about changes after the effective date must be dealt with by a supersession (see p223).

Young non-resident parents

A face-to-face interview is likely to be arranged with a young non-resident parent – ie, one under 16 years of age (or aged 16 or over but under 20 and treated as a child – see p13). The parent is asked to confirm parentage, but no calculation can be made until s/he ceases to be treated as a child. An adult must be present at the interview. This is because, although there is no calculation for under-16-year-olds (and some young parents aged 16–19), a parentage statement is needed.

3. Parentage investigations

Note: the information in this section relates mainly to applications dealt with by the Child Maintenance Service (CMS) under the '2012 rules', but also applies to any outstanding parentage disputes dealt with by the Child Support Agency (CSA) for '2003 rules' or '1993 rules' cases.

Disputes about whether a person is a parent of a qualifying child can arise before or after a child support calculation is made. The dispute can be about one or all of the qualifying children.

Where the parentage of a qualifying child is denied or is in doubt, a child support application cannot be decided unless the CMS can assume parentage (see p11) or parentage is determined.

An alleged non-resident parent may deny parentage during the initial phone contact with the CMS or in writing before a calculation is made (a 'pre-calculation' case).

The CMS can proceed with the calculation for any children for whom parentage is accepted or assumed while investigations are taking place for others.

If a presumption of parentage cannot be made, the CMS cannot make a calculation until parentage has been resolved. For details of when parentage may be assumed, see p11. The CMS carries out investigations to determine whether parentage may be established or assumed. Both the non-resident parent and person with care are given the opportunity to submit evidence to resolve the dispute, and may be interviewed. The qualifying child's other parent may also be interviewed if s/he is not a person with care. The CMS may seek a DNA test or court action to establish parentage (although this is unlikely). The person with care or alleged non-resident parent may also pursue court action at any time.

If an alleged non-resident parent has completed an enquiry form, s/he is treated as having accepted parentage. Neither the CMS/CSA nor the First-tier Tribunal can then cancel the calculation unless a court decides that s/he is not in fact the parent.[37]

Once a calculation has been made (a 'post-calculation' case), the non-resident parent may dispute parentage and seek a revision. However, the person named as the non-resident parent of the child will have to pay child support until s/he provides conclusive evidence that s/he is not the parent.[38] If the decision is not revised, the non-resident parent may have to apply to court for a declaration/ declarator of parentage. A decision to refuse to revise can be challenged, but parentage can only ultimately be established by the court.

If the non-resident parent disputes parentage, s/he is asked to provide evidence.[39] It is not sufficient in post-calculation cases simply to deny parentage; evidence must be given to raise doubt – eg, if the parent with care was having another relationship when the child was conceived. In all cases, documentary evidence is preferred. If the evidence is a previous negative DNA test or declaration/declarator of parentage, this is sufficient proof.[40] The calculation is cancelled and any payments made may be refunded. The CMS states that whether or not all payments made are refunded in post-calculation cases may depend on how long after the calculation was made the alleged non-resident parent disputed parentage, and a refund may only be made from the date that parentage was denied.[41] The person with care may then be re-interviewed to identify another alleged non-resident parent.

If a doubt is raised, the parent with care is contacted by the CMS for comments on the non-resident parent's evidence. If the parent with care:

- accepts that there may be doubt about parentage, a DNA test may be offered;
- disputes the non-resident parent's evidence, the decision is not revised. The non-resident parent is advised to obtain a DNA test or declaration/declarator of non-parentage; the CMS does not offer a DNA test in this case.[42] S/he is informed of the right to appeal to a court.

Interviews where parentage is disputed

Interviews can be carried out by phone or in person. If parentage is denied after initial contact, the parent with care may be interviewed in order to establish the case to be put to the alleged non-resident parent. In other cases, sufficient information may already be available to contact the non-resident parent. However, both parties are interviewed before offering DNA tests (see p69) and, even if the parent with care has already been interviewed or parentage is assumed, s/he may be re-interviewed to see how s/he responds to the alleged non-resident parent's version of events. If the parent with care has already filled in a parentage statement, s/he is only re-interviewed if the alleged non-resident parent introduces new evidence.

In the case of a face-to-face interview, if the interviewee does not want to attend the local office, s/he can be interviewed at home or at a friend's or relative's house. It is not compulsory to attend any interview, but see p56 for who can be required to provide what information.

If the parent with care or alleged non-resident parent is under 16 (or under 20 and treated as a child), her/his parent or guardian must consent to the case progressing. The young person must have a face-to-face interview in the presence of a parent or guardian. A calculation is not made for a non-resident parent under 16 (or aged 16 and over but under 20 and treated as a child – see p13), but a parentage statement is required for future use. Additional information may be sought about an alleged non-resident parent aged 16–19 to determine whether or not s/he should be treated as a child – eg, details of current education or training.

Interview with an alleged non-resident parent

If parentage is denied, the alleged non-resident parent is asked whether s/he has evidence that s/he is not the parent. There is no guidance on whether oral or documentary evidence should be required. A face-to-face interview may be arranged, although this is relatively unusual. The alleged non-resident parent may ask for further time to obtain documentary evidence; seven days are usually allowed.

If documentary evidence cannot be supplied, the person with care may be interviewed to gather her/his evidence. If no evidence can be provided to assume parentage, the case may progress to DNA testing.

Parentage is most commonly disputed by alleged non-resident fathers. In an interview with an alleged father, the CMS could ask for information such as:

- whether he was in the country at any time between the date of conception and the child's birth;
- whether he had sex with the mother and, if so, over what period of time;
- if conception was assisted, whether he agreed to the treatment;
- how long the relationship lasted and whether he lived with the woman as husband and wife;
- whether or not he has had any contact with the child(ren);
- his reasons for thinking that he is not the father; *and*
- any other information which might support his view.

This is not an exhaustive list. The alleged non-resident parent need only answer such questions if he denies parentage and the information is needed to decide the issue.

The alleged non-resident parent is sent information about disputing parentage and the reduced-cost DNA test (see p67) before the interview. At the interview, the possibility of DNA testing is explained and his agreement sought.[43] The alleged non-resident parent is told that he is responsible for the costs of the tests for the parent with care and child(ren), as well as his own, if he is found to be the parent. He is also told that, if he is found not to be the parent, he can reclaim any costs incurred from the CMS. If the alleged non-resident parent states that he cannot afford to pay for the test, the CMS pays. However, the fee must be paid back if the test shows that he is the parent.[44]

If the alleged non-resident parent accepts parentage, the CMS proceeds to make a child support calculation.

Interviewing officers should take notes, and details of the interview (including any statement made by the non-resident parent) should be recorded.

If the alleged non-resident parent does not comply with requests to be interviewed, the CMS may consider a home visit or court action.

Interview with a parent with care

If someone has been named as the parent of a qualifying child and denies it, the CMS informs the parent with care of this and explains the procedures that follow. The interview is usually conducted by phone or, if the parent does not want to be interviewed in this way, it may be conducted in the CMS office or at her/his home.

The parent with care is asked for any documentary evidence from which the CMS could assume parentage – eg, birth or marriage certificate.[45] S/he is also questioned about her/his relationship with the alleged non-resident parent.

If no evidence can be provided to assume parentage, the parent with care is asked if s/he is willing to take a DNA test (see p67).

The CMS enquires about the alleged relationship and the circumstances of conception and birth. The parent with care is likely to be asked personal questions.

Most commonly, the parent with care is the mother and the alleged non-resident parent a man. In this case, the CMS may ask the parent with care questions such as:

- the place the child was born and whether the pregnancy was full term;
- who are named as the child's parents on the birth certificate;
- the man's reaction to the pregnancy;
- whether she and the alleged non-resident parent ever lived together and, if so, when and where;
- whether she considered them to be a couple at the time the child was conceived;
- whether the alleged non-resident parent has ever acknowledged the child;
- whether the alleged non-resident parent has ever paid any maintenance;
- whether there is, or has been, any contact with his family;
- whether she has any letters or cards acknowledging the child, or witnesses to her association with the alleged non-resident parent;
- whether the child's conception was assisted and, if so, whether the man agreed to the treatment and gave notice of this;
- whether she has any photographs of him; *and*
- whether she is willing to give evidence in court.

If a parent considers the question(s) inappropriate, she should ask the interviewer about the point of them. If the interviewer insists, the person with care could ask to end the interview to consider whether to give the information requested. She can ask the interviewer to write down the questions and the reason for them. If, at the interview or later, she refuses to answer any of the questions, she should indicate that she has given all the information that is necessary to trace and identify the father.

A parent with care may also be asked to make a parentage statement. S/he can refuse to sign this and the refusal forms part of the evidence, along with any reasons given. The parent may ask for a copy of the parentage statement or reasons for failing to sign the statement. This statement is added to the report of the interview and can be used in court proceedings (see p69).

Interviewing a person with care who is not the parent

If both parents are non-resident and an alleged non-resident parent continues to deny parentage after an interview, the person with care may be interviewed. The questions depend on the person with care's relationship with the alleged parents – eg, a grandparent is likely to know the length of the relationship between the parents. S/he is asked for the addresses of both parents, and any letters or cards from them. S/he is also asked why s/he is looking after the child(ren), whether there is any documentation about the care arrangements and whether s/he gives her/his consent for the child(ren) in her/his care to undergo a DNA test (see below) if s/he has parental responsibility.

DNA testing

DNA testing involves taking a cell sample from the parent with care, alleged non-resident parent and qualifying child. The test establishes the genetic fingerprint of the individual and is virtually conclusive. The test is usually done by taking a cheek cell sample, which is gathered from the inside of the mouth using a swab. It is possible for blood to be taken for the DNA test instead, but all parties must use the same method. If young children are involved, a cheek cell sample will usually be preferred.

DNA testing is used in cases where parentage cannot be presumed and the parties involved give consent. In cases where the CMS has applied to court for a declaration/declarator of parentage, the court may order DNA testing.

The CMS has special arrangements with a private testing agency, Cellmark, and reduced testing rates may apply.[46] There are special rules that apply if an alleged non-resident parent wishes to arrange her/his own test.

Consent

If there is a dispute about parentage, both the parent with care and the alleged non-resident parent are asked to agree to a DNA test. Written consent must be obtained before a test can be carried out. If the qualifying child is under 16, the parent or guardian must give consent.

Refusal to take the test has consequences.

- If the parent with care accepts DNA testing, but refuses consent for the child, a court can direct DNA testing if it is in the best interests of the child, but it cannot force the child to take the test.
- An alleged non-resident parent may be assumed to be the parent (see p11).[47]
- If a non-resident parent already assumed to be the parent refuses to take a test, the CMS does not revise the calculation.
- If an applicant refuses consent for her/himself and/or a qualifying child, the case may be closed.
- There is no guidance on what happens when a parent or guardian of a child applicant in Scotland refuses consent, but DWP policy indicates that action may be taken to get a declarator of parentage.

The reason for any refusal must be explored. As the DNA test usually involves taking a cheek cell sample, any objections (eg, to blood tests on medical or religious grounds) may not be viable.

If the alleged non-resident parent agrees to the test, but fails to attend the appointment, parentage is assumed unless there are good reasons – eg, s/he was in hospital, did not receive the test notification or was ill.

If a qualifying child aged 16 or over refuses consent, the non-resident parent must apply to the court for a declaration/declarator of non-parentage.

Paying for the DNA test

The CMS offers discounted tests to alleged non-resident parents who are prepared to take it in advance. These are known as voluntary cases. The alleged non-resident parent must agree to the results being passed to the CMS.

If the court directs the DNA test to be taken, a non-discounted fee is charged.

The cost of tests varies according to the number of people tested. At the time of writing this *Handbook*, the child maintenance section of the gov.uk website states that the discounted fee for a test for three people is £190.80 and the non-discounted fee is £258.60.[48]

If the alleged non-resident parent is found not to be the parent, a full refund of the cost of the test is made.[49]

If the alleged non-resident parent says s/he cannot afford to pay for the test in advance, the CMS may pay for the test initially if s/he agrees to accept the results, and to repay the fee should the test show that s/he is the parent. If s/he still refuses to take the DNA test, parentage may be assumed (see p11).

The CMS can recover the costs of the test from the alleged non-resident parent if the test does not exclude her/him from being the parent and:[50]

- s/he does not now deny that s/he is the parent; *or*
- a court has now made a declaration/declarator of parentage.

Private testing

An alleged non-resident parent may arrange the test her/himself either through Cellmark or another company. In the meantime, the CMS may still assume parentage if the CMS test has been refused.[51] In this case, no discount or CMS non-discounted rate is offered. Prices vary depending on which company is used, but are likely to be at least £300–£400. This fee is not refunded if the test proves negative.

The test must be carried out by an approved agency and proper security measures must be in place; otherwise, even if the test is negative, the CMS and court may not accept the result.

Tests must involve the parent with care; a test with only the alleged non-resident parent and the qualifying child is not accepted. No action can be taken against a parent with care who does not consent to a private test. If the alleged non-resident parent cannot arrange a private test because s/he does not know the address of the person with care, the CMS does not provide contact details to her/him.

DNA test results

Once the DNA-testing company has received all the samples, the test usually takes 10 days. The results are sent by post to the parent with care, the alleged non-resident parent and the CMS. The results are confidential and are not given by phone.[52]

If the alleged non-resident parent is shown to be the parent, s/he is also sent notification by the CMS. The CMS also asks for any additional information needed. (The 'effective date' of liability for child support remains the date two days after the original notification of the application was sent.) If the alleged non-resident parent still does not accept parentage, s/he will have to take court action to obtain a declaration/declarator of non-parentage. The CMS may make a calculation, or refuse to revise one, because a positive DNA test is grounds to assume parentage.

If the DNA tests confirm that the person who took the test as the alleged non-resident parent is not the parent, action is taken to confirm the identity of the person tested. If the alleged non-resident parent sent someone else to take the test, the CMS passes the case to the fraud team. If the wrong person has been traced, the CMS pursues further tracing. If the identity is confirmed, the parent with care may be re-interviewed about any other possible non-resident parent.[53]

Court proceedings

When all possible action and investigations have been completed, the CMS decides whether to apply to a court for a declaration/declarator of parentage.[54] Court action is rare, as there are other ways by which parentage can be assumed. Examples of situations where court action may be taken include:

- if a DNA test is inconclusive;
- cases involving fertility treatment where an alleged non-resident father denies he consented to the treatment;
- in post-calculation cases, where the parent with care disputes the non-resident parent's non-conclusive evidence. In this instance, the non-resident parent must apply to court (the CMS may not be involved in this action, but may be informed of the outcome).

If the CMS decides not to take court action, the person with care may initiate proceedings.[55] The person with care or non-resident parent may start court proceedings at any time.

The CMS *or* the person with care can apply to court for a declaration/declarator of parentage. If the CMS is willing to do so, the person with care should normally not also apply, because s/he would probably have to pay her/his own legal costs (and those of the alleged non-resident parent) if s/he loses (see p70). If the CMS suspends the case, but the person with care wants to go to court her/himself, s/he should consider taking legal advice.

Only the courts have the power to order blood tests (including DNA tests – see p67) in any civil proceedings in which parentage is an issue.[56] If convinced that blood testing would be against the child's interests, the court should not order it.[57] A court can direct that blood tests be used to establish whether or not someone is a parent of the child, but cannot force anyone to give a blood sample. It can, however, overrule a child's lack of consent if it believes it is in the child's interests.[58] However, the court may draw its own adverse conclusions if a person fails to comply, depending on all the circumstances of the case.[59] Courts can only order DNA or blood testing if a party applies for it and agrees to pay. However, if that party wins the case, the court usually orders the losing party to pay costs, which can include the costs of any test. In Scotland, if an alleged non-resident parent applies for a declarator of non-parentage and the CMS does not defend the action, no expenses can be awarded against the CMS.[60]

Outcome of the court proceedings

Once a declaration/declarator of parentage is issued, if no calculation has been made, the CMS contacts the non-resident parent to gather the information needed to make a calculation.[61]

If the court finds that the person is not the parent, the parent with care is approached to establish whether a different alleged non-resident parent can be named.[62] Unless the parent can name an alternate alleged non-resident parent, the case may be closed.

The court can order any party to pay some, or all, of the legal costs of another party. Usually, the losing party is ordered to pay the other party's costs. However, an order for costs cannot normally be made against a party who is legally aided. In addition to the costs of any test, the CMS usually asks the court to order the losing party to pay towards its own presentation costs – eg, a solicitor's fees and witnesses' costs.

4. **Further investigations**

The Child Maintenance Service (CMS) or Child Support Agency (CSA) may make further enquiries when considering an application, revision or supersession. In practice, the CMS/CSA usually makes no further investigation if:
- parentage is accepted; *and*
- information is provided to make a calculation; *and*
- any documents requested are provided – eg, copy of maintenance agreement, pay slips or tax calculation notice.

Even if one parent challenges the details provided by the other, the CMS/CSA may be reluctant to make any further enquiries unless the parent can provide sufficient evidence to give it reasonable grounds to trigger a revision or supersession.

Corroboration of evidence (ie, other evidence to support what the CMS/CSA already has) should not be requested unless the evidence the CMS/CSA has is self-contradictory, improbable or contradicted by other evidence.[63]

Evidence can include documentary, written and oral information.

Verifying information

There are specific rules on how the CMS gathers evidence of gross income for '2012 rules' cases (see Chapter 6).

For '1993 rules' and '2003 rules' cases, the CSA seeks to verify certain types of information. Verification of housing costs (in '1993 rules' cases) and earnings is routinely sought by the CSA. However, if every effort to obtain verification of earnings has failed, the amounts provided are accepted as long as they are reasonable.

Verification of earnings from a non-resident parent's employer can only be requested if the employee cannot or does not provide it.

Self-employed earnings are usually taken from the self-assessment return to HM Revenue and Customs (HMRC), or from a tax calculation notice. If not supplied, attempts are made to obtain the information by phone or a face-to-face interview with the parent, or through accountants, companies for whom the parent works, an inspector's visit, or a request to HMRC for self-assessment details where all other means to obtain the information have failed.

Verification of benefits, other income and costs (the latter where needed in relation to a '1993 rules' assessment) is only sought if the amounts appear to be disproportionate or there is another reason to doubt them.

For cases under all three child support schemes, it is an offence for a person who is required to provide information to fail to do so (see p58).

Asking the Child Maintenance Service/Child Support Agency to investigate

The CMS/CSA is not under a general duty to investigate issues relating to child support applications. The CMS/CSA may, however, be under a duty to obtain information that is available to it but not to the applicant.[64] The CMS/CSA may also be under a duty to investigate if there is a contradiction in the evidence.

The CMS/CSA should take into account the nature of any application rather than whether it is in the correct legal form. For example, if a parent with care provides information to the CMS/CSA, it may treat it as an application for a variation if the information and circumstances justify this, even if the application did not expressly ask for a variation.[65]

In some cases, the CMS/CSA may fail to investigate to the satisfaction of one party. If, at any stage, a person believes that the CMS/CSA ought to make more enquiries, s/he should ask it to do so. S/he should phone the CMS/CSA and explain all the information, ask what enquiries have already been made and suggest further ones. Reference should be made to the CMS/CSA's power to require information (see p54) and to use an inspector to conduct investigations (see p72). If the CMS/CSA refuses to say what steps have been taken or to make further enquiries, a complaint can be made (see Chapter 15) and judicial review may be possible (see p215). If an appeal is made, the First-tier Tribunal can make enquiries (see Chapter 13). It has more powers than the CMS/CSA and it may be easier to persuade it to use them.

A person who is dissatisfied with CMS/CSA enquiries can also make her/his own and pass the information to the CMS/CSA. For example, a person with care applying for a court order for maintenance for a spouse or civil partner may obtain information about the non-resident parent's circumstances.

The inspectors

The CMS/CSA can appoint inspectors to obtain the information required.[66] The inspector must have a certificate of appointment, which must be produced when entering premises.[67]

Powers of inspectors

Inspectors can enter premises (except those used only as a home)[68] to make enquiries and to inspect documents.[69] 'Premises' can include vehicles, aircraft, moveable structures and offshore installations.[70] Inspectors cannot enter premises by force. Premises include ones where: [71]

- the non-resident parent is, or has been, employed;
- the non-resident parent carries out, or has carried out, a trade;
- there is information held by someone whom the inspector has reasonable grounds for suspecting has information about the non-resident parent acquired in the course of her/his own trade, profession, vocation or business.

An inspector can question any person aged 18 or over found on the premises[72] and request all such information and documents s/he might reasonably require from:[73]

- an occupier of the premises;
- an employer or employee working there;
- anyone else whose work or business is based there;
- an employee or agent of any of the above.

No one is required to give any evidence or answer any question that might incriminate her/him or her/his spouse or civil partner.[74] Deliberately delaying or obstructing an inspector carrying out her/his duties is an offence. Failing or refusing to answer a question or to provide evidence requested is also an offence, unless there is a good reason for not doing so.[75] The maximum fine is currently £1,000.[76]

A solicitor is entitled to claim 'privilege' concerning information about a client's confidential affairs and can refuse to give information. The CMS/CSA has also given assurances that the powers of inspectors will not be used for other representatives. This does not apply to information required from an employer about an employee.

5. **Change of circumstances**

There is no general duty to give information about any change of circumstances to the Child Maintenance Service (CMS) or Child Support Agency (CSA). This is different from social security benefits, where there is a continuing duty to disclose any relevant changes.

However, there is a duty to disclose information to the CMS/CSA in the circumstances described below and where the CMS/CSA has the right to request the information.

In all cases, the non-resident parent must notify the CMS/CSA within seven days if s/he changes address.[77] The non-resident parent must also inform the CMS/CSA of changes when a deduction from earnings order is in force (see p295).

A person with care also has a duty to tell the CMS/CSA if s/he believes that a calculation has ceased to have effect.[78] This may be because:

- the person with care, non-resident parent or qualifying child has died;
- the person with care, non-resident parent or qualifying child is no longer within CMS/CSA jurisdiction – ie, habitually resident in the UK (see p35);
- the non-resident parent is no longer a non-resident parent of the child or, if there is more than one, all the children named in the calculation – eg, because the child has been adopted;
- a child no longer counts as a child, or as a qualifying child (see p13); *or*
- the person with care has stopped being a person with care in relation to the child or, if there is more than one, all the children named in the calculation.

The person with care must give the reasons for her/his belief in writing, and may be required to give further information to allow a decision to be made.

The person with care is not required to inform the CMS/CSA until the change has taken place.

In '2012 rules' cases, the CMS may also require the non-resident parent to notify it of increases in gross income in certain circumstances (see Chapter 6).

For the consequences of failing to disclose information when required, see p58.

In practice, any party may want to tell the CMS/CSA of changes or new information that may affect the calculation.

6. **Disclosure of information**

In the course of its investigations, the Child Maintenance Service (CMS) or Child Support Agency (CSA) collects information and evidence about people affected by child support applications. The non-resident parent and person with care (and a child applicant in Scotland) must be given details of how the calculation has been worked out (see p205). Some other forms of disclosure are part of the CMS/CSA's duties, such as giving information to courts, the First-tier Tribunal, other parts of the Department for Work and Pensions (DWP) and local authorities.

The CMS/CSA may disclose information given to it by one party (see below) to a child support calculation to another party to explain:[79]

- why an application for child support, or for revision or supersession, has been rejected; *or*
- why an application cannot proceed or why a calculation will not be made; *or*
- why a calculation is cancelled or ceases to have effect; *or*
- how a calculation has been worked out; *or*
- why a decision has been made not to arrange for collection of child support, or to stop collection; *or*
- why a particular method of enforcement has been used; *or*
- why enforcement methods have not been used or enforcement has ceased; *or*
- why a decision has been made not to accept part payment in satisfaction of liability for arrears; *or*
- why a decision has been made not to write off arrears in certain circumstances.

For the purposes of the CMS/CSA's disclosure of information, the '**parties**' are the person with care, the non-resident parent and a qualifying child. If one of these people has died, and a revision, supersession, appeal or variation request is pending but not decided at the date of death, a representative who was dealing with the request on behalf of the person is also a party.[80] Any request for the above information must be made in writing to the CSA/CMS, giving reasons, but the CSA/CMS can provide the information without a request.[81]

The CSA/CMS must only disclose a person's address, or other information which could reasonably be expected to lead to that person's being located, if the person concerned has given written permission.[82] (If a case is appealed, a party should notify the First-tier Tribunal if s/he does not want her/his address or other information disclosed – see Chapter 13.[83]) Also, the CMS/CSA must not disclose information which could reasonably be expected to lead to the identification of any person other than a person with care, non-resident parent, parent treated as non-resident or a qualifying child.[84]

The CMS/CSA can disclose any information it has to the First-tier Tribunal, court and anyone with a right of appeal, if it is for proceedings under the child support or benefits legislation.[85]

In practice, in a child support appeal, CMS/CSA papers are included in the CMS/CSA submission sent to each party (see p235). The CMS/CSA can also disclose information to a court which has made, varied or revived a maintenance order or agreement, if that information is required in relation to those proceedings or other matters arising from them.[86] The CMS/CSA can also disclose information it has to local authorities for their use in administering housing benefit.[87]

In certain circumstances, the CMS/CSA can also disclose information about the non-resident parent to a credit reference agency (see below).

Otherwise, information cannot be given to third parties without the written permission of the person to whom it relates. Any unauthorised disclosure of information is a criminal offence (see p76).

Anyone wishing to see a copy of the information on her/him held by the CMS/CSA can apply in writing. This information must normally be supplied within 40 days.[88] A fee of £10 is likely to be charged for supplying this information. If anyone has concerns about the collection, retention, accuracy or use of this information, the Information Commissioner's Office can be contacted.[89]

Disclosure to other government departments

The CMS/CSA can disclose information to government departments dealing with benefits, including DWP agencies.[90] This includes information obtained using its powers, or information disclosed to the CMS/CSA voluntarily.

As the DWP has close links with the Home Office, disclosure may create problems for people from abroad, in particular possible illegal entrants and those prohibited from having recourse to public funds. If a person has doubts about whether information ought to be disclosed to the CMS/CSA, s/he should get advice first from a law centre or independent advice centre dealing with immigration issues (see Appendix 3). A person cannot be prosecuted for refusing to give information unless it was requested by the CMS/CSA or an inspector (see p72).

CMS/CSA staff can exchange information with their counterparts in Northern Ireland and vice versa.

Disclosure to credit reference agencies

In certain circumstances, the CMS/CSA can disclose information that it holds about a non-resident parent to credit reference agencies. This information can then be used by the agencies in the credit assessment of individuals, meaning that any arrears of child support are likely to have the same effect on a parent's credit assessment as other debts s/he may have.

The parent must consent to the information being passed to the agency, unless a liability order (see p306) is in force against her/him.[91]

The following information can be passed to a credit reference agency:[92]
- the parent's name, last known or notified address and date of birth;

- the CMS/CSA reference number for the parent's case;
- the date any liability order in force against the parent was made;
- the amount covered by the liability order;
- the address stated in the liability order, if different from the last known or notified address.

Before passing any of the above information to an agency, the CMS/CSA must notify the parent in writing by post to her/his last known or notified address (if s/he can be traced) that it intends to do so. The notification must be sent at least 21 days before the information is passed to an agency.[93]

The CMS/CSA can also pass the following information to a credit reference agency without first notifying the non-resident parent:[94]

- that the amount covered by the liability order has been paid, and the date it was paid;
- that a liability order against the parent has been set aside or quashed.

Unauthorised disclosure

Unauthorised disclosure of information is a criminal offence. This offence applies to anyone who is, or has been, a child support officer, a DWP employee working for the CMS/CSA, a civil servant carrying out a function under the Child Support Acts (eg, a Jobcentre Plus officer helping the CMS/CSA make enquiries), First-tier Tribunal staff, various ombudsmen and their staff, staff at the National Audit Office and anyone who, whether or not a civil servant, is providing services to the DWP.[95] It does not apply to members of the First-tier and Upper Tribunals.

It is not an offence to disclose information if:[96]

- the CMS/CSA can do so, or already has done so, under any legal requirement or court order;
- it is in the form of a summary or statistics and it cannot be related to any particular person; *or*
- the person to whom the information relates gives consent or, if that person's affairs are being dealt with under a power of attorney, a receiver under the Mental Health Act, a mental health appointee or a Scottish mental health guardian, the attorney, receiver, guardian or appointee gives consent.

A person who has broken these rules has a defence if s/he can prove that s/he believed s/he was making the disclosure under these rules, or believed that disclosure under these rules had already been made, and had no reason to think otherwise.[97]

On summary conviction, the maximum sentence is six months' imprisonment and/or a fine of up to £5,000. On conviction on indictment, the maximum sentence is two years' imprisonment and/or a fine.[98]

Notes

1. Information-seeking powers
1 s14 and Sch 2 CSA 1991
2 s12 CSPSSA 2000
3 ss4(4), 6(9) and 7(5) CSA 1991; reg 3 CSI Regs
4 Reg 4(1) CSI Regs
5 Reg 7(1) CSI Regs
6 Regs 3 and 4 CSI Regs
7 Reg 3(2) CSI Regs
8 Reg 5 CSI Regs
9 Reg 6 CSI Regs
10 Order 1 r3 CCR 1981
11 See s3 SSA 1998
12 Sch 2 para 1 CSA 1991; Sch 6 para 2 CMOPA 2008
13 Sch 5 TCA 2002
14 s6 and Sch 1 Taxes Management Act 1970; s182 Finance Act 1989
15 Reg 4(2)(b) and (3) CSI Regs
16 Reg 4(2)(c) and (3) CSI Regs
17 Reg 4(2)(d) CSI Regs
18 Reg 4(2)(f) CSI Regs – credit reference agencies are as defined by s145(8) Consumer Credit Act 1974
19 Reg 4(2)(g) CSI Regs
20 s122D SSAA 1992
21 Reg 4(2)(h)(i) CSI Regs
22 Reg 4(2)(h)(ii) CSI Regs
23 Reg 4(2)(i) CSI Regs
24 Reg 4(j) and (k) CSI Regs
25 Reg 7(1) CSI Regs
26 Reg 7(2) CSI Regs
27 s14A CSA 1991
28 s14A(4) CSA 1991
29 Reg 8 CSI Regs
30 Reg 9 CSI Regs
31 s14A CSA 1991; s36 CMOPA 2008

2. Contacting the non-resident parent
32 Regs 7, 11 and 12 CSMC Regs
33 Reg 3(1)(a) CSI Regs
34 CCS/2288/2005
35 Reg 11 CSMC Regs
36 *The Child Support Maintenance Calculation Regulations 2012: a technical consultation on the draft regulations,* CMEC, December 2011

3. Parentage investigations
37 R(CS) 13/98
38 *What Happens if Someone Denies They Are the Parent of a Child?* CSL304, October 2013 (2003 rules) or CMSB010GB, October 2013 (2012 rules)
39 s26 CSA 1991
40 *What Happens When Someone Denies They Are the Parent of a Child?* CMSB010GB, October 2013
41 *What Happens When Someone Denies They Are the Parent of a Child?* CMSB010GB, October 2013
42 s26 CSA 1991
43 *What Happens When Someone Denies They Are the Parent of a Child?* CMSB010GB, October 2013
44 *What Happens When Someone Denies They Are the Parent of a Child?* CMSB010GB, October 2013
45 *What Happens When Someone Denies They Are the Parent of a Child?* CMSB010GB, October 2013
46 *What Happens When Someone Denies They Are the Parent of a Child?* CMSB010GB, October 2013
47 s26 CSA 1991, Case A3(b)
48 www.gov.uk/dna-testing-parentage-disagreements
49 *What Happens When Someone Denies They Are the Parent of a Child?* CMSB010GB, October 2013
50 s27A CSA 1991
51 *What Happens When Someone Denies They Are the Parent of a Child?* CMSB010GB, October 2013
52 *What Happens When Someone Denies They Are the Parent of a Child?* CMSB010GB, October 2013
53 *What Happens When Someone Denies They Are the Parent of a Child?* CMSB010GB, October 2013
54 s27 CSA 1991
55 ss27 and 28 CSA 1991
56 s20 FLRA 1969; *Re H (Paternity: Blood Test)* [1996] 2 FLR 65
57 *W v Official Solicitor* [1972] AC 24
58 s21 FLRA 1969

59 s23 FLRA 1969; *Re A(Paternity: Refusal of Blood Test)* [1994] 2 FLR 463
60 s28(2) CSA 1991; s7 LR(PC)(S)A 1986; r152 AS(CSA) (AOCSCR)
61 *What Happens When Someone Denies They Are the Parent of a Child?* CMSB010GB, October 2013
62 *What Happens When Someone Denies They Are the Parent of a Child?* CMSB010GB, October 2013

4. Further investigations

63 *DB v CMEC* [2010] UKUT 356 (AAC)
64 *DB v CMEC* [2010] UKUT 356 (AAC), citing R(SF) 1/04
65 *DB v CMEC* [2010] UKUT 356 (AAC)
66 s15(1) CSA 1991
67 s15(8) CSA 1991
68 s14(4A) CSA 1991
69 s15(4) CSA 1991
70 s15(11) CSA 1991
71 s15(4A) CSA 1991
72 s15(5) CSA 1991
73 s15(6) CSA 1991
74 s15(7) CSA 1991
75 s15(9) CSA 1991
76 s15(9) CSA 1991

5. Change of circumstances

77 Reg 9 CSI Regs
78 ss44 and 55 and Sch 1 para 16 CSA 1991; reg 10 CSI Regs

6. Disclosure of information

79 Reg 13 CSI Regs, as amended by reg 3 CS(MPA)A Regs; R(CS) 1/00
80 Reg 13(2)(d) CSI Regs
81 Reg 13(3) CSI Regs
82 Reg 13(4) CSI Regs
83 r19(3) TP(FT) Rules
84 Reg 13(4) CSI Regs
85 Reg 12 CSI Regs
86 Reg 12(3) CSI Regs
87 s122C(2)(a) SSAA 1992
88 s7 Data Protection Act 1998
89 https://ico.org.uk
90 s3 SSA 1998
91 s49D CSA 1991
92 Reg 14A(1)(a)-(e) CSI Regs
93 Reg 14A(2) and (3) CSI Regs
94 Reg 14A(1)(f) and (g) and (2) CSI Regs
95 s50 CSA 1991; reg 14 CSI Regs
96 s50 CSA 1991
97 s50(3) CSA 1991
98 s50(4) CSA 1991

Part 3

....

The '2012 rules'

Chapter 5

....

Introduction of the '2012 rules'

This chapter covers:
1. New applications (below)
2. Closure of existing cases (p83)

1. New applications

Since 25 November 2013, all new applications to the statutory child support system have been dealt with by the Child Maintenance Service (CMS) under a new scheme. This scheme was introduced on 10 December 2012 and was phased in, opening gradually to a wider group of applicants (see below). The scheme is referred to as the '2012 rules' scheme in this *Handbook*. It is sometimes also referred to as the 'gross income scheme'.

Existing '1993 rules' or '2003 rules' cases (ie, cases with a child support calculation or assessment in force, or where an application for a calculation or assessment has been made but not yet decided) continue to be dealt with under the '1993 rules' or the '2003 rules' until:[1]

- they are closed as part of the case closure process (see p83);
- they come to an end naturally – eg, because the youngest or only qualifying child becomes too old to count as a qualifying child; *or*
- they are cancelled for some other reason.

Phased introduction of the '2012 rules'

The '2012 rules' scheme was introduced on 10 December 2012. From this date, new applications were initially dealt with by the CMS under the '2012 rules' if they were for at least four qualifying children with the same person with care and same non-resident parent (and provided there was no existing case relating to the same person with care and non-resident parent who were parties to the new application).[2] From 29 July 2013, this was extended to applications for two or three qualifying children, with the same conditions.[3] Since 25 November 2013, *all* new applications have been dealt with under the '2012 rules'.[4]

During the phased introduction of the '2012 rules' scheme, if a new application was made under the '2012 rules', certain existing '1993 rules' and '2003 rules' cases that were related to the new application were also automatically transferred and dealt with under the '2012 rules' without the need for a separate new application. Any arrears outstanding on the related case remain due. If a variation was applied to an existing case, this does not continue to apply when the case is transferred.

A case is a 'related case' if:[5]

- the non-resident parent in a new application under the '2012 rules' is also a non-resident parent in an existing case with a different parent with care; *or*
- the non-resident parent in a new application under the '2012 rules' has a partner who is a non-resident parent in an existing case, and either one (or both) of the non-resident parents receives income support, income-based jobseeker's allowance, income-related employment and support allowance, pension credit or universal credit calculated on the basis that s/he does not have any earned income.

Example 5.1

Neil and his wife Stacey have one child, Rebecca. They separate and in January 2014 Stacey applied for child support for Rebecca. The application is dealt with under the '2012 rules'. The effective date of the calculation for the new application is 17 January 2014.

For several years, Neil has also been paying child support under the '2003 rules' to his former partner, Sarah, for his daughter, Nicola. This existing child support case for Nicola is classed as a related case. It is transferred and also calculated under the '2012 rules', with effect from 17 January 2014, so that all cases involving Neil as the non-resident parent are dealt with by the CMS under the '2012 rules'.

Since 30 June 2014 these rules on automatic transfer of related cases no longer apply.[6] From this date, when a new application is made, related cases are closed as part of the case closure process (see p83).

Note: if, after the date the '2012 rules' were introduced for a particular type of case, an applicant in an existing '2003 rules' or '1993 rules' case asks for that case to be cancelled and then makes a new application within 13 weeks, the new application is treated under the same rules as the cancelled calculation/assessment rather than under the '2012 rules'. This applies whether or not a decision has been made on the existing case.[7]

2. **Closure of existing cases**

The Department for Work and Pensions (DWP) can close existing cases and require parents to choose whether or not to apply to the '2012 rules' scheme.[8] The rules allowing this to happen came into force on 30 June 2014.

Parents whose case is being closed must choose either to make their own private family-based arrangements for child maintenance or to apply to the Child Maintenance Service (CMS) under the '2012 rules'.

Most cases are expected to be closed by the end of 2017, by which time all statutory child support cases will be managed by the CMS under the '2012 rules'.

Note: if an application under the '1993 rules' or '2003 rules' is outstanding and has not yet been decided, and none of the parties apply under the '2012 rules' before the date the existing case is due to close, the Child Support Agency (CSA) may treat the existing application as withdrawn and not make any decision on it.[9]

When cases will be closed

The DWP can set the rules for the order in which cases will be closed over the transition period, and set a date for when the transition period will end. It can revise these arrangements.[10] The current rules on how cases will be closed were issued on 3 December 2014.[11]

The process of closing existing cases will take place in stages (see p84) over a transition period.[12] This is expected to last for over three years (from 30 June 2014 until 31 December 2017), but it may be extended.[13]

Two types of existing cases will not be dealt with proactively in this staged process over the transition period: cases that are due to close anyway and those that are 'related' to a new application.

Cases that are due to close before the end of the transition period because the only or youngest qualifying child in the assessment or calculation has reached the age of 20 (see p13) are not closed as part of the staged process.[14] These continue until they are due to end. This means that a significant number of '1993 rules' cases, in particular, are likely to continue until they naturally come to an end.

If a new application is made under the '2012 rules' during the transition period, the application triggers the closure of an existing 'related' case (see p82).[15] This is intended to ensure that all child support cases involving the same non-resident parent are assessed using the same set of rules. The parties in the existing case are notified that the case is to close and must choose either to make their own private family-based arrangements for child maintenance or to apply to the CMS under the '2012 rules' (see p85).

If an applicant in an existing case that will not be closed proactively, or is not yet due to close under the staged process, asks the CSA to cease acting and then applies under the '2012 rules' scheme within 13 weeks of the existing case closing, the new application is treated as if it were still an existing case and is not dealt with under the '2012 rules'.[16] This means that a person with care who considers that the '2012 rules' scheme would be advantageous to her/him can voluntarily transfer to the '2012 rules'. However, s/he must wait at least 13 weeks and loses child support for this period unless a private family-based arrangement for child maintenance can be made for this period. The new application is subject to the 'gateway' and the application fee (see p42).

If, on or after 30 June 2014, the person with care (or child applicant in Scotland) in a case in which all the qualifying children will reach the age of 20 before the end of the transition period (ie, before 31 December 2017) requests that the case be cancelled, the non-resident parent cannot make an application for 13 weeks after the date of cancellation. This only applies if the non-resident parent makes an application in respect of a child who was a qualifying child in the cancelled case. This rule is designed to prevent a non-resident parent making a new application that forces the case still to be dealt with as an existing case under the '1993 rules' or '2003 rules'. The rule does not apply if the non-resident parent was the applicant in the original case, or is making an application because s/he is now a person with care.[17]

The staged case closure process

All cases (except those that are due to close anyway and those related to new applications) will be closed in stages over the transition period. They will be closed in tranches, and the DWP can give priority to certain cases.[18]

Cases are being closed in the following stages (which the DWP calls 'segments').[19]

- Segment one: cases in which child support liability is nil. A number of '1993 rules'and '2003 rules' cases will be selected each day, with the oldest cases generally being selected first. Cases from this segment began being selected on 30 June 2014, with the first cases ending in January 2015.
- Segment two: cases in which the non-resident parent has a liability to pay child support but is not paying or there is no payment schedule in place. Again, a number of '1993 rules' and '2003 rules' cases will be selected each day, with the oldest cases generally being selected first. Cases from this segment began being selected on 26 January 2015, with the first cases due to close in August 2015. Cases where enforcement action is being pursued are part of segment five rather than segment two.
- Segments three and four: cases that are dealt with clerically as they cannot be managed on the main computer systems, and all cases that are dealt with on the main computer systems, except those that fall into segments one, two or five. Segments three and four are being dealt with together. Again, a number of '1993 rules' and '2003 rules' cases will be selected each day, with the oldest cases generally being selected first. At the time of writing, it was not known

when cases in these segments will begin to be selected. It is expected that 'pathfinder' groups will be selected first to test systems.

- Segment five: all 'enforcement cases'. Non-compliant cases will be dealt with first, followed by partially compliant cases and then fully compliant cases. 'Enforcement cases' are those where the method of payment is via a deduction from earnings order, deduction from earnings request or regular deduction order (see p292), or where other enforcement action (such as lump-sum deduction orders, liability orders and action resulting from them – see p292) is currently in progress.

This order of dealing with cases is intended to minimise the risk of disruption to the payment of child support in existing cases, particularly where payment is being made as a result of certain enforcement action.

There are approximately 100,000 to 200,000 cases to close in each segment, so during each segment cases will be selected randomly over time. Other criteria may be applied – eg, the oldest cases within each segment may be selected first. Although it intends to follow these five main segments, the DWP has also said that it may select a small number of 'pathfinder' cases from each segment to test systems and the reactions of parties, and may revise the scheme at any time.[20]

If the circumstances of a case change so that it would come into an earlier segment, it will be selected at the next earliest opportunity. If a change means that a case that has already been selected now comes into a later segment, the process of case closure continues (unless the DWP withdraws the closure notice – see p86).[21]

If a group of cases is linked (eg, different cases with the same non-resident parent) and the cases would come into different segments, all those cases are likely to be selected in the latest segment that applies to any of the cases.[22]

How cases are closed

The CSA notifies the parties (ie, person with care, non-resident parent and child applicant in Scotland) in writing of the date that liability for child support under the existing case ends (ie, the date the case will close). A person is treated as having received the notification on the second day after it was sent to her/his last known address. The parties must then choose whether they wish to stay in the statutory child support scheme or make a private family-based arrangement for paying child maintenance. The notice must include information on how to choose to stay in the statutory scheme.[23]

Existing cases normally close between 180 days and 272 days (ie, between approximately six and nine months) after the parties are notified. This is usually 180 days, but a longer period of up to 272 days may be used in cases where the non-resident parent has been given the chance to demonstrate her/his ability to pay voluntarily in order to be allowed the opportunity to pay by 'direct pay' under a new '2012 rules' case. If the existing case is closing because it is related (see p83) to a new application under the '2012 rules', it closes on a day no less than 30 days after the parties are notified.[24] These periods are intended to:

- give the parties to the existing case time to consider whether they can make a private family-based arrangement or whether the person with care wants to apply to the '2012 rules' scheme and pay the application fee; *and*
- minimise the delay before liability in the new application begins.

If the parties in an existing case have received a notice that the case is to close and it then becomes a related case, the CSA may change the date for the existing case to end by issuing a new notice to say that the case will close on a day at least 30 days later.[25]

Information on any outstanding arrears will also be sent to the parties. A reminder letter will be sent to the parties one month before the case is due to close. A final letter confirming that the case has closed and liability ended is also sent.

The CSA can withdraw a notice that a case will close if:[26]

- it decides that it was issued in error – ie, it should not have been selected, or should have been selected for a later segment; *and*
- it is withdrawn more than 30 days before the date the case is due to close.

It is understood that the CSA intends to use this power to withdraw notices only in exceptional cases. Before doing so, it considers the circumstances, including the wishes of the parties and whether there is likely to be disruption to payments or disadvantage caused by continuing with the case closure process. If a notice is withdrawn, the case continues under the existing rules until it would close anyway or is selected at a future date.[27] If a notice is withdrawn and a party has already applied under the '2012 rules', any application fee already paid must be reimbursed.[28]

Choosing to stay in the statutory scheme

If the parties in a case that is being closed want to stay in the statutory scheme with no break in child support liability, they must apply under the '2012 rules' before the date the existing case is due to close.[29]

The application is treated in the same way as any other new application under the '2012 rules' (see Chapter 3), and the 'gateway' and the application fee apply (see p42).[30]

Note: if one of the parties in a case chooses to stay in the statutory scheme and make an application, this proceeds even if the other party does not want to do so.[31]

Once a new application has been made, the address of the non-resident parent has been verified and any application fee due has been paid, the CMS must notify the non-resident parent in writing as soon as reasonably practical after the date that is 39 days before the existing case is due to close.[32]

Information to determine the new application is gathered afresh and entered on the new computer system. The parties may be required to provide information to enable the application to be considered, even if this was previously provided for the existing case that is closing.[33]

The decision under the '2012 rules' normally takes effect from the day after the existing case is closed. However, the calculation is made at the time the new application is made, using information that applied on the 'effective date' of the new application – ie, the day the non-resident parent was notified in writing of the new application.[34] As with other cases, the CMS can take account of changes in circumstances.

If a deduction from earnings order (DEO) or regular deduction order was in place for the existing case, the new case under the '2012 rules' is treated as a continuation of the existing case and the DEO or regular deduction order continues to apply.[35] If the existing case was an arrears-only case, and there is no ongoing child support liability, the liability in a new application begins immediately – ie, on the date the non-resident parent is given written notification of the application.

Note: there is no provision to phase in the new child support liability if parties whose existing case is due to close choose to apply under the '2012 rules'. The amount due under the '2012 rules' may be significantly different from the amount due under the existing case. Some cases may have been calculated several years ago and not been changed since, and so liability under the '2012 rules' may be considerably higher. In other cases, liability under the '2012 rules' may be lower due to changes in the way income is calculated.

Arrears in closed cases

The DWP has said that it will use the closure of existing '1993 rules' and '2003 rules' cases to validate arrears and prioritise recovery action.[36]

If a case has been closed and there are arrears, but no ongoing liability for child support in a new '2012 rules' case, action to recover the outstanding arrears is expected to be treated as a low priority by the CSA.

Arrears that arise from '1993 rules' or '2003 rules' cases remain outstanding unless the person with care states that s/he does not want them to be collected. As part of the transition process, the CSA asks the person with care whether s/he wants the arrears written off, and the CSA also considers whether any arrears should be written off (see p291). The parties are informed of any balance of arrears that is transferred to the new case.

Arrears are only transferred to be managed by the new computer system if there is an ongoing liability for child support under a '2012 rules' application. Before being transferred, the arrears are checked for accuracy. Only arrears that have been validated in this way are transferred. This process could take up to six months. Existing CSA enforcement is expected to continue while this is going on.

Once arrears have been validated and transferred, no new enforcement action is started by the CMS unless the non-resident parent has failed to pay her/his ongoing liability. This means that, once enforcement action in the existing case has ended, it does not begin until the CMS accepts that a direct payment arrangement is not suitable in the case.[37]

Notes

1. **New applications**
    1 Art 3 CMOPA(Comm 12)O
    2 Art 3 CMOPA(Comm 10)O
    3 Art 3 CMOPA(Comm 11)O
    4 Art 2 CMOPA(Comm 12)O
    5 Art 3(3) and (4) CMOPA(Comm 10)O;
       Art 3(3) and (4) CMOPA(Comm 11)O;
       Art 5 CMOPA(Comm 12)O
    6 Art 5(1) CMOPA(Comm 12)O; Arts 6
       and 7 CMOPA(Comm 14)O
    7 Art 3(5) CMOPA(Comm 10)O; Art 3(5)
       CMOPA(Comm 11)O; Art 4
       CMOPA(Comm 12)O

2. **Closure of existing cases**
    8 s19 and Sch 5 para 1(1) CMOPA 2008
    9 Reg 8 CS(ELEC) Regs
    10 Reg 3 CS(ELEC) Regs
    11 *Child Support Scheme for Timing and
       Related Matters in Relation to Ending
       Liability in Existing Cases ('the ending
       liability scheme'),* DWP, 3 December
       2014
    12 Reg 4(1) CS(ELEC) Regs
    13 *Child Support Scheme for Timing and
       Related Matters in Relation to Ending
       Liability in Existing Cases ('the ending
       liability scheme'),* DWP, 3 December
       2014
    14 Reg 4(3) CS(ELEC) Regs
    15 Reg 4(2) CS(ELEC) Regs
    16 Art 4 CMOPA(Comm 12)O
    17 Art 3 CMOPA(Comm 14)O
    18 Reg 4(4) CS(ELEC) Regs

    19 *Child Support Scheme for Timing and
       Related Matters in Relation to Ending
       Liability in Existing Cases ('the ending
       liability scheme'),* DWP, 3 December
       2014 , paras 20-28
    20 *Child Support Scheme for Timing and
       Related Matters in Relation to Ending
       Liability in Existing Cases ('the ending
       liability scheme'),* DWP, 3 December
       2014, para 29 and Annex A
    21 *Child Support Scheme for Timing and
       Related Matters in Relation to Ending
       Liability in Existing Cases ('the ending
       liability scheme'),* DWP, 3 December
       2014, para 18
    22 *Child Support Scheme for Timing and
       Related Matters in Relation to Ending
       Liability in Existing Cases ('the ending
       liability scheme'),* DWP, 3 December
       2014, para 19
    23 Sch 5 para 1(1) CMOPA 2008; reg 5
       CS(ELEC) Regs
    24 Reg 6(1) CS(ELEC) Regs; *Child Support
       Scheme for Timing and Related Matters in
       Relation to Ending Liability in Existing
       Cases ('the ending liability scheme'),*
       DWP, 3 December 2014, paras 11 and
       12
    25 Reg 6(2) CS(ELEC) Regs
    26 Reg 5(7) CS(ELEC) Regs
    27 *Child Support Scheme for Timing and
       Related Matters in Relation to Ending
       Liability in Existing Cases ('the ending
       liability scheme'),* DWP, 3 December
       2014, paras 32-35
    28 Reg 5(8) CS(ELEC) Regs

29 Reg 5(5) CS(ELEC) Regs
30 Reg 7(1) CS(ELEC) Regs
31 Sch 5 para 4 CMOPA 2008
32 Reg 11(5)-(8) CSMC Regs
33 Reg 5(6) CS(ELEC) Regs
34 Reg 7(3) CS(ELEC) Regs
35 Reg 7(4) CS(ELEC) Regs
36 *Supporting Separated Families: securing children's futures*, Cm 8399, DWP, July 2012; *Preparing for the Future, Tackling the Past: child maintenance – arrears and compliance strategy 2012-2017*, DWP, January 2013
37 *Supporting Separated Families: securing children's futures*, Cm 8399, DWP, July 2012

Chapter 6

The child support calculation ('2012 rules')

This chapter covers:
1. Calculating child support (below)
2. Gross income (p94)
3. Shared care (p106)

1. Calculating child support

The amount of child support is calculated under the '2012 rules' in a similar way as for the '2003 rules' (see Chapter 8). The main difference is that the non-resident parent's gross income rather than net income is used in the '2012 rules' (see p94).

Child support is calculated for each non-resident parent separately. This means that a person with care could receive, for example, the flat rate of child support from one non-resident parent and an amount worked out using the basic rate from another non-resident parent.

The child support calculation is based on the same kinds of factors as for '2003 rules' cases (see p129).

The amount of child support calculated is a weekly amount. In all cases, fractions of a penny are disregarded if they are less than a half, or rounded up to the next penny if a half or over.[1]

Rates of child support

There are four rates of child support:
- nil rate (see below);
- flat rate (see p91);
- reduced rate (see p91);
- basic rate, including 'basic rate plus' (see p91).

Nil rate

The nil rate applies in the same circumstances as for the '2003 rules' (see p132), except that:[2]

- prisoners who are liable for the nil rate include those serving a prison sentence who are detained in hospital;
- full-time students do not automatically qualify for the nil rate under the '2012 rules';
- gross income (including income from benefits) is used to decide whether a person has income of less than £7 a week (before 25 November 2013 this was £5 a week).

Flat rate

From 25 November 2013, the flat rate under the '2012 rules' is £7 a week.[3] The flat rate applies in the same circumstances as for the '2003 rules' (see p133). It can also be halved or apportioned in the same circumstances (see p133).[4]

Reduced rate

The reduced rate applies in the same circumstances, and is calculated in the same way, as for the '2003 rules' (see p134), except that:[5]

- gross income is used to decide whether a person has income of less than £200 but more than £100 per week;
- the percentages of income used are different (see table below), to reflect the fact that gross income is used. The percentages were changed on 25 November 2013 when the flat rate was increased to £7;
- it is the flat rate of £7 that is added to the percentage of income;
- the rules on relevant non-resident children are different (see p94).

Reduced rate percentages

Number of relevant other children	Number of qualifying children (including relevant non-resident children)		
	One	Two	Three or more
None	17%	25%	31%
One	14.1%	21.2%	26.4%
Two	13.2%	19.9%	24.9%
Three or more	12.4%	18.9%	23.8%

If the non-resident parent shares the care of any qualifying children, the reduced rate may be decreased by applying the shared care rules (see p106).

Basic rate

The basic rate applies if none of the other rates (nil, flat or reduced) apply. The basic rate applies in similar circumstances, and is calculated in a similar way, as for the '2003 rules' (see p135). However, under the '2012 rules':

- gross income is used to decide the parent's weekly income;

- the percentages of income used are different, to reflect the fact that gross income is used;
- there is an additional step if gross weekly income is more than £800;
- the rules on relevant non-resident children are different (see p94).

If the non-resident parent has a gross weekly income of £200 or more, child support is calculated using the basic rate. If her/his gross weekly income is over £800, the 'basic rate plus' applies. The basic rate is a percentage of gross income, depending on the number of qualifying children. How much is paid also depends on the number of relevant other children.

Basic rate percentages[6]

Number of qualifying children (including relevant non-resident children)	Percentage of gross income up to £800	Percentage of gross income above £800
One	12%	9%
Two	16%	12%
Three or more	19%	15%

If the non-resident parent has one or more relevant other children, her/his gross income is reduced before the basic rate is calculated. The basic rate is therefore worked out in two steps, depending on the circumstances.

Number of relevant other children	Percentage by which gross income is reduced
One	11%
Two	14%
Three or more	16%

Step one

Work out the gross income of the non-resident parent. Reduce this by 11 per cent, 14 per cent or 16 per cent, depending on the number of relevant other children.

Step two

Work out the amount of child support as a proportion of this remaining gross income, depending on the number of qualifying children.

- If gross income is £800 or less, the basic rate child support is 12 per cent, 16 per cent or 19 per cent of this gross income.

- If gross income is over £800, 'basic rate plus' child support is 12 per cent, 16 per cent or 19 per cent of £800 plus 9 per cent, 12 per cent or 15 per cent of the amount over £800.

Example 6.1

Alfie and Susan have separated and their two children, Tracey and Jon, live with Susan. Alfie lives with his new partner and her daughter Donna. Alfie's gross income is £450 a week. Donna is a relevant other child, and Tracey and Jon are the qualifying children.

Step one	Alfie's gross income is £450. There is one relevant other child, so this is reduced by 11 per cent.
	11% x £450 = £49.50
	£450 – £49.50 = £400.50
Step two	There are two qualifying children, so child support is 16 per cent of the remaining gross income.
	16% x £400.50 = £64.08

Alfie therefore pays £64.08 in child support to Susan.

Alfie's gross income is now £980, so the basic rate plus applies.

Step one	Alfie's gross income is £980. There is one relevant other child, so this is reduced by 11 per cent.
	11% x £980 = £107.80
	£980 – £107.80 = £872.20
Step two	This amount is over £800 and there are two qualifying children. So child support is 16 per cent of £800 plus 12 per cent of the 'excess' above £800 – ie, 12 per cent of £72.20.
	16% x £800 = £128
	12% x £72.20 = £8.66

Alfie therefore now pays £136.66 (£128 + £8.66) in child support to Susan.

If there is more than one person with care

If there is more than one person with care in relation to a non-resident parent, the amount of child support may be apportioned between them in the same way as under the '2003 rules' (see p137).[7]

Divided families

If a couple has more than one child together and at least one child is living with each parent, child support liability is still calculated for both parents. However, as with '2003 rules' cases, the amounts are offset so that only the parent with the higher liability makes a balancing payment, while the other parent does not pay anything.[8] The Child Maintenance Service may use the term 'split care' when referring to this situation.

Relevant non-resident children

A non-resident parent may have other relevant non-resident children (see p24). This affects the child support calculation in the same way as under the '2003 rules' (see p137). However, for the '2012 rules', the definition of 'relevant non-resident children' is wider and includes all children who are the subject of a maintenance agreement involving the non-resident parent (see p24).

2. Gross income

The child support calculation under the '2012 rules' is based on the non-resident parent's gross weekly income.

'Gross weekly income' is calculated by using either the non-resident parent's 'historic income' or 'current income' at the 'effective date' and converting this into a weekly amount.[9] The rules on the type of income that is taken into account are complex and are based on how income is treated for income tax purposes.

Income from sources other than those described in this section is not counted. Taxable social security benefits are not included, except that incapacity benefit (IB), contributory employment and support allowance (ESA), jobseeker's allowance (JSA) and income support (IS) are included in the historic income figure provided by HM Revenue and Customs (HMRC). **Note:** unlike the '2003 rules', working tax credit is *not* counted as part of the non-resident parent's income.

In some cases, income that is not counted in gross income for the calculation can be taken into account by a variation (see Chapter 7). For example, if a non-resident parent has unearned income from property or investments, a variation could be sought on the grounds that s/he has additional income. However, in many cases, an application for a variation is only likely to be made if a person with care is aware that the non-resident parent has other sources of income.

Contributions to an approved personal or occupational pension scheme (ie, a scheme registered with HMRC) by the non-resident parent in the relevant tax year are deducted when calculating gross weekly income. No other deductions are taken into account.

There is no limit on the amount of pension contributions that can be deducted. If a person with care is aware of the amount of contributions and considers them to be excessive, or that arrangements have been set up deliberately to reduce liability for child support (eg, if the non-resident parent has made a salary sacrifice arrangement in return for increased employer contributions), s/he can apply for a variation on the grounds of diversion of income (see p111).

The parties to the calculation decision are notified of the income figure used. This applies whether the calculation is based on historic income or current income (including if current income is estimated), but does not include a breakdown of the types of income included.[10] See p205 for further details on the notification of decisions.

Note: if the Child Maintenance Service (CMS) does not have sufficient information to make a calculation, it may make a 'default maintenance decision' (see p204).

There are special rules for annual reviews of income (see p101), periodic checks if current income is being used (see p103) and for reporting changes to current income (see p104).

Historic income

In most cases, the calculation uses a non-resident parent's 'historic' income. The CMS aims to avoid having to obtain information on income from the parent or her/his employer, and information on historic income is provided by HMRC using an automated system. This is intended to reduce the possibility of delay, the supply of inaccurate information and demands on employers.

The CMS requests a historic income figure for the latest available tax year from HMRC no more than 30 days before the initial effective date. The 'latest available tax year' is, on the date the CMS requests the information, the most recent tax year for which HMRC has received information on the non-resident parent under either:[11]

- the Pay As You Earn (PAYE) scheme, for which employers complete end-of-year returns on the taxable earnings of their employees; *or*
- the annual self-assessment returns completed by individual taxpayers on various sources of income.

The latest available tax year must be one of the six tax years before the date the information is sought.[12]

The CMS does not have discretion to use different income figures – eg, if there is evidence that the non-resident parent has under-reported her/his income on the self-assessment. The CMS is not expected to receive a breakdown of the historic income figure automatically. It may request a breakdown from HMRC if one party queries the figure. It does not normally provide the breakdown to the parties, but may give it to the non-resident parent.

The historic income figure takes into account the non-resident parent's taxable income from:[13]

- employment – ie, her/his income from earnings (see p99);
- pensions (see p100);
- the taxable amount of the following social security benefits – IB, contributory ESA, JSA and IS; *and*
- her/his profits from self-employment (see p100).

Self-assessment information is usually available to the CMS by February or March in the year following the end of the tax year on 5 April. Information from PAYE returns is available earlier. If HMRC has information from both the PAYE scheme and a self-assessment for the latest available tax year, information from the self-assessment is used, as it is expected to be more comprehensive.[14]

Contributions to an approved personal or occupational pension scheme (ie, a scheme registered with HMRC) by the non-resident parent in the relevant tax year are deducted by HMRC when providing the historic income figure. If the non-resident parent has made pension contributions during the relevant tax year that have not been deducted under net pay arrangements (eg, payments made directly to a personal pension scheme), s/he can request that the weekly average amount of these is deducted from the gross income figure.[15] The CMS may require her/him to provide further information. Because tax relief is given on pension contributions, actual contributions are less than the gross amount included in the pension plan. It is the higher gross amount that should be deducted from gross income. If a gross amount including higher rate tax relief is being claimed, the CMS is likely to require evidence in the form of an HMRC calculation notice.

The rules on the type of income included are intended to ensure that parents are treated consistently, whether the information held on them by HMRC comes from the PAYE scheme or from self-assessment.

The use of historic income information from HMRC means that taxable payments to those in the following occupations or offices are *not* disregarded (as is the case for '2003 rules' cases):

- auxiliary coastguards;
- part-time firefighters and lifeboat crew members;
- reserve or territorial force members;
- local authority councillors.

Maintaining consistency, however, means that some types of income captured by self-assessment are not counted as gross weekly income for the calculation, even though HMRC may hold reliable information about them. This includes some taxable social security benefits and some allowances claimed by employees against taxable earnings.[16]

If a parent is both employed and self-employed, it is possible that at the time the calculation is made PAYE details are available for the most recently completed tax year, but self-assessment only for the year before this. Information on employment income is, therefore, likely to reflect the parent's current circumstances more accurately.

Income from employment

When HMRC provides information on historic income from employment, gross pay is used. 'Gross pay' is all payments, such as salary, wages, fees, bonuses, commission, tips and overtime, before any income tax or national insurance contributions are deducted. HMRC deducts contributions to an approved personal or occupational pension scheme. No other deductions are permitted.[17]

Statutory sick pay, statutory maternity pay, statutory adoption pay, statutory paternity pay and statutory shared parental pay are treated as employment income.

Anything of direct monetary value to the employee that derives from the employment or office is also treated as earnings.[18] There are certain exemptions.[19]

Income from self-employment

Historic income from self-employment is based on the taxable profits from any 'trade, profession or vocation' in the latest available tax year for which a self-assessment has been completed – ie, the profits in the accounting period that ended in the tax year.[20] For example, if a self-employed parent's accounting year ends in June, the self-assessment for that period will not be returned until the January 19 months later.[21]

If a business is run on a commercial basis and has made a loss, gross income is nil for that tax year. In certain circumstances, a loss in a previous year can be carried forward and deducted from profits in the next and later tax years. HMRC deducts such losses when determining the historic income figure for self-employment.[22]

Pension income

Income (before tax) from a personal or occupational pension, or an annuity or other kind of taxable pension income, counts towards gross weekly income.[23]

The full details of pension income that is taxable are complex.[24] Tax-free lump sums paid under an approved personal pension scheme, retirement annuity contract or tax-exempt pension scheme are ignored completely.[25] A lump sum counts if it is for cashing in a small pension, if the fund is too small to pay a pension (within the 'trivial commutation' limit) or if an occupational pension scheme winds up.[26] If a pension is paid because of a work-related illness or disability caused by an injury on duty, only the amount that would have been paid had the parent retired on non-work-related ill-health grounds counts. Any extra amount paid is ignored.[27] Various war disablement pensions are also not counted.[28]

Pension income for these purposes does not include UK social security pensions, even though they are taxable and appear on a self-assessment return.[29] This means that the following are not counted:[30]

- retirement pension;
- graduated retirement benefit;
- industrial death benefit;
- widowed mother's allowance;
- widowed parent's allowance;
- widow's pension.

Current income

In certain cases, historic income information may not be available or may differ significantly from the non-resident parent's current circumstances. In this case, the calculation is based on the non-resident parent's current income. The CMS approaches the parent to verify her/his employment or self-employment details and, in some cases, may contact her/his employer or accountant for information.

The CMS can seek information on current income if:[31]

- no historic income figure is available – ie, HMRC does not have information for any one of the six tax years before the date of the CMS's request;[32]
- the CMS is unable, for whatever reason, to request or obtain the required information from HMRC – eg, because of problems with the automatic data-sharing system; *or*
- there is at least 25 per cent difference between the current income and historic income.

Note: the CMS accepts a historic income figure of nil from HMRC and does not use current income in this case. If a non-resident parent with nil historic income is believed to have current earnings, a revision or supersession can be requested. If the non-resident parent has *any* current income, it is automatically treated as at least 25 per cent different from the nil historic income figure and a new calculation decision can be made.[33]

The most likely stage at which a parent may dispute the accuracy of the historic income figure used and ask for current income to be considered is once an application has been made and information from the non-resident parent starts to be gathered.

'Current income' is the total, calculated or estimated income from:[34]

- employment;
- self-employment; *and*
- pensions.

Income from taxable benefits included in historic income is not counted in current income. A parent currently receiving one of these benefits normally qualifies for the flat rate.

Contributions to an approved personal or occupational pension scheme (ie, a scheme registered with HMRC) by the non-resident parent in the relevant tax year are deducted. In many cases, these will already have been deducted by her/his employer in her/his pay. In this case, the deductions are not included in gross income.[35]

If the non-resident parent has income from employment or self-employment and has made pension contributions during the relevant tax year that have not been deducted by her/his employer (eg, they were made directly to a personal pension scheme), the weekly average amount of these can be deducted from the gross income figure.[36] Because tax relief is given on personal pension contributions, actual contributions are less than the gross amount included in the pension plan. It is the higher gross amount that should be deducted from current income. The CMS does not deduct a higher gross amount to reflect higher rate tax relief, as granting this relief requires a decision by HMRC that it will not yet have been able to make at the time that current income is being assessed.

If any payment is made in a currency other than sterling, charges for converting it to sterling are deducted from the current income figure.[37]

Estimating current income

The CMS can estimate current income if the information about it is insufficient or is unreliable and:[38]

- the historic income is nil and there is any current income – ie, current income is automatically treated as being 25 per cent different from historic income; or
- no historic income information is available, or the CMS is unable, for whatever reason, to request or obtain the required information from HMRC.

The CMS is likely to use this power to encourage non-resident parents to co-operate in providing details of their current income. It can base an estimate on any assumptions about any facts. Assumptions may be based on any information already held about the non-resident parent's circumstances. If the CMS is satisfied that s/he works in a particular occupation, it can assume that s/he has the average weekly income of a person engaged in that occupation in a particular area of the UK.[39] It may use information such as the Office for National Statistics' *Annual Survey of Hours and Earnings*, which gives average earnings for occupations and regions. This can apply to income from employment or self-employment.

A parent who works part time or has lower than average wages for any reason should make sure the CMS is aware of this.

If there is no historic income information available, the CMS has not been able to gather information about current income and it does not have enough information to estimate current income, it may make a 'default maintenance decision' (see p204).

Income from employment

Income from employment is defined for current income purposes in the same way as for historic income (see p96). Gross earnings are taken into account, not including approved pension contributions.

Current income is intended to be assessed in a way that, wherever possible, results in a stable amount of child support liability being set. If the non-resident parent receives any income from a salary, wages or other periodic payments and the CMS considers that this is a settled regular amount likely to continue for the foreseeable future, it converts this into a weekly amount.[40]

If earnings are less frequent, fluctuate or are not a regular settled amount for some other reason, the CMS averages the amounts over an appropriate period before the effective date of the decision and converts this to a weekly amount. Averaging is likely to be used if, for example, the parent is a seasonal worker or has an irregular pattern of hours, shifts or overtime.[41]

Some taxable amounts may be paid at different intervals from regular pay. The total of any bonus or commission payments in the last 12 months that have been paid separately or for a different period than other income is also converted to a weekly amount.[42]

The detailed rules on what income from employment is taxable are complex. Anything of direct monetary value to an employee that derives from her/his employment or office is also treated as earnings, and the amount received in the past 12 months converted into a weekly amount.[43] There are certain exemptions that are not treated as earnings.[44]

Income from self-employment

Income from self-employment is defined for current income purposes in the same way as for historic income – ie, as the taxable profits from any 'trade, profession or vocation' (see p97).

Profits are determined for the most recently completed tax year or accounting period that a parent would normally report in a self-assessment. If no full tax year or accounting period has been completed, the profits are estimated for the current period. The total profit for the period is converted into a weekly amount.[45] The current income of an established business is normally expected to relate to an annual period equal to that covered by most self-assessments. A shorter period is only expected to be used for a new business. In this case, the CMS tries to identify estimated or projected annual profits – eg, using any completed profit and loss accounts to date and business plans.

It is the profits from the self-employment in which the non-resident parent is engaged on the effective date that are determined. If the CMS accepts that the parent had ceased trading on the effective date, s/he is assessed as having no profits, so her/his current income is nil if s/he has no other source of income. If the parent is a partner in a business, the profits are apportioned according to her/his share.[46]

Pension income

Pension income is defined for current income purposes in the same way as for historic income (see p97). If current income is being used, the CMS averages pension income over an appropriate period to give a weekly amount.[47]

Income from outside the UK

Income from outside the UK is included in gross income if it falls into one of the categories of taxable income from employment, self-employment or pensions.

The detailed rules on what income is taxable are complex. The following are some types of income that are disregarded:

- social security payments from outside the UK, equivalent to tax-free UK benefits;[48]
- one-tenth of the amount of any overseas pension or of a pension payable in the UK by the governments of certain other countries;[49]
- tax-free lump-sum payments under an overseas pension scheme;[50]
- income the parent is prevented from transferring to the UK by law or by the government of the country where the income arises or because foreign currency cannot be obtained in that country.[51]

Annual reviews

The CMS must conduct an annual review of gross weekly income. This is done whether gross income is based on historic income or current income.[52]

The review date is normally on the anniversary of the initial effective date, but the CMS can use a different date for a particular case or type of case.[53]

If a child support calculation is already in force and a new application is made in relation to the same non-resident parent for a different qualifying child, the review dates for the two cases are aligned. This allows the non-resident parent's income to be assessed at the same time for all cases in which s/he is involved. The first review date for the new case is on the next review date for the calculation already in force.[54] If both parents are non-resident and applications for child support from both have been treated as one application (see p48), the CMS can use different review dates for each non-resident parent.[55]

In order to conduct the review, the CMS requests an updated historic income figure for the latest available tax year from HMRC.[56] It can request this no earlier than 30 days before the review date.[57]

If the gross weekly income shown by the updated figure is different from the historic income figure previously used, the CMS supersedes the calculation decision. The supersession decision takes effect from the review date.[58]

If gross weekly income is based on current income, the current income is compared with the updated historic income figure. If current income is still at least 25 per cent different from the updated historic income, the current income figure is still used. If it is within 25 per cent, the updated historic income figure is used and the calculation is superseded, with effect from the review date.

If a variation to the calculation on the grounds of additional income is in force, the CMS may also request updated information on unearned income in the latest available tax year when it asks HMRC for the updated historic income figure. If unearned income has changed, a supersession decision can be made. This takes effect from the review date.[59]

When the CMS gets the updated historic income figure, it writes to the person with care and non-resident parent (and child applicant in Scotland) giving details of the income figure to be used for the coming year. This includes a breakdown of the calculation, including details such as qualifying children, relevant other children, other maintenance arrangements taken into account and shared care. This notification is not a formal decision that can be challenged, but a notification that the calculation is expected to be based on this information. The parties have 30 days to notify the CMS of any changes and provide any additional information or evidence.[60]

The formal decision on the child support calculation for the coming year is then issued to the parties on the effective date of the annual review. This formal decision can be challenged by the parties.

Any changes reported by any of the parties during this 30-day period may also result in a supersession of the current child support calculation from the date the change is reported.

Example 6.2

The situation is as in Example 6.1. Alfie is paying £64.08 a week child support to Susan. This is based on historic income information, showing his gross weekly income to be £450. The annual review date is 8 March.

On 6 February (30 days before the annual review), the CMS receives updated historic income information, showing a gross weekly income of £500 and notifies Alfie and Susan. The CMS receives evidence from Alfie on 12 February, showing that he has changed his working pattern and that his current gross weekly income is now £320.

This current income figure varies by more than 25 per cent from the updated historic income figure of £500, so Alfie's new child support liability from 8 March is based on the current income figure of £320 gross weekly income.

Step one	Alfie's gross weekly income is £320. There is one relevant other child, which means this is reduced by 11 per cent.
	11% x £320 = £35.20
	£320 – £35.20 = £284.80
Step two	There are two qualifying children, so child support is 16 per cent of the remaining gross income.
	16% x £284.80 = £45.57

Alfie will, therefore, pay £45.57 a week in child support to Susan from the review date. The CMS also compares the new current income figure of £320 with the historic income figure used in Alfie's existing child support liability (£450). This is also more than 25 per cent different, so there are grounds for a supersession of the existing liability. Alfie's liability from the date he reported the change (12 February) until the review date (8 March) is changed to £45.57 a week.

Periodic checks of current income

The CMS can undertake a 'periodic check' of a parent's current income if:[61]
- her/his gross weekly income has been based on current income; *and*
- no supersession decision changing the amount has been made for at least 11 months.

A periodic check is likely to happen if the current income figure has not been updated at the annual review and is still at least 25 per cent different from the updated historic income figure obtained at the review.

This periodic check is separate from the annual review process and is not normally done at the same time. If current income is used to determine gross weekly income, in some cases this may only have been in place for a short time at the annual review date. Once it has been in place for 11 months, a periodic current income check takes place.

If current income has previously been used, but the annual review results in historic income now being used, a periodic check of current income is not undertaken. Therefore, if a periodic check is due to take place around the same time as the annual review, the annual review is done first.

The non-resident parent must provide updated evidence of her/his current income for the periodic check.[62] Any updated evidence on current income is compared against the updated historic income figure for the latest available tax year that was provided at the most recent annual review. Any information provided by a person with care can also be considered.

If the person with care requests a supersession while the periodic review is being conducted and provides any relevant information, this is considered to be part of the periodic review.[63]

If the evidence provided by the non-resident parent is sufficient to make a new decision on current income, a supersession of the calculation decision is made.[64] If the evidence shows that the up-to-date current income figure varies by at least 25 per cent from the most recently updated historic income figure, the calculation continues to be based on current income. If the current income is no longer at least 25 per cent different, a supersession decision is made with gross weekly income based on the updated historic income figure. If the non-resident parent fails to provide evidence for the periodic review, the CMS may decide to supersede the calculation decision and use the updated historic income figure for gross weekly income.[65]

The effective date of a supersession decision arising from a periodic review of current income is the day the decision is made.[66] This is usually expected to be 30 days after the CMS writes to the non-resident parent to request her/his updated income details.[67]

If there has been a change in current income that should have been reported by the non-resident parent (ie, a change of 25 per cent or more that s/he should reasonably have understood to be likely to lead to increased liability for child support – see below), the effective date for the supersession decision is the date the income changed.[68]

Change of circumstances

The CMS intends calculations to remain in place for a reasonable period. In many cases, a calculation based on historic income is likely to remain in force for the year ahead.

If gross weekly income is based on current income, a change of circumstances does not result in a supersession decision unless a parent's current income has changed by at least 25 per cent.[69] Calculations are not adjusted for smaller changes in income. The CMS also intends calculations to be in place for a reasonable period of time, and so does not supersede calculations because of short-term fluctuations in income – eg, due to temporary sickness, temporary promotion and seasonal work.

If current income has changed by at least 25 per cent, a supersession decision is made, even if the change means that current income is now less than 25 per cent different from the historic income figure for the latest available tax year.[70]

Example 6.3

The situation is as in *Example 6.1*. Alfie is paying £64.08 a week child support to Susan. This is based on current income information, showing his gross weekly income to be £450. Alfie's current income was used at the time the calculation was made as it was more than 25 per cent different from the historic income data provided by HMRC, which showed his gross weekly income as £300.

After the calculation has been in force for a few months, Alfie provides the CMS with new evidence, showing that he has changed his working pattern and his current gross weekly income is now £320.

This new current income figure is more than 25 per cent different from the current income figure used to make the calculation decision. The CMS makes a supersession decision and calculates his child support liability based on a gross weekly income of £320. This takes effect from the date it received the new evidence. This can be done even though £320 is less than 25 per cent different from the most recent historic income figure.

Even if current income has not changed by 25 per cent, a supersession decision can still be made if:[71]

- the supersession results from changes that are considered by the CMS at an annual review or periodic check; *or*
- the supersession is made on the grounds that the original decision was based on an error of law; *or*

- the CMS supersedes a calculation that was based on an estimate of current income.

Certain changes to historic income (eg, if the historic income information is changed by HMRC, or if the non-resident parent amends a self-assessment) are grounds for the calculation to be revised.[72] However, HMRC does not routinely inform the CMS of minor changes, and so a revision is only likely to be done if a party queries the accuracy of the historic income figure.

For full details of revisions and supersessions of decisions, see Chapter 12.

Reporting changes in income

As with the '1993 rules' and '2003 rules', parents are not required to report changes in their circumstances on a routine basis, except in specific instances – eg, if a qualifying child dies. See p73 for the changes that must be reported. In addition, under the '2012 rules' there are specific duties on non-resident parents to report certain changes in their income.

If a parent's gross weekly income is based on her/his current income, s/he may be informed by the CMS that s/he must report relevant changes of circumstances. The parent is informed of this in the written notification of the child support calculation decision. S/he must report any such change in writing within 14 days of its occurring. The CMS may specify a longer period.[73] Failure to provide the required information may be an offence (see p58).[74]

If the non-resident parent is paying child support at the basic, reduced or flat rate and gross weekly income is based on her/his current income from employment, s/he must tell the CMS if s/he:[75]

- starts a new job; *or*
- receives a new rate of pay for her/his existing job; *or*
- changes her/his working pattern in her/his existing job.

These changes must be reported if the parent could reasonably be expected to know that they may lead to an increased amount of child support being due. This duty does not apply to those who are self-employed.

Fluctuations in wages from week to week or month to month may not necessarily need to be reported. However, the parent must tell the CMS if her/his wages increase so that over a longer period (ie, five payments if paid weekly, three if paid fortnightly, and two if paid four-weekly or monthly) the average payment is at least 25 per cent more than the gross weekly income that was taken into account in the calculation.[76]

If the non-resident parent is liable for the nil rate and gross weekly income is based on current income, s/he must tell the CMS if her/his gross weekly income increases to £7 or more. This duty applies to income from employment, self-employment or pensions (including income from any of the benefits that qualify for the flat rate).[77]

If gross weekly income is based on historic income, there is no duty on the non-resident parent to notify the CMS if her/his current income becomes (at some point during the year after the calculation decision is made) more than 25 per cent different from the most recent historic income figure. However, if this does happen, one of the parties in the case could apply for the calculation to be superseded. If the person with care alleges that the current income is at least 25 per cent more than the historic income figure used in the calculation, the CMS is only likely to investigate this if the person with care provides information that gives reasonable grounds to do so.

3. **Shared care**

If the non-resident parent shares, or is expected to share, the care of a qualifying child for at least 52 nights per year, the amount of child support due may be decreased. In most respects, shared care under the '2012 rules' scheme is dealt with in the same way as for the '2003 rules' (see p145).[78]

The care must be provided overnight, and the non-resident parent and the child must stay at the same address. The Child Maintenance Service (CMS) determines the number of nights that count for shared care. For the '2012 rules', this is based on the number of nights the non-resident parent is expected to provide overnight care for the qualifying child(ren) during the 12 months starting with the effective date of the calculation.[79]

The CMS can use a shorter period than this if appropriate – eg, if the parties have agreed a pattern of shared care for a shorter period.[80] If a shorter period is used, the number of nights of care in that period must be in the same ratio as 52 nights is to 12 months.

In determining the number of nights of shared care, the CMS must consider:[81]

- the terms of any agreement between the person with care and the non-resident parent, or the terms of any court order providing for contact between the non-resident parent and the qualifying child;
- if there is no such agreement or order, any pattern of care that has been established over the previous 12 months (or a shorter period that the CMS thinks is appropriate to use).

If the CMS accepts that the person with care and non-resident parent have agreed to share care, but there is not enough evidence to determine the number of nights of shared care, the CMS can assume that the non-resident parent provides care for one night per week. This assumption can be made if the parties provide conflicting evidence and the number of nights of shared care cannot be determined, even if both parties agree that shared care is provided on more than one night per week. The assumption is applied until a supersession is sought and there is sufficient evidence to determine the actual number of nights of shared care.[82]

The CMS does not review whether agreed shared care arrangements are being kept to. If it is reported that an agreement about shared care is not being complied with, the CMS may seek further evidence from the parties to allow a revision of the calculation.

If the qualifying child is a boarder at a boarding school or a hospital inpatient, any night spent there counts as a night with the person who would normally have been looking after the child were s/he not a boarder or inpatient on that night. Any such nights are treated in the same way as under the '2003 rules' (see p153).

The proportions by which the child support due is reduced, depending on the number of nights of shared care provided by the non-resident parent, are the same as under the '2003 rules' (see p149).

If each parent provides sufficient care to be classed as a parent with care, the rules for treating one parent as non-resident are the same as under the '2003 rules' (see p19). However, under the '2012 rules', a parent who shares day-to-day care is only treated as 'non-resident' if s/he does so to a lesser extent than the other parent. If care is deemed to be shared exactly equally, no one is treated as the non-resident parent and there is no liability for child support.[83] This is the case regardless of whether the income of one parent is significantly higher than the other. In case there is a dispute about whether care is shared equally, parents may wish to keep a detailed diary of the care pattern. As with all shared care, the CMS requires evidence to verify the pattern of care if the parties do not agree.

Care provided partly by a local authority

If a local authority cares for a child for 52 nights or more in the 12-month period ending with the effective date of the calculation decision, the child support to be paid by the non-resident parent is decreased in the same way as under the '2003 rules' (see p154).[84] This also applies if it is intended that a local authority will care for a child for 52 nights or more in the 12-month period beginning with the day after the effective date.[85] The CMS can use a shorter or longer period than 12 months if appropriate. The child support paid is reduced if the number of nights of local authority care is in the same ratio as 52 nights is to 12 months.[86]

A local authority cannot be a person with care.[87]

Notes

1. Calculating child support
1 Reg 45 CSMC Regs
2 Sch 1 para 5(b) CSA 1991; reg 45 CSMC Regs
3 Sch 4 para 4 CMOPA 2008
4 Reg 44(3) CSMC Regs
5 Reg 43 CSMC Regs
6 Sch 1 para 2(1) and (3) CSA 1991; reg 2 CSM(CBR) Regs
7 Sch 1 Part 1 para 6 CSA 1991
8 Reg 5 CS(MPA) Regs

2. Gross income
9 Reg 34(1) CSMC Regs
10 Reg 25(1)(b) CSMC Regs
11 Reg 4(1) CSMC Regs
12 Reg 4(1) CSMC Regs
13 Reg 36(1) CSMC Regs
14 Reg 36(5) CSMC Regs
15 Reg 35(3) CSMC Regs
16 Reg 36(1)(c) and (2)(b) CSMC Regs
17 Reg 36(2) CSMC Regs
18 Part 3 IT(EP)A 2003
19 Part 4 IT(EP)A 2003
20 Reg 36(1)(d) CSMC Regs; s5 IT(TOI)A 2005
21 s198 IT(TOI)A 2005
22 Reg 36(4) CSMC Regs
23 Reg 36(1)(b) CSMC Regs
24 Part 9 IT(EP)A 2003
25 s637 IT(EP)A 2003
26 s637 IT(EP)A 2003
27 s644 IT(EP)A 2003
28 ss638-41 IT(EP)A 2003
29 Reg 36(3) CSMC Regs
30 s577(1) IT(EP)A 2003
31 Reg 34(2) CSMC Regs
32 Reg 4(2) CSMC Regs
33 Reg 34(2A) CSMC Regs
34 Reg 37(1) CSMC Regs
35 Reg 38(5) CSMC Regs
36 Reg 40 CSMC Regs
37 Reg 37(2) CSMC Regs
38 Reg 42(1) CSMC Regs
39 Reg 42(2) CSMC Regs
40 Reg 38(2)(a) CSMC Regs
41 Reg 38(2)(b) CSMC Regs
42 Reg 38(3) CSMC Regs

43 Part 3 IT(EP)A 2003; reg 38(4) CSMC Regs
44 Part 4 IT(EP)A 2003
45 Reg 39(2), (3) and (4) CSMC Regs
46 Reg 39(1), (5) and (6) CSMC Regs
47 Reg 41 CSMC Regs
48 s681 IT(EP)A 2003
49 ss567 and 615 IT(EP)A 2003
50 s637 IT(EP)A 2003
51 s575(2)(b) IT(EP)A 2003
52 Reg 19(1) CSMC Regs
53 Reg 19(2) CSMC Regs
54 Reg 19(3) CSMC Regs
55 Reg 19(4) CSMC Regs
56 Reg 20(1) CSMC Regs
57 Reg 35(2)(b) CSMC Regs
58 Reg 20(2) CSMC Regs
59 Reg 21(2) CSMC Regs
60 *The Child Support Maintenance Calculation Regulations 2012: a technical consultation on the draft regulations,* CMEC, December 2011
61 Reg 22(1) CSMC Regs
62 Reg 22(1) CSMC Regs
63 *The Child Support Maintenance Calculation Regulations 2012: a technical consultation on the draft regulations,* CMEC, December 2011
64 Reg 22(3) CSMC Regs
65 Reg 22(2) CSMC Regs
66 Reg 22(4) CSMC Regs
67 *The Child Support Maintenance Calculation Regulations 2012: a technical consultation on the draft regulations,* CMEC, December 2011
68 Reg 22(5) CSMC Regs
69 Reg 23(1) and (2) CSMC Regs
70 Reg 23(4) CSMC Regs
71 Reg 23(3) CSMC Regs
72 Reg 14(1)(f) CSMC Regs
73 Reg 9A(1), (4) and (5) CSI Regs
74 s14A(3A) CSA 1991
75 Reg 9A(2) and (6)(a) CSI Regs
76 Reg 9A(2) and (6)(b) CSI Regs
77 Reg 9A(3), (9) and (10) CSI Regs

3. Shared care
78 Regs 46, 47 and 50-55 CSMC Regs
79 Reg 46 CSMC Regs

80 Reg 46(3) CSMC Regs
81 Reg 46(4) CSMC Regs
82 Sch 1 para 9(2) CSA 1991; reg 47 CSMC
    Regs
83 Reg 50(2) CSMC Regs
84 Reg 53(2)(a) CSMC Regs
85 Reg 53(2)(c)(i) CSMC Regs
86 Reg 53(2)(b) and (c)(ii) CSMC Regs
87 Reg 78(1)(a) CSMC Regs

Chapter 7

Variations ('2012 rules')

This chapter covers:
1. Variations (below)
2. Grounds for a variation (p111)
3. Applying for a variation (p118)
4. Procedure (p119)
5. The decision (p123)

1. Variations

A variation allows circumstances that are not taken into account by the usual child support calculation to be considered by the Child Maintenance Service (CMS). If the variation is agreed, the calculation may be adjusted.

Under the '2012 rules' scheme, an application for a variation to the child support calculation can be made on certain grounds. These grounds are similar to some of those for '2003 rules' cases (see Chapter 9). There are, however, significant differences, mainly due to the different way in which income is assessed. This chapter concentrates on areas where the '2012 rules' are different.

A variation can only be made under a ground specified in the legislation and only if it would be 'just and equitable' to do so (see p111).

An application for a variation can be made before a calculation is made or once a calculation is in force.[1] An application may be rejected automatically in certain specific circumstances, either at a preliminary consideration or at a later stage (see p119). In certain cases, the CMS may refer the application to the First-tier Tribunal for a determination (see p122).

If an application is successful, it may result in a child support calculation being made or, if a calculation already exists, being revised or superseded with the variation incorporated (see p124).

Note: there is no separate variation decision; the decision is whether to revise or supersede the child support calculation decision or to refuse to revise or supersede the calculation with or without a variation element. This means that any subsequent challenge is simply against the revised or superseded decision or against the refusal to revise or supersede.

Variations are one of the areas of child support law in which disputes frequently arise. There is caselaw on many of the issues, and the principles established for variations in '2003 rules' cases (see Chapter 9) also apply to variations in '2012 rules' cases.

2. **Grounds for a variation**

A variation can be made for:
- special expenses (see below);
- additional income (see p113).

Special expenses

A non-resident parent can apply for a variation to have her/his child support liability reduced on the grounds that s/he has certain special expenses. The expenses that can be considered are the same as those for '2003 rules' variations (see Chapter 9) – ie:[2]
- costs of maintaining contact with children for whom the calculation is, or will be, in force;
- costs of a long-term illness or disability of a 'relevant other child';
- previous debts, incurred before the couple separated;
- boarding school fees paid for children for whom an application for a child support calculation has been made;
- costs of paying a mortgage on the home of the person with care and qualifying child.

Except for costs associated with an illness or disability of a relevant other child, there is a threshold amount that must be exceeded before special expenses can be considered. The way this operates is slightly different from the '2003 rules'. The threshold is £10, regardless of the income of the non-resident parent. If expenses are being considered in more than one category, the threshold applies separately to each. If the expenses in any category are less than £10 a week, a variation is not allowed on that ground. If the expenses in any category are £10 or more a week, the whole amount is counted in full (not just the excess over £10) – ie, the £10 threshold is not a 'disregard' as it is for the '2003 rules'.[3]

The Child Maintenance Service (CMS) can also substitute a lower amount for any special expenses costs it considers are unreasonably high or have been unreasonably incurred. This may be below the threshold amount or nil. In the case of contact costs, any reduced amount must not be so low that it makes it impossible for the non-resident parent to maintain contact with the child at the level of frequency stated in any court order, provided that contact is actually taking place.[4]

Contact costs

A variation can be considered on the basis of costs related to the non-resident parent's contact with the qualifying child.[5]

The circumstances in which costs can be included, and the types of costs that qualify, are the same as for the '2003 rules' (see p161). However, under the '2012 rules', expenses for contact costs may be considered, even if the contact is also being counted as part of a shared care arrangement.

Costs of a relevant other child's long-term illness or disability

A variation can be considered on the basis of the costs of a long-term illness or disability of a relevant other child (see p23).[6]

The circumstances in which costs can be included, and the types of costs that qualify, are the same as for the '2003 rules' (see p162), except that, for the purposes of determining whether a child is disabled, the definition of 'blind' in the '2012 rules' has not been changed to 'certified as severely sight impaired or blind by a consultant opthalmologist' and remains as 'registered blind'.

Note: in order for a child to count as having a disability, someone must receive (or would receive but for the fact that the child is in hospital) disability living allowance (DLA) care component, personal independence payment (PIP) daily living component or armed forces independence payment on her/his behalf. Unlike for the '2003 rules', the mobility component of DLA or PIP does not count.

Debts of the relationship

A variation can be considered on the basis of the cost to the non-resident parent of repaying debts incurred before s/he became a non-resident parent of the qualifying child and when that parent and the person with care were a couple. The type of debts that qualify are the same as for the '2003 rules' (see p163).[7]

Boarding school fees

The maintenance element of boarding school fees incurred, or expected to be incurred, by the non-resident parent for the qualifying child may be considered as a special expense. The way that such costs are calculated is the same as for the '2003 rules' (see p164).[8]

Payments for mortgages, loans or insurance policies

A variation can be considered on the basis of payments made to a mortgage lender, insurer or person with care for a mortgage or loan from a qualifying lender in the same circumstances as for the '2003 rules' (see p165).[9]

Variations for additional income

A variation to increase child support liability can be considered on the grounds that the non-resident parent has certain additional income that has not been taken into account in the calculation. A variation results in such income being added to gross weekly income for the calculation.

Variations on additional income grounds under the '2012 rules' are substantially different from the additional cases variations under the '2003 rules'. This is because the '2012 rules' use gross income in the calculation, and because the way in which income is assessed and information about income gathered is different.

A variation can be considered if the non-resident parent:

- has unearned income – ie, income that has not been counted in gross weekly income (see below);
- is on the nil or flat rate in certain circumstances, but has gross weekly income of more than £100 (see p117);
- has diverted income (p117).

Note: the additional cases grounds under the '2003 rules' relating to assets over £65,000 and having a lifestyle that is inconsistent with declared income (see Chapter 9) do not apply to '2012 rules' cases. Instead, the above additional income grounds are intended to reflect actual additional income rather than a notional figure derived from assets or assumed from lifestyle.

Unearned income

A variation can be considered if the non-resident parent has certain types of taxable unearned income of £2,500 or more a year (see p114).[10]

The definitions of the different types of income that are classed as unearned for this purpose are extremely complex and rely on how the sources of the income are treated for income tax purposes. This chapter includes only a summary of some of the main types.

Information on unearned income is collected by HM Revenue and Customs (HMRC) through self-assessment tax returns, and details of the amount in the latest available tax year are provided by HMRC to the CMS. However, the CMS only requests this following an application for a variation.

The CMS can decide the amount of unearned income based on the most recent tax year if:[11]

- the latest available tax year is not the most recent tax year; *or*
- the information for the latest available tax year does not include a self-assessment; *or*
- the CMS is unable, for whatever reason, to request or obtain the information from HMRC – eg, because there has been a failure in the automatic data-sharing system.

The CMS should only do this if it is satisfied that there is sufficient evidence to do so. It should base its decision on information that would need to be provided on a tax self-assessment form.

The CMS bases the variation decision on actual unearned income figures for a complete tax year, rather than notional amounts based on the non-resident parent's assets and lifestyle. The use of HMRC figures also means that the CMS no longer relies on the person with care to provide evidence of the non-resident parent's financial circumstances to support an application for a variation.

There are no grounds for a variation on the basis of the value of assets themselves if they do not produce income. Also, the fact that assets have been sold for a capital gain that would be taxable is not a ground for a variation.

If the CMS accepts that the non-resident parent had unearned income in a past tax year but no longer has unearned income in the current tax year (eg, if s/he has sold property that generated income), it can treat the parent as having no unearned income.[12]

If the CMS agrees to make a variation on this ground, the unearned income is converted into a weekly amount and added to the existing gross weekly income.[13] If the non-resident parent has paid approved pension contributions that have not otherwise been taken into account in the child support calculation, the average weekly amount of these contributions is deducted from the unearned income amount. The pension contributions must have been made in the same tax year to which the unearned income relates.[14]

What counts as unearned income

Not all taxable other income counts. 'Unearned income' for this purpose is income that would be subject to UK income tax from:[15]
- property (see below);
- savings and investments (see p115);
- other miscellaneous sources (see p116).

Income from land or property

Any taxable income from the use of property or land in the UK or elsewhere counts as additional income. The capital value of property or land is ignored.

In most cases, property income is the rent from tenants or licensees from furnished, unfurnished, commercial and domestic premises, and from any bare land. Certain other payments also count, including:[16]
- ground rent and feu duties;
- if property is let furnished, any payment by the tenant for the use of the furniture;
- premiums and other similar lump sums received for granting certain leases;
- income from caravans or houseboats where these are not moved around various locations;

- service charges from tenants for certain services normally provided by a landlord – eg, cleaning of communal areas, fuel and heating, and arranging repairs;
- deposits/bonds from tenants.

Any expenses incurred wholly and exclusively for the purpose of the property business and that are not of a capital nature (such as the cost of furniture, appliances and improvements to the property) are first deducted from the taxable income.[17] Some of the main categories of allowable expenses include:[18]

- council tax, business rates and water charges, if the agreement specifies that these are the responsibility of the landlord;
- the cost of maintenance and repairs (but not improvements);
- in some cases, the cost of certain energy efficiency measures installed before 6 April 2015;
- for fully furnished properties, certain costs for the wear and tear or renewal of furnishings;
- insurance premiums for contents, building and loss of rent;
- interest on a mortgage or loan taken out to purchase the property;
- the cost of providing services, including the wages of gardeners and cleaners;
- letting agent fees, and certain legal and accountancy fees;
- rent, ground rent and service charges;
- other direct costs – eg, phone calls, stationery and advertising for new tenants.

If only part of a property is let and part is occupied by the landlord, a suitable proportion of the charges can be deducted. Any loss on a property business can usually be set against the property business profits of the following year.[19]

Rent and other receipts from properties outside the UK are treated in the same way. Losses on overseas property cannot be offset against profits on UK property, and vice versa.

If a person rents furnished accommodation in her/his only or main home under the 'rent-a-room' scheme, the first £4,250 income a year is not taxable. (For the tax year 2016/17, this figure will increase to £7,500.) When calculating the income in this case, expenses cannot be deducted.[20]

Income from property rented as a business (eg, running a hotel, B&B or guest house), or from services not normally offered by a landlord (such as meals, laundry or room cleaning), usually counts as trading income – ie, income from self-employment (see Chapter 6). Rental income from tied houses and caravan sites, and income from other land-related activity, such as farming and market gardening, are also treated as trading income.[21]

Income from savings and investments

Any taxable income from savings and investments counts as additional income. The capital value of any savings or investments is ignored.

The main types of income that count are:[22]

- interest on invested money, including outside the UK – eg, interest on savings in a bank or building society (including income from selling a right to receive interest);
- dividends and other distributions from UK companies (including the tax credit payable with the dividend), and foreign dividends;
- discounts from securities – ie, the profit from trading in securities such as government stocks and bonds;
- income from government stocks and bonds;
- taxable payments from a life assurance policy, life annuity contract or capital redemption policy;
- payments from a trust;
- payments from the estate of a deceased person;
- interest arising from a debt;
- artificial transactions in futures and options.

Certain types of income are exempt from tax and therefore disregarded. These include:[23]
- interest, dividend or bonus from an individual investment plan, such as an ISA;
- income from certified Save As You Earn (SAYE) schemes;
- interest under an employee share scheme;
- income from national savings certificates and tax reserve certificates;
- venture capital trust dividends;
- tax-exempt annual payments made by an individual in the UK not for commercial reasons – eg, from a covenant;
- periodical payments or annuity payments of personal injury damages;
- annuity payments under a Criminal Injuries Compensation Scheme award;
- gains from dealing in certain commodities, financial futures and options;
- the capital element of purchased life annuities;
- tax-free health and employment insurance or immediate-needs annuity payments.

Miscellaneous income

Any taxable income from other miscellaneous sources may count as additional income. This can include, for example, casual income from one-off jobs, royalties and other income from intellectual property such as sales of patent rights, and other recurring income not included in the other categories above.[24]

Certain types of income that are exempt from tax are not counted, including:[25]
- income from an educational bursary or scholarship;
- payments to adopters;
- certain foreign maintenance payments;
- certain compensation payments to World War Two victims;

- income from domestic electricity microgeneration;
- winnings from premium bonds, lotteries and gambling.

Income of a non-resident parent liable for the nil or flat rate

In certain circumstances, if a non-resident parent is on the nil rate or flat rate and has income which would otherwise be taken into account in a child support calculation, a variation can be considered on the grounds of income not taken into account.

A variation on this ground is possible if the non-resident parent has gross weekly income of more than £100 that would normally be taken into account were it not for the fact that the parent is liable for:[26]

- the nil rate because s/he is:
  - a child; *or*
  - a prisoner; *or*
  - receiving an allowance for work-based training for young people; *or*
  - resident in a care home or independent hospital, or is being provided with a care home service and/or independent healthcare service and receiving one of the qualifying benefits for the flat rate (see p133), or has the whole or part of the cost of her/his accommodation met by a local authority; *or*
- the flat rate because s/he receives a qualifying benefit (see p133).

If the CMS agrees to make a variation on this ground, the non-resident parent is treated as having the whole amount of the income for the purpose of calculating a new child support liability. Child support is calculated on this income at the reduced rate, basic rate or basic rate plus as appropriate. The liability calculated this way is added to the nil rate or flat rate.[27]

If a variation has been agreed on this ground, information about the additional income is sought and treated in the same way as for gross weekly income used in the child support calculation. Historic income information from HMRC for the latest available tax year is normally used. If current income is at least 25 per cent different from the historic income, current income can be used for the variation. If current income is used, the non-resident parent must notify the CMS if it changes by 25 per cent or more (see p105).

Diversion of income

A variation on the grounds of diversion of income can be considered if:[28]

- the non-resident parent can control, whether directly or indirectly, the amount of income that s/he receives or that is taken into account as her/his gross income; *and*
- the CMS is satisfied that the parent has unreasonably reduced the amount of income that s/he would have received (and which would have been taken into

account in the child support calculation or under a variation) by diverting it to someone else or for some other purpose.

This applies to income that would count as gross weekly income and to unearned income.

The way that diversion of income is interpreted is the same as for the '2003 rules' (see p169).

The full weekly equivalent amount of any diverted income is added to gross weekly income when calculating child support.[29]

Changes in additional income

As variations on unearned income grounds are based on historic income information provided by HMRC, they are considered at the annual review (see p101).

The CMS seeks updated information on this income from HMRC as part of the annual review process and can make a supersession decision on the basis of that information. The supersession decision takes effect from the review date.[30]

If the CMS accepts that the non-resident parent had unearned income in a past tax year but no longer has unearned income in the current tax year (eg, if s/he has sold a property), it can treat the parent as having no unearned income.[31]

A variation on the ground that the non-resident parent has gross weekly income of more than £100 based on current income can be superseded before the annual review date if her/his current income changes by at least 25 per cent.

There is no obligation on parents who have unearned income included in their gross weekly income to report changes in this.

A variation based on diversion of income is not reviewed routinely, as it is not based on income information provided by HMRC. A party to the child support calculation can apply for a supersession at any time if the circumstances relating to the diversion of income change.

3. **Applying for a variation**

The rules on applying for a variation under the '2012 rules' are the same as under the '2003 rules' (see p172), except that if the Child Maintenance Service (CMS) requests further information or evidence from the applicant in order to decide on a variation, s/he is given 14 days (rather than one month) in which to supply the information requested.[32] If this is not supplied within the timescale (or any longer period that the CMS considers reasonable), the application may be determined without the further information and may be rejected.

Two or more applications for a variation may be considered at the same time.[33] In addition, if appropriate, an application made on one ground may be treated as an application on a different ground.[34]

4. Procedure

Once an application has been made, the procedure involves the same steps as under the '2003 rules'.

- There is a preliminary consideration of the application (see below).
- Unless rejected, other parties may be notified and asked to make representations. This is known as 'contesting' (see p120).
- An interim maintenance decision may be made (see p121).
- A regular payment condition may be imposed (see p121).
- The decision is considered (see p121).

After the preliminary consideration, a case may also be passed to the First-tier Tribunal for a determination (see Chapter 13).

The application proceeds for determination unless it has already failed. It may fail (ie, the Child Maintenance Service (CMS) may refuse to consider it further) before this point because, for example:[35]

- one of the grounds for rejection is established on the preliminary consideration (see below);
- it is withdrawn; *or*
- the regular payment condition has not been met.

Preliminary consideration

Once an application is properly made, the CMS may give preliminary consideration to the case.[36] At this point, the CMS may reject the application and decide:

- to revise or supersede the child support calculation, or to refuse to revise or supersede it; *or*
- make the calculation, or make a default maintenance decision.

A parent can challenge any decision, including a decision not to revise.[37]

Grounds for rejecting an application

The CMS may reject an application for a variation after the preliminary consideration if:[38]

- there are no grounds for a variation;
- the CMS has insufficient information to decide the child support application and so a default maintenance decision is likely to be made;
- the applicant does not state a ground or provide sufficient information to allow a ground to be identified;
- the requirements of the stated ground are not met, or no information has been given that supports the ground or that is sufficient to allow further enquiries to be made;
- a default maintenance decision is in force;

- the non-resident parent is liable to pay the nil or flat rate because s/he, or her/his partner, receives one of the prescribed benefits (see p133);
- a variation was sought on additional income grounds but gross weekly income was already the capped amount of £3,000; *or*
- the non-resident parent has made the application on special expenses grounds and:
  – the amount of the expenses is below the threshold (see p111);
  – s/he is already paying an amount of child support equal to or less than £7;
  – after deducting special expenses, the gross weekly income is still above the capped amount of £3,000; *or*
  – the gross weekly income has been estimated because insufficient information was available.

Note: rejecting an application for a variation on preliminary consideration for one of the above reasons is a power, not a duty.[39]

Note also: under the '2012 rules', an application is not automatically rejected because the non-resident parent or her/his partner is in receipt of working tax credit, as is the case for additional cases variations under the '2003 rules'.

In some cases, if a default maintenance decision applies, an application for a variation may contain sufficient information to revise the default decision and replace it with a calculation.

Contesting the application

If an application has not been rejected on preliminary consideration, the CMS usually notifies the other relevant parties. This may be done orally or in writing and must include:[40]

- the grounds on which the application has been made; *and*
- any relevant information given by the applicant or obtained by the CMS, except information that must not be disclosed. The rules on non-disclosure of information for variations are the same as for '2003 rules' cases (see p176).[41]

The CMS may invite the other parties to make representations within 14 days about anything to do with the application. If the CMS is satisfied that it is reasonable, the 14-day time limit may be extended.[42]

The CMS does not need to notify the other parties if:[43]

- it is satisfied that, on the available information, the application for a variation would not be agreed to;
- the application is on the grounds of unearned income, the latest available tax year information from HM Revenue and Customs (HMRC) does not show unearned income above the threshold and the CMS does not have further information that justifies making further enquiries; *or*
- a previously agreed variation can be reinstated without an application (see p126).

The CMS tends to inform the other parties in writing. If an application has been made by phone, the evidence may be a transcript of the call.

The other parties may respond orally or in writing, although the CMS may require it in writing. If no contesting information is provided, the CMS may make a decision on the application as it stands.[44]

Any information provided by another party, other than that which may not be disclosed (see p176), may be forwarded to the applicant if the CMS considers this reasonable. The applicant is given 14 days to comment on the evidence or information supplied by the other party. This 14-day time limit may also be extended if the CMS is satisfied that it is reasonable. The application must not be decided until this period is over.[45]

It is possible that the applicant may supply further information outside the 14-day time limit and the CMS may already have decided in the meantime to proceed with the application and notify the other parties. In this case, the further information is likely to be passed to the other parties and a further 14 days from the date of this notification (or longer if the CMS is satisfied that it is reasonable) allowed for representations.

Interim maintenance decision

If an application for a variation is made before the child support calculation decision has been made, an interim maintenance decision may be made in the same way as under the '2003 rules' (see p176).[46]

Regular payment condition

If a non-resident parent has applied for a variation, s/he may have a regular payment condition imposed after the preliminary consideration. The rules for this are the same as under the '2003 rules' (see p176).[47]

Considering the decision

The CMS has some discretion in deciding whether to make a variation to the child support calculation. It must bear in mind the general principles that:[48]
- a parent is responsible for maintaining her/his children when s/he can afford to do so;
- a parent is responsible for maintaining all her/his children equally;
- the welfare of any child affected by an application for a variation must be taken into account.

In addition, the CMS must be satisfied that:[49]
- the grounds are met; *and*
- it is just and equitable to agree to the variation.

The CMS must take into account any representations made by any of the relevant parties to the application.[50]

If the variation application is made by the person with care and the CMS considers that further information would affect its decision, the onus is on the CMS to investigate. There is no onus on the person with care to prove that a variation is justified. The CMS must consider any information that is available to it (eg, information that it can obtain from HMRC), and must take appropriate steps to obtain any such further information.[51]

The CMS must not agree to make a variation if:[52]

- it has insufficient information to make a child support calculation and so would make a default maintenance decision; *or*
- any of the circumstances apply that would lead to a variation application being rejected after the preliminary consideration (see p119).

A decision may be made to agree to the variation in full or to refuse it. This may result in a revision or supersession of the decision or a replacement of the interim maintenance decision. The revision/supersession is dealt with under the usual rules (see p124).[53]

Just and equitable

Even though the grounds are met, a variation is only agreed if it is 'just and equitable' to do so.[54]

The '2012 rules' do not include a list of factors that must be taken into account in deciding whether it is just and equitable to make a variation. The factors taken into account for '2003 rules' cases (see p178) are likely to be relevant for '2012 rules' cases, but this list is not exhaustive and the CMS must make this discretionary decision based on the individual circumstances of the case.

The following must not be taken into account:[55]

- whether or not the child's conception was planned;
- who was responsible for the breakdown of the relationship between the non-resident parent and the person with care;
- whether the non-resident parent or person with care is in a new relationship with someone who is not the qualifying child's parent;
- any contact arrangements and whether or not they are being kept to;
- the income or assets of anyone other than the non-resident parent;
- any failure of the non-resident parent to pay child support or maintenance under a court order or written agreement; *or*
- representations from individuals other than the person with care, non-resident parent, or a qualifying child applicant in Scotland.

Referral to the First-tier Tribunal

Once the application has passed the preliminary consideration and contest stage, the case may be passed to the First-tier Tribunal for a determination on whether or not to agree to the variation.[56] This normally only occurs if a novel or particularly contentious issue is being considered.

The First-tier Tribunal applies the same rules as the CMS and decides that the variation should be either agreed to or refused.[57] In doing so, it must make a revision or supersession decision, but may pass it back to the CMS to make the child support calculation.[58] This decision by the CMS (ie, to revise or supersede, or to refuse to revise or supersede, the child support calculation) may then be challenged in the normal way (see Chapters 12 and 13).

5. **The decision**

A variation is an element of the child support calculation. The Child Maintenance Service (CMS) may agree to, or refuse, an application for a variation. In either case, it may result in a decision to:[59]

- revise or supersede the calculation/replace the interim maintenance decision (IMD), or refuse to revise or supersede;
- make a calculation (this may replace an IMD) or default maintenance decision.

In some cases, a variation may be agreed which makes no difference to the amount of child support calculated. A revision or supersession is still carried out, as each decision gives further appeal rights.

Once a variation is made, it continues to be considered each time there is a revision or supersession of the calculation, under the normal revision/supersession rules (see Chapter 12). Because of some changes in circumstances, the variation may cease to have effect, in which case the calculation may be suspended or cancelled in order to remove the variation element. In certain cases, if there is a further change in circumstances, the variation may be reinstated by the CMS without an application. In other cases, a new request for a variation may need to be made.

The effect of the variation

The effect of the variation should not reduce the total amount of child support to less than £7, and the maximum amount of gross income that can be taken into account is the capped amount of £3,000.

Special expenses

All special expenses amounts are aggregated (taking account of the threshold rules). This total amount of the non-resident parent's relevant expenses is converted into a weekly amount and deducted from the gross weekly income of the non-resident parent. The calculation is then carried out as normal, using this amount.

If the effect of the variation would be to reduce the child support liability to below the flat rate of £7, the non-resident parent is liable to pay £7 (apportioned between the persons with care if appropriate).[60]

As under the '2003 rules' (see p180), if the gross weekly income is the capped amount, the effect of the variation is worked out by subtracting the special expenses from the actual gross weekly income. If this results in a figure above the capped amount of £3,000, the special expenses variation is refused.[61]

Additional income

The amount of any additional income is converted to a weekly amount and added to the gross weekly income of the non-resident parent. If this would result in a gross income figure above the capped amount, the gross income to be taken into account is restricted to the capped amount of £3,000.[62]

If a variation on additional income grounds is agreed and the child support without the variation would be the flat rate or £7, the amount of child support is the amount that would be calculated on the additional income plus £7.[63]

Concurrent variations

If there is more than one variation element (ie, on both special expenses and additional income grounds) to be applied, the results are aggregated.[64] The calculation is carried out as follows.

- Work out the amounts for each variation element.
- Aggregate any special expenses with any additional income.
- Add the aggregate figure to the actual gross weekly income, capping the income at £3,000.
- Work out the child support due, applying any apportionment or reduction for shared care or part-time local authority care.[65]
- Check the total amount of child support is not less than £7. If it is, £7 is payable and is apportioned between the persons with care, if appropriate.[66]

Revisions and supersessions

A variation is not a separate decision to be challenged; it is applied by a decision revising or superseding the child support calculation decision. If a variation is agreed and applied to the calculation, this decision may be challenged by applying for a revision within 30 days. Any change of circumstances, whether in relation to the variation or other factors, can result in a revision or supersession of the calculation under the normal rules, depending on the circumstances (see Chapter 12). This also applies to decisions referred by the CMS to the First-tier Tribunal for a decision – eg, contentious cases.[67]

The variation is taken into account in any reconsideration. However, there may be changes of circumstances which mean that the effect of the variation ceases to be applied. In certain circumstances, the CMS has discretion to reinstate a previous variation to the calculation without an application (see p126).

When a variation takes effect

If the ground for the variation existed at the initial effective date of the child support calculation (ie, when the non-resident parent was notified of the application), the variation takes effect on the initial effective date of the calculation if either:

- the application is made before the calculation is made;[68] *or*
- the application is made within 30 days of the date the calculation decision was notified, or within a longer period if the CMS allows a late application for a revision.[69]

The exception to this is if the non-resident parent applied for a variation on the grounds of prior debts or payments in respect of certain mortgages, loans or insurance policies before the child support calculation was made, and payments towards these are treated as voluntary payments in the initial payment period. In this case, the variation takes effect from the date on which the non-resident parent was notified of the amount of her/his child support liability.[70]

If the ground did not apply at the initial effective date of the child support calculation, the variation takes effect from:

- the date the ground arose, if this is after the initial effective date but before the calculation is made;[71] *or*
- the date of the variation application;[72] *or*
- the date on which the ground is expected to arise, if the application for variation is made in advance.[73]

If an application for a variation is made before the child support calculation is made and the ground has ceased to exist by the date the calculation is made, the variation is applied for the period the ground existed.[74]

A case may have a number of different grounds, agreed over time, and each may have a different date from when it takes effect.

When a variation is not applied

The effect of a variation is not applied for any period when:[75]

- the non-resident parent is liable for the flat or nil rate because s/he or her/his partner receives one of the prescribed benefits (see p133); *or*
- a variation was sought on additional income grounds but gross weekly income was already the capped amount of £3,000; *or*
- the non-resident parent applied for the variation on special expenses grounds and:
  - the amount of the expenses is below the threshold (see p111); *or*
  - the non-resident parent is already paying an amount of child support equal to or less than £7; *or*
  - after deducting special expenses, the gross weekly income is still above the capped amount of £3,000; *or*

– the gross weekly income has been estimated because insufficient information was available.

When a variation ceases to have effect, a supersession is carried out which takes effect from the day on which the change occurred. If there is a later change, unless the CMS has discretion to reinstate the variation, a further application may need to be made.

Discretion to reinstate a variation

In some cases, the CMS may revise or supersede a child support calculation to reinstate a variation that has previously been agreed, without the need for a new application. This is most likely to apply to variations on special expenses grounds, as this discretion can be applied if:[76]

- a variation ceases to have effect, because a change of circumstances means that:
  - the non-resident parent's liability is reduced to the nil rate or another rate that means that the variation cannot be taken into account; *or*
  - the child support calculation has been replaced with a default maintenance decision;

then:

- a subsequent change of circumstances means the calculation has been revised or superseded so that the non-resident parent is now liable for a rate which can be adjusted to take the variation into account.

Examples of situations where this could apply include if:

- the non-resident parent is sentenced to a prison term and so becomes liable for the nil rate, but subsequently returns to a basic or reduced rate;
- a variation is agreed and on a subsequent application for a revision or supersession the non-resident parent fails to provide information. Therefore, the child support calculation is replaced by a default decision. Later, the information required is provided and this default maintenance decision is replaced with a calculation. The variation may then be reapplied without a fresh application.

If the calculation ceases, this discretion does not apply. For example, if the parent moves abroad and the CMS ceases to have jurisdiction, but then s/he returns to the UK, a subsequent application must be made for a child support calculation, including an application for a variation. However, in some circumstances, the CMS may be able to reinstate the variation without its being contested (see p120).

The CMS can reinstate a variation straight away without checking whether the circumstances relating to it have changed. If any party is aware of such changes of circumstances, s/he could apply for a revision or supersession.[77]

Revising or superseding a variation

If a variation has been agreed, it may subsequently be revised or superseded. If an application is made for a revision or a supersession of such a decision:[78]

- the application is not subject to a preliminary consideration;
- the usual rules on seeking further information and allowing the application to be contested apply; *and*
- the same factors must not be taken into account when considering whether it would be just and equitable to agree to a variation (see p122).

However, the CMS does not have to notify the other parties and invite representations if:[79]

- the revised or superseded decision would not be to the advantage of the applicant; *or*
- it considers that representations from the other parties would not be relevant to the application.

The CMS may decide to revise or supersede, or not to revise or supersede, the decision and notifies the applicant and any relevant parties, as appropriate.

Appealing a decision

Decisions on the child support calculation in response to a variation application, or if a variation element is reinstated into a calculation, may be appealed under the normal procedure. An application for a revision (a 'mandatory reconsideration') must normally be made before there is a right of appeal. As with other appeals, if, following the appeal application, there is a revision of the appealed decision that is to the advantage of the person appealing, the appeal lapses.[80] For further details on appeals, see Chapter 13.

Notes

1. Variations
1 ss28A(1) and (3) and 28G(1) and (2) CSA 1991; ss28A-28F and Schs 4A and 4B CSA 1991, as modified by CS(V)(MSP) Regs

2. Grounds for a variation
2 Sch 4B CSA 1991; regs 63-67 CSMC Regs
3 Reg 68 CSMC Regs

4 Reg 68(3) and (4) CSMC Regs
5 Reg 63 CSMC Regs
6 Reg 64 CSMC Regs
7 Reg 65 CSMC Regs
8 Reg 66 CSMC Regs
9 Reg 67 CSMC Regs
10 Sch 4B para 4(1) CSA 1991; reg 69(1) CSMC Regs
11 Reg 69(5) CSMC Regs
12 Reg 69(6) CSMC Regs

13 Reg 69(7) CSMC Regs
14 Reg 69(8) and (9) CSMC Regs
15 Reg 69(2) CSMC Regs; Parts 3-5
   IT(TOI)A 2005
16 Part 3 IT(TOI)A 2005; *Property Income
   Manual*, HMRC
17 ss33 and 272 and IT(TOI)A 2005
18 Part 3 IT(TOI)A 2005; *Property Income
   Manual*, HMRC
19 Reg 69(4) CSMC Regs; s118 ITA 2007
20 ss309, 784, 786, 788(2) and 789(4)
   IT(TOI)A 2005; Income Tax (Limit for
   Rent-a-Room Relief) Order 2015,
   No.1539
21 ss9, 19, 20, 267 and 273 IT(TOI)A 2005
22 Part 4 IT(TOI)A 2005; *Savings and
   Investment Manual*, HMRC
23 Part 6 IT(TOI)A 2005; *Savings and
   Investment Manual*, HMRC
24 ss579, 587, 683 and 687 Part 5 IT(TOI)A
   2005
25 Part 6 IT(TOI)A 2005
26 Reg 70 CSMC Regs
27 Reg 70(2) CSMC Regs
28 Reg 71 CSMC Regs
29 Reg 71(2) CSMC Regs
30 Reg 21 CSMC Regs
31 Reg 69(6) CSMC Regs

3. **Applying for a variation**
32 Reg 58(2) CSMC Regs
33 Reg 56(3) CSMC Regs
34 Reg 56(4) CSMC Regs

4. **Procedure**
35 s28D CSA 1991
36 s28B CSA 1991
37 *RB v CMEC* [2009] UKUT 53 (AAC)
38 s28B CSA 1991; reg 57(1) CSMC Regs
39 *CR v CMEC* [2009] UKUT 111 (AAC)
40 Reg 59(1)(a) CSMC Regs
41 Reg 59(1)(a) and (5) CSMC Regs
42 Reg 59(1)(b) CSMC Regs
43 Reg 59(2) CSMC Regs
44 Reg 59(4) CSMC Regs
45 Reg 59(3) CSMC Regs
46 ss12 and 28F(5) CSA 1991
47 s28C CSA 1991; reg 62 CSMC Regs
48 ss28E(1) and (2) and 28F(2)(a) CSA
   1991
49 s28F(1) CSA 1991
50 s28E(3) CSA 1991
51 s28D(2A) and (2B) CSA 1991
52 s28F(3) CSA 1991; reg 57(2) CSMC
   Regs
53 ss28D(1) and 28F CSA 1991
54 s28F(1) CSA 1991

55 s28F(2)(b) CSA 1991; reg 60 CSMC
   Regs
56 s28D(1)(b) CSA 1991
57 s28D(3) CSA 1991
58 R(CS) 5/06

5. **The decision**
59 ss28B(2) and 28F(3) and (4) CSA 1991
60 Reg 74(1A) CSMC Regs
61 Reg 72(2) CSMC Regs
62 Reg 73(1) CSMC Regs
63 Reg 73(2) CSMC Regs
64 Reg 74(1) CSMC Regs
65 Reg 74(3) CSMC Regs
66 Reg 74(4) CSMC Regs
67 ss16(1A)(c) and 17(1)(d) CSA 1991;
   regs 14(1)(a)(ii) and 17(3) CSMC Regs
68 Reg 13(1) CSMC Regs
69 s28G CSA 1991; regs 14(1)(a) and 15
   CSMC Regs
70 Reg 13(2) CSMC Regs
71 Reg 13(1)(b) CSMC Regs
72 ss17(4) and 28G CSA 1991
73 Reg 18(2) CSMC Regs
74 Reg 13(3) CSMC Regs
75 Regs 57(1)(d)-(f) and 74(5) CSMC Regs
76 Reg 75 CSMC Regs
77 Reg 75(2) CSMC Regs
78 Reg 61(1) CSMC Regs
79 Reg 61(2) CSMC Regs
80 s16(6) CSA 1991; Sch para 1(1) CSMC
   Regs

Part 4

The '2003 rules'

Chapter 8

The child support calculation ('2003 rules')

This chapter covers:
1. Calculating child support (below)
2. Net income (p138)
3. Shared care (p145)

All new applications for child support are now dealt with under the '2012 rules' (see Chapter 6). Some existing '2003 rules' cases are also converted automatically to the '2012 rules' if they are linked to a new application (see p81). However, many existing cases will continue to be dealt with under the '2003 rules' until the process of closing existing cases and inviting people to apply under the '2012 rules' is complete (see Chapter 5). This is expected to be some time in 2017. The parties in existing '2003 rules' cases can still apply for a variation to the calculation (see Chapter 9), or for it to be revised or superseded (see Chapter 12). The information in this chapter is intended to assist with such applications.

1. Calculating child support

Child support is calculated for each non-resident parent separately. This means that a person with care may receive child support from one non-resident parent, worked out using one rate, and from another non-resident parent, worked out using a different rate.

The child support calculation is based on the following information:[1]
- the number of qualifying children;
- the number of relevant other children (see p23);
- the number of any relevant non-resident children (see p137);
- the number of persons with care;
- benefits (if any) received by the non-resident parent;
- whether the non-resident parent meets the conditions for the nil rate (see p132);
- the income of the non-resident parent (see p138);

- the number of nights (if any) the non-resident parent has care of a qualifying child (see p147);
- the number of nights (if any) a local authority has care of a qualifying child (see p154).

In all cases, the amount of child support calculated is a weekly amount.[2] Rounding rules apply to the different rates as follows.[3]

- In basic rate and reduced rate cases, fractions of a pound are disregarded if less than a half, or rounded up to the next pound if a half or over.
- In all other cases (ie, if there is apportionment or shared care), fractions of a penny are disregarded if less than a half, or rounded up to the next penny if a half or over.

Rates of child support

There are four rates of child support:
- nil rate (see below);
- flat rate (see p133);
- reduced rate (see p134);
- basic rate (see p135).

Nil rate

This applies if the non-resident parent is:[4]
- a full-time student;[5]
- a child;
- a prisoner;
- a 16/17-year-old receiving income support (IS), income-based jobseeker's allowance (JSA) or income-related employment and support allowance (ESA) (or her/his partner is);
- a 16/17-year-old and receiving universal credit (UC) calculated on the basis that s/he has no earned income (or a member of a couple and her/his partner is receiving UC calculated on this basis);
- receiving an allowance for work-based training for young people. Work-based training includes schemes such as Entry to Employment and Modern Apprenticeships. Young people may receive a training allowance or an education maintenance allowance;
- resident in a care home or independent hospital, or being provided with a care home service or/and independent healthcare service, and receiving one of the prescribed benefits for the flat rate (see p133) or has all or part of the cost of her/his accommodation met by a local authority;
- a person with net income (including from any of the prescribed benefits for the flat rate listed p133) of less than £5 a week.

Example 8.1

Kerry is a parent with care of two children, Mia and Lewis. Her ex-partner, Craig, is in prison. In this case, the nil rate applies. When he comes out of prison, Kerry could ask for a supersession.

Flat rate

The flat rate of £5 applies if the non-resident parent does not qualify for the nil rate and:[6]

- has weekly income of £100 or less; *or*
- receives one of the following:[7]
  - bereavement allowance;
  - retirement pension;
  - incapacity benefit or contributory ESA;
  - carer's allowance;
  - maternity allowance;
  - severe disablement allowance;
  - industrial injuries benefit;
  - widowed parent's allowance;
  - widow's pension;
  - contribution-based JSA;
  - a training allowance (other than for work-based learning for young people);
  - war disablement pension;
  - war widow's, war widower's or surviving civil partner's war pension;
  - payments under the Armed Forces Compensation Scheme;
  - a social security benefit paid by a country other than the UK;[8]
  - IS, income-related ESA or income-based JSA (or her/his partner does);
  - UC calculated on the basis that s/he does not have any earned income;
  - pension credit (PC).

The flat rate can be halved for couples if the non-resident parent's partner is also a non-resident parent with a child support application in force, and receives IS, income-based JSA, income-related ESA, UC calculated on the basis that s/he does not have any earned income, or PC.[9] If the non-resident parent is in a polygamous relationship and there is more than one partner who is also a non-resident parent and the non-resident parent or her/his partner receives one of these benefits, the flat rate is apportioned between them.

Note: the flat rate is not reduced to take account of any relevant other children or relevant non-resident children.

There are special rules about shared care (see p145).

Example 8.2

Craig has now come out of prison and gets income-based JSA. Kerry requests a supersession and Craig has a flat rate £5 child support deducted from his benefit each week.

If Craig moved in with Josie and claimed income-based JSA as a couple, the flat rate of £5 still would apply and Kerry would receive £5 a week. However, if Josie were also a non-resident parent, the flat rate would be halved. In this case, Kerry would receive £2.50 a week. If Josie had two persons with care (Alison and Penny), each caring for one qualifying child, they would find their child support reduced, as the flat rate of £2.50 is then apportioned. Alison and Penny would receive £1.25 each.

Reduced rate

This applies if neither the flat nor the nil rate applies and the non-resident parent has an income of less than £200 but more than £100.[10] The flat rate of £5 is added to a percentage of the parent's income between £100 and £200.[11] This means that only the income above £100, but under £200, is used in the calculation – eg, if net income is £150, the percentage is applied to £50. The percentage depends on the number of qualifying children and the number of relevant other children – ie, one for whom the non-resident parent or her/his partner receives child benefit.[12] Rounding is to the nearest pound.

Reduced rate percentages

Number of relevant other children	Number of qualifying children (including relevant non-resident children)		
	One	Two	Three or more
None	25%	35%	45%
One	20.5%	29%	37.5%
Two	19%	27%	35%
Three or more	17.5%	25%	32.5%

Step one

Work out the net income over £100 but less than £200.

Step two

Work out the relevant percentage, depending on the number of relevant other children and qualifying children. Apply this percentage to the income worked out in Step one and add this to £5, rounding to the nearest pound.

Step three

If there is more than one person with care, apportion this amount between them, depending on the number of qualifying children each cares for, rounded to the nearest penny. **Note:** if there is more than one person with care in relation to a qualifying child, child support can only be apportioned if a request to do so has been agreed by the Child Support Agency (CSA).

Example 8.3

Simon is due to pay child support to Fiona for two qualifying children, John and Margaret. Simon lives with his new partner, Julie, and their baby, Paul. Simon's net income is £180 a week. The reduced rate of child support applies.

Step one	Net income = £180
	Income between £100 and £200 = £80
Step two	Relevant percentage for one relevant other child and two qualifying children is 29 per cent.
	£5 + (29% x £80) = £5 + £23.20 = £28.20 (rounded to £28)

Simon is due to pay £28 child support to Fiona.

If the situation were as above except that Margaret were cared for by Fiona and John stayed with his grandmother, there would still be two qualifying children but there would be two persons with care. The child support calculated would need to be apportioned between them.

Step three	Each person cares for one qualifying child, so the child support is divided by two.
	£28 ÷ 2 = £14

Simon now pays Fiona £14 and the grandmother £14.

If the non-resident parent shares the care of any qualifying children, the reduced rate may be decreased by applying the shared care rules (see p145).

Basic rate

The basic rate applies if none of the other rates apply – eg, if the non-resident parent has a net weekly income of £200 or more.[13] The basic rate is a percentage of net income depending on the number of qualifying children. How much is paid also depends on the number of relevant other children. There may be other relevant non-resident children who are taken into account (see p137).

Basic rate percentages

Number of qualifying children (including relevant non-resident children)	Percentage of net income	Number of relevant other children	Percentage by which net income is reduced
1	15%	1	15%
2	20%	2	20%
3 or more	25%	3 or more	25%

If the non-resident parent has one or more relevant other children, her/his net income is reduced by an equivalent percentage (see p134) before the basic rate is calculated. Therefore, the basic rate is worked out in two steps.

Step one

Work out the net income of the non-resident parent. Depending on the number of relevant other children, reduce this by 15 per cent, 20 per cent or 25 per cent.

Step two

Depending on the number of qualifying children, child support is a proportion of this remaining net income, rounded to the nearest pound.

Step three

If there is more than one person with care, apportion this amount between them depending on the number of qualifying children each cares for, rounded to the nearest penny. **Note:** if there is more than one person with care in relation to a qualifying child, child support can only be apportioned if a request to do so has been agreed by the CSA.

Example 8.4

Simon now has a net income of £240 a week. Paul is a relevant other child, and John and Margaret are the qualifying children.

Step one   Net income is £240. One relevant other child means this is reduced by
15 per cent.
15% x £240 = £36
£240 – £36 = £204

Step two   There are two qualifying children, so child support is 20 per cent of
remaining net income.
20% x £204 = £40.80 (rounded to £41)

Simon therefore pays £41 in child support to Fiona.

If Margaret were cared for by Fiona and John stayed with his grandmother, this £41 would be split equally between Fiona and the grandmother.

Step three   £41 is apportioned between two persons with care. Each receives
£20.50 from Simon.

If the non-resident parent shares the care of any of the qualifying children, the child support calculated may be decreased further by applying the shared care rules (see p145).

If there is more than one person with care

If there is more than one person with care in relation to a non-resident parent, the amount of child support may be apportioned between them in relation to the number of qualifying children of each person.[14]

If this occurs and rounding provisions would result in the total amount of child support being different from the total amount before apportionment, the amount due is adjusted.[15] This may mean that child support due to one person with care must be reduced by a penny, so that no one person with care is disadvantaged. This reduction is reallocated between the persons with care from time to time.[16]

Apportionment occurs after the calculation of child support at the appropriate rate and before any decrease for shared care (see p151).[17]

In basic and reduced rate cases, if an adjustment is made that reduces the non-resident parent's liability to less than £5 (eg, because of shared care or a variation), the amount payable is £5 apportioned between the persons with care.

If there is more than one person with care in relation to a qualifying child, the child support due for this child may be further apportioned between them, but only if a request to do so has been agreed by the CSA (see p134).

Relevant non-resident children

A non-resident parent may have other relevant non-resident children (see p24).

If child support is payable at either the basic or reduced rate, or is calculated at one of these rates after applying a variation (see Chapter 9) and would otherwise have been the flat or nil rate, the relevant non-resident child is counted as a qualifying child.[18] The amount of child support calculated is then apportioned between the persons with care in relation to the number of qualifying children they care for, including any adjustment for shared care.[19] If the total amount payable by the non-resident parent is less than £5, s/he pays £5 instead, apportioned between the persons with care as appropriate.[20]

No payment is actually made for a relevant non-resident child. There is also no adjustment of the notional amount worked out for a non-resident child because of the non-resident parent sharing care or the child being in local authority care for part of the time.[21]

Example 8.5

James lives with his new partner, Amanda, and her son, Liam. He has three other children. Two (Emma and Joshua) are cared for by Elizabeth; one (Rachel) is cared for by Hilary. James has a court order for child maintenance for Rachel. Hilary cannot apply for child support as the court order is in force (if it was made after 3 March 2003, she could apply for child support if the order has been in force for one year; otherwise the order must cease before she can apply). In this case:

Emma and Joshua are qualifying children.

Liam is a relevant other child (even though he is not James's child, James' new partner, Amanda, gets child benefit for him).

Rachel is a relevant non-resident child.

If James had a net income of £275 a week, his child support worked out using the basic rate would be as follows.

Step one   £275 – (15% x £275) = £275 – £41.25 = £233.75

Step two   25% x £233.75 = £58.44 (rounded to £58)

Step three   Apportionment applies between Elizabeth and Hilary. Elizabeth receives two-thirds of the child support calculated – ie, £38.67 (when apportioning, rounding applies to the nearest penny).

Hilary receives her normal court order maintenance.

Note: if Hilary could apply for child support, she would receive £19.33.

---

2. Net income

A non-resident parent's net weekly income includes earned income, self-employed earnings, tax credits and payments from a pension scheme, retirement annuity or another scheme providing an income in retirement,[22] less any relevant deductions. Only these forms of income are included. All other income is ignored.

Note: a 'default maintenance decision' (see p204) may have been made if the Child Support Agency (CSA) did not have enough information to make a calculation.

From 30 April 2012, if evidence is not available or is unreliable, the CSA can assume that a parent's income is the average for her/his occupation in the area where s/he lives. This applies to both employed and self-employed earners.[23]

Also from 30 April 2012, the CSA can take into account the earnings of a non-resident parent who is habitually resident in the UK, even if s/he is paid abroad. This applies to both employed and self-employed earners, provided the earnings are taxable in the UK.[24]

Calculating income for child support purposes is one of the areas where errors are frequently made and should, therefore, be checked carefully. There is much caselaw on this area.

The CSA may make separate child support calculations for different periods in a particular case.[25]

Disregarded income

If a payment is made in a currency other than sterling, bank charges or commission for changing the payment into sterling are disregarded.[26] In addition, a payment made in a country outside the UK that prohibits currency transfer to the UK is ignored.[27]

Earnings from employment

Earnings are 'any remuneration or profit derived from employment' and, as well as wages, includes:[28]
- payments for overtime;
- profit-related pay;
- bonuses or commission;
- royalties or fees;
- holiday pay (except that payable more than four weeks after ending employment);
- retaining fees;
- statutory sick pay, statutory maternity pay, statutory adoption pay, statutory paternity pay and (from 5 April 2015) statutory shared parental pay;
- pay in lieu of notice.

Earnings do not include:[29]
- payments of expenses 'wholly, exclusively and necessarily' incurred in carrying out the duties of the job. It may be possible to argue that these can be apportioned between private and work use if they are necessary to carry out the duties of the job;[30]
- tax-exempt allowances paid by an employer;
- gratuities paid by customers – ie, tips;
- payments in kind;
- advance earnings or loans made by an employer;
- payments made by an employer when the employee is on strike;
- payments for duties as an auxiliary coastguard, part-time firefighter, or within the lifeboat services, territorial army or reserve forces;
- payments made by a local authority to local councillors for performing their duties;
- payments made after employment ends which relate to a specific period of time, provided that a period of equal length has elapsed between the job ending and the effective date;
- earnings from a previous job if they are paid in the same week or period in which earnings from a second job are received.

Dividends on shares are not taken into account as earnings, provided they derive genuinely from share ownership and are not intended to be in lieu of earnings.[31] However, in some cases, they may be classed as earnings derived from employment.[32]

Calculating normal weekly earnings

Averaged earnings are used in the child support calculation.[33] When calculating or estimating average earnings in the relevant week (see p25), the CSA considers evidence of the person's earnings over any appropriate period, beginning not more than eight weeks before the relevant week and ending not later than the date of the calculation. The CSA may also consider cumulative earnings in the tax year in which the relevant week falls to the date of the calculation.

If the CSA believes that the amount of weekly earnings does not accurately reflect the person's usual earnings, another period can be used, taking into account earnings received and those due to be received (from past, present or future employment) and the duration and pattern (or expected duration and pattern) of any employment.[34]

The CSA must be satisfied that the calculation of earnings in the relevant week produces a figure which is normal,[35] and that the period chosen reflects the parent's usual pattern of work – eg, the amount of overtime worked or sick leave.[36] A future period can be used – eg, to take into account earnings from a job which has not yet begun. The CSA must also consider the expected duration and pattern of any employment. A parent may want to suggest an alternative period to the CSA, giving reasons, as the CSA cannot be expected to consider this without substantial grounds and a prompt by one of the parents.[37] The CSA must use one continuous period.[38] If earnings during a year ending with the relevant week include a bonus or commission which is paid separately from, or for a longer period than, the other earnings with which it is paid, these payments are totalled over the year and divided by 52.[39]

The CSA must take into account any change of circumstances it is aware of between the relevant week and the effective date (see p206).[40] However, it must first calculate earnings as above for the relevant week in order to determine whether there has been a change of circumstances.[41] For changes after this date, see p202.

Calculating net earnings

Net earnings from employment are counted as net income in full. Net earnings are gross earnings less:[42]
- income tax;
- Class 1 national insurance (NI) contributions;
- all contributions made to an occupational or personal pension scheme (unless the scheme is intended partly to pay off a mortgage on the parent's home, in which case 75 per cent of contributions).

Income tax is the actual amount deducted, including any tax in relation to payments not included as earnings.[43] If a person avoids tax and NI, the amount that should have been due must be deducted when calculating net earnings. However, a variation on the grounds of having a 'lifestyle inconsistent with level of income' could be sought (see Chapter 9).[44]

Pension contributions are only deducted if they are made to a scheme approved by HM Revenue and Customs (HMRC).

Earnings from self-employment

Income from self-employment is assessed on the basis of either:
* taxable profits from self-employment shown on a tax calculation notice issued by HMRC; *or*
* in a small number of cases, the income from self-employment as calculated from gross receipts less relevant deductions.[45]

The non-resident parent must provide a tax calculation notice (or any revised notice) on demand.[46] The demand should explain the consequences of failing to provide the information. This may be an offence (see p58).

If there is evidence of a change of circumstances in the usual or long-term average income of a self-employed parent, the CSA can make a supersession decision without waiting for the end of the relevant accounting period and the submission of the tax return.[47]

Earnings calculated using taxable profits less deductions

The net earnings taken into account are the total taxable profits from self-employment less:[48]
* income tax (calculated using the personal allowances and tax rates applicable at the effective date[49]);
* Class 2 and Class 4 NI contributions (at the rates applicable at the effective date[50]);
* any personal pension premiums or retirement annuity contract premiums (but only 75 per cent of such premiums if the scheme is intended to pay off a mortgage).

Net weekly earnings can only be worked out as outlined above if they are for a period not more than 24 months before the relevant week.[51]

Earnings calculated using gross receipts less deductions

Earnings can be calculated by using gross receipts less deductions if:[52]
* the 24-month condition is not met (see above); *or*
* the CSA accepts that it is not reasonably practicable for a non-resident parent to provide the forms submitted to, or issued or revised by, HMRC.

It is relatively rare for a case to be assessed based on gross receipts rather than using figures submitted to HMRC. The CSA does not consider revising or superseding a decision based simply on the fact that using the gross receipts method would produce a greater amount of child support due to a person with care than that calculated using the tax calculation notice. However, if a non-resident parent's earnings were assessed by the gross receipts method, but s/he now has self-assessment details or a tax calculation notice, the CSA may supersede the decision.

Net earnings are the gross receipts less:[53]

- income tax and NI;
- any premiums paid in respect of a pension or retirement annuity contract (or 75 per cent of such premiums if the scheme is intended to pay off a mortgage);
- any VAT paid in excess of VAT received in the same period as that over which the earnings are assessed; *and*
- any expenses which are reasonably incurred and which are wholly and exclusively for the business. If the CSA is not satisfied that the full expense was appropriate or necessary to the business, it allows that part considered reasonable. If an expense is partly business and partly private (eg, a car), the CSA decides on the breakdown between the two uses on the evidence available.

If a non-resident parent provides board and lodgings, gross earnings include all of the board or lodgings payments if this is her/his only or main source of income.[54]
Income tax and NI are calculated in the same way as for taxable profit.[55]
Business expenses include:[56]

- repayments of capital on loans used to replace or repair a business asset (but not for loans taken out for any other business purpose or if the costs are met by payments from an insurance policy);
- any income used to repair a business asset;
- any payment of interest on loans taken out for business purposes (this does not include loans taken out to acquire a share of a business or to pay business tax liabilities).[57]

Business expenses do *not* include capital expenditure, nor any expenses incurred in providing business entertainment.[58]
The net weekly income of a self-employed earner is averaged over the 52 weeks up to and including the relevant week or, if a person has been self-employed for less than a year, over the period s/he has been self-employed (including the relevant week).[59]
A self-employed person may be asked to provide other evidence of business receipts and expenses, such as business books, receipts of bills, bank statements, records of wages paid, HMRC forms and VAT bills.
If the CSA believes that the above calculation would produce an amount that does not accurately represent a parent's true earnings, another period can be used.[60] This should not be used just because earnings fluctuate, receipts are irregular, trade is slow at times or work non-existent for a period, nor should a different period be used just because it is known that earnings will subsequently change.[61] In such cases, the CSA takes into account earnings received or due to be received, and the duration and pattern (or expected pattern) of any self-employment.[62]
Since most calculations are based on the self-assessment form or tax calculation notice, this alternative method is only used if there has been a major change in

trading which has resulted in higher or lower earnings, or if a person has recently become self-employed.[63]

A person may still be classed as a self-employed earner even if her/his profits are not taxable – eg, in certain circumstances if s/he spends a significant amount of time gambling. In such a case, however, it may be very difficult to demonstrate that the activities amount to self-employment that generates profits and, in practice, a person with care may have to consider applying for a variation from the calculation on the grounds that the non-resident parent's lifestyle is inconsistent with her/his income (see Chapter 9).[64]

Challenging self-employed earnings

There have often been delays in self-employed parents producing all the information necessary to work out the child support due. The CSA can impose penalties and a default decision (see p204) while waiting for the information. The person with care may want to request that this is done if there have been problems in the past, and can complain if the CSA refuses to do so (see Chapter 15). However, s/he cannot force a penalty to be imposed.

A person with care may allege that a self-employed non-resident parent is disguising her/his true income. If a person with care wants to challenge the earnings, once a calculation has been made s/he can apply for a revision (see p217) and ask the CSA to use an inspector (see p72) to obtain more detailed information. In practice, if a non-resident parent's accounts have been accepted by HMRC, it is very unlikely that the CSA will consider it worthwhile to undertake further investigations. However, HMRC's declaration of income is not necessarily conclusive, and the CSA is not required to use the figures used by HMRC in the tax calculation if there is evidence that they are not reliable.[65] The true and full amount of profits defined as taxable should be taken into account, not any lower amount that a person may pay as a result of the correct law not being applied for any reason.[66]

The CSA may also refuse to revise the calculation if a person with care cannot substantiate the allegations. This can be challenged if the belief is reasonably held, as it is very difficult for one party to obtain definitive details of the other's income. The CSA is much better placed to obtain such details.

If a person with care takes a case to the First-tier Tribunal (see Chapter 13), details of income appear in the appeal papers and s/he may be able to argue that some of the expenses included are not reasonable or not wholly connected with the business. The First-tier Tribunal may adjourn the hearing for further information to be collected. Alternatively, it can estimate net earnings based on the available evidence, including oral evidence from the person with care[67] or data about earnings in different sectors and in particular localities.[68]

The person with care can apply for a variation on the grounds that a person's lifestyle is inconsistent with her/his level of income or that assets that do not currently produce income are capable of doing so (see Chapter 9).

Tax credits

Working tax credit

Working tax credit (WTC) is counted as the income of the non-resident parent if it is based solely on her/his work and earnings.[69] The rate of WTC used is that payable at the effective date and includes any element for childcare costs.[70]

If both members of a couple meet the conditions for WTC, they can choose who receives it, but this is not reflected in the rules for calculating child support. If both members of a couple are working, WTC is treated as the income of the partner with the higher earnings over the period used for assessing earnings for tax credit purposes, or halved if their earnings are equal.[71] The earnings used for determining WTC are the ones used to determine who is treated as having WTC included in their income.[72] This means that, should the earnings change later, the non-resident parent could be treated as having more income than s/he has. For example, if s/he is earning more than her/his partner when WTC is worked out, WTC counts in full as her/his income. If the partner's income later increases, but the non-resident parent does not notify HMRC during the tax year and waits for an end-of-year adjustment, s/he still has WTC counted as her/his income, even though her/his partner currently earns more than s/he does. **Note:** it is not compulsory to report changes of income during the tax year, although it may be advisable if there is a large increase.

If their respective incomes change so that a non-resident parent's income becomes lower than that of her/his partner, s/he can ask for a revision of the tax credit award to reflect the new income during the year. Otherwise, it is based on the previous tax year. If s/he asks for a revision, s/he can then apply for a supersession of the child support calculation on the basis that WTC should no longer be treated as her/his income. However, s/he should seek advice before asking for the tax credit award to be revised. As income for the current tax year is an estimate, asking for an in-year income revision of a tax credit award can lead to overpayments as well as underpayments. See CPAG's *Welfare Benefits and Tax Credits Handbook* for more details.

Child tax credit

Any child tax credit paid to the non-resident parent or her/his partner counts in full as income, at the rate payable at the effective date.[73]

Other income

Periodic or other payments from an occupational or personal pension, retirement annuity or other scheme to provide income in retirement count in full as income. Payments to compensate for the failure of pension schemes (Financial Assistance Scheme and Pension Protection Fund payments) are treated in the same way. Income is calculated or estimated on a weekly basis using the 26-week period ending in the relevant week (see p25).[74] If the income has been received during each week of the period, the total received over the 26 weeks is divided by 26. In other cases, the total received is divided by the number of complete weeks for which the payment was received. However, the CSA can use a different period if the amount produced by the above calculation does not accurately reflect actual income.[75] Furthermore, a change occurring between the relevant week and the effective date (see p206) must be taken into account by the CSA if it is aware of the change, in the same way as for earnings (see p139).

Periodic 'drawdown' of capital (eg, monthly repayments of a loan to a parent) is not counted as income.[76]

If a person has capital assets that produce income (eg, rent from property), the income is taken into account as earnings from self-employment (see p141) if the assets are held as part of a trade or business.[77]

Maximum amount of net weekly income

The maximum amount of net weekly income that can be included in the calculation of child support is £2,000.[78] This includes all income, whether from earnings, tax credits, self-employment, or a pension and other payments. Even if a variation is being applied, the amount of net income cannot exceed this maximum figure.

This means that the maximum weekly amount of child support that can ever be paid is £500 – ie, if the non-resident parent has three or more children and no other relevant children.

Maximum child support payable (using the basic rate)

Number of relevant children	One qualifying child	Two qualifying children	Three or more qualifying children
None	£300	£400	£500
One	£255	£340	£425
Two	£240	£320	£400
Three or more	£225	£300	£375

3. **Shared care**

For the shared care rules to apply in '2003 rules' cases, there must be:
- a non-resident parent who shares care – ie, looks after the qualifying child at least 52 nights a year on average (see p147); *or*
- a parent with care (ie, with day-to-day care of a qualifying child because s/he cares for the child at least 104 nights a year on average) who is treated as a non-resident parent (see p19); *or*
- a qualifying child cared for by a local authority for part of the time (see p154).

One, or all, of these situations may apply in any individual case. See p21 for the definition of 'shared care', and p15 for the definition of 'day-to-day care'.

If there are two or more persons with care (of a child for whom an application has been made) and at least one of them is a parent, special rules apply and a parent with care may be treated as a non-resident parent (see p19).

The Child Support Agency (CSA) calculates the amount of shared care by looking at regular weekly patterns, exceptional weeks and other occasional nights within a 12-month period. It is the actual care provided that counts, whether or not it is authorised or agreed.

If a non-resident parent provides some care but not sufficient for it to qualify as shared care, an application for a variation may be made on the grounds that her/his contact costs are 'special expenses' (see p161).

Who receives child support

If there are two or more people in different households who both have day-to-day care of a qualifying child, either can make an application for child support, provided both or neither have parental responsibility.[79] If only one has parental responsibility, that person must be the applicant. If s/he decides not to apply, the other person with care could lose out on child support, unless there is an application from the non-resident parent (or a child in Scotland).

If both/all the persons with care make an application, only one is accepted, depending on the order of priority (see p48). This may include a parent with care who is subsequently treated as non-resident for the calculation.

If none of the persons with care is a parent who is treated as non-resident, the person whose application is accepted receives all the child support calculated.[80] The applicant or other person with care may request that the payment be apportioned between them.[81] In making the decision, the CSA considers all the circumstances of the case and representations from the persons with care.[82] If agreed, the child support payable is apportioned in relation to the amount of care provided (see *Example 8.9*).

If one of the persons with care is treated as a non-resident parent, this apportionment cannot take place. The deemed non-resident parent is liable to pay child support, and the entire amount is paid to the person with care whose application has been given priority (see p48) or who provides care for the greater amount of time. In other words, a person with care who provides care for the lesser amount of time can never receive child support from a deemed non-resident parent, irrespective of the amount being paid. The person with care who receives child support could decide on an informal basis to pass some of it on to the other person(s) with care, but this cannot be enforced.

This may seem illogical, particularly if the application has been made by a parent with care who is then treated as non-resident, or if applications have been made by both persons with care but one is then treated as the non-resident parent.

A parent with care who applies to the CSA for child support from the non-resident parent but ends up being deemed non-resident and paying child support can request that the application be withdrawn (see p208). However, s/he may find that the other person with care makes another new application (if that person has parental responsibility).

When a non-resident parent shares care

In '2003 rules' cases, a non-resident parent shares care if s/he looks after a qualifying child at least one night a week on average.[83] The care must be provided overnight and the non-resident parent must stay at the same address as the child.[84] This means that the care could be provided away from the non-resident parent's normal home – eg, while on holiday or at a relative's home. It also includes the situation where the non-resident parent looks after the child overnight in the parent with care's home while the parent with care is away from home during the relevant nights.[85]

The number of nights is averaged over the 12 months ending with the relevant week.[86] A shorter period may be used – eg, because there is no pattern for the frequency or there is an intended change in frequency.[87] The number of nights of care in that period must be in the same ratio as 52 nights is to 12 months – eg, 26 nights in six months or 13 nights in three months.[88]

The effect of shared care on the flat rate

If a non-resident parent shares care with one or more persons with care, it must be established whether s/he is liable for the flat rate because her/his income is less than £100. If so, there is no adjustment of the child support liability, regardless of how many nights of shared care there are. However, the amount of child support due to the person with care of that qualifying child is nil if a non-resident parent:[89]

- is liable to pay the flat rate because s/he is in receipt of a relevant benefit (see p133) or s/he or her/his partner receives income support (IS), income-based jobseeker's allowance, income-related employment and support allowance (ESA), universal credit calculated on the basis that the parent does not have any earned income, or pension credit (including cases where a reduced flat rate of £2.50 applies); *and*
- cares for a qualifying child for at least 52 nights a year.

If there is more than one person with care, the flat rate is apportioned in relation to the number of qualifying children before any adjustment for shared care is made. This may mean that a non-resident parent's liability reduces to nil for one person with care because of shared care. However, s/he is still liable for the remaining amounts to the other person(s) with care, in which case s/he pays an amount which is less than £5. The process is as follows.

- **Step one:** check the reason why the flat rate applies.

- **Step two:** apportion the flat rate between the persons with care on the basis of the number of qualifying children. Where appropriate, apply any apportioning in relation to a qualifying child if there is more than one person with care.
- **Step three:** apply any reduction to nil because of shared care.

Note: apportioning and rounding may result in adjustments of a penny in some calculations done by the CSA (see p131).

Example 8.6

Alistair is the non-resident parent of Keith, who lives with his older brother Neil, and Katie, who lives with her mother, Rachel. Alistair looks after Katie one or two nights a week. Both Neil and Rachel apply for child support. Alistair receives income-related ESA.

Step one   Alistair is due to pay child support at the flat rate of £5, as he receives income-related ESA.

Step two   Apportion the flat rate of £5 between the persons with care in relation to the qualifying children each cares for – ie, the amount is halved.
To Neil for Keith = £2.50
To Rachel for Katie = £2.50

Step three   Alistair cares for Katie over 52 nights a year so the amount due reduces to nil.
Alistair remains liable to pay £2.50 in child support to Neil for Keith.

The situation is as above but now Keith goes to stay with his grandfather two nights a week. Neil asks for child support to be split between them and the CSA agrees to do this.

Step one   Remains the same.

Step two   Rachel is due £2.50, but now the £2.50 for Keith is split between Neil and his grandfather.
Neil looks after Keith five nights out of seven; his grandfather looks after him two out of seven, therefore:
5/7 x £2.50 is due to Neil = £1.79
2/7 x £2.50 is due to the grandfather = £0.72

Step three   The amount due to Rachel reduces to nil as Alistair cares for Katie over 52 nights a year.
Alistair remains liable to pay £1.79 to Neil and £0.72 to Keith's grandfather.

In total, this means that Alistair is due to pay £2.51. This is more than the amount before apportioning because of the rounding provisions. Therefore, the child support is adjusted by one penny to one of the persons with care. Neil has his adjusted to £1.78 for a period, after which the adjustment is made to the grandfather's. He receives £0.71 and Neil receives £1.79.

The effect of shared care on the basic and reduced rate

If a non-resident parent, or parent with care who is treated as non-resident, shares care of a qualifying child for 52 or more nights a year, the amount of child support s/he is due to pay is reduced by a suitable fraction, depending on the number of nights of shared care.[90] The amount depends on the relevant band.[91]

Number of nights	Fraction to subtract
52 to 103	One-seventh
104 to 155	Two-sevenths
156 to 174	Three-sevenths
175 or more	One-half

If a non-resident parent shares care of a qualifying child for a sufficient number of nights for the one-half fraction to apply, an additional £7 decrease in child support must also be applied.[92] This is known as **'abatement'**. Abatement is applied for each child for whom at least 175 nights of shared care applies.

If the decrease results in a non-resident parent being liable to pay a person with care less than £5, s/he pays the flat rate of £5 instead.[93] This includes the situation where the total amount of child support due to all persons with care is decreased to less than £5. In this case, the £5 is apportioned between the persons with care in relation to the number of qualifying children.

When applying the decrease for shared care, the rounding provisions apply to the nearest penny.[94]

Example 8.7

Alex shares care of Mark with the person with care, Diane. He looks after Mark on average two nights at the weekend and a couple of weeks in school holidays. Although Alex is a parent with care, he is treated as a non-resident parent as he is not the principal provider of care. Alex's net income is £240.

Step one	**Basic rate** = 15% x £240 = £36
Step two	**Apply decrease for shared care**
	Alex shares care in the 104–155 band (two-sevenths).
	£36 child support must be decreased by two-sevenths – ie, £36 – £10.29 = £25.71

Alex pays Diane £25.71.

Alex increases the amount of time he shares care of Mark to three nights one week and four nights the next. In this case, Alex shares care for over 175 nights and the one-half fraction is applied. Alex's child support calculated under the basic rate remains £36.

Step two	£36 decreased by one-half and a further £7 subtracted – ie, £18 – £7 = £11

Because of the increase in shared care, Alex pays £11 to Diane.

Alex's circumstances change and he now has income of £160.

Step one   **Reduced rate** of child support = £5 + (25% x £60) = £5 + £15 = £20

Step two   **Apply decrease for shared care**

The fraction to apply remains at one-half and there is an abatement of £7.

(50% x £20) – £7 = £10 – £7 = £3

Step three   **Child support due** is below £5, so Alex pays £5 a week to Diane.

More than one qualifying child

If a person with care and non-resident parent have more than one qualifying child, the fractions that apply for shared care for each qualifying child are added together, then divided by the number of qualifying children.[95] This applies where care is shared for some, but not all, of the qualifying children or there are different shared-care arrangements for each qualifying child.

Example 8.8

Pat is the non-resident parent of Lea and Dylan. Both are cared for by their grandmother, Jean. Lea does not like staying with Pat and only does so occasionally. However, Dylan stays with him on Friday and Saturday nights. Both children stay with him for a few days at Christmas and during the school holidays. Pat has a net income of £220.

Step one   **Basic rate** for two children = 20% x £220 = £44

Step two   **Apply decrease for shared care**

Lea does not stay with Pat sufficient days for it to count as shared care.

Dylan is in the 104–155 band (two-sevenths).

The fractions which apply are added together and divided by two, as there are two qualifying children for whom Jean cares.

(0 + 2/7) ÷ 2 = 2/14

Pat's child support is decreased by 2/14 (ie, £6.29).

Because of the shared care, Pat must pay £37.71 (£44 – £6.29) to Jean.

Note: if Pat has costs for keeping in contact with Lea, he may be able to apply for a variation (see Chapter 9).

Lea increases the amount of time she spends with her father and now this counts as shared care.

Step two   Lea is in the 52–103 band (one-seventh).

Dylan is in the 104–155 band (two-sevenths).

The fractions are added together and divided by two – ie, 3/7 ÷ 2 = 3/14

The child support due is, therefore, decreased by 3/14 because of shared care.

Pat's child support is decreased by 3/14 (ie, £9.43).

Because of shared care, Pat must pay £34.57 (£44 – £9.43) to Jean.

Dylan stays with his father more often and increases the amount of care, so that:

Step two   Lea is in the 52–103 band (one-seventh).

Dylan is in the 175 or more band (one-half).

The decrease is $(1/7 + 1/2) \div 2 = 9/28$; $9/28 \times £44 = £14.14$

$£44 - £14.14 = £29.86$. However, because care is shared equally for one qualifying child, the abatement of £7 applies and child support due is decreased by a further £7.

Pat now pays Jean £22.86 ($£29.86 - £7$).

More than one person with care: apportionment

A non-resident parent may be due to pay child support to more than one person with care because there:

- are several qualifying children with different persons with care (known as 'multiple maintenance units');
- is more than one person with care in relation to a qualifying child(ren).

One or both of these situations may apply in any one case, and the non-resident parent may share care with only one or all of the persons with care. In these cases, there may be apportioning and shared-care adjustments made throughout the calculation (see p137).

Example 8.9

Ivan is the non-resident parent of two children – Holly, whose parent with care is Ellen, and Jamie, whose parent with care is Laura. Ivan looks after Holly when Ellen is on night shifts, which is every other week apart from holidays, and takes her camping with him on the odd weekend. Jamie and Laura live further away, so Ivan only sees Jamie for a long weekend once a month when he visits his parents and two weeks in the summer holidays. Ivan's net income is £230.

Step one   The **basic rate** applies for two qualifying children. There are no relevant other children and net income is £230.

$20\% \times £230 = £46$

There is apportionment between the persons with care. They each care for one qualifying child so halve the child support between them.

To Ellen for Holly = £23

To Laura for Jamie = £23

Step two	**Apply decrease for shared care**

Child support paid to Ellen for Holly

Holly is in the 156–174 band (three-sevenths).

3/7 x £23 = £9.86

£23 – £9.86 = £13.14

Child support paid to Laura for Jamie

Jamie is in the 52–103 band (one-seventh).

1/7 x £23 = £3.29

£23 – £3.29 = £19.71

Step three **Total child support due** is £13.14 (to Ellen) + £19.71 (to Laura) = £32.85.

The situation is as above but now Laura has a new job which means she is away from home on average two nights a week and the occasional weekend. Her sister (Alice) looks after Jamie and Laura asks the CSA to split the child support between her and Alice.

Step one **Basic rate** is £46.

Apportion between the persons with care (there are two qualifying children but three persons with care – Ellen for Holly, and Laura and Alice for Jamie).

To Ellen for Holly = £23

Between Laura and Alice for Jamie = £23

Alice looks after Jamie two nights a week on average (2/6 – ie, one-third).

To Alice for Jamie = £7.67 (1/3 x £23)

Laura looks after Jamie for the remaining four nights (4/6 – ie, two-thirds).

To Laura for Jamie = £15.33 (2/3 x £23)

Step two **Apply decrease for shared care**

Child support paid to Ellen for Holly

Ivan's care for Holly is in the 156–174 band (three-sevenths).

3/7 x £23 = £9.86 (ie, £23–£9.86 = £13.14)

Child support paid to Alice for Jamie

Ivan's care for Jamie is in the 52–103 band (one-seventh).

1/7 x £7.67 = £1.10; £7.67 – £1.10 = £6.57

Child support paid to Laura for Jamie

Ivan's care for Jamie is in the 52 – 103 band (one-seventh).

1/7 x £15.33 = £2.19; £15.33 – £2.19 = £13.14

Step three **Total child support due** is £13.14 (to Ellen) + £6.57 (to Alice) + £13.14 (to Laura) = £32.85.

Overall, Ivan pays exactly the same amount as before, but it is split between three people.

A qualifying child is in hospital or at boarding school

If a qualifying child is in hospital or at boarding school, any night spent there counts as a night with the person who would normally provide care at that time.[96] This includes nights normally spent with a non-resident parent,[97] person with care or local authority.[98]

These nights count in determining whether a non-resident parent or local authority shares care. They also count when establishing who is a person with care or which parent is to be treated as non-resident.

Example 8.10

Nick, who has been living with his mother during the week and spending Friday nights with his father, goes to boarding school. The time as a boarder continues to be treated as if he were living with his mother. Even if the care arrangement changes, so that Nick spends alternate weekends with his father, the nights at school still count as having been spent with his mother.

If the parents agree, or the periods involved are infrequent, the case may be straightforward. However, if the arrangements break down, a normal pattern cannot be established or the parents disagree, the CSA must make a decision on shared care.

Example 8.11

Ella is a qualifying child cared for most of the time by her mother, Sarah, although her father, Stuart, looks after her on Wednesday and Saturday nights. Over the past year Ella has undergone treatment for cancer, which has resulted in her spending periods in hospital. Because of this, Stuart has only looked after Ella for 42 nights in the year. On 16 of the remaining nights that Ella should have stayed with him, she was in hospital. On the other nights that Ella should have stayed with Stuart, she was unwell and wanted to stay with Sarah. The CSA must decide whether to consider Ella as staying with Stuart for 58 nights or accept that the intention was for her to stay with Stuart on 104 nights in the year. Both parents have the right to appeal against the CSA's decision.

If, having counted these nights, a person is not a person with care, a non-resident parent who shares care or a local authority who has part-time care, the night is treated as if the child is in the care of the principal provider of day-to-day care.[99] For example, if a babysitter looks after a child one night a week, then the child goes into hospital, the babysitter is not a person with care, non-resident parent or local authority. Therefore, that night is treated as one normally spent with the principal provider of day-to-day care.

Care provided partly by a local authority

Part-time local authority care has no effect on the flat rate of child support. This section therefore only applies if:

- a non-resident parent is liable to pay the basic or reduced rate (including if a variation has been made which results in her/him paying child support at either of these rates);[100] *and*
- a qualifying child is cared for by a local authority at least one night a week on average but not more than five (see below).

A local authority cannot be a person with care.[101] Therefore, if a child is in the care of a local authority for more than five nights a week, no child support is payable by the non-resident parent because there is no person with care. If a child is at a boarding school, even if this is publicly funded education provision, s/he does not count as being in local authority care.[102]

If a local authority cares for the child for 52 nights or more in the 12-month period ending with the relevant week, the child support to be paid by the non-resident parent is decreased.[103] The CSA may use a different period if it considers it to be more representative of the current arrangements. A future period may also be considered if the qualifying child is to go into local authority care on or after the effective date.[104] If an alternative period is used, the number of nights of care must be in the same ratio as 52 nights to 12 months.[105] (Nights spent in hospital or at boarding school which normally would have been spent in care are included – see p153.)

Local authority care only affects the calculation of child support when it applies to a qualifying child. If a relevant other child is in local authority care (whether full or part time), this does not affect how s/he is treated, provided the non-resident parent or her/his partner receives child benefit for her/him (or has elected not to receive child benefit because s/he would be liable for the 'high income child benefit charge' in income tax).[106]

The decrease for part-time local authority care

If a local authority has part-time care of a qualifying child, the basic or reduced rate child support calculated for a non-resident parent is decreased in relation to the number of nights the qualifying child spends in local authority care.

This calculation may be carried out either on its own, if a non-resident parent does not share care, or alongside one carried out because a non-resident parent shares care (see p147).

The effect of part-time local authority care

Number of nights	Fraction to subtract
52 to 103	One-seventh
104 to 155	Two-sevenths
156 to 207	Three-sevenths
208 to 259	Four-sevenths
260 to 262	Five-sevenths

If a person with care and non-resident parent have more than one qualifying child, the fractions that apply for each qualifying child in local authority care are added together and divided by the number of qualifying children for whom child support is calculated.[107] This applies if the local authority cares for one or all qualifying children or there are different care arrangements for each qualifying child.

If the decrease because of part-time local authority care would reduce the amount of child support to less than £5 for the only or all of the persons with care, the amount due is £5.

Example 8.12

Jake is the non-resident parent for Michael and Leanne. Michael has just been placed under local authority supervision, which means that over the next six months he will spend four nights a week in a residential unit and the rest of the time with his mother, Naomi. Jake has net income of £280 and currently pays child support of £56 (basic rate child support). This must be superseded because of local authority care. The CSA supersedes the decision, considering the ratio in the six-month period.

Step one   Work out amount of child support due
Basic rate = 20% x £280 = £56

Step two   Work out the decrease because of part-time local authority care
Local authority care for Michael is in the 208–259 band (four-sevenths). The fractions which apply are added together and divided by the number of qualifying children – ie, (0 + 4/7) ÷ 2 = 4/14. Jake's child support is decreased by 4/14 – ie, £16.

Jake now pays Naomi £40 (£56 – £16).

If Leanne were also in care for two nights a week:

Step one   Same as above.

Step two   Local authority care for Leanne is in the 104–155 band (two-sevenths). Local authority care for Michael is in the 208–259 band (four-sevenths). The fractions are added together and divided by two:
(2/7 + 4/7) = 6/7 ÷ 2 = 6/14
Jake's child support decreases by 6/14 = £24.

Jake now pays Naomi £32 (£56 – £24).

A non-resident parent shares care and the local authority has part-time care

If a non-resident parent shares care of a qualifying child and a local authority has part-time care of a qualifying child in relation to the same person with care, the appropriate fractions are worked out under each provision and are added together.[108] The amount of child support due from the non-resident parent is then decreased by this fraction.

If this decrease would result in a non-resident parent being due to pay less than £5 to the only or all of the persons with care, s/he pays £5.[109]

This calculation is carried out at Step two.

Example 8.13

The situation is as in *Example 8.12*, except that Leanne spends one night a week with Jake, but Michael does not.

Step two   Jake cares for Leanne in the 52–103 band (one-seventh).

The fractions which apply are added together and divided by the number of qualifying children:

$(0 + 1/7) \div 2 = 1/14$

Jake's child support because of shared care should be reduced by 1/14. Because Michael is in local authority care, the child support due should be reduced by 4/14. This is added to the amount because of shared care.

$1/14 + 4/14 = 5/14$

Jake's child support is reduced by £20 (5/14 x £56).

Jake now pays Naomi £36 (£56 – £20).

If Leanne is also in care two nights a week but still spends one night a week with Jake:

Step two   Jake's child support because of shared care should reduce by 1/14 (as above).

Local authority care for Michael and Leanne should reduce child support by 6/14 (see *Example 8.12*).

These fractions are added together:

$1/14 + 6/14 = 7/14 = 1/2$

Jake's child support is reduced by £28 (1/2 x £56).

Jake now pays Naomi £28 (£56 – £28).

Notes

1. Calculating child support

1 Sch 1 CSA 1991; reg 2(5) CS(MCSC) Regs
2 Reg 2(1) CS(MCSC) Regs
3 Reg 2(2) and (3) CS(MCSC) Regs
4 Sch 1 Part 1 para 5 CSA 1991; reg 5 CS(MCSC) Regs
5 Reg 1(2) CS(MCSC) Regs
6 Sch 1 Part 4 CSA 1991
7 Reg 4 CS(MCSC) Regs
8 Reg 4(1)(c) CS(MCSC) Regs
9 Sch 1 Part 1 para 4(2) CSA 1991; reg 4(3)(a) CS(MCSC) Regs
10 Sch 1 Part 1 para 3 CSA 1991
11 Reg 3 CS(MCSC) Regs
12 Sch 1 Part 1 para 10C CSA 1991
13 Sch 1 Part 1(1) CSA 1991
14 Sch 1 Part 1 para 6 CSA 1991
15 Reg 6 CS(MCSC) Regs
16 Reg 6 CS(MCSC) Regs
17 Sch 1 Part 1 para 1(2) CSA 1991
18 Reg 11(2) and (3) CS(MCSC) Regs
19 Reg 11(3) CS(MCSC) Regs
20 Reg 11(5) CS(MCSC) Regs
21 Reg 11(4) CS(MCSC) Regs

2. Net income

22 Sch Part I para 1 CS(MCSC) Regs
23 Sch Parts II para 6A and III para 9A CS(MCSC) Regs
24 Reg 1(2) CS(MCSC) Regs; *AT v SSWP and JN (CSM)* [2013] UKUT 614 (AAC)
25 Sch 1 Part II para 15 CSA 1991
26 Sch Part I para 2(a) CS(MCSC) Regs
27 Sch Part I para 2(b) CS(MCSC) Regs
28 Sch Part II para 4(1) CS(MCSC) Regs
29 Sch Part II para 4(2) CS(MCSC) Regs
30 CCS/137/2007
31 R(CS) 4/05
32 CCS/623/2005
33 Sch Part II para 6(1) CS(MCSC) Regs
34 Sch Part II para 6(4) CS(MCSC) Regs
35 CCS/16/1994; CCS/11873/1996
36 CCS/6810/1995
37 CCS/511/1995
38 CCS/7312/1995; CCS/556/1995; CSCS/1/1996; CSCS/6/1996
39 Sch Part II para 6(3) CS(MCSC) Regs
40 Reg 2(4) CS(MCSC) Regs
41 CCS/2750/1995

42 Sch Part II para 5 CS(MCSC) Regs
43 Sch Part II para 5(2) CS(MCSC) Regs
44 *WM v CMEC (CSM)* [2011] UKUT 226 (AAC)
45 Sch Part III para 7(1) and (1A) CS(MCSC) Regs
46 Sch Part III para 7(2) CS(MCSC) Regs
47 *LW v CMEC* [2010] UKUT 184 (AAC)
48 Sch Part III para 7(3) CS(MCSC) Regs
49 Sch Part III para 7(4) CS(MCSC) Regs
50 Sch Part III para 7(5) CS(MCSC) Regs
51 Sch Part III para 7(6) CS(MCSC) Regs
52 Sch Part III para 8(1) CS(MCSC) Regs
53 Sch Part III para 8(2) CS(MCSC) Regs
54 Sch Part III para 10 CS(MCSC) Regs
55 Sch Part III para 8(4) CS(MCSC) Regs
56 Sch Part III para 8(3)(a) CS(MCSC) Regs
57 CCS/15949/1996
58 Sch Part III para 8(3)(b) CS(MCSC) Regs
59 Sch Part III para 9(2) CS(MCSC) Regs
60 Sch Part III para 9(3) CS(MCSC) Regs
61 CCS/3182/1995; CCS/6145/1995; CCS/3428/2002
62 Sch Part III para 9(3) CS(MCSC) Regs
63 *How is Child Maintenance Worked Out?* CSL303, June 2011
64 *Hakki v SSWP* [2014] EWCA Civ 530
65 CCS/1263/2008; *KB v CMEC* [2010] UKUT 434 (AAC); *Gray v SSWP* [2012] EWCA Civ 1412
66 *DB v CMEC (CSM)* [2011] UKUT 202 (AAC)
67 CCS/7966/1995
68 CCS/13988/1996; CCS/2901/2002
69 Sch Part IV para 11(1) CS(MCSC) Regs
70 Sch Part IV para 11(1) CS(MCSC) Regs; CCS/2049/2007
71 Sch Part IV para 11(2) CS(MCSC) Regs
72 Sch Part IV para 11(2A) CS(MCSC) Regs
73 Sch Part IV para 13A CS(MCSC) Regs; *SSWP v RH* [2008] UKUT 19 (AAC), reported as R(CS) 3/09
74 Sch Part V para 16 CS(MCSC) Regs
75 Sch Part V para 16(2) CS(MCSC) Regs
76 R(CS) 2/08
77 CCS/2128/2001; R(CS) 2/06
78 Sch 1 para 10 CSA 1991

3. Shared care

79 s5(1) CSA 1991
80 Reg 14(2)(a) CS(MCSC) Regs
81 Reg 14(2)(b) CS(MCSC) Regs
82 Reg 14(2)(c) CS(MCSC) Regs
83 Sch 1 Part 1 paras 7 and 8 CSA 1991
84 Reg 7(1) CS(MCSC) Regs
85 R(CS) 7/08
86 Reg 7(3) CS(MCSC) Regs
87 Reg 7(4) CS(MCSC) Regs
88 Reg 7(5) CS(MCSC) Regs
89 Sch 1 Part 1 para 8 CSA 1991
90 Sch 1 Part 1 para 7 CSA 1991
91 Sch 1 Part 1 para 7(4) CSA 1991
92 Sch 1 Part 1 para 7(6) CSA 1991
93 Sch 1 Part 1 para 7(7) CSA 1991
94 Reg 2(2) CS(MCSC) Regs
95 Sch 1 Part 1 para 7(5) CSA 1991
96 Reg 12 CS(MCSC) Regs
97 Reg 7(6) CS(MCSC) Regs
98 Reg 9(10) CS(MCSC) Regs
99 Reg 1(2)(b)(i) CS(MCSC) Regs,
    definition of 'day-to-day care'
100 Reg 9(1) CS(MCSC) Regs
101 Reg 21(1)(a) CS(MCP) Regs
102 R(CS) 1/04; R(CS) 2/04
103 Reg 9(2) and (4) CS(MCSC) Regs
104 Reg 9(2)(c) CS(MCSC) Regs
105 Reg 9(5) CS(MCSC) Regs
106 Regs 8(3) and 10 CS(MCSC) Regs
107 Reg 9(7) CS(MCSC) Regs
108 Reg 9(8) CS(MCSC) Regs
109 Reg 9(9)(a) CS(MCSC) Regs

Chapter 9

Variations ('2003 rules')

This chapter covers:
1. Variations (below)
2. Grounds for a variation (p160)
3. Applying for a variation (p172)
4. Procedure (p173)
5. The decision (p180)

1. Variations

A variation allows circumstances that are not taken into account by the usual child support calculation to be considered by the Child Support Agency (CSA). If the variation is agreed, the calculation may be adjusted.

An application for a variation to the child support calculation may have been made before the calculation was made, or after it came into force.[1]

A variation can only be made on one of the grounds specified in the legislation and only if it is 'just and equitable' to do so (see p177).

An application may be rejected automatically in certain circumstances, either at the preliminary consideration of the application or at a later stage (see p174). In certain cases, the CSA may refer the application to the First-tier Tribunal (see p179).

If an application is successful, it may result in a child support calculation being made or, if a calculation already exists, in its being revised or superseded with the variation incorporated (see p182).

Variations are one of the areas of child support law in which disputes frequently arise. There is much caselaw on the issues.

The grounds and procedures for variations set out in this chapter are very similar to those for variations under the '2012 rules' (see Chapter 7).

2. **Grounds for a variation**

A variation can be made for:[2]
- special expenses (see below);
- additional cases (see p165).

Special expenses

A variation can be considered on the grounds that there are special expenses if there are:[3]
- costs of maintaining contact with children for whom the calculation is, or will be, in force;
- costs of a long-term illness or disability of a relevant other child;
- prior debts, incurred before the couple separated;
- boarding school fees being paid for children for whom an application for a child support calculation has been made;
- costs from paying a mortgage on the home of the person with care and qualifying child.

Except for costs associated with a relevant child's illness or disability, the costs must be more than a certain amount.[4] If the net income of the non-resident parent is:
- £200 or more, the threshold is £15;
- below £200, the threshold is £10.

The threshold applies to one ground or, if there is more than one relevant ground, the sum of those costs. This also means that the first £10 or £15 of these special expenses are disregarded when calculating the variation and any subsequent adjustment to the calculation.[5] The fact that the contact costs that can be taken into account are restricted in this way has been held not to breach the non-resident parent's human rights, even if the result could be regarded as unfair and a disincentive to the non-resident parent keeping in touch with her/his children.[6] The disregard does not apply to the costs associated with an illness or disability of a relevant child.

The Child Support Agency (CSA) can substitute a lower amount for any special expenses that it thinks are unreasonably high or have been unreasonably incurred.[7] This may be below the threshold amount or nil. In the case of contact costs, any reduced amount must not be so low that it makes it impossible for contact to occur at the level of frequency stated in any court order, provided the visits are taking place.[8]

A variation for special expenses reduces the net weekly income of the non-resident parent that is taken into account in the child support calculation.[9]

Contact costs

Costs related to the non-resident parent's contact with the qualifying child can be included.[10] They can be for the non-resident parent or the child. The cost of a travelling companion can also be included – eg, because of disability, long-term illness or the child's age. Costs of contact with another child (eg, a child who might have been a qualifying child but for the fact that s/he does not live in the UK) do not count.[11]

Costs of contact do not include those that arise if the non-resident parent shares care of the child and which are already taken into account under the shared-care provisions.[12] This means, for example, that the cost of travel to collect the child from an overnight stay which counts as a night of shared care cannot be grounds for a variation, as that contact is already taken into account in the child support calculation.[13]

The following count as contact costs:[14]

- public transport fares;
- fuel for a private car;
- taxi fares, but only if the illness or disability of the non-resident parent or qualifying child makes it impractical to use another form of transport;
- car hire, if the cost of the journey would be less than by public transport or taxis, or a combination of both;
- accommodation costs for the parent or the child for overnight stays, if a return journey on the same day is impractical, or the pattern of care includes contact over two or more days;
- minor incidental costs associated with travelling, such as road or bridge tolls or fees. This may include parking fees and ticket reservation fees if it was necessary to incur these to maintain contact with the child. Other costs necessary to maintain contact with the child, such as fees for a contact centre if a court required contact to be supervised, do not count.[15]

The costs are based on an established pattern of visits, if one exists.[16] If there is no current established pattern, a previous one may be referred to if contact is to begin again, or an intended pattern, agreed between the non-resident parent and person with care, may be used. The pattern set out in a court order may also be used. When contact is set out in a court order, it may only specify an upper limit on visits.

The costs are calculated as an average weekly amount. This is based on a 12-month, or shorter, period that ends just before the first day of the maintenance period in which the variation would take effect.[17] In other cases, it can be based on anticipated costs. If it is based on a pattern that ends before the child support calculation, the CSA considers the costs incurred between the effective date of the variation and the date on which it would cease (ie, the date on which the circumstances giving rise to the variation ended) and the date of the interim maintenance decision/child support calculation.[18]

To determine whether the cost for fuel is reasonable, the CSA may compare the amount claimed with an average figure.

If a non-resident parent returns from abroad and contact is only one reason for the trip, the CSA may limit costs to those of travel from her/his home in the UK. The CSA may only allow those costs that are a necessary and integral consequence of maintaining contact with the child.

Overnight costs only include reasonable accommodation costs if an overnight stay is necessary. They do not cover the cost of meals and sundries.

Changes in contact may mean the variation is also changed. If contact stops, even through no fault of the non-resident parent, the calculation may be superseded to reflect this (see p182).

Example 9.1

Bronwen has net income of £428 and pays basic rate child support of £86 a week to Ivan for Ursula and Gretchen. She claims a special expenses cost for contact with her children, amounting to £450 over a six-month period since the girls attend boarding school. This includes travel from Northern Ireland by ferry, petrol and overnight stays in hotels, amounting to 18 nights over the six-month period. As this is fewer than 26 nights in six months, the contact costs are not for nights that could be classed as shared care (see p145).

The amounts included are deemed reasonable in the circumstances and the weekly amount is calculated:

£450 ÷ 26 = £17.30 a week on average.

This is above the threshold of £15. Therefore, a variation of £2.30 (£17.30 − £15) for contact costs may be considered, and Bronwen's net income reduced by this amount.

Costs of a relevant other child's long-term illness or disability

A variation can be considered on the grounds of the costs of a long-term illness or disability of a relevant other child – ie, a child for whom the non-resident parent or her/his partner receives child benefit (or if s/he has elected not to receive child benefit because s/he would be liable for the 'high income child benefit charge' in income tax).[19]

A long-term illness is one current at the date of the variation application or from the date the variation would take effect. It must be likely to last for at least a further 52 weeks or be terminal.[20] A child is considered disabled if:[21]

- disability living allowance (DLA), personal independence payment (PIP) or armed forces independence payment is paid for her/him;
- s/he would receive DLA or PIP but for the fact that s/he is in hospital; or
- s/he is certified as severely sight impaired or blind by a consultant ophthalmologist.

The reasonable additional costs of any of the following count:[22]

- personal care, attendance or communication needs;
- mobility;
- domestic help;
- medical aids that cannot be provided on the NHS;[23]
- heating, clothing and laundry;
- food essential for a diet recommended by a medical practitioner;
- adaptations to the non-resident parent's home;
- day care, respite care or rehabilitation.

If an aid or appliance can be provided on the NHS (by health services or a local authority), a variation is not normally agreed, even if the item is not available because of a lack of funds at a particular time. However, a variation may be considered if there is likely to be a serious delay in supplying an item which would prevent the child's condition from seriously deteriorating. The CSA may also consider the cost of the aid and whether it can be obtained at a cheaper price.

Any financial help towards these costs from any source, paid to the non-resident parent or a member of her/his household, is deducted if it relates to the expense claimed.[24] Any DLA, PIP or armed forces independence payment being paid for the relevant other child is also deducted from the costs. If DLA, PIP or armed forces independence payment has been applied for, but is not in payment, it can be included if, when awarded, it will cover the date the variation starts.

Debts of the relationship

A non-resident parent may be repaying a debt incurred *before* s/he became a non-resident parent (see p17) of the qualifying child. This can count as special expenses, provided it was incurred when that parent and the person with care were a couple (see p24). The debt must have been taken out for the benefit of at least one of the following: [25]

- the non-resident parent and person with care, jointly;
- the person with care alone, if the non-resident parent is liable for the repayments;
- a person who is not a child, but at the time the debt was incurred:
  - was a child;
  - lived with the non-resident parent and person with care; *and*
  - was the child of the non-resident parent, person with care or both of them;
- the qualifying child;
- any child other than the qualifying child who at the time the debt was incurred:
  - lived with the non-resident parent and person with care; *and*
  - is a child of the person with care.

Loans only count if they are from a qualifying lender, or from a non-resident parent's current or former employer.[26] Qualifying lenders include banks, building societies or other registered lenders – eg, hire purchase.[27]

The following do *not* count as debts for this purpose:[28]
- debts incurred to buy something which the non-resident parent kept for her/his own use after the relationship ended;[29]
- a debt for which the applicant took responsibility under a court order or a financial settlement with the ex-partner;
- a debt for which a variation has previously been agreed, but which has not been repaid in the period for which the variation has been applied to the calculation;
- debts of a business or trade;
- secured mortgage repayments, except for amounts incurred to buy, repair or improve the home of the person with care and qualifying child;
- endowment or insurance premiums, except if incurred to buy, repair or improve the home of the person with care and qualifying child.

Payments on a debt taken out to pay off any negative equity on the former joint home once it has been sold do not count as debts, as the person with care no longer lives there.

The following also do *not* count as debts:[30]
- gambling debts;
- legal costs of the separation, divorce or dissolution of the civil partnership;
- credit card repayments;
- overdrafts, unless taken out for a specified amount repayable over a specified period;
- fines imposed on the applicant;
- any debt incurred to pay off one of the above;
- any other debt the CSA considers reasonable to exclude.

A debt incurred to pay a former debt which would have counted may be included. However, only that part which could have counted is included as special expenses.[31]

A variation is normally based on the original debt repayment period; any rescheduling of the debt is usually ignored. However, if the applicant has been unemployed or ill and the creditors have agreed to extend the repayment period, the CSA can take the extended period into account. It has discretion on the length of time over which the debt may be extended when setting the period for which the variation for prior debts applies to the calculation.

Boarding school fees

The maintenance element of boarding school fees incurred, or expected to be incurred, by the non-resident parent for the qualifying child can be included as a special expense.[32] Only term-time costs for non-advanced education at a recognised educational establishment can be included.[33]

If the maintenance element cannot be distinguished from other costs, the CSA can decide what to include, but this should not exceed 35 per cent of the total fees.[34]

If the non-resident parent receives financial help to pay the fees, or only pays part of the fees with someone else, a proportion of the costs are included. This is calculated in the same ratio as the maintenance element to overall fees.[35]

In all cases, a variation for boarding school fees should not reduce the amount of income used to calculate child support by more than 50 per cent.[36]

Example 9.2
Bronwen claims special expenses for her contribution to the costs of boarding school for Ursula and Gretchen. She pays the school £1,500 a term – ie, £4,500 a year. Ivan pays the rest of the fees – ie, £4,500 a year. Her weekly net income is £428.
The fees for each child per term are £1,500 and the maintenance element is £500 a term. Bronwen's contribution to the maintenance element of the fees is worked out as £250 a child each term – ie, £500. Over the three terms this amounts to £1,500, which is converted into a weekly figure (£1,500 ÷ 365 x 7 = £28.77). This is above the threshold of £15, so a variation for a contribution to boarding school fees of £13.77 may be considered.
Note: if this is accepted, it does not reduce her net income by more than 50 per cent.

Payments for mortgages, loans or insurance policies

A variation can be considered on the basis of payments made to a mortgage lender, insurer or person with care for a mortgage or loan if:[37]

- it was taken out to facilitate the purchase of, or repairs/improvements to, the property by someone other than the non-resident parent; *and*
- the payments are not made because of a debt or other legal liability of the non-resident parent for the period in which the variation is applied; *and*
- the property was the person with care's and non-resident parent's home when they were a couple, and it is still the home of the person with care and qualifying child; *and*
- the non-resident parent has no legal or financial rights in the property – eg, a charge or equitable interest.

Payments may also be considered for an insurance or endowment policy taken out to discharge a mortgage or loan as above, except if the non-resident parent is entitled to any part of the proceeds when the policy matures.[38] See p277 for more information.

Additional cases

There are additional situations in which a variation may be applied for (usually by a person with care or a child applicant in Scotland). These are if the non-resident parent has:[39]

- assets over £65,000;
- income that has not been taken into account in the calculation;
- diverted income; *or*
- a lifestyle which is inconsistent with her/his stated income.

The effect of a variation on these grounds is to increase the net weekly income of the non-resident parent taken into account in the calculation.[40] **Note:** the maximum net weekly income, after including any amount for a variation, cannot exceed the capped amount of £2,000.

If the non-resident parent is in receipt of certain benefits that attract the flat rate, there are special rules on the maximum amount payable – known as the 'better-buy' provision (see p181).

Assets over £65,000

For a variation to be possible, the CSA must be satisfied that the asset:[41]

- is under the non-resident parent's control, or is one in which s/he has a beneficial interest; *or*
- has been transferred to trustees, but the non-resident parent is the beneficiary of the trust, and the transfer was made to reduce the amount of assets which could be considered under a variation application; *or*
- is subject to a trust of which the non-resident parent is a beneficiary. This can include assets in a discretionary trust of which the parent is a beneficiary.[42]

'**Assets**' mean:[43]

- money – eg, cash, deposits in a bank, building society or Post Office account, premium bonds or savings certificates; *or*
- legal estate, interest in or rights over land; *or*
- stocks and shares; *or*
- claims that are reasonable to enforce; *or*
- in Scotland, money due or an obligation owed that would be reasonable to enforce; *and*
- any of the above located outside Great Britain.

The CSA does not count assets if:[44]

- their total value is £65,000 or less after repaying any mortgage or charge on them. If an asset is worth less than an outstanding mortgage on it, the 'negative equity' cannot be offset against the value of another asset the parent has. However, the CSA may consider this when deciding whether it is just and equitable to agree a variation (see p178).[45] Any asset in respect of which income is taken into account under the 'income not taken into account or diverted income' ground (see p168 and p169) is first deducted from the non-resident parent's total assets;

- it is satisfied that the non-resident parent is holding them for a reasonable purpose – eg, cash from the sale of a home that is intended to purchase a new home. In considering what is reasonable, the financial circumstances of both parents can be taken into account;[46]
- they are compensation for personal injury;
- they are used for a trade or business (except a legal estate or interest in or rights over land, which produces income that is not part of the non-resident parent's net weekly income). Shares are not used in the course of a business or trade if the trade or business is not that of the non-resident parent – eg, if s/he has invested in a company or even owns one, but it is not her/his trade or business.[47] Income generated from business assets may, however, be classed as self-employed earnings for the child support calculation;[48]
- it is the home of the non-resident parent or her/his child; *or*
- they are payments from certain trusts, which would be ignored if the non-resident parent were on income support (IS).[49]

The way that money is held in a business may indicate that an asset should be taken into account. For example, if a parent has shares in a company into which s/he has diverted assets but from which no earnings or dividends have been paid, the capital value of the shares may be counted as an asset.[50] If an asset is owned by a partnership in which the parent is a partner, it can be assumed that the parent has an equal share in the asset and the notional income unless there is specific agreement or evidence that a different share should apply.[51]

The income assumed from the assets is determined using the statutory rate of interest which applies on the effective date. This is currently 8 per cent.[52] If the non-resident parent works abroad for a UK-based employer, the rate is based on the locality of the employer. The weekly value is added to other income, including benefits, bearing in mind the better-buy rules for those on benefit (see p181).[53]

Example 9.3

Graham has net income of £480 a week and pays £96 a week in child support to Andie. Andie applies for a variation on the grounds that Graham has substantial assets, including a holiday home in Spain and savings.

The property in Spain is worth £52,000 and Graham has savings and investments of £17,000. The total value of his assets is £69,000, which is above the threshold of £65,000. This is calculated to have a weekly value of £106.15 (ie, £69,000 x 8% ÷ 52). A variation may, therefore, be considered on the basis that Graham has £106.15 more net income.

If Graham owned the property in Spain jointly with his new partner, Nadia, the total value of his assets would be £26,000 + £17,000 = £43,000, which is below the threshold.

Income not taken into account and diverted income

The person with care (or a child applicant in Scotland) may apply for a variation in certain circumstances on the grounds that the non-resident parent has income that has not been taken into account in the calculation or has reduced the income taken into account by diverting it in some way.

Income not taken into account: non-resident parent is on benefit but has other income

If the flat or nil rate of child support applies because the non-resident parent receives a prescribed benefit (see p132) but has income which would otherwise be taken into account in the calculation, a variation can be considered. The CSA must be satisfied that the non-resident parent is in receipt of income which would be taken into account in the child support calculation if s/he were not liable for the flat or nil rate because of receipt of benefit.[54] A variation can also apply if a non-resident parent would pay the flat rate but is paying less than this (or nothing) because of shared care (see p145).

Income not taken into account: non-resident parent is able to control income

If a non-resident parent is able to control income, a variation may be considered. This can apply if s/he is liable to pay child support at any rate without the variation. This variation may apply if:[55]

- the non-resident parent can control how much income s/he receives from a company or business, including earnings from employment or self-employment; *and*
- the income from that company or business would not otherwise be taken into account in the child support calculation.

For example, a variation on these grounds may apply if a parent is a company director and has arranged to take income in the form of dividends instead of wages or salary.[56] It could also apply to other forms of income received from a company or business (reimbursement of legitimate business expenses is ignored) and if a non-resident parent has reduced her/his net income to an unreasonable extent by making substantial pension contributions.[57] The additional income received from the company or business is added to the net weekly income for the purposes of the child support calculation.

General rules for income not taken into account

For a variation to be made, the income not taken into account must be net weekly income of over £100. This can be from either of the situations described above or, if a variation is considered under both cases, income from both can be added together.[58]

Note: income from renting out property does not count as earnings unless the activity is classed as a business enterprise. The income cannot be taken into account for a variation.[59]

When working out the earnings of students for the purpose of this type of variation, the total income for the year, ending with the relevant week, is added together and divided by 52 to give a weekly amount. An alternative period may be used if the CSA considers it more representative.

The weekly value of any additional income is added to other income from benefits, bearing in mind that the better-buy provision applies to those on benefit when calculating the maximum child support due.[60] Benefits include those prescribed for the flat rate (except IS/income-based jobseeker's allowance (JSA)/ income-related employment and support allowance (ESA)/universal credit (UC) calculated on the basis that the non-resident parent has no earned income/ pension credit (PC)), less any disregards.[61] For an explanation of disregards for these purposes, see the better-buy provision on p181.

Example 9.4

Joel is a mature student who works part time in a care home. He is on the nil rate for child support. Kaliani applies for a variation on the grounds that he has income not taken into account. Kaliani looks after one child, Selim.

Joel's student grant and loan do not count as income, so only his part-time earnings are considered. Over the year, Joel's net earnings are £9,367.80, which are converted into a weekly amount (ie, £9,367.80 ÷ 52 = £180.15). As this is over £100, a variation may be considered using a weekly amount of £180.15. If the variation to the calculation is agreed, instead of paying nothing, Joel will now be due to pay a reduced rate of £25 (£5 + (25% x £80.15) = £25.04 rounded to the nearest pound).

Diverted income

A variation on the ground of diversion of income can be considered if:[62]

- the non-resident parent can control the income s/he receives, including earnings from self-employment; *and*
- the CSA is satisfied that the non-resident parent has unreasonably reduced the amount of income s/he would have received (and which would have been taken into account in the child support calculation or under a variation) from a company or business (see p168) by diverting it to someone else or for some other purpose. The diversion does *not* have to have been arranged specifically to avoid child support responsibilities. The CSA (or First-tier Tribunal) has a broad discretion to judge what is unreasonable in the circumstances.[63]

The non-resident parent may have diverted income:

- to a third party – eg, a new partner or close family member;
- to a business (eg, if the non-resident parent takes a lower income[64]) or to a pension scheme from which the non-resident parent will benefit later. In this situation, it must be reasonable to make a variation;

- towards other purposes – eg, if the non-resident parent uses company assets for private use or business funds for day-to-day expenditure.

Diverting earnings from a form that counts as income to one that results in their being excluded (eg, taking earnings as a benefit in kind, such as a company car) in the calculation can be classed as diverting income.[65]

Example 9.5

Marcus runs his own import/export business, employing his new partner, Shamira, and his brother. Each has a company car, in his case a Jaguar. His brother is paid £600 a week and he and Shamira each receive £400. His ex-wife, Helene, gets basic rate child support of £80 for their two children. Helene applies for a variation because she thinks Marcus is diverting income via the company, especially as Shamira does not seem to do any work.

Part of Marcus's day-to-day expenses are included in business expenses – eg, the car and business lunches. Shamira's salary could also be a token payment, as Marcus takes less from the business than he pays his brother. The CSA considers that, on balance, there could be diversion of income via the company and Shamira's wages. Given its contentious nature, the case is referred to the First-tier Tribunal.

The full weekly equivalent amount of any diverted income is added to net weekly income when working out child support.[66]

Deciding whether a parent has the ability to control the income s/he receives or whether a reduction in income received is unreasonable can be difficult. Many cases may require detailed investigation of the circumstances – eg, if a parent is a director, employee or shareholder of a small business. The way that money is held and distributed in the business is important, particularly whether this follows recognised business and accounting practices and/or is done for justified business reasons.[67]

Lifestyle inconsistent with declared income

A person with care (or a child applicant in Scotland) can obtain a variation on this ground if the CSA is satisfied that the income used (or which would have been used) in the calculation is substantially lower than that needed to support the non-resident parent's lifestyle.[68] A variation can be granted in cases where the flat rate applies because of benefit income, but not if it applies because of receipt of IS, income-based JSA, income-related ESA, UC calculated on the basis that the non-resident parent has no earned income, or PC.

A variation is not granted if it is clear that the non-resident parent's lifestyle is paid for by:[69]

- income that is, or would be, disregarded in the child support calculation;
- income that could be considered as having been diverted (see p169);

- income that could be considered as not taken into account from a company or business (see p168);
- assets, or income from assets; *or*
- a partner's income or assets, except if the non-resident parent can influence or control the amount of income, assets or income from the assets.

A variation cannot be granted if an inconsistent lifestyle is financed by borrowing, as this would not meet the requirement that the variation decision be just and equitable (see p178).[70] If a lifestyle is supported by an amount of tax and national insurance (NI) that should have been due on income but was not paid, this may be taken into account through a variation on this ground.[71]

In addition to the above situations, if the calculation is not based on net weekly income, a variation is not allowed if the person's lifestyle is paid for from income of £100 or less, or which could be considered on the ground of income not taken into account (see p168).[72]

The amount of income taken into account is the difference between:[73]

- the amount the non-resident parent needs to support her/his overall lifestyle; *and*
- the amount taken into account (or which would have been taken into account) in the child support calculation.

This includes any income from benefits prescribed for the flat rate (except for IS/income-based JSA/income-related ESA/UC calculated on the basis that the non-resident parent has no earned income/PC) less disregards, bearing in mind the better-buy rules for those on benefit (see p181).

This ground is most likely to be used if a non-resident parent is self-employed or is suspected of working without fully declaring income for tax and NI purposes.[74] The CSA is unlikely to investigate a parent's lifestyle. If there appear to be grounds for investigation, it may refer the case to the First-tier Tribunal, which could direct the parties to provide evidence (see Chapter 13). The specific lifestyle factors considered, the level of income required to fund them, and the difference between that level and the income used in the calculation must be identified.[75] The costs of the lifestyle should be considered from the effective date of the original calculation, not earlier (or based on assumptions or evidence of lifestyle before a couple separate).[76]

Note: it is not sufficient to show that the non-resident parent pursued one extravagant activity, as there may be good reasons for this. S/he must have an overall lifestyle that, in most respects, is inconsistent with the declared income – eg, a large, expensively furnished home, expensive car, frequent foreign holidays and expensive leisure activities.

Example 9.6

The situation is as in *Example 9.5*. Helene applies for a variation because Marcus is able to afford to live in central London and drive a new Jaguar (changing cars every two or three years). He plays polo (keeping three ponies in stables), is a member of an exclusive golf club, and he and Shamira frequently travel abroad.

Some of the expenses are included in his business expenses – eg, the car and travel abroad on business trips, and the golf club membership is used for corporate entertaining. Shamira's income is under Marcus's control, although her wages are equivalent to those of other staff. The CSA considers that, on balance, his lifestyle does appear inconsistent with his income. However, it also considers that income could be being diverted. Given its contentious nature, the case is referred to the First-tier Tribunal.

If Shamira were independently wealthy, owning the business and paying for their lifestyle, including paying Marcus's wages, a variation could be refused. Helene could appeal, although a variation may not be possible on this ground. The CSA would need to consider whether there had been a diversion of income or assets which Marcus could control.

3. **Applying for a variation**

Only a relevant person (ie, a person with care, a non-resident parent or a qualifying child in Scotland) can apply for a variation. An authorised representative may also make an application. The Child Support Agency (CSA) also has discretion to reinstate a previous variation without an application in certain circumstances (see p185).

An application for a variation can be made either orally or in writing.[77] This means an applicant may give details over the phone, although the CSA may ask for a written application – eg, because complicated special expenses are being considered. The CSA may provide a form, or the applicant can send the application in another written form which the CSA accepts as sufficient.[78] If a written application is required, this should be provided within 14 days. If the time limit is exceeded without good cause, the effective date of the variation may be affected.

The application must state the grounds on which it is made.[79] If it does not, or at least give a reason, it is not accepted as properly made.

Example 9.7

Joe applies for a variation because he believes his child support is too high. The CSA does not accept it as a properly made application.

Joe applies for a variation because he believes his child support is too high and he cannot afford it because of the high cost of pet food. The CSA accepts the application as properly made, but then rejects it as it is not on one of the specified grounds.

Joe applies for a variation because he believes his child support is too high because he cannot now afford the kennel costs he incurs when he travels to see his children. The CSA accepts the application as properly made and it is given a preliminary consideration. It rejects the application as kennel costs are not one of the specified grounds. Had Joe referred to his other contact costs (eg, his travel costs), his application would probably have proceeded.

If a calculation is already in force and a new application is made by the same person, the CSA may (but is not obliged to) treat it as a request for a variation, depending on the circumstances and the information contained in the application.[80] An appeal can also be treated as an application for a variation if it is more advantageous to the appellant. The CSA must bear in mind, however, that what is advantageous to the appellant may not be to another party.[81]

If an application is made, but there is insufficient information to decide whether to proceed, the CSA may request further information.[82] The applicant is given one month from the date of notification in which to supply the information.[83] This time limit may be extended in special circumstances – eg, if the applicant is in hospital. If the information is not provided, the CSA has the discretion either to reject the application or proceed.[84]

An application for a variation may be amended or withdrawn at any time before a decision is made.[85] This may be done orally or in writing. No amendment can be made if the change relates to a period after the effective date of the application, but a new application for a variation could be made.[86]

Two or more applications for a variation may be considered at the same time.[87] In addition, if appropriate, an application made on one ground may be treated as an application on a different ground.[88]

4. **Procedure**

Once an application has been made, the procedure is as follows.
- There is a preliminary consideration of the application (see p174).
- Unless rejected, other parties may be notified and asked to make representations, known as 'contesting' (see p175).
- An interim maintenance decision may be made (see p176).
- A regular payment condition may be imposed (see p176).
- The decision is considered (see p177).

After the preliminary consideration, a case may also be passed to the First-tier Tribunal for a determination (see p179).

An application proceeds for determination unless it has already failed.[89] It may fail (ie, the Child Support Agency (CSA) may refuse to consider it further) before this point because, for example:
- one of the grounds for rejection is established on preliminary consideration (see below);
- it is withdrawn; *or*
- the regular payment condition has not been met.

Preliminary consideration

Once an application is properly made, there is a preliminary consideration of the case.[90] At this point, the CSA may reject the application and decide:
- to revise or supersede the child support calculation, or to refuse to revise or supersede it;[91] *or*
- to make the calculation, or to make a default maintenance decision.[92]

Any decision, including a decision not to revise, can be challenged (see Chapter 12).[93]

When an application for a variation is rejected

An application for a variation may be rejected on preliminary consideration because:[94]
- the requirements of the stated ground are not met;
- in special expenses cases, the threshold is not exceeded;
- in additional assets cases, their value does not exceed £65,000;
- in income not taken into account cases, this does not exceed £100 per week;
- information requested by the CSA has not been provided within the one-month time limit;
- a default maintenance decision is in force. In some cases, if there is a default maintenance decision, an application for a variation may contain sufficient information to revise the default decision and replace it with a calculation;
- the application is made by the person with care or qualifying child in Scotland on additional cases grounds and the capped amount of income is already applied, or the non-resident parent or her/his partner are in receipt of working tax credit;
- the application is made by the non-resident parent on special expenses grounds and, after deducting these, net income exceeds the capped amount;
- the flat rate applies to the non-resident parent as s/he or her/his partner is on income support (IS), income-based jobseeker's allowance (JSA), income-related employment and support allowance (ESA), universal credit (UC) calculated on the basis that the non-resident parent has no earned income, or pension credit (PC) but is due to pay less than the flat rate, or nil because of shared care;
- the non-resident parent is due to pay the flat rate because of part-time care by a local authority;

- the application is made by the non-resident parent and:
  - the nil rate applies; *or*
  - the flat rate applies because s/he receives a prescribed benefit (other than IS/income-based JSA/income-related ESA/UC calculated on the basis that s/he has no earned income/PC) or has income of £100 or less; *or*
  - the flat rate of £5 (or less if apportioned) applies because of shared care, including care by a local authority.

Note: rejecting an application for a variation at preliminary consideration for one of the above reasons is a power and not a duty.[95]

Contesting the application

If an application has not been rejected on preliminary consideration, the other relevant parties are usually notified. However, in some situations where the CSA has discretion to reinstate a previous variation, it does not need to notify or invite representations (see p185).

The notification may be done orally or in writing and must:[96]

- state the grounds on which the application has been made and provide any information or evidence the applicant has given to support it; *and*
- not contain information that should not be disclosed.

In practice, non-applicants are informed in writing and supplied with the evidence. If the application has been via a phone call, the evidence may be a transcript of the conversation.

The notification may invite other parties to make representations about the circumstances within 14 days.

In some cases, the applicant may supply further evidence or information outside the one-month time limit and, in the meantime, the CSA may have notified the other parties. The information may be passed to them later and they are given a further 14 days from the date of this later notification to make representations.[97] If the CSA is satisfied that it is reasonable, this time limit may be extended.[98]

The other parties may respond orally or in writing, although the CSA may require it to be in writing. If no contesting information is provided, the CSA may make a determination on the application as it stands.[99]

Any information provided by another party, other than that which may not be disclosed (see p176), may be forwarded to the applicant if the CSA considers this reasonable.[100] The applicant is given 14 days to comment on the evidence or information supplied by the other party.

Information that cannot be disclosed

In addition to the general rules on disclosing information (see p74), there are additional rules for variations. Supporting evidence or information from one party is not notified to another party if it contains:[101]

- details of an illness or disability of a relevant other child if the non-resident parent has requested that this not be disclosed and the CSA agrees;
- medical evidence that has not been disclosed to the applicant or a relevant person (ie, person with care, non-resident parent or qualifying child in Scotland) and which would be harmful to her/him;
- the address of a relevant person or qualifying child, or information that could lead to that individual or child being located, and there is a risk of harm or undue distress to that person or child or any other child(ren) living with that person.

If an applicant requests that information not be disclosed, this is discussed with her/him. It may be possible to make an amended application which does not include the relevant details. If an applicant refuses to disclose information that is relevant for the other party to contest the application, the application could be rejected. However, there may be a good reason for non-disclosure, and each case should be considered on its own merits.

When representations are not required

Representations from the other relevant parties are not required if:[102]

- the CSA is reinstating a variation at its own discretion (see p185);
- a variation is agreed and the calculation is replaced by a default decision, but this is subsequently replaced with a calculation.

Interim maintenance decision

If an application for a variation was made before the child support calculation, an interim maintenance decision (IMD) may have been made.[103] The amount of the IMD is the child support calculated in the normal way, ignoring the variation. This is to allow the variation application to be considered. An IMD may be replaced by a calculation, which is made whether or not a variation has been agreed. The effective date of the calculation is the same as the IMD.

An IMD can be challenged in the usual way. However, when a calculation is made which replaces this, any appeal against the IMD may lapse.[104] If the IMD is superseded, the usual rule tolerating a 5 per cent change in net income (see p224) does not apply.

Regular payment condition

If a non-resident parent has applied for a variation, s/he may have a regular payment condition (RPC) imposed after the preliminary consideration.[105] The CSA is likely to do so if a non-resident parent has:

- a poor payment record or arrears;
- failed to make payments while the variation application was being contested and considered; *or*
- special expenses that make it difficult for her/him to meet her/his child support liability.

The amount due under an RPC is either:[106]
- the child support calculated, including that set under an IMD; *or*
- the amount that would be due if the variation were agreed.

This means that if the CSA believes that the variation application will be successful, it may set an RPC that adjusts the child support calculated to reflect the variation, reducing the financial burden on the parent. However, if it believes that the application will be unsuccessful and an RPC is imposed, it is set at the calculation rate.

An RPC does not affect the amount of child support the non-resident parent is liable to pay. Therefore, if the set amount is lower than the amount due, there will be arrears if the variation application fails.

The RPC is set independently of any other arrears arrangement the parent may have. It ends either when the CSA makes a final decision on the calculation (whether or not the variation is agreed) or when the variation application is withdrawn.[107]

When an RPC is imposed, the non-resident parent, person with care and/or qualifying child applicant in Scotland are sent written notification.[108] This makes it clear that if the RPC is not met, the application may lapse.[109]

If a non-resident parent does not meet the RPC within one month of this notification, written notification of this is sent to all the relevant parties.[110] If the RPC has not been met, the CSA may refuse to consider the application for a variation.[111] A refusal to consider the application cannot be appealed.

Considering the decision

The CSA has discretion when considering a variation. It must bear in mind the general principles that:[112]
- a parent is responsible for maintaining her/his children when s/he can afford to do so; *and*
- a parent is responsible for maintaining all her/his children equally.

The CSA must take into account any representations made by the parties – ie, the person with care, non-resident parent and child applicant in Scotland.[113]

To agree to make a variation, the CSA must be satisfied that:[114]
- the grounds are met; *and*
- it is just and equitable to do so (see p178).

The CSA must refuse to make a variation if it does not have sufficient information to make a child support calculation, and so would make a default maintenance decision (see p204).[115]

The CSA may agree to the variation in full or refuse it. This may result in a revision or supersession of the decision or a replacement of the IMD.[116] The revision or supersession decision is dealt with under the usual rules (see p182).

Just and equitable

Even though the grounds are met, a variation is only made if it is 'just and equitable' to do so.[117] Certain factors must be taken into account when making the decision. These include:[118]

- the welfare of any child likely to be affected if the variation is agreed;
- whether agreeing to a variation would lead the non-resident parent or parent with care to give up employment;
- if the applicant is the non-resident parent, whether there is any liability to pay child maintenance under a court order or agreement before the effective date of the child support calculation;
- if the non-resident parent has applied for a special expenses variation, whether s/he could make financial arrangements to cover those expenses or could pay for them from money currently spent on non-essentials.

The above list is not exhaustive and other factors may be considered when deciding what is just and equitable. As the child support legislation expressly leaves it to the courts to make orders that a parent pay towards tuition fees, the fact that a non-resident parent pays for school fees cannot be taken into account when deciding whether it is just and equitable to agree to a variation.[119]

The following must *not* be taken into account:[120]

- whether or not the child's conception was planned;
- who was responsible for the breakdown of the relationship between the non-resident parent and the person with care;
- whether the non-resident parent or person with care is in a new relationship with someone who is not the qualifying child's parent;
- any contact arrangements, and whether or not they are being kept to;
- the income or assets of anyone other than the non-resident parent, other than any income or assets of the parent's partner taken into account in an application made on the grounds of a lifestyle inconsistent with declared income;
- any failure of the non-resident parent to pay child maintenance under CSA arrangements, a court order or written agreement; *and*
- representations from individuals other than the person with care, non-resident parent, or a qualifying child applicant in Scotland.

The CSA must reach a positive conclusion that it is just and equitable to agree to a variation, and not simply that there is no reason not to do so.[121] All factors should be considered, but the CSA (or the First-tier Tribunal on a referral) decides what weight to give to them.[122] This may mean taking into account circumstances for which either party could have sought a variation, even if s/he did not. For example, since contact costs affect the financial circumstances of a non-resident parent, it may be just and equitable to take these into account when deciding on the variation, even if the application was about something else (and may have been made at the request of the person with care).[123] However, if such circumstances are taken into account, it must be made clear to all parties on what basis the variation has been decided.

The just and equitable rule can never be used to increase the amount of a variation above the amount justified by the relevant ground.[124] However, the amount may be reduced – eg, by applying a lower rate than the statutory rate of interest to an asset.[125] As well as considering whether a variation is just and equitable, the CSA must also take into account all the principles of child support law, including the duty of parents to maintain their children and the welfare of all children who may be affected.[126]

Referral to the First-tier Tribunal

Once the application has passed the preliminary consideration and contest stage, the case may be passed to the First-tier Tribunal for a determination on whether or not to agree to the variation.[127] This normally only occurs if a novel or particularly contentious issue is being considered. The First-tier Tribunal should consider the grounds stated in the following order:[128]
- assets over £65,000;
- income not taken into account;
- diversion of income;
- lifestyle inconsistent with declared income.

If a referral is made, it can only be withdrawn by the CSA. The First-tier Tribunal can proceed, even if the parties come to an agreement.[129] It is also possible for an applicant to add a further ground of variation to an application before it is decided by the First-tier Tribunal on referral.[130] The First-tier Tribunal applies the same rules as the CSA and determines whether the variation should be agreed or refused.[131] In doing so, it must make a revision or supersession decision, but may pass it back to the CSA to make the child support calculation.[132] This decision by the CSA (ie, to revise/supersede, or to refuse to revise/supersede, the child support calculation) may then be challenged in the usual way (see p186).

5. The decision

A variation is an element of the child support calculation. The Child Support Agency (CSA) may agree to, or refuse, an application for a variation. In either case, it may result in a decision to:[133]

- revise or supersede the calculation/replace the interim maintenance decision (IMD), or refuse to revise or supersede;
- make a calculation (this may replace an IMD) or default maintenance decision.

In some cases, a variation may be agreed that does not affect the amount of child support calculated. A revision or supersession is still carried out, as each decision gives further appeal rights.

Once a variation is made, it continues to be considered each time there is a revision or supersession of the calculation, under the usual revision/supersession rules (see Chapter 12). As a result of certain changes in circumstances, the variation may cease to have effect, in which case the calculation may be suspended or cancelled to remove the variation element. If there is a further change in circumstances, the variation may be reinstated by the CSA without an application. In other cases, a new request for a variation may need to be made.

The effect of the variation

The effect of the variation should not reduce the total amount of child support to less than £5,[134] and the maximum amount of net income that can be taken into account is the capped amount of £2,000.[135] The following sections examine the effect of a variation on different grounds, including where there is more than one ground. The CSA calls these 'concurrent variations'.

Special expenses

The total amount of any special expenses (less any threshold amounts) is deducted from the net weekly income of the non-resident parent and the calculation is carried out as normal using this amount.[136] If there is more than one special expense included, the amounts are aggregated and only one threshold is applied (where applicable).[137]

If the net income is the capped amount, the effect of the variation is worked out by subtracting the special expenses from the actual net weekly income.[138] If this results in a figure above the capped amount of £2,000, the special expenses variation is refused.

Example 9.8
Bronwen has a net income of £428 a week and pays basic rate child support of £86 to Ivan for Ursula and Gretchen. She claims special expenses costs for contact with her children,

amounting to £450 over a six-month period, and for the contribution to their boarding school fees of £1,500 a term.

Her special expenses are worked out as £17.30 for contact and £28.77 for boarding school costs, totalling £46.07. The threshold of £15 applies and £15 is deducted from the total, leaving £31.07.

This is deducted from her weekly net income: £428 – £31.07 = £396.93

Her child support is now worked out in the usual way: 20% x £396.93 = £79.39 (rounded to £79)

Her variation for special expenses has reduced her child support from £86 a week to £79.

Additional cases

If a variation is made on additional cases grounds, the amount of any additional income is added to the net income of the non-resident parent.[139] If this results in a net income figure above the capped amount, the net income is restricted to the capped amount of £2,000.

Example 9.9

The case in *Example 9.5* is referred to the First-tier Tribunal. The First-tier Tribunal determines that there should be a variation for additional income, with a weekly value of £360 for both diversion of income and a lifestyle inconsistent with declared income. This amount is added to Marcus's net income used in the child support calculation of £400. His net income is now £760 a week. The amount he is now due to pay Helene is £152 a week.

Variations on the grounds of having assets over £65,000, income not taken into account and of diverting income should be applied in a way that avoids 'double counting' – eg, income that is counted as diverted should not also be counted as increasing the value of an asset.[140]

If the non-resident parent is in receipt of a benefit (other than income support (IS), income-based jobseeker's allowance (JSA), income-related employment and support allowance (ESA), universal credit (UC) calculated on the basis that s/he has no earned income, or pension credit (PC)) that attracts the flat rate, even though s/he may not pay this because of shared care or because s/he qualifies for the nil rate (except on income grounds), there are special rules on the maximum amount payable when a variation is agreed.[141] This is known as the 'better-buy' provision (see below).

'Better-buy'

The maximum amount of child support a non-resident parent on benefit (other than IS, income-based JSA, income-related ESA, UC calculated on the basis that s/he has no earned income, or PC) must pay after a variation on additional cases grounds is the lesser of:[142]

- the flat rate plus the amount calculated under the usual rules on additional income (exclusive of the benefit income); *or*
- the amount calculated under the usual rules on total income (including any benefit that attracts the flat rate liability, less disregards).

The amounts disregarded in benefit income are:[143]
- constant attendance and exceptionally severe disablement allowances in industrial injuries benefits;
- constant attendance, exceptionally severe disablement, severe occupational and mobility supplement allowances in war disablement pensions;
- unemployability allowances in service pensions.

Example 9.10

Adam gets a retirement pension of £115.95 and is due to pay Carol the flat rate of £5 for one child. He has an occupational pension of £98.50 a week and a personal pension of £39 a week, providing a further £137.50 a week. Adam's total income is £253.45. Carol applies for a variation on the grounds that Adam has income that is not taken into account. As he has income over £100, the better-buy calculation is carried out:

Flat rate (£5) + £5 + (25% x £37.50, rounded to the nearest pound = £9) = £19

Normal rules calculation on total income: £115.95 + £137.50 = £253.45

Basic rate child support is 15% x £253.45 = £38.02 (rounded to £38)

Better-buy means that a variation may be considered which would result in child support of £19 – ie, the lesser of the two amounts.

Concurrent variations

If there is more than one variation element (ie, special expenses and additional cases) to be applied, the calculation is carried out as follows.
- Work out the amounts of each element.
- Apply the additional cases element, capping the income at £2,000. A variation on the grounds of income not taken into account or diversion of income should be considered before a variation on the grounds of lifestyle inconsistent with declared income.[144]
- Apply the special expenses element.
- Work out the child support due, applying any apportionment or reduction for shared care or part-time local authority care.
- Check that the total amount of child support is not less than £5. If it is, £5 is payable (apportioned between the persons with care, if appropriate).

Revisions and supersessions

A variation is not a separate decision to be challenged; it is a variation of the child support calculation. If a variation is agreed and applied to the calculation, this decision may be challenged by applying for a revision within one month. Any change of circumstances, whether in relation to the variation or other factors, can result in a revision or supersession of the calculation under the usual rules, depending on the circumstances (see Chapter 12). This also applies to decisions referred by the CSA to the First-tier Tribunal for a decision – eg, contentious cases.[145]

The variation is taken into account in any reconsideration. However, there may be changes of circumstances which mean that the variation ceases to have effect. In certain circumstances, a previous variation to the calculation may be reinstated, without an application, at the discretion of the CSA (see p185).

Date the variation takes effect

If the ground existed at the effective date of the child support calculation (ie, when the non-resident parent was notified of the application or the application was treated as made), the date the variation takes effect is the effective date of the calculation if either:

- the application is made before the calculation is made;[146] *or*
- the application is made within one month of the calculation, or meets the usual rules on revisions (eg, misrepresentation or failure to disclose information that meant the decision was to the person's advantage) or erroneous decisions.[147]

The exception to this is if the non-resident parent applies for a variation on the grounds of previous debts or payments in respect of certain mortgages, loans or insurance policies and these are treated as voluntary payments in the initial payment period.[148] In this case, the variation takes effect from the maintenance period following the date on which the non-resident parent was notified – ie, the start of the second week of liability.

If the ground did not apply at the effective date of the child support calculation, the variation takes effect from:

- the first day of the maintenance period in which the ground arose, if this is after the effective date but before the calculation is made;[149]
- the first day of the maintenance period in which the relevant person requested the variation.[150] However, if the CSA requests that the application is made in writing and this is not supplied within 14 days, the date the request was made is the date the application is received, unless the CSA accepts that the delay was unavoidable;[151]
- the first day of the maintenance period in which the ground will arise, if the application for variation is made in advance.[152]

A case may have a number of different grounds, agreed over time, and each may have different dates from when they take effect.

Example 9.11

Tara claims child support. The effective date is 26 August 2012. She is notified of her calculation on 19 September 2012. She takes advice and applies for a variation on the basis that an additional cases ground applied on 26 August 2012. She makes this application on 8 October 2012 – ie, within one month of her notification of the decision. The variation is agreed and the calculation is revised on 14 November 2012, with effect from 26 August 2012.

Juan, her ex-partner, takes advice and on 3 December 2012 applies for a variation on the grounds that he has been paying off a loan for a car which they bought before splitting up and which Tara needs, as she lives in a secluded cottage. He is also just about to start paying boarding school fees for their eldest child in late December. The variation is agreed and a revision is made on 3 January 2013 in which the elements for previous debts take effect from 2 December and the boarding school fees take effect from 16 December 2012. Even though the variation for previous debts only applies from December, Juan could ask that the amounts he paid towards the car before the calculation was made be considered as voluntary payments to offset initial arrears. Had Juan taken advice at the same time as Tara and applied for a variation at the same time as she did on the grounds of prior debts and that his repayments on the car loan were voluntary payments, there could have been a further variation to the calculation, with the decision taking effect from 26 August 2012.

When a variation ceases to have effect

A variation ceases to have effect when the ground no longer applies or if any of the reasons for refusing a variation is met. For example, a variation in favour of the person with care always ceases to have effect and is suspended when the non-resident parent or her/his partner starts to receive working tax credit (WTC).[153] When a variation ceases, a supersession is carried out, which takes effect from the first day in the maintenance period in which the change occurred.

If there is a later change, unless the CSA has discretion to reinstate the variation, a further application may need to be made.

Situations in which a further application for variation is required

Ground	When variation ceases	When a further application could be made following a later change
Special expenses	Net income after any variation is more than £2,000.	Net income after variation would be less than £2,000.
Additional cases	Net income before any variation is more than £2,000. The non-resident parent or her/his partner receives WTC.	Net income before variation would be less than £2,000. Neither receives WTC.

Discretion to reinstate a previous variation

In some cases, the CSA may revise or supersede a child support calculation to reinstate a variation that has previously been agreed. This discretion may be applied if there is:[154]

- a change of circumstances which means the non-resident parent's liability is reduced to nil or another rate and the variation cannot be taken into account; *and then*
- a subsequent change of circumstances means the liability can now be adjusted to take the variation into account.

Examples of situations when this could apply include where:

- the non-resident parent becomes a full-time student and so becomes liable for the nil rate, but subsequently returns to a basic or reduced rate;
- a variation is agreed and on a subsequent application for a revision or supersession the non-resident parent fails to provide information. Therefore, the child support calculation is replaced by a default decision. S/he provides the required information later and this default maintenance decision is replaced with a calculation. The variation may then be reapplied without a fresh application.

Note: if the calculation ceases, this discretion does not apply. For example, if the parent moves abroad and the CSA ceases to have jurisdiction, then s/he returns to the UK, a subsequent application must be made for a child support calculation, including an application for variation. However, in some circumstances, the CSA may be able to reinstate the variation without contest (see p176).

In exercising its discretion to reinstate a previous variation, the CSA must be satisfied that there has been no material change in circumstances which affects the earlier variation.[155] If so, the previous variation can be reinstated without an application or any further contact with the relevant persons – ie, they are not invited to make representations. There is no obligation to investigate, so decisions are made based on the information available to the CSA. There is no time limit on the period between the variation ceasing to apply and being reinstated, provided the circumstances that gave rise to the variation remain unchanged.

Example 9.12

Joe applies for, and obtains, a variation from his basic rate child support on the grounds of contact costs with his children. He is later convicted of a criminal offence and sentenced to six months in prison. He becomes liable to pay the nil rate. On his release, he becomes liable at the reduced rate. The CSA is not satisfied that the circumstances relating to eligibility are still the same and does not reinstate the variation. Joe must make a new application for a variation on the grounds of contact costs.

Had the variation been granted on the grounds of previous debts of the relationship, the CSA could probably have reinstated the variation without Joe having to make a further application, as there is no reason why this ground and its effect should be changed by his imprisonment.

Revision and supersession of a previously agreed variation

If a variation has been agreed, it may subsequently be revised or superseded. When a request is received to revise or supersede such a decision, the CSA may notify the other relevant parties and invite them to make representations.[156] This need not be done if the CSA thinks it would not agree to vary the calculation or that a revision or supersession would not be to the advantage of the applicant.

If contest does take place, the usual procedure is followed (see p175).[157]

The CSA may decide to revise or supersede, or not to revise or supersede, the decision and notify the applicant and any relevant parties, as appropriate.

Challenging a decision

Decisions on the child support calculation following a variation application or where a variation element is reinstated, may be challenged in the usual way. For further details, see Chapters 12 and 13.

Notes

1. Variations
1 s28A(1) CSA 1991. Certain modifications apply if an application is made after a calculation is in force. In such cases, ss28A-28F and Schs 4A and 4B must be read in light of the CS(V)(MSP) Regs.

2. Grounds for a variation
2 Sch 4B CSA 1991, as substituted by s6 CSPSSA 2000
3 Sch 4B para 2(3) CSA 1991, as substituted by s6 CSPSSA 2000
4 Reg 15 CS(V) Regs
5 Reg 15(1) CS(V) Regs
6 *R (Qazi) v SSWP* [2004] EWHC 1331 (Admin), reported as R(CS) 5/04
7 Reg 15(2) CS(V) Regs
8 Reg 15(3) CS(V) Regs

9 Reg 23 CS(V) Regs
10 Reg 10(1) CS(V) Regs
11 *CMEC v NC (CSM)* [2009] UKUT 106 (AAC), reported as [2010] AACR 1
12 Reg 10(4) CS(V) Regs
13 CCS/821/2006
14 Reg 10(1) CS(V) Regs
15 R(CS) 5/08; *SM v SSWP and FS (CSM)* [2013] UKUT 445 (AAC)
16 Reg 10(3)(a) CS(V) Regs
17 Reg 10(3)(b) CS(V) Regs
18 Reg 10(3)(b) CS(V) Regs
19 Reg 11 CS(V) Regs; reg 1(3) CS(MCSC) Regs
20 Reg 11(2)(c) CS(V) Regs
21 Reg 11(2)(a) CS(V) Regs
22 Reg 11(1) CS(V) Regs
23 Reg 11(2)(b) CS(V) Regs

24 Reg 11(3) CS(V) Regs
25 Reg 12(2) CS(V) Regs
26 Reg 12(3)(k) and (6)(a) CS(V) Regs
27 Reg 12(6)(a) CS(V) Regs (see also CCS/3674/2007, para 23); s376(4) ICTA 1988
28 Reg 12(3) CS(V) Regs
29 CCS/3674/2007, para 19
30 Reg 12(3)(c)-(g), (j) and (m) CS(V) Regs
31 Reg 12(5) CS(V) Regs
32 Reg 13(1) CS(V) Regs
33 Reg 13(5) CS(V) Regs
34 Reg 13(2) CS(V) Regs
35 Reg 13(3) CS(V) Regs
36 Reg 13(4) CS(V) Regs
37 Reg 14(2)(a) CS(V) Regs
38 Reg 14(2)(b) CS(V) Regs
39 Sch 4B para 4 CSA 1991
40 Reg 25 CS(V) Regs
41 Reg 18(1) CS(V) Regs
42 *CA v SSWP and EG (CSM)* [2014] UKUT 359 (AAC)
43 Reg 18(2) CS(V) Regs
44 Reg 18(3) CS(V) Regs
45 *GL v SSWP and IL (CSM)* [2014] UKUT 209 (AAC)
46 CCS/1129/2005
47 CCS/1026/2006
48 R(CS) 2/06
49 Reg 18(3)(f) CS(V) Regs
50 CCS/1047/2006
51 CCS/1246/2002
52 Reg 18(6) CS(V) Regs
53 Regs 18(5) and 25 CS(V) Regs
54 Reg 19(1) CS(V) Regs
55 Reg 19(1A) CS(V) Regs
56 CCS/2979/2008; *SSWP v Wincott* [2009] EWCA Civ 113, reported as R(CS) 4/09
57 *DW v CMEC* [2010] UKUT 196 (AAC), following CCS/2707/2007 and CCS/2708/2007 and disagreeing with CCS/289/2008
58 Reg 19(2) CS(V) Regs
59 *MZ v SSWP and NK (CSM)* [2013] UKUT 528 (AAC)
60 Regs 19(5)(a) and 25 CS(V) Regs
61 Reg 26(3) CS(V) Regs
62 Reg 19(4) CS(V) Regs
63 *G'OB v CMEC (CSM)* [2010] UKUT 6 (AAC)
64 *TB v SSWP and SB (CSM)* [2014] UKUT 301 (AAC)
65 R(CS) 6/05; CCS/1769/2007
66 Reg 19(5)(b) and 25 CS(V) Regs
67 See, for example, *RC v CMEC and WC* [2009] UKUT 62 (AAC), reported as [2011] AACR 38; CCS/1320/2005; CCS/409/2005

68 Reg 20(1) and (2) CS(V) Regs
69 Reg 20(3) and (4)(a) CS(V) Regs
70 CCS/2018/2005
71 *WM v CMEC (CSM)* [2011] UKUT 226 (AAC)
72 Reg 20(4) CS(V) Regs
73 Reg 20(5) CS(V) Regs
74 See, for example, *WM v CMEC (CSM)* [2011] UKUT 226 (AAC); *RC v SSWP* [2009] UKUT 62 (AAC), reported as [2011] AACR 38
75 R(CS) 3/01; CCS/2786/2005; CCS/2082/2004; CCS/2152/2004; CCS/821/2003
76 CCS/1944/2005; CCS/1440/2004

3. Applying for a variation
77 s28A(4) CSA 1991
78 Reg 4(1) CS(V) Regs
79 s28A(4)(b) CSA 1991
80 *DB v CMEC* [2010] UKUT 356 (AAC)
81 R(CS) 2/06
82 Reg 8(1) CS(V) Regs
83 Reg 8(1) CS(V) Regs
84 Regs 6(2)(c) and 8(2) CS(V) Regs
85 Reg 5(1) CS(V) Regs
86 Reg 5(2) CS(V) Regs
87 Sch 4B para 5(1) CSA 1991; reg 9(9) CS(V) Regs
88 Reg 9(8) CS(V) Regs

4. Procedure
89 s28D CSA 1991
90 s28B(1) CSA 1991
91 Reg 6(1) CS(V) Regs
92 s28B CSA 1991; reg 7 CS(V) Regs
93 *RB v CMEC* [2009] UKUT 53 (AAC)
94 s28B CSA 1991; regs 6 and 7 CS(V) Regs
95 *CR v CMEC* [2009] UKUT 111 (AAC)
96 Reg 9(1) CS(V) Regs
97 Reg 9(4)(a) CS(V) Regs
98 Reg 9(1) CS(V) Regs
99 Reg 9(5) CS(V) Regs
100 Reg 9(4) CS(V) Regs
101 Reg 9(2) CS(V) Regs
102 Reg 9(3) CS(V) Regs
103 s12 CSA 1991
104 s28F(5) CSA 1991
105 s28C CSA 1991
106 s28C(2) CSA 1991; reg 31(1) CS(V) Regs
107 s28C(4) CSA 1991
108 s28C(3) CSA 1991
109 s28C(5) CSA 1991
110 s28C(7) CSA 1991
111 Reg 31(2) and (3) CS(V) Regs
112 ss28E and 28F(2)(a) CSA 1991
113 s28E(3) CSA 1991
114 s28F(1) CSA 1991

115 s28F(3) CSA 1991
116 ss28D(1) and 28F CSA 1991
117 s28F(1) CSA 1991
118 Reg 21(1) CS(V) Regs
119 *DB v CMEC* [2010] UKUT 356 (AAC)
120 Reg 21(2) CS(V) Regs
121 R(CS) 3/01
122 CSCS/16/2003
123 CCS/1131/2005
124 R(CS) 5/06
125 *DDH v SSWP and DAH (CSM)* [2013] UKUT 299 (AAC)
126 *RC v CMEC and WC* [2009] UKUT 62 (AAC), reported as [2011] AACR 38
127 s28D(1)(b) CSA 1991
128 *HB v SSWP* [2009] UKUT 66 (AAC)
129 *Milton v SSWP* [2006] EWCA Civ 1258
130 R(CS) 3/01
131 s28D(3) CSA 1991
132 R(CS) 5/06

5. The decision
133 ss28B(2) and 28F(3) and (4) CSA 1991
134 Reg 27(5) CS(V) Regs
135 Reg 25 CS(V) Regs
136 Reg 23(1) CS(V) Regs
137 Reg 15(1) CS(V) Regs
138 Reg 23(2) CS(V) Regs
139 Reg 25 CS(V) Regs
140 CCS/1047/2006
141 Reg 26 CS(V) Regs
142 Reg 26(1) CS(V) Regs
143 Reg 26(3) CS(V) Regs
144 CCS/1047/2006
145 ss16(1A)(c) and 17(1)(d) CSA 1991
146 Reg 22 CS(V) Regs
147 s28G CSA 1991; reg 3A SS&CS(DA) Regs
148 Reg 22(2) CS(V) Regs
149 Reg 22(1)(b) CS(V) Regs
150 s28G CSA 1991; regs 6A(6) and 7B(6) SS&CS(DA) Regs
151 Reg 4 CS(V) Regs
152 Regs 6A(3) and 7B(5) SS&CS(DA) Regs
153 Regs 7(5)(b) and 27(6) CS(V) Regs; *AW v SSWP (CSM)* [2014] UKUT 462 (AAC)
154 Reg 29 CS(V) Regs
155 Reg 9(3) CS(V) Regs
156 Reg 15B SS&CS(DA) Regs
157 Reg 15B SS&CS(DA) Regs

Part 5

The '1993 rules'

Chapter 10

The '1993 rules' formula

This chapter covers:
1. Introduction (below)
2. The five steps of the formula (p192)
3. Minimum child support (p194)
4. Non-resident parents on certain benefits (p195)
5. Special cases (p196)

1. Introduction

If an application was made before 3 March 2003, it will normally be a '1993 rules' case. Some '1993 rules' cases were converted to the '2003 rules'. See Chapter 10 of the 2013/14 edition of this *Handbook* for more details.

All new applications for child support are now dealt with under the '2012 rules' (see Chapter 6). Some existing cases will continue to be dealt with under the '1993 rules' until the process of closing existing cases and inviting parents to consider whether they want to apply under the '2012 rules' is complete (see Chapter 5). Some '1993 rules' cases are also converted automatically to the '2012 rules' if they are 'linked' to a new application (see p81).

There is a statutory formula for calculating child support under the '1993 rules'. There is a right of appeal against the assessment, but an appeal is only likely to be successful if the Child Support Agency (CSA) has made a mistake, or if a different interpretation of the law is possible.

The amount of child support payable depends on the circumstances and the income of both parents, but particularly the income of the non-resident parent. Understanding the way in which the formula works is important for explaining the result of an assessment as well as forecasting the effect of any change of circumstances, and deciding whether to apply for a revision or supersession.

This chapter summarises the main aspects of the formula. For full details of the '1993 rules', see previous editions of this *Handbook*.

Note:

- If a non-resident parent is on income support (IS), income-based jobseeker's allowance, income-related employment and support allowance or pension credit, or receives universal credit on the basis that s/he has no earned income, the formula is not used to calculate her/his contribution towards child support (see p195).
- In some cases where the CSA did not have enough information to carry out a full assessment using the formula (eg, because someone did not provide the information required), an 'interim maintenance assessment' may have been imposed.
- There are usually penalty assessments, which are set at a higher rate than would be likely under the formula.
- It may be possible to request a change to the standard formula in certain circumstances. This is called **'departure'** and is a way of taking into account a financial factor particular to that family. Although the decision on whether to take the factor into account (and to what extent) is discretionary, an adjusted statutory formula is then used to obtain the final assessment.
- The child support payable under the '1993 rules' formula is given as a weekly rate and all stages of the calculation use weekly figures.[1] In most aspects of the calculation, fractions of a penny are disregarded if less than one-half, or rounded up to the next penny if equal to or more than one-half.[2]
- The formula for assessing child support is based on IS personal allowances and premiums. The IS rates used in a particular calculation are those that apply on the date the assessment came into effect, known as the 'effective date'.[3] Benefit rates increase in April each year. The assessment is not automatically altered at the annual April uprating, but if a reassessment is requested after a change of circumstances, the new rates are then used.
- Since the formula was introduced in April 1993, there have been several changes to it. Unless there is a specific provision, the general rule is that the calculation must be done using the regulations which applied on the effective date of the assessment.[4]

2. **The five steps of the formula**

The '1993 rules' formula is long and complex, but it is not advisable to skip any steps without checking them.

Although it is only a non-resident parent who is liable to pay child support, the formula involves the income of both parents.

If the person with care is *not* the legal parent of the child, the income of that person does not affect the amount of child support payable.

Step one: the child support maintenance requirement

The child support 'maintenance requirement' represents the minimum day-to-day expenses of maintaining children. However, this is neither the minimum nor the maximum amount of child support payable. Under the formula, a non-resident parent might be assessed as liable to pay less or more than the maintenance requirement.

The main significance of this step is that a non-resident parent pays 50 per cent of assessable income (see below) in child support until the maintenance requirement figure has been met. From this point on, a lower percentage of any remaining assessable income is paid.

Step two: exempt income

Exempt income represents the minimum day-to-day living expenses of the parent and covers the housing costs of the family with whom s/he lives. However, it only includes amounts for living expenses of any of the parent's *own* children who are living with her/him, *not* the living expenses of a new partner or stepchildren.

Each parent can keep income equal to the exempt income before being expected to pay any child support.

Step three: assessable income

Assessable income is income that is available to pay child support. It is the amount of the parent's income which remains after exempt income has been taken into account. If a non-resident parent has no assessable income, s/he may still have to pay the minimum payment.

Step four: proposed child support

'Proposed child support' is the amount of child support the non-resident parent is expected to pay, provided it does not bring her/his income below the protected income level (Step five).

A non-resident parent pays 50 per cent of her/his assessable income in child support until s/he has met the maintenance requirement figure of Step one. Once the maintenance requirement is met, s/he pays 15, 20 or 25 per cent of any further assessable income, depending on the number of children for whom s/he is being assessed to pay child support.

The assessable income of the parent with care can reduce the proposed child support.

There is an upper limit to the amount of child support payable under the formula (although it may be possible for the parties to go to court to seek additional child maintenance).

Step five: protected income

The protected income step ensures that a non-resident parent's disposable income does not fall below a certain level as a result of paying the proposed child support.

At this stage, the whole family's expenses and income are taken into account, including those of a new partner and stepchildren.

A non-resident parent is not expected to pay more than 30 per cent of her/his own net income.

3. **Minimum child support**

There is a standard minimum amount of child support that a non-resident parent must pay if the formula results in an amount less than this minimum.[5]

The amount of the minimum payment is currently £7.40. This is calculated by rounding 5 per cent of the income support personal allowance for someone aged 25 or over (£73.10) up to the next 5 pence and doubling it.[6]

If a non-resident parent has been assessed under the formula as liable to pay less than £7.40, s/he must pay child support of £7.40 a week.

This minimum payment must be made unless the non-resident parent falls into a category which is specifically exempt (see below), in which case s/he pays nothing.

A non-resident parent is only required to pay one minimum payment even if s/he has qualifying children being looked after by more than one parent or person with care.[7] If a non-resident parent has qualifying children who are being cared for in different households, the minimum payment is divided between the persons with care in the same ratio as their respective maintenance requirements.

Exempt non-resident parents

Some non-resident parents do not have to pay any child support at all. If a non-resident parent has been assessed under the formula as having to pay £7.40 or less, s/he is exempt from paying any child support if s/he:[8]

- has the family premium included in the calculation or estimation of her/his protected income level – ie, a child is a member of her/his family for at least two days a week; *or*
- is a prisoner; *or*
- receives (or would receive if s/he satisfied the national insurance contribution conditions or did not receive an overlapping benefit):
  - incapacity benefit or statutory sick pay;
  - maternity allowance or statutory maternity pay;
  - severe disablement allowance;
  - disability living allowance, personal independence payment, armed forces independence payment or attendance allowance;
  - an industrial injuries disablement benefit;
  - a war disablement benefit or payment from the Armed Forces Compensation Scheme;

- carer's allowance; *or*
- payments from the Independent Living Funds; *or*
- is under 16 years old, or under 20 and in full-time, non-advanced education or child benefit is payable for her/him – ie, s/he is a child for child support purposes (see p13); *or*
- has a net weekly income of less than £7.40. Trainees on approved training whose income consists solely of a training allowance (or an education maintenance allowance, where still payable),[9] or students whose only income is a grant or student loan,[10] have these payments ignored when calculating net income for child support purposes. This means they are usually exempt from paying child support.

4. **Non-resident parents on certain benefits**

If a non-resident parent is in receipt of income support (IS), income-based jobseeker's allowance (JSA), income-related employment and support allowance (ESA) or pension credit (PC), or receives universal credit (UC) on the basis that s/he has no earned income, the formula is not used. Instead, the Department for Work and Pensions (DWP) can make a deduction from one of those benefits paid to her/him as a contribution towards child support.[11] The deduction can be made from a partner's benefits if the partner of a non-resident parent is claiming one of these benefits for the couple.[12]

When deductions cannot be made

Deductions cannot be made if a non-resident parent is exempt. In this case, s/he will pay nothing. A non-resident parent is exempt if s/he:[13]
- is aged under 18; *or*
- qualifies for the family premium and/or has day-to-day care (see p15) of any child; *or*
- receives any of the benefits that exempt a non-resident parent from having to pay any child support (see p194), or would receive one of those benefits except for the national insurance contribution conditions or overlapping benefit rules.

Amount of the deduction

The deduction for a non-resident parent on IS/income-based JSA/income-related ESA/PC who is not exempt is an amount equal to the minimum payment (see p194), irrespective of her/his age.[14] This is currently £7.40 a week. In some cases, half of this amount may be deducted. The deduction for a non-resident parent who receives UC calculated on the basis that s/he has no earned income and who is not exempt is 5 per cent of the relevant standard allowance.[15] Whether the deduction is actually made by the DWP, and how much is deducted, depends on the number of other deductions of higher priority being made from the benefit. For more information about how deductions are made, see p285.

Only one deduction for child support can be made, even if there is more than one person with care looking after the non-resident parent's qualifying children. In this case, the minimum payment is apportioned between the persons with care in the same ratio as their respective maintenance requirements.[16]

What the deduction is for

Technically, deductions from benefit are not payments of child support, but payments in lieu of child support.[17] Deductions are not the result of an assessment, and the rules that apply to assessments do not apply to these contributions. In particular, liability for the contributions is not backdated to the effective date and arrears do not accrue if the DWP is unable to make the full deduction because there are other deductions with higher priority.

No more than one deduction for child support can be made at any one time from an IS/income-based JSA/income-related ESA/PC or UC claim.[18] In addition, because deductions can only be made where there is a non-resident parent with current liability, no amount for child support arrears can ever be deducted from these benefits. Arrears of child support could still be collected by other methods (see Chapter 14), but usually the arrears are held in abeyance until the non-resident parent comes off these benefits. However, if s/he is in receipt of contribution-based JSA or contributory ESA, an amount can be deducted from these benefits towards arrears (see p285).

Challenging decisions

Child Support Agency (CSA) decisions about the liability of non-resident parents on certain benefits can be challenged in the same way as other CSA decisions[19] – ie, by a revision[20] or supersession[21] (see Chapter 12) and by appealing to the First-tier Tribunal (see Chapter 13).[22] This includes decisions on whether a non-resident parent can have an amount deducted from her/his IS/income-based JSA/income-related ESA/PC/UC, given other higher priority deductions. See CPAG's *Welfare Benefits and Tax Credits Handbook* for more details.

Note: a revision (a 'mandatory reconsideration') must be sought before an appeal can be made to the First-tier Tribunal.

---

5. **Special cases**

The child support legislation uses the phrase 'special cases' to cover situations that are not as straightforward as those in which there is one non-resident parent and one person with care looking after all the qualifying children[23] – eg, where:

- both parents are non-resident;
- more than one person with care applies for child support from the same non-resident parent;
- a person cares for children of more than one non-resident parent.

If care of a child is being shared between different people, several modifications of the formula are necessary.

'Shared care' is different from the situation where different children of the same family have different homes. If the children of a family are divided between two households (eg, if one child lives with one parent and another child with the other parent), this involves two assessments. In one assessment, the first parent is the parent with care and the second parent is the non-resident parent. In the second assessment the roles are reversed. This situation is referred to as 'divided families' in this *Handbook*. The Child Support Agency may refer to this as 'split care'.

Notes

1. Introduction
1 Reg 33(1) CS(MAP) Regs; reg 2(1) CS(MASC) Regs
2 Reg 2(2) CS(MASC) Regs
3 Regs 3(2), 9(5) and 11(5) CS(MASC) Regs
4 Reg 2(3) CS(MASC) Regs; CCS/7312/1995

3. Minimum child support
5 Sch 1 para 7 CSA 1991
6 Reg 13 CS(MASC) Regs
7 Reg 22(4) CS(MASC) Regs
8 Reg 26 and Sch 4 CS(MASC) Regs
9 Sch 2 paras 21 and 36 CS(MASC) Regs
10 Reg 7(3) CS(MASC) Regs

4. Non-resident parents on certain benefits
11 s43 and Sch 1 para 5(4) CSA 1991
12 Sch 9 para 7A(1) SS(C&P) Regs
13 Reg 28 CS(MASC) Regs
14 Reg 28(2) CS(MASC) Regs; Sch 9 para 7A(3) SS(C&P) Regs
15 Sch 6 para 10 UC,PIP,JSA&ESA(C&P) Regs

16 Reg 28(2) CS(MASC) Regs
17 s43(2)(a) CSA 1991
18 Sch 9 para 7A(2) SS(C&P) Regs; Sch 6 para 10(3) UC,PIP,JSA&ESA(C&P) Regs
19 s43(3) CSA 1991
20 Sch 4C para 1(a) CSA 1991
21 Sch 4C para 2(1)(a) CSA 1991
22 Sch 4C para 3(1)(a) CSA 1991

5. Special cases
23 Part III CS(MASC) Regs

Part 6

Decisions, challenges and enforcement

Chapter 11

Decisions

This chapter covers:
1. Making the initial child support decision (below)
2. Default maintenance decisions (p204)
3. Notification of decisions (p205)
4. When the first calculation begins (p206)
5. When a calculation ends (p208)

This chapter mainly covers how the Child Maintenance Service makes decisions on applications for child support under the '2012 rules'. However, as many cases are still dealt with under the '2003 rules', it also covers some information on decisions by the Child Support Agency under these older rules. For full details of decisions under the '2003 rules', see previous editions of this *Handbook*. Also see previous editions for full details of decisions under the '1993 rules', which are significantly different from decisions under the '2012 rules' and '2003 rules'.

For information on revision and supersession decisions, see Chapter 12.

---

1. Making the initial child support decision

Once an effective application has been made and the Child Maintenance Service (CMS) has obtained, or tried to obtain, the necessary information, it can:[1]
- make a calculation;
- make a 'default maintenance decision' (see p204); *or*
- refuse to make a calculation (p203).

Details of the case are entered on the CMS computer system and child support is calculated automatically.

Waiting for the calculation decision

If the person with care can provide contact details, the CMS aims to start gathering information from the non-resident parent as soon as possible. It aims to make an accurate decision within six weeks of an application, but some cases may take up to 26 weeks.[2] If the CMS has to trace the non-resident parent, it is likely to take longer before it can make a decision.

Delays in dealing with applications

Much of the contact with parents to collect and check information needed to make a calculation and collect payments is done by telephone.

Applicants are contacted at certain stages during the progress of the case – eg, to let them know about negotiations with the non-resident parent about collection or if they have made a complaint. The CMS aims to keep people informed about the progress on a case. However, a parent should contact the CMS regularly for progress reports on an application.

A delay after the non-resident parent is contacted about the application does not normally delay the starting date of any calculation (see p206), but the date of the decision may be delayed. If the non-resident parent has liability under an order or agreement, this continues and remains enforceable. Other non-resident parents should consider putting money aside or making voluntary payments (see p281). Parents who are already contributing voluntarily should check whether these payments might be used to offset initial arrears (see p275).

If the non-resident parent is not co-operating, the CMS should make a default maintenance decision (see p204) and may impose a criminal sanction. If the CMS does not make a default maintenance decision, the person with care should request that one be made. If this does not happen, a complaint should be made (see p323). In certain circumstances in a '2012 rules' case, the CMS also has the option of making a calculation based on an estimate of the non-resident parent's income (see Chapter 6).

Withdrawing the application

If an application is withdrawn or treated as withdrawn (see p47), the CMS cannot make a calculation. If a calculation is made after withdrawal, it can be challenged (see Chapters 12 and 13).

The application cannot be withdrawn after a decision has been made, but the applicant can ask the CMS to cease acting, in which case the calculation is cancelled (see p208).

Change of circumstances

There is no general requirement to notify the CMS or Child Support Agency (CSA) of changes in circumstances. However, both the person with care and the non-resident parent are required to notify the CMS/CSA of some changes (see p73). It is an offence for a non-resident parent not to notify the CMS/CSA of a change of address.[3]

In practice, any party may want to tell the CMS/CSA of changes or new information that might affect the calculation.

In '2012 rules' cases, there are specific rules for when changes of income must be disclosed and which changes result in a calculation being changed (see Chapter 6).

If the CMS/CSA is told about a change or given new information that relates to *before* the effective date, it has discretion on whether to take this information into account. This can be done in the initial calculation, or by making two or more calculations for the different periods.[4]

In '2003 rules' cases, if the date or period normally used (eg, for earnings) is before the effective date and the CSA knows about a relevant change which happened after that date or period but before the effective date, it must take that change into account.[5] If the change is after the normal 'relevant week' (see p25), the relevant week for each later calculation is the week before the date the CSA was notified of the relevant change.[6]

Any information about a change *after* the effective date but before the calculation can lead to a series of calculations in respect of different periods. In '2012 rules' cases, the effective date of each calculation is normally the date the change occurred or is expected to occur.[7] In '2003 rules' cases, the effective date of each calculation is the beginning of the maintenance period in which the change occurred or is expected to occur.[8]

Changes that occur after a calculation is made may result in a revision or supersession, depending on when the change is notified and its significance (see Chapter 12).

Refusal to make a calculation

The CMS *must* refuse to make a calculation if:
- the application was made by a person who is *not* a non-resident parent or a person with care (or, in Scotland, a qualifying child aged 12 or over) (see p33);
- there is a pre-3 March 2003 court order (registered agreement in Scotland) or written agreement (see p37);
- there is a post-3 March 2003 court order (registered agreement in Scotland) that has been in force for less than one year (see p38);
- not all the parties are habitually resident in the UK (see p34);
- there is no non-resident parent, either because both parents live in the same household as the child (see p18) or because the CMS does not accept that the person named is a parent of the child (see p11); *or*
- there is no qualifying child (see p13).

The CMS can also delay making a calculation pending the outcome of a test case (see p260). Otherwise, the CMS must make a calculation.[9]

If there is a change of circumstances so that one of these situations applies for a period beginning after the effective date, the CMS makes a calculation that ends on the date of the change.

In '2012 rules' cases, if a child in respect of whom an application has been made dies before the calculation is made, a decision is still made for the period from the effective date to the date of death (see p47).

The CMS cannot refuse to make a calculation just because it has insufficient information or because it may affect the welfare of a child.[10] The CMS may make a default maintenance decision (see below). If the CMS refuses to make a calculation, the applicant (and, if the applicant is a child in Scotland, any person with care or non-resident parent who had been notified of the application) must be notified in writing of the decision, how to apply for a revision or supersession (see Chapter 12) and the right of appeal (see Chapter 13).[11]

A fresh application may be made after the refusal – eg, if there is a change of circumstances, such as the non-resident parent returning to live in the UK.

2. **Default maintenance decisions**

If the Child Maintenance Service (CMS) does not have enough information to make a calculation, or to revise or supersede a decision, it may make a 'default maintenance decision'.[12]

The amount of the default maintenance decision depends on the number of qualifying children applied for.

In a '2012 rules' case, the amount of the default maintenance decision is:[13]

- £39 per week if there is one qualifying child;
- £51 per week if there are two qualifying children; *or*
- £64 per week if there are three or more qualifying children.

Some default maintenance decisions made by the Child Support Agency (CSA) under the '2003 rules' may also still be in force. In a '2003 rules' case, the amount of the default maintenance decision is:[14]

- £30 per week if there is one qualifying child;
- £40 per week if there are two qualifying children; *or*
- £50 per week if there are three or more qualifying children.

These amounts may be apportioned if there is more than one person with care. Any relevant non-resident children are ignored.

The effective date of a default maintenance decision is the same as it would have been for a child support calculation decision.

Note: default maintenance decisions apply only under the '2012 rules' and '2003 rules'. Under the '1993 rules', if the CSA did not have sufficient information to make a full assessment using the formula, it may have made an interim maintenance assessment (IMA). For full details of IMAs, see previous editions of this *Handbook*.

When a default maintenance decision ends

A default maintenance decision may be revised at any time – eg, when it is replaced by a calculation.[15] In practice, this only happens when the CMS/CSA has sufficient information to determine the case properly (ie, to make a calculation) from the effective date. In a '2003 rules' case, if the CSA does not have sufficient information to do this but has enough information from a later date, it can make a calculation that takes effect from the first day in the maintenance period in which the information is received.[16]

3. **Notification of decisions**

The Child Maintenance Service (CMS) or Child Support Agency (CSA) must notify the person with care and non-resident parent (and child applicant in Scotland) once a child support calculation or interim maintenance decision (IMD) has been made.[17] This also includes default maintenance decisions (but see below). There are similar rules on notifying revision and supersession decisions (see Chapter 12). If the CMS/CSA corrects an accidental error in a decision or in the record of a decision (see p213), it must also notify the person with care and non-resident parent (and child applicant in Scotland) in writing as soon as practicable.[18]

The notification of the calculation or IMD *must* include information on:[19]

- the effective date;
- for the '2012 rules', where relevant, the gross weekly income of the non-resident parent, including:
  - whether gross income is based on historic or current income; *and*
  - if it is based on current income, whether this has been estimated (see Chapter 6);
- for the '2003 rules', where relevant, the net weekly income of the non-resident parent;
- the number of qualifying children;
- the number of relevant other children;
- the weekly rate of child support and any collection fees;
- any variations;
- any adjustments for apportionment, shared care by the non-resident parent or part-time local authority care, or maintenance to another relevant non-resident child; *and*
- the rules for requesting a revision, supersession and appeal.[20]

Notification of a default maintenance decision must state the effective date, the default date, the number of qualifying children, details of any apportionment and the information needed to make a child support calculation.[21] It should also include details of rights to request a revision, supersession or an appeal.[22]

Unless there is written permission, a notification should not contain:[23]
- the address of anyone else other than the recipient or information that could lead to her/his being located; *or*
- information on anyone other than persons with care, non-resident parents or qualifying children.

If there are errors or someone disagrees with the decision, s/he may challenge it (see p217 and Chapter 12). The CMS/CSA can also, at any time, correct an accidental error in a decision or in the record of a decision (see p213).

If there is a court order for maintenance, the court is notified of the calculation.

4. When the first calculation begins

The date a child support calculation takes effect is called the **'effective date'** (see below).[24]

There are different rules for effectives dates in the '2012 rules' and the '2003 rules'.

There are also different rules for effective dates after a supersession (see Chapter 12) and for calculations replacing default maintenance decisions (see p204).

The effective date in '2012 rules' cases

Effective dates for '2012 rules' cases are intended to be much simpler than those for the '2003 rules'.[25] The date a child support calculation under the '2012 rules' first comes into force and liability begins is called the 'initial effective date'. The **'initial effective date'** is specified in the notice issued to the non-resident parent informing her/him that an effective application has been made (see p46). The Child Maintenance Service (CMS) may telephone the non-resident parent on or before the initial effective date and then confirm this in writing to the parent's last known address. If the CMS does not telephone the parent, it must send written notice to the parent's last known address at least two days before the initial effective date.[26] The initial effective date is normally expected to be two days after the written notice is issued.[27] **Note:** there is no different effective date in a case where a child support application is made when a court order is in force. See p207 for the effective date in such cases under the '2003 rules'.

There are different rules for effective dates after a supersession (see Chapter 12).

The effective date in '2003 rules' cases

Unless there is a maintenance order in force in relation to all the qualifying children (see p207), the effective date of the calculation depends on who made the application.

If the application was made by the person with care or a child applicant in Scotland, the effective date is:[28]

- the date the non-resident parent is notified of the application; *or*
- if the non-resident parent has intentionally avoided notification, the date on which notification would have been given but for the avoidance.

The non-resident parent is normally notified of the application by phone. In some cases, a maintenance enquiry form may be issued, in which case, notification is treated as given or sent on the day it is given or posted.[29]

An alleged non-resident parent cannot delay the effective date of a calculation by disputing parentage. The Child Support Agency does not make a calculation until the issue of parentage is resolved (see p12) but, if it later decides that the person is in fact a non-resident parent, the calculation is backdated to the effective date.

If the non-resident parent made the application, the effective date of the first calculation is the date of the effective application.[30]

If there are multiple applications for child support and these are treated as a single application (see p48), the effective date is set by the earlier or earliest application.[31]

If there is, or has been, a calculation (or '1993 rules' assessment) in force, and a new application is then made under the '2003 rules', special rules may apply. See previous editions of this *Handbook* for details relevant to any such cases that are still to be decided.

Court orders

The effective date is two months and two days after the date on which the application was made if:[32]

- there was no calculation in force for either the parent with care or the non-resident parent;
- there was a maintenance order in force for all of the qualifying children named in the calculation (this means that if the court order covered some, but not all, of the qualifying children, this rule does not apply);
- the maintenance order was made on or after 3 March 2003; *and*
- the maintenance order had been in force for at least one year.

If the maintenance order ceased to be in force after the application but before the effective date worked out under the above rule, the effective date was the day after the maintenance order ceased to be in force.[33]

Liability for maintenance continues until the order stops being in force, so the non-resident parent should continue making payments while waiting for the calculation. Payments are treated as payments of child support (see also p280) if:[34]

- a calculation is made; *and*
- an order made on or after 3 March 2003 has been in force for at least a year; *and*

- the non-resident parent makes payments due under the order but after the effective date of the calculation (and so will have been making them retrospectively after the order ceased to have effect).

For collection and enforcement of arrears, see Chapter 14.

5. **When a calculation ends**

A calculation continues until the Child Maintenance Service (CMS) or Child Support Agency (CSA):
- cancels it following a request. In effect, this is a supersession decision as a result of a change of circumstances – ie, there has been a change in what the applicant wishes the CMS/CSA to do (see below);
- supersedes it because it has ceased to have effect (see p209);
- revises it (see p217); *or*
- supersedes it for another reason (see p223).

In some circumstances, this means that the calculation is replaced by another; in others, no further calculation is made. When the cancellation takes effect depends on the grounds on which the supersession or revision was made, or the nature of the request (see p210). Any arrears remaining after a calculation ends may still be collected (see Chapter 14). If an application is made for a child of the non-resident parent who is not named in the existing calculation, the new calculation replaces the old one.

Note: '1993 rules' and '2003 rules' cases may also be cancelled by the CSA as part of the introduction of the '2012 rules' and the process of closing existing cases. See p83 for details.

Request to cancel a calculation

A calculation must be cancelled when the applicant requests that the CMS/CSA cease acting.[35]

The request may be made verbally or in writing. If the request is made, the CMS/CSA must stop all action, including collecting and enforcing arrears, although the person may specifically ask for action for arrears to continue.

Note: if, after the date the '2012 rules' were introduced for a particular type of case (see Chapter 5), the applicant asks for an existing '2003 rules' calculation or '1993 rules' assessment to be cancelled and then makes a new application within 13 weeks, the new application is treated under the same rules as the cancelled calculation/assessment.

Living together

When the request is made, reasons need not be given. However, if the reason is that the parent with care and non-resident parent are living together, the CMS/CSA should be told. This is because, once all the parties share a household, the non-resident parent is no longer non-resident (see p17), so the child is no longer a qualifying child and the calculation ceases to have effect (see below).

The calculation ceases to have effect

Some changes of circumstances lead to a termination of the calculation, whether or not a request is made. The CMS/CSA may be aware of a change from, for example, a request or a notification by the parent with care under her/his duty to do so (see p73). The CMS/CSA *must* supersede the decision and cancel a calculation (including a default decision) if the calculation ceases to have effect. The calculation ceases to have effect if:[36]

- the non-resident parent or person with care dies;
- the only, or all, qualifying child(ren) is (are) no longer a qualifying child(ren); *or*
- the non-resident parent ceases to be a parent of the only, or all, qualifying child(ren).

This means cancellation occurs, for example, when:

- a child aged 16 or over leaves non-advanced education or becomes too old to count as a child (see p13);
- the qualifying child, non-resident parent and parent with care start living together (see p17);
- the qualifying child goes to live with someone else and, as a result, the person with care no longer counts as a person with care;
- the qualifying child is adopted, in which case the non-resident parent is no longer a parent; *or*
- the non-resident parent is no longer considered a parent because of the results of a DNA test or a declaration/declarator of parentage.

Other cancellations

The CMS/CSA must cancel the calculation if the person with care, non-resident parent or qualifying child is no longer habitually resident in the UK (see p34).[37]

A non-resident parent who has successfully contested parentage has any calculation cancelled and, if s/he has paid any child support, may obtain a refund (see p63).

If an applicant fails to provide the CMS/CSA with enough information to make a revision or supersession decision, the CMS/CSA *may* cancel the calculation.

Date cancellation takes effect

Cancellation of a calculation requires a decision by the CMS/CSA, either at its own initiative or following a request or application (see p208).[38]

If a calculation **under the '2012 rules'** is cancelled because it ceases to have effect or because of another relevant change (including the circumstances on p209), the cancellation takes effect from the date the change occurred.[39]

If a calculation **under the '2003 rules'** is cancelled because it ceases to have effect or because of another relevant change, the cancellation takes effect from the first day in the maintenance period in which the change occurred. This includes if:

- the person with care is no longer the person with care for the child(ren) named in the calculation;[40] *or*
- a party is no longer habitually resident in the UK;[41] *or*
- the qualifying child dies or ceases to be a qualifying child;[42] *or*
- the non-resident parent ceases to be a parent.[43]

If the cancellation is because the non-resident parent is not considered to be the parent because of a DNA test or declaration/declarator of parentage, the effective date is the effective date of the original calculation.[44]

Cancellation following a request

In '2012 rules' cases, a calculation is normally cancelled with effect from the date the request was received (in '2003 rules' cases, the first day of the maintenance period in which the request was received). A different date may apply, depending on the reason for the cancellation.[45] A later date may be appropriate if an applicant has asked that the calculation end on a later date.

Notification of the cancellation decision

When the CMS/CSA cancels a calculation or refuses to cancel one, it must notify the non-resident parent, person with care and child applicant in Scotland, and must also provide information on revisions and supersessions and on the right of appeal.[46]

If the calculation was made following an application from a child in Scotland and that child is no longer a qualifying child, the CMS/CSA must notify the person with care, non-resident parent and other children aged 12 or over who are potential child applicants that the calculation has been cancelled.[47]

Cancelling '1993 rules' assessments

The rules on ending '1993 rules' assessments are similar to those for the '2012 rules' and '2003 rules'. There are some important differences, including the following.

- Under the '1993 rules', if a child applicant in Scotland is no longer habitually resident in Scotland, the assessment is cancelled.[48] This takes effect from the first day in the maintenance period in which the change occurred.
- Under the '1993 rules', in some cases the CSA determines the effective date of the cancellation – eg, if the person with care and non-resident parent are living together (see p17).[49]
- Before cancelling an assessment, the CSA must, if possible, give written notice to the person with care and non-resident parent (and any child applicant in Scotland) of its intention to cancel the assessment, and allow 14 days from the date the notice is sent before cancelling.[50]
- The full amount of the assessment is due for the maintenance period in which the cancellation date falls.[51]

For full details of decisions on '1993 rules' cases, including when interim maintenance assessments (see p204) are cancelled, see previous editions of this *Handbook*.

Notes

1. Making the initial child support decision
1 s11 CSA 1991
2 www.gov.uk/child-maintenance/how-to-apply
3 s14A(3A) CSA 1991
4 Sch 1 para 15 CSA 1991
5 Reg 2(4) CS(MCSC) Regs; CCS/2750/1995
6 Reg 1(2) CS(MCSC) Regs (see the exception to definition (c) of 'relevant week')
7 Reg 18(2)-(4) CSMC Regs
8 Reg 25(5) CS(MCP) Regs
9 s11(2) CSA 1991
10 R(CS) 2/98
11 **2012 rules** Reg 24 CSMC Regs
 2003 rules Reg 23(4) CS(MCP) Regs

2. Default maintenance decisions
12 s12(1) CSA 1991
13 Reg 49 CSMC Regs
14 Reg 7 CS(MCP) Regs

15 s16(1B) CSA 1991
 2012 rules Reg 14(3) CSMC Regs
 2003 rules Reg 3A(5) SS&CS(DA) Regs
16 Reg 29A CS(MCP) Regs

3. Notification of decisions
17 **2012 rules** Regs 24 and 25 CSMC Regs
 2003 rules Reg 23 CS(MCP) Regs
18 **2012 rules** Reg 27A(3) CSMC Regs
 2003 rules Reg 9B(3) SS&CS(DA) Regs
19 **2012 rules** Regs 24(1) and 25(1) CSMC Regs
 2003 rules Reg 23(1) CS(MCP) Regs
20 **2012 rules** Reg 24(2) CSMC Regs
 2003 rules Reg 23(4) CS(MCP) Regs
21 **2012 rules** Reg 25(2) CSMC Regs
 2003 rules Reg 23(2) CS(MCP) Regs
22 **2012 rules** Reg 24(2) CSMC Regs
 2003 rules Reg 23(4) CS(MCP) Regs
23 **2012 rules** Reg 25(3) CSMC Regs
 2003 rules Reg 23(3) CS(MCP) Regs

4. When the first calculation begins

24 Reg 1(2) CS(MCP) Regs
25 *The Child Support Maintenance Calculation Regulations 2012: a technical consultation on the draft regulations,* CMEC, December 2011
26 Regs 7, 11 and 12 CSMC Regs
27 Reg 12 CSMC Regs
28 Regs 1(2) and 25(3) and (4) CS(MCP) Regs
29 Reg 2 CS(MCP) Regs
30 Reg 25(2) CS(MCP) Regs
31 Reg 4(3) CS(MCP) Regs
32 Reg 26 CS(MCP) Regs
33 Reg 28 CS(MCP) Regs
34 Reg 8A CS(MAJ) Regs

5. When a calculation ends

35 ss4(5) and (6) and 7(6) and (7) CSA 1991
36 Sch 1 para 16 CSA 1991
37 s44(1) CSA 1991
38 *SM v CMEC* [2010] UKUT 435 (AAC); *GR v CMEC* [2011] UKUT 101 (AAC)
39 Reg 18(3) CSMC Regs
40 Sch 3D para 3(b) SS&CS(DA) Regs
41 Sch 3D para 3(c) SS&CS(DA) Regs
42 Sch 3D, para 3(a) SS&CS(DA) Regs
43 Sch 1 para 16(1)(c) CSA 1991
44 s16(3) CSA 1991
45 s17(4) CSA 1991
46 **2012 rules** Regs 24(2) and 27 CSMC Regs
   2003 rules Reg 15C(4) and (5) SS&CS(DA) Regs
47 **2012 rules** Reg 27(2) CSMC Regs
   2003 rules Reg 15C(5)(b) SS&CS(DA) Regs; reg 24 CS(MCP) Regs
48 Sch 1 para 16(5) CSA 1991; reg 7(1) CS(MAJ) Regs; reg 32A(1) CS(MAP) Regs
49 Sch 1 para 16(7) CSA 1991
50 Reg 32B CS(MAP) Regs
51 Reg 33(5) CS(MAP) Regs

Chapter 12

Revisions and supersessions

This chapter covers:
1. Changing decisions (below)
2. Revisions (p217)
3. Supersessions (p223)

This chapter covers the rules on when a decision can be revised or superseded, and the date from which a supersession takes effect, for '2012 rules' and '2003 rules' cases. While revisions and supersessions of '1993 rules' cases are broadly similar, there are some small differences.[1]

For information on revisions and supersessions outstanding at conversion of a '1993 rules' case to the '2003 rules', or revisions or supersessions of conversion decisions, see Chapter 10 of the 2013/14 edition of this *Handbook*.

1. Changing decisions

Most decisions can be changed or challenged by revision or supersession. However, there are some decisions that cannot (see p215).

From 23 March 2015, the Child Maintenance Service (CMS) or Child Support Agency (CSA) can also correct at any time an accidental error in a decision or in the record of a decision. The correction is then treated as part of the record of the decision.[2]

A supersession or revision is a decision that changes an earlier decision. As with all decisions, they are made by officials who work for the CMS/CSA and who make decisions on behalf of the Secretary of State for Work and Pensions. A revision or supersession normally happens because the CMS/CSA is told that something is wrong or has changed since the initial decision was made. The CMS/CSA itself may also initiate a revision or supersession.

The table on p214 shows when decisions are revised and superseded. The main difference between a revision and supersession is:
- a revision means the decision which is wrong or has been challenged is itself changed, and the revised decision normally takes effect from the date the original decision had effect;

- a supersession means that a new decision is made that takes effect from a later date.

If a decision is challenged within 30 days ('2012 rules') or one month ('2003 rules') of the decision (or of the date an accidental error in the decision was corrected), it may be revised. Outside this time period, a decision can only be revised if a late application for revision is accepted (see p219), or in special circumstances where the original decision was wrong in such a way that it can be revised at any time – eg, if there has been official error (see p220). If these special circumstances are not met, the decision may be superseded instead.

If the original decision is not incorrect, but the CMS/CSA has not dealt with the case properly in some way, a complaint can be made at any time (see Chapter 15). In some cases where the original decision is wrong (eg, where maladministration has led to an official error), it may be appropriate to make a complaint as well as applying for the decision to be revised.

Revisions and supersessions

Why is the decision being challenged?	When?	What can be done?
The decision is wrong for any reason.	Within 30 days ('2012 rules') or one month ('2003 rules') of being told the decision.	The decision can be revised.
The CMS/CSA made a mistake ('official error'), was misled, did not know about something that would have affected the decision or someone was not a parent of a child to whom a calculation relates.	At any time.	The decision can be revised. If the CMS/CSA did not know something or was misled, the decision can only be revised in certain circumstances (see p217). If these do not apply, the decision can be superseded.
The decision is wrong for any reason (other than one of the reasons in the above row).	More than than 30 days ('2012 rules') or one month ('2003 rules') after being told the decision.	The decision may be superseded, but the person can make a late application for a revision to be considered (see p219).
Something that affects the decision has changed.	At any time.	The decision can be superseded.

Variations are an element of the child support calculation. This means that any change relating to a variation can lead to a revision or supersession of the calculation. See Chapter 7 for variations under the '2012 rules' and Chapter 9 for variations under the '2003 rules'.

For changing decisions on deductions of child support from benefits, see CPAG's *Welfare Benefits and Tax Credits Handbook*.

Decisions of the First-tier Tribunal and the Upper Tribunal (see Chapter 13) (and of an appeal tribunal or child support commissioner before 3 November 2008) can also be superseded or revised, but only in certain circumstances (see p218 and p224).

If a non-resident parent thinks the revision or supersession may reduce the amount of the calculation, s/he may try to negotiate lower payments pending the decision, although this is usually difficult (see p284).

Challenging decisions that cannot be revised or superseded

Decisions that cannot be revised or superseded are mainly in the areas of information gathering, collection and enforcement (including decisions about fees), and in other circumstances, such as refusals to make an interim or default maintenance decision.

The CMS/CSA can be given further information and asked to reconsider. If the CMS/CSA refuses to change the decision, a complaint can be made. An accidental error in a decision or in the record of a decision can also be corrected at any time.[3]

There may be other occasions that do not involve a decision, but where the behaviour of CMS/CSA staff or others is unsatisfactory – eg, if there is intimidating or unnecessarily intrusive questioning, or unwarranted demands for evidence and documentation. In these cases, a complaint can be made (see Chapter 15).

Some decisions on the enforcement of arrears cannot be revised or superseded, but can be appealed to a court (see p293).

Judicial review

Judicial review is the legal procedure that allows a court to examine the way in which a public body has exercised its discretionary decision-making power to ensure that it has done so for the lawful purpose of the power.[4] A person affected by a decision or action of a public body or one of its officers can ask the High Court (or Court of Session in Scotland) to carry out a judicial review of the decision or action.

A judicial review looks at the validity of the process by which a decision was made rather than the actual result of the decision.

The court can 'set aside' the decision and can also order the public body which made the decision to consider it again in a lawful way. Judicial review cannot usually be brought if there is a right to raise the issue in an appeal to the First-tier Tribunal, Upper Tribunal or court. Otherwise, judicial review of a CMS/CSA decision (eg, on enforcement) may be sought. Legal advice *must* be taken as soon as possible after the decision is made.

In England and Wales, an application must be made to the High Court promptly and, in any event, within three months of the decision being challenged.[5] In Scotland, there is currently no time limit, but an application should be made as soon as possible.[6] **Note:** a time limit of three months (or a longer time if the Court of Session considers it equitable in the circumstances), and a requirement to seek the court's permission before making an application, will be introduced in Scotland with effect from 22 September 2015.[7]

Judicial review of a child support decision may succeed if:[8]

- the CMS/CSA makes an error in law ('illegality') – eg, does something it has no power to do; *or*
- the CMS/CSA fails to have regard to a relevant matter or has regard to an irrelevant matter, or where a decision is 'so outrageous in its defiance of logic or of accepted moral standards that no sensible person who had considered the question could have arrived at it' (irrationality); *or*
- there has been procedural unfairness.

Challenging decisions about benefit entitlement

Some CMS/CSA decisions depend on a decision of another part of the Department for Work and Pensions (DWP). For example, a non-resident parent in receipt of income support, income-based jobseeker's allowance, income-related employment and support allowance, universal credit calculated on the basis that s/he has no earned income, or the guarantee credit of pension credit pays the flat rate ('2012 rules' and '2003 rules' – see p91 and p133) or the minimum rate ('1993 rules' – see p194) of child support. Provided the DWP pays one of these benefits, even if the non-resident parent has other income, there can be no application for a variation on additional income grounds (see p168). A parent who believes that the other parent should not be allowed to claim a benefit (eg, because s/he is working full time) cannot directly challenge a DWP decision to award it, but can raise the issue with the CMS/CSA, which contacts the other part of the DWP, which then investigates. The result is reported to the CMS/CSA, but not to the person who made the allegation. That person cannot appeal to the First-tier Tribunal against the DWP decision,[9] although a judicial review could be sought.

---

2. **Revisions**

The Child Maintenance Service (CMS) or Child Support Agency (CSA) can revise a decision if:

- a person applies within 30 days ('2012 rules') or one month ('2003 rules') of the decision (or of the date an accidental error in the decision or in the record of the decision was corrected); *or*
- a person applies for a variation within 30 days/one month, provided the grounds for variation existed from the date of the decision under revision; *or*
- if the CMS/CSA initiates the revision within 30 days/one month of the original decision.

The CMS/CSA can also revise a decision if a person applies for, and is granted, an extension of time (see p219). In addition, there are certain situations in which the original decision was wrong in such a way that it can be revised at any time (see p219). A revised decision normally takes effect from the date the original decision had effect.

For most decisions made on or after 28 October 2013, an appeal to the First-tier Tribunal can only be made if an application for a revision has first been requested. The CMS/CSA calls this '**mandatory reconsideration**' (see p235). See previous editions of this *Handbook* for the rules if mandatory reconsideration does not apply. The CMS/CSA provides a notice of the result of the request for a revision (a '**mandatory reconsideration notice**'), which must be sent to the First-tier Tribunal with the appeal.

Note: from 23 March 2015, the CMS/CSA can correct an accidental error in a decision or in the record of a decision at any time.[10] A mandatory reconsideration of the corrected decision must be requested before an appeal to the First-tier Tribunal can be made. Previously, if the CMS/CSA agreed to correct an accidental error, this was done by a revision, meaning that an appeal could be made to the First-tier Tribunal against the corrected decision straight away without the need for a further revision.

Decisions that can be revised

Most child support decisions can be revised, including:[11]

- a decision made by the CMS/CSA that makes a calculation (including a variation on a calculation), an interim decision or a default maintenance decision;
- a CMS/CSA decision not to make a calculation, unless it has made an interim or default maintenance decision instead (in which case, it is that decision which can be revised). A refusal to make an interim or default maintenance decision cannot be revised;[12]

- a decision of the First-tier Tribunal (or of an appeal tribunal before 3 November 2008) to make, or refuse to agree, a variation to a calculation following a referral by the CMS/CSA;[13]
- any supersession decision made by the CMS/CSA (see p223);[14]
- a decision which has previously been revised if any of the above circumstances apply to the revised decision.[15]

When a decision can be revised

The CMS/CSA can revise a decision on any grounds if, within 30 days ('2012 rules') or one month ('2003 rules') of notification of the decision (or of the notification that an accidental error in the decision or in the record of the decision has been corrected):[16]

- it starts action leading to a revision; *or*
- a person (person with care, non-resident parent or child applicant in Scotland) applies for a revision; *or*
- a person applies for a variation.

'**Month**' means a complete calendar month from the date of notification.[17]

Days falling before the date an accidental error is corrected do not count towards the time limit.[18] If the 30-day/one-month time limit is missed, a person can ask for a late application to be accepted (see below).[19]

At any time outside this 30-day/one-month period, the CMS/CSA can revise a decision if:

- an appeal is made in time (or within the time allowed for late appeals if the application meets those conditions) and the appeal has not yet been determined.[20] If an appeal is lodged, the CMS/CSA checks to see whether the decision should be revised;
- there has been 'official error' (see p220);[21]
- the decision is wrong because of a misrepresentation or failure to disclose a material fact (see p221) and, because of this, the decision is more advantageous to the person who misrepresented or failed to disclose than it would otherwise have been;[22]
- it is an interim maintenance decision or default maintenance decision;[23]
- the decision is wrong because a person with respect to whom the child support calculation has been made was not, at the time the calculation was made, a parent of a child to whom the calculation relates;[24]
- the person applied for a revision within a month of the decision (or correction of an accidental error in the decision or in the record of the decision) but it was refused because there was insufficient information or evidence to carry out a revision and the person has provided the further information within a month (or such longer period as is reasonable in the circumstances) of being notified of the refusal. **Note:** this ground is stated for the '2003 rules', but not

specifically provided for in the '2012 rules'.[25] In a '2012 rules' case, the CMS may allow a person more time to provide information. (If no statutory timescale applies, the CMS generally allows 14 days to provide information and extends this to 16 days to allow for the time taken to reach the CMS by post.) Otherwise, the CMS could still revise the decision if it accepts a late application for revision (see below).

If the CMS/CSA makes a decision which is appealed and, while that appeal is pending the CMS/CSA makes a second decision on the same case, when the First-tier Tribunal decides the appeal on the first decision, the CMS/CSA can revise its second decision at any time if it would have been made differently had the CMS/CSA known about the First-tier Tribunal's decision.[26] For example, if a non-resident parent's income is calculated in a particular way in the first decision, a second decision is likely to follow that also. If the First-tier Tribunal changes that for the first decision, the second decision can be revised at any time.

Under the '2012 rules', the CMS can also revise a decision at any time if the information on historic income (or unearned income for the purposes of a variation) given to it by HM Revenue and Customs (HMRC) has since been amended.[27]

A decision cannot be revised because of a change in circumstances after the date the decision was made, or because of an expected change.[28] Instead, the decision may be superseded (see p223) or a new application should be made.

For revisions of default maintenance decisions, see p205.

Under the test case rules (see p260), the CMS/CSA may refuse to follow the law as decided by the Upper Tribunal or the courts, or even suspend a decision on revision while an appeal is being brought in another case.

Late applications

Because a supersession (see p223) cannot usually lead to a decision being backdated to the original effective date, a late application for a revision may need to be made. However, in case it is not accepted, an application for a supersession can be made at the same time, if appropriate. For example, a decision may be based on the wrong mortgage payment details. If the person concerned missed the deadline for applying for a revision, s/he can make a late application (giving special reasons – see p220) and also apply for a supersession on the grounds that there has been a mistake of fact (see p224).

The CMS/CSA can extend the 30-day/one-month period for applying for a revision if it considers that:[29]

- the application has merit; *and*
- it was not practicable to apply within the time limit because of 'special circumstances' (see p220); *and*
- it is reasonable to grant the application.

'Special circumstances' are not defined, but they are not the same as the special circumstances needed for the CMS/CSA to accept a late appeal (see p238).

In '2003 rules' cases, the person applying for a revision must apply for an extension within 13 months of the notification.[30] However, if s/he has asked for written reasons for the decision s/he is seeking to revise, the 13 months can be extended. If the statement of reasons is provided within one month of the notification of the decision, the 13-month period is extended by 14 days. If the statement of reasons is provided after one month, the 13 months plus 14 days run from the date it is provided.[31] These rules do not apply to '2012 rules' cases; there is no absolute time limit for seeking a revision under the '2012 rules'. When the CMS/CSA is considering a late application, no account is taken of days falling before the correction of an accidental error in a decision or in the record of a decision.[32]

The longer the delay in applying for a revision, the more compelling the special circumstances must be.[33]

An application for an extension must identify the decision that it seeks to revise and explain why an extension should be granted.[34]

An application that is refused may not be renewed,[35] although the CMS/CSA may have power to reconsider a refusal to extend.[36] There is no right of appeal against a refusal to allow a late application for a revision. If a late application for a revision is refused, the CMS/CSA considers whether the decision can be revised on one of the grounds on which a decision can be revised at any time or whether it can be superseded.[37]

Judicial review of a refusal to extend the time limit for making a revision may also be possible (see p215).

Official error

'Official error' is a mistake made by an officer of the CMS/CSA, another part of the Department for Work and Pensions, HMRC or a designated authority, which was not caused, or contributed to, by anyone outside these bodies.[38] This includes mistakes of law (see p226), except those only shown to be an error by a decision of the Upper Tribunal or court, as well as mistakes of fact, such as:

- a mistake of arithmetic;
- a wrong assumption about a person's circumstances where there was no evidence for it;
- a mistake made because CMS/CSA staff did not pass information or evidence to the officer who made the decision, when they should have done.

Note: if the official error appears to be an accidental error (eg, a mistake of arithmetic), the CMS/CSA can be asked to correct this. The CMS/CSA can correct an accidental error in a decision, or in the record of a decision, at any time. If the CMS/CSA does this, the time limit for requesting a revision of the decision begins from the date of the correction.[39]

Misrepresentation and failure to disclose

A **'misrepresentation'** is a written or spoken statement of fact which is untrue.[40] This applies to an untrue statement, even if the person making it believes it to be true.[41]

There is only a **'failure to disclose'** a fact if there is a legal duty to report that fact to the CMS/CSA.[42] Therefore, a person who is asked to give information, but does not, has failed to disclose that information. However, if a person is not asked for the information, there can be no failure to disclose unless it is one of the facts that a parent with care or non-resident parent must always report. There is no general duty to report all changes of circumstances to the CMS/CSA, but there are some changes which must be reported (see p73).

The decision that the CMS/CSA wishes to revise must have been wrong because of a fact that was misrepresented or not disclosed and was more advantageous to the person who misrepresented or failed to disclose.[43] Therefore, if the CMS/CSA ignored that fact or if that fact made no difference, it cannot base a revision on misrepresentation or failure to disclose.

Example 12.1

When Amy applied for child support under the '2003 rules', she also applied for a variation on the grounds that Shaun had assets over £65,000. However, the variation was not agreed and her calculation was made without this element, based on the information Shaun provided. A few months later, Amy discovers that Shaun had inherited a property from his aunt a few weeks before her application. She informs the CSA, it investigates and confirms that he failed to disclose this when he was asked to provide information for the variation element. Because he failed to disclose the inheritance, his calculation is less than it would have been with the variation element. Since there was a failure to disclose that resulted in a decision that was more advantageous to him, the CSA revises the original calculation.

However, had Shaun inherited the property some time after he was asked for information in relation to the variation application, the CSA could not decide that he had failed to disclose information. In this case, the child support calculation could not be revised, but it may be superseded if Amy asks for a variation to be considered.

Procedure for revising

A notification of a decision sets out how to ask the CMS/CSA to revise that decision.[44] The request may be made by telephone. However, unless the issue is straightforward, it is best to follow up any telephone call with a letter to the CMS/CSA, confirming the reason for the request.

There is no general requirement for the CMS/CSA to notify the parties that it is considering a revision or to inform one party that the other has applied for a revision. However, if an application for variation has passed preliminary consideration[45] or there is a request for a revision of a calculation with a previously agreed variation,[46] the other parties are usually contacted and asked for their representations.

The rules about disclosure apply to the information given in any notification (see p74).

If a revision has been requested, the burden of proof is on the applicant.[47] In cases where a revision is sought within 30 days ('2012 rules') or one month ('2003 rules') or a late application is accepted, a person does not have to show any specific grounds for the revision. It is enough that s/he simply thinks that the decision is wrong, although a full explanation of reasons for seeking the revision, and any supporting information or evidence, should always be provided.

If the applicant in a '2003 rules' case fails to provide sufficient information or evidence to make a decision, the CSA notifies her/him of this. S/he may be invited to reapply, usually within one month of this notification, providing sufficient information or evidence. The time limit may be extended if the CSA considers this reasonable.[48] These rules do not specifically apply to '2012 rules' cases. However, the CMS may allow a person more time to provide information. Otherwise, the CMS could still revise the decision if it accepts a late application for revision (see p219).

The CMS/CSA may decide to:
- revise the decision; *or*
- make a default maintenance decision; *or*
- refuse to revise the decision.

If a default decision would be less than the current calculation, the CMS/CSA may refuse to revise rather than make a default decision. For further information on default maintenance decisions, see p204.

If an appeal has been lodged (see Chapter 13) following a mandatory reconsideration decision, the CMS/CSA can still consider whether the decision should be revised. If it is revised and the revised decision is more advantageous for the person appealing (the appellant), the appeal lapses.[49] The appellant can then decide to appeal against the revised decision within the usual time limits. The CMS/CSA should try to inform all the relevant people that the appeal has lapsed.[50] If the revised decision does not benefit the appellant, it is still carried out and the appeal does not lapse but continues against the decision as revised.[51]

The revised decision

The revised decision normally has the same effective date as the decision it replaces.[52] However, if the effective date of that decision was wrong, the revised decision has the effective date that the replaced decision should have had.[53]

Notification

If the decision is revised, whether or not this results in a fresh or new calculation (including a default maintenance decision), the parties must be notified of the decision and given the usual details (see p205).[54] If there is more than one person with care in relation to a non-resident parent, this means all of them must be notified. The normal rules on information disclosure apply (see p74).[55]

If the request for revision is refused, the notification of the decision must include reasons for the refusal and details of appeal rights.

The time limit for appealing against a decision that has been revised runs from the date of the notice of the revised decision. If the request for a revision is refused, the time limit for appealing runs from the date on which this refusal is notified, provided the request was made within 30 days ('2012 rules') or a month ('2003 rules') of the original decision being notified, or from the date a late application for revision was accepted.[56]

3. **Supersessions**

The Child Maintenance Service (CMS) or Child Support Agency (CSA) can supersede a decision at any time, with or without an application, if certain rules are met. Usually a decision is superseded because of a change in circumstances. The main difference between a revision and a supersession is that a superseded decision generally takes effect from the date on which it is made, whereas a revision generally takes effect from the effective date of the decision being revised. However, there are numerous exceptions to this general rule. There is no general duty to tell the CMS/CSA of all changes of circumstances. See p73 for the changes that must be notified.

Cases under the '**2012 rules**' are likely to be subject to regular supersession. See Chapter 6 for the rules about annual reviews and periodic current income checks.

Cases under the '**2003 rules**' and '**1993 rules**' are not automatically reviewed at intervals. If a supersession has not been carried out, the calculation or assessment may have been in place for several years and be based on circumstances that may have since changed.

Decisions that can be superseded

Most child support decisions (whether made by the CMS/CSA, the First-tier Tribunal or the Upper Tribunal, or by an appeal tribunal or the child support commissioners before 3 November 2008) can be superseded.

Decisions that can be superseded include:[57]

- a decision to make a child support calculation (including a variation on a calculation), an interim decision or a default maintenance decision (see p205);

- a decision of a First-tier Tribunal on a CMS/CSA referral of a variation application;
- any decisions made on revision (see p217).

It may also be possible to supersede other CMS/CSA decisions, depending on how the CMS/CSA (or the First-tier Tribunal or Upper Tribunal) interprets the rules. For decisions which may be revised, see p217.

When a decision can be superseded

The CMS/CSA can *normally* supersede a decision if:[58]
- there has been a relevant change of circumstances since the decision had effect, or it is expected that there will be such a change, and there would be a significant change in the amount of the calculation;
- the decision was made in ignorance of, or was based on a mistake about, a material fact; *or*
- there is an application for a variation to the calculation.

A decision made by the CMS/CSA can also be superseded if it is wrong in law (see p226). If a person thinks that a decision of the First-tier Tribunal or Upper Tribunal is wrong in law, s/he must appeal against it.[59]

Any information or evidence on which a superseding decision is to be based must be known to the CMS/CSA and not be based on supposition.[60] If a change of circumstances has taken place, or is expected, this must be based on fact and not on probability.

When the CMS/CSA is notified of a change of circumstances, it does not have to consider anything not raised by the application (or, if the CMS/CSA is acting on its own initiative, anything which did not cause it to act).[61] This means that it does not have to investigate whether all the other circumstances are still correct. However, the CMS/CSA might decide to incorporate the supersession action into a case check, which could result in other changes or errors being identified, and subsequent revisions or supersessions being carried out.

Under the test case rules, the CMS/CSA may refuse to follow the law as decided by the Upper Tribunal or courts, or even suspend a decision on supersession, while an appeal is being brought in another case. See p260 for details.

When a decision cannot be superseded

The CMS/CSA cannot supersede a decision:
- which can be revised instead (see p217);[62]
- refusing to make or cancelling a child support calculation.[63] A further application for a calculation should be made instead.

In a '2012 rules' case in which gross income is determined on the basis of current income (see Chapter 6), a decision cannot be superseded on the basis that there has been, or it is anticipated that there will be, a change of circumstances relating to the current income of the non-resident parent, unless there is a change of 25 per cent or more in the current income.[64] This 'tolerance level' does not apply if the superseding decision:[65]

- is made by the CMS as part of an annual review of gross income or a periodic check of current income;
- is made because of an error of law; *or*
- supersedes a calculation decision that was based on an estimate of current income.

In a '2003 rules' case, a decision cannot be superseded on the basis that there has been, or it is anticipated that there will be, a change of circumstances relating to the net income of the non-resident parent unless there is a change of 5 per cent or more in the net income used in the calculation.[66] However, this 'tolerance level' does not apply if the superseding decision:[67]

- is on the outcome of a variation application;
- affects a variation ground in a calculation, or a revised/superseded decision on this;
- is made on an interim maintenance decision, or on the revised/superseded decision;
- is made by the CSA acting on its own initiative on the basis of information or evidence which was also the basis of a Department for Work and Pensions decision on a benefit claim or a revision or supersession of a decision on a claim for or an award of benefit;[68]
- is made following an application on more than one ground, and the grounds that do not relate to the net income of the non-resident parent lead to a superseding decision. The change in income can also be taken into account.[69]

A different 'tolerance level' applies to supersessions in **'1993 rules' cases**. See the 2002/03 edition of this *Handbook* for further information.

For all cases, the tolerance rules are not applied to other changes of circumstances – eg:

- relevant children joining or leaving the household;
- applications for other qualifying children;
- changes in shared-care arrangements;
- changes notified by a third party – eg, Jobcentre Plus;
- if the person with care, non-resident parent or qualifying child are no longer habitually resident in the UK; *or*
- if the person with care and non-resident parent start living together.

In '2003 rules' cases, if an application for a supersession is made to which the tolerance rule would apply and a further application is then made on a ground(s) that does not relate to the net income of the non-resident parent, a superseding decision can be made as if the two applications had been made at the same time – ie, so that the change in income can be taken into account.[70]

In '2003 rules' cases, if the tolerance rule is satisfied (ie, net income changes by 5 per cent or more), the CSA makes decisions on additional changes of circumstances without applying the tolerance rule to each of the further changes.[71]

In '2012 rules' cases, the CMS intends calculations to remain in place for a reasonable period. In many cases, the calculation is likely to remain in place for the year ahead.

Wrong in law

A decision that is wrong in law can constitute an official error and also be grounds for a revision (see p220). A decision is wrong in law if:[72]

- when making it, the CMS/CSA misinterpreted or overlooked part or all of an Act of Parliament, a regulation or relevant caselaw;
- there is no evidence to support it;
- the facts are such that no reasonable person applying the law could have come to such a conclusion;
- there is a breach of 'natural justice' – ie, the procedure used has led to unfairness, or the officer who took the decision appeared to be biased;[73]
- the CMS/CSA has not given sufficient reasons for the decision;
- when exercising its discretion, the CMS/CSA took into account something irrelevant or ignored something relevant – eg, the welfare of the child (see p27).[74]

A decision is wrong in law if the regulation under which it is made was not made lawfully. Such a regulation is said to be *ultra vires* (outside the powers). The courts and tribunals can decide that a regulation is *ultra vires*,[75] and the First-tier and Upper Tribunals have done so in benefit cases.

A decision is also wrong in law if it is contrary to European law – ie, European Union (EU) law and the European Convention on Human Rights (ECHR). EU law will rarely be relevant to child support issues. Caselaw has established that European law on the equal treatment of men and women in social security matters does not apply to child support.[76]

ECHR law is more likely to be relevant. The CMS/CSA, courts and the First-tier and Upper Tribunals are required to interpret Acts of Parliament consistently with the ECHR as far as possible.[77] They cannot use the ECHR to overrule an Act of Parliament, but the courts can issue a 'declaration of incompatability'.[78] Courts and tribunals can override regulations which are incompatible with the provisions of the ECHR. It is unlawful for the CMS/CSA, courts or tribunals to act in a way which is incompatible with an ECHR right.[79] In practice, however, few challenges using these principles have succeeded.

Procedure for superseding

A party to the calculation can apply for a supersession at any time. There are no time limits, but any superseding decision runs from the date on which ('2012 rules') or the beginning of the maintenance period in which ('2003 rules') the application is made, unless one of the special situations described on p228 applies.[80] If an application is made, the CMS/CSA must consider it and supersede if the conditions set out above are met.

The CMS/CSA itself can initiate a supersession. It must take into account the welfare of the child (see p27) when considering whether or not to do so. The CMS/CSA learns of some changes automatically from Jobcentre Plus or may do so from a third party.

If the CSA is considering a supersession on its own initiative in a '2003 rules' case, it must notify the relevant parties – ie, the person with care, non-resident parent and a child applicant in Scotland.[81] The supersession cannot take effect until 28 days after this notice has been given, unless it is a decision based on information which was also used to make a benefit decision.[82] This rule does not apply to '2012 rules' cases.

If the supersession is in relation to an application for a variation that has passed preliminary consideration (see p174),[83] or a supersession of a previously agreed variation,[84] the other relevant parties are contacted and notified of the grounds of the application and any relevant information or evidence the applicant has given. They are not told details of any long-term illness or disability of a relevant other child (if the application for variation was made on that basis), or harmful medical evidence or the address of a relevant person or qualifying child if that would cause a risk of harm or undue distress.[85]

Otherwise, the other party may not be notified of the application for a supersession. The normal rules about disclosure apply to the information given in any notification (see p74).[86]

The CMS/CSA does not have to check all the facts again and so can just consider the issues raised in the application.[87] An application for a supersession should, therefore, include all available information and evidence that supports the case for the decision to be changed. Information provided may need to be verified in the normal way (see Chapter 4). Remember that some changes will not lead to a supersession because of the 'tolerance rules' (see p224).

The superseding decision

The CMS/CSA may decide that:
- there are no grounds for supersession and so refuse to supersede;
- there are grounds for supersession, but the calculation remains unchanged;
- there are grounds for supersession and the calculation is changed; *or*
- the calculation should be cancelled.

Effective date of the superseding decision

The general rule is that a supersession takes effect from the day on which ('2012 rules') or the first day in the maintenance period in which ('2003 rules') the decision is made or the application for the supersession/variation was made.[88] However, the effective date may be different in certain circumstances, as shown in the table below. This does not cover all circumstances in which a calculation is cancelled (see p208). The rules about the effective date for supersessions in '1993 rules' cases are a little different and are not covered in this table.

Circumstances	Effective date
'2012 rules' cases only	
Gross income is based on current income and the non-resident parent is required to report a change because current income has changed by at least 25 per cent.	The day on which the change occurred.[89]
There is a new qualifying child in relation to the non-resident parent.	The day that would be the initial effective date (ie, two days after the day on which written notification would be sent to the non-resident parent) if a new application were made for that child, if there were no calculation already in force.[90]
The application is made by one of the parties.	The day the application is received by the CMS.[91]
The CMS has acted on its own initiative.	If the CMS acts on the basis of information provided by a third party, the day that information is provided.[92] In any other case, the day on which the decision is made.[93]
'2012 rules' and '2003 rules' cases	
An application for an anticipated change in circumstances.	The first day in the maintenance period in which/day on which the change is expected to occur.[94]
The relevant circumstance is that a variation ground is expected to occur.	The first day in the maintenance period in which/day on which the ground is expected to occur.[95]
A qualifying child dies or ceases to be a qualifying child.	The first day in the maintenance period in which/day on which the change occurred.[96]

A relevant other child (or, for '2012 rules' cases, a child supported under other maintenance arrangements) dies or ceases to be a qualifying child for child support purposes.	The first day in the maintenance period in which/day on which the change occurred.[97]
A person with care ceases to be a person with care in relation to a qualifying child.	The first day in the maintenance period in which/day on which the change occurred.[98]
A person with care, non-resident parent or a qualifying child ceases to be habitually resident in the UK.	The first day in the maintenance period in which/day on which the change occurred.[99]
A non-resident parent (or her/his partner) becomes or stops being entitled to a benefit that qualifies her/him for the flat rate.	The first day in the maintenance period in which/day on which the change occurred.[100]
The CMS/CSA is superseding a decision of the First-tier Tribunal or the Upper Tribunal given following the CMS/CSA's having served notice that a test case which could have affected that decision was pending before the Upper Tribunal or a court.	The beginning of the maintenance period following the date on which/day on which the decision of the First-tier Tribunal or Upper Tribunal would have taken effect had it been decided in accordance with the decision in the test case.[101]
The CMS/CSA is superseding a decision of the First-tier Tribunal or the Upper Tribunal (or a decision of an appeal tribunal or the child support commissioners made before 3 November 2008) on the ground that it is wrong because of a misrepresentation about, or a failure to disclose, a material fact, and the decision is more advantageous to the person who misrepresented or failed to disclose than it would otherwise have been but for that error.	The date on which the First-tier Tribunal or Upper Tribunal (or appeal tribunal or child support commissioner) decision took, or was to take, effect.[102]
A decision of the CMS/CSA is superseded because it is shown to have been wrong as a result of an Upper Tribunal or court decision in which the CMS/CSA lost.	The date of the relevant Upper Tribunal or court decision.[103]

'2003 rules' cases only

A non-resident parent starts to be liable, or stops being liable, to pay for half of the flat rate – ie: – her/his partner is also a non-resident parent; *and* – there is a child support application in force in respect of the partner; *and* – either s/he or her/his partner receive income support, income-based job-seeker's allowance, income-related em-ployment and support allowance, universal credit calculated on the basis that the non-resident parent has no earned income, or pension credit.	The first day in the maintenance period in which the change occurred.[104]
The CSA has acted on its own initiative.	If the CSA acts on information or evidence which also led Jobcentre Plus or the Pension Service to make a decision on a claim for or an award of benefit, the effective date is the first day in the maintenance period in which the CSA became aware of the information or evidence.[105] In all other cases, the decision takes effect from the first day of the maintenance period which includes the date 28 days after the date on which notice that the CSA is proposing to supersede is given to the relevant persons.[106]
There is a further qualifying child in relation to the same non-resident parent and person with care.	If this is brought to the attention of the CSA by the non-resident parent, the first day of the maintenance period in which the CSA is told about the child.[107] If this is brought to the attention of the CSA by the person with care, the first day of the maintenance period in which the non-resident parent is given notification of the application for that child.[108]

A non-resident parent has another qualifying child with a different parent with care and an application for child support is made by either the non-resident parent or the new parent with care.	The beginning of the maintenance period in which notification of the calculation is given to the non-resident parent.[109]
A non-resident parent or person with care applies for a supersession and the CSA decides when superseding that different amounts of child support need to be calculated in respect of different specified periods.	The beginning of the maintenance period in which the change of circumstances to which the calculation relates occurred or is expected to occur, unless that change occurred before the date of the application for supersession and was notified after that date. In which case, the effective date is the beginning of the maintenance period in which the application for supersession is made.[110]

Notification

If the decision results in a supersession, whether or not a new calculation is made (including an interim maintenance decision or default maintenance decision), the parties must be notified of the decision and given the usual details (see p205).[111] The notice must also state how to seek a revision, supersession and appeal.[112]

If the decision is to refuse to supersede, notification is given, including the reasons for refusal and rights to challenge the decision.[113]

A party can ask for a supersession decision to be revised and can then, if the decision is one against which there is a right of appeal, appeal to the First-tier Tribunal (see Chapter 13). **Note:** in most cases, an appeal against a decision can only be made if the CMS/CSA has first considered an application for a revision (a 'mandatory reconsideration' – see p235).

If the CMS/CSA intends to cancel the case, it must notify each party and, if the reason for cancellation is a child applicant in Scotland's ceasing to be a qualifying child, inform other potential child applicants.[114]

Whether to request supersession

Before requesting a supersession because of a change of circumstances, a parent may wish to work out whether a fresh calculation would be to her/his advantage. Unless it is a change that must be reported to the CMS/CSA (see p73), s/he need only tell the CMS/CSA about the changes in her/his favour. If the change only relates to one party, the CMS/CSA may not tell the other person; but if it does, that party might tell the CMS/CSA about other changes. These may cancel out the effect of the changes which led the other to ask for a supersession.

If a person believes that another person's circumstances have changed (eg, a non-resident parent no longer has children living with her/him), s/he can ask for a supersession and for the CMS/CSA to investigate (see Chapter 4). The CMS/CSA does not have to, but any changes it is aware of must be taken into account when it decides whether or not to supersede.

Notes

1 Regs 17-24 CS(MAP) Regs contain the detailed rules on supersessions and revisions for 1993 rules cases.

1. Changing decisions
2 **2012 rules** Reg 27A CSMC Regs
2003 rules Reg 9B SS&CS(DA) Regs
3 **2012 rules** Reg 27A CSMC Regs
2003 rules Reg 9B SS&CS(DA) Regs
4 *West v Secretary of State for Scotland*, 1992 SC 385, 1992 SLT 636 (reported as *West v Scottish Prison Service*, 1992 SCLR 504)
5 r54.5 Civil Procedure Rules
6 See *Hanlon v Traffic Commission* [1988] SLT 802 and *Perfect Swivel v Dundee District Licensing Board* (No.2) [1993] SLT 112
7 s89 Courts Reform (Scotland) Act 2014, inserting s27A into the Court of Session Act 1988; Art 4 Courts Reform (Scotland) Act 2014 (Commencement No.3, Transitional and Saving Provisions) Order 2015, No.247
8 *Council of Civil Service Unions v Minister for the Civil Service* [1984] 1 WLR 1174, [1984] 3 All ER 935
9 s12(2) SSA 1998; reg 25 SS&CS(DA) Regs

2. Revisions
10 **2012 rules** Reg 27A(1) CSMC Regs
2003 rules Reg 9B(1) SS&CS(DA) Regs
11 s16 CSA 1991
12 Reg 3A(8) and (9) SS&CS(DA) Regs
13 Reg 3A(3) SS&CS(DA) Regs

14 s16(1A)(a) CSA 1991 and reg 3A(3) SS&CS(DA) Regs
15 Reg 3A(3) SS&CS(DA) Regs
16 **2012 rules** Reg 14(1)(a) and (d) CSMC Regs
2003 rules Reg 3A(1)(a) and (d) SS&CS(DA) Regs
17 R(IB) 4/02
18 **2012 rules** Reg 27A(4) CSMC Regs
2003 rules Reg 9B(4) SS&CS(DA) Regs
19 **2012 rules** Reg 15 CSMC Regs
2003 rules Regs 3A(1)(a) and 4 SS&CS(DA) Regs
20 **2012 rules** Reg 14(1)(c) CSMC Regs
2003 rules Reg 3A(1)(cc) SS&CS(DA) Regs
21 **2012 rules** Reg 14(1)(e) CSMC Regs
2003 rules Reg 3A(1)(e) SS&CS(DA) Regs
22 **2012 rules** Reg 14(1)(b) CMSC Regs
2003 rules Reg 3A(1)(c) SS&CS(DA) Regs
23 **2012 rules** Reg 14(3) CSMC Regs
2003 rules Reg 3A(4) and (5) SS&CS(DA) Regs
24 **2012 rules** Reg 14(1)(g) CSMC Regs
2003 rules Reg 3A(1)(f) SS&CS(DA) Regs
25 Reg 3A(1)(b) SS&CS(DA) Regs
26 **2012 rules** Reg 14(3A) CSMC Regs
2003 rules Reg 3A(5A) SS&CS(DA) Regs
27 Reg 14(1)(f) CSMC Regs
28 **2012 rules** Reg 14(2) CSMC Regs
2003 rules Reg 3A(2) SS&CS(DA) Regs

29 **2012 rules** Reg 15(4) CSMC Regs
    2003 rules Reg 4(4) SS&CS(DA) Regs
30 Reg 4(3)(b) SS&CS(DA) Regs
31 Reg 4(3)(b) SS&CS(DA) Regs
32 **2012 rules** Reg 27A(4) CSMC Regs
    2003 rules Reg 9B(4) SS&CS(DA) Regs
33 **2012 rules** Reg 15(5) CSMC Regs
    2003 rules Reg 4(5) SS&CS(DA) Regs
34 **2012 rules** Reg 15(3) CSMC Regs
    2003 rules Reg 4(3)(a) SS&CS(DA)
    Regs
35 **2012 rules** Reg 15(7) CSMC Regs
    2003 rules Reg 4(7) SS&CS(DA) Regs
36 See CIS/93/1992
37 *Mandatory Consideration of Revision
    Before Appeal: government response to
    public consultation*, DWP, September
    2012
38 **2012 rules** Reg 14(4) CSMC Regs
    2003 rules Reg 1(3) SS&CS(DA) Regs
39 **2012 rules** Regs 14(1)(a) and 27A
    CSMC Regs
    2003 rules Regs 3A(1)(a) and 9B
    SS&CS(DA) Regs
40 R(SB) 9/85
41 R(SB) 2/92 (*Page and Davis v CAO*)
42 CCS/15846/1996
43 **2012 rules** Reg 14(1)(b) CSMC Regs
    2003 rules Reg 3A(c) SS&CS(DA) Regs
44 **2012 rules** Reg 24(2) CSMC Regs
    2003 rules Reg 23(4) CS(MCP) Regs
45 **2012 rules** Reg 57 CSMC Regs
    2003 rules Reg 9 CS(V) Regs
46 **2012 rules** Reg 61 CSMC Regs
    2003 rules Reg 15B SS&CS(DA) Regs
47 R(I) 1/71
48 Reg 3A(1)(b) SS&CS(DA) Regs
49 s16(6) CSA 1991
    2012 rules Sch para 1(1) CSMC Regs
    2003 rules Reg 30(1) and (2)(f)
    SS&CS(DA) Regs
50 Reg 15C(12) SS&CS(DA) Regs
51 **2012 rules** Sch para 1(2) CSMC Regs
    2003 rules Reg 30(3) SS&CS(DA) Regs
52 s16(3) CSA 1991
53 **2012 rules** Reg 16 CSMC Regs
    2003 rules Reg 5A SS&CS(DA) Regs
54 **2012 rules** Reg 26(1) CSMC Regs
    2003 rules Reg 15C SS&CS(DA) Regs
55 **2012 rules** Reg 25(3) CSMC Regs
    2003 rules Reg 15C(3) SS&CS(DA)
    Regs
56 r22(2) and Sch 1 TP(FT) Rules

3. **Supersessions**
57 s17(1) CSA 1991
58 **2012 rules** Reg 17(1)-(3) CSMC Regs
    2003 rules Reg 6A(2)-(4) SS&CS(DA)
    Regs
59 **2012 rules** Reg 17(1)(c) CSMC Regs
    2003 rules Reg 6A(2)(c) SS&CS(DA)
    Regs
60 CCS/162/2006
61 **2012 rules** Reg 17(6) CSMC Regs
    2003 rules s17(2) CSA 1991
62 **2012 rules** Reg 17(4) CSMC Regs
    2003 rules Reg 6A(5) SS&CS(DA) Regs
63 **2012 rules** Reg 17(5) CSMC Regs
    2003 rules Reg 6A(6) SS&CS(DA) Regs
64 Reg 23(1) and (2) CSMC Regs
65 Reg 23(3) CSMC Regs
66 Reg 6B(1) SS&CS(DA) Regs
67 Reg 6B(4) SS&CS(DA) Regs
68 Reg 6B(4)(e) and Sch 3D para 4
    SS&CS(DA) Regs
69 Reg 6B(3) SS&CS(DA) Regs
70 Reg 6B(5) SS&CS(DA) Regs
71 Reg 6B(4)(f) SS&CS(DA) Regs
72 R(A) 1/72; R(SB) 11/83
73 *R v Gough* [1993] AC 646, [1993] 2 WLR
    883, [1993] 2 All ER 724
74 *Wednesbury Corporation v Ministry of
    Housing and Local Government (No.2)*
    [1965] 3 WLR 956, [1965] 3 All ER 571
75 *CAO v Foster* [1993] AC 754, [1993] 2
    WLR 292, [1993] 1 All ER 705
76 R(CS) 3/96; R(CS) 2/95; CCS/17/1994.
    These concerned the application of Art
    141 of the EC Treaty (formerly Art 119),
    and Council Directives 75/117 and 79/
    7. The Sex Discrimination Act 1975 also
    has no effect. CCS/6/1995
77 s3 HRA 1998
78 s4 HRA 1998
79 s6 HRA 1998
80 s17(4) CSA 1991
81 Reg 7C SS&CS(DA) Regs
82 Sch 3D para 9 SS&CS(DA) Regs
83 **2012 rules** Reg 59 CSMC Regs
    2003 rules Reg 9 CS(V) Regs
84 **2012 rules** Reg 61(1) CSMC Regs
    2003 rules Reg 15B SS&CS(DA) Regs
85 **2012 rules** Reg 59(1)(a) and (5) CSMC
    Regs
    2003 rules Reg 15B(2) SS&CS(DA)
    Regs
86 **2012 rules** Reg 25(3) CSMC Regs
    2003 rules Reg 15B SS&CS(DA) Regs
87 **2012 rules** Reg 17(6) CSMC Regs
    2003 rules s17(2) CSA 1991
88 s17(4) CSA 1991
89 Reg 18(4) CSMC Regs

90 Reg 18(5) CSMC Regs
91 Reg 18(6)(a) CSMC Regs
92 Reg 18(6)(b) CSMC Regs
93 Reg 18(6)(c) CSMC Regs
94 **2012 rules** Reg 18(2) CSMC Regs
    2003 rules Sch 3D para 2 SS&CS(DA) Regs
95 **2012 rules** Reg 18(2) CSMC Regs
    2003 rules Sch 3D para 2 SS&CS(DA) Regs
96 **2012 rules** Reg 18(3)(a) CSMC Regs
    2003 rules Sch 3D para 3(a) SS&CS(DA) Regs
97 **2012 rules** Reg 18(3)(a) CSMC Regs
    2003 rules Sch 3D para 3(aa) SS&CS(DA) Regs
98 **2012 rules** Reg 18(3)(b) CSMC Regs
    2003 rules Sch 3D para 3(b) SS&CS(DA) Regs
99 **2012 rules** Reg 18(3)(c) CSMC Regs
    2003 rules Sch 3D para 3(c) SS&CS(DA) Regs
100 **2012 rules** Reg 18(3)(d) CSMC Regs
    2003 rules Sch 3D para 3(e) SS&CS(DA) Regs
101 **2012 rules** Reg 30 CSMC Regs
    2003 rules Sch 3D para 10 SS&CS(DA) Regs
102 **2012 rules** Reg 31 CSMC Regs
    2003 rules Sch 3D para 11 SS&CS(DA) Regs
103 **2012 rules** Reg 32 CSMC Regs
    2003 rules Sch 3D para 12 SS&CS(DA) Regs
104 Sch 3D para 3(d) SS&CS(DA) Regs
105 Sch 3D para 4 SS&CS(DA) Regs
106 Sch 3D para 9 SS&CS(DA) Regs
107 Sch 3D para 6(a) SS&CS(DA) Regs
108 Sch 3D para 6(b) SS&CS(DA) Regs
109 Sch 3D para 7 SS&CS(DA) Regs
110 Sch 3D para 8 SS&CS(DA) Regs
111 **2012 rules** Reg 26(1) CSMC Regs
    2003 rules Reg 15C SS&CS(DA) Regs
112 **2012 rules** Reg 24(2) CSMC Regs
    2003 rules Reg 15C(4) SS&CS(DA) Regs
113 **2012 rules** Regs 24(2) and 26(2) CSMC Regs
    2003 rules Reg 15C(9)-(11) SS&CS(DA) Regs
114 **2012 rules** Reg 27 CSMC Regs
    2003 rules Reg 15C(5) SS&CS(DA) Regs

Chapter 13

· ·

Appeals

This chapter covers:
1. Decisions that can be appealed (below)
2. Appealing to the First-tier Tribunal (p237)
3. The appeal procedure (p240)
4. Preparing a case (p248)
5. Hearings (p249)
6. Decisions (p252)
7. Changing a First-tier Tribunal decision (p254)
8. Appealing to the Upper Tribunal (p256)
9. Test case rules (p260)

This chapter applies to cases under all three child support schemes.

For further details about appeal procedures and tactics for preparing for an appeal, see CPAG's *Welfare Benefits and Tax Credits Handbook*.

---

1. Decisions that can be appealed

Most decisions made by the Child Maintenance Service (CMS) or Child Support Agency (CSA) can be appealed to an independent appeal tribunal: the First-tier Tribunal (Social Entitlement Chamber).

An application for a revision must normally be made before a decision (including a decision in which an accidental error has been corrected by the CMS/CSA – see p217) can be appealed. This is known as a **'mandatory reconsideration'** and applies to all child support decisions issued on or after 28 October 2013, provided that:[1]
- the CMS/CSA has issued a written notice of the decision; *and*
- the decision notice includes a statement that there is only a right of appeal after the CMS/CSA has considered an application for a revision of the decision, and gives information on the time limit for seeking an 'any grounds' revision (see p218).

This means that, to be sure of having a right of appeal, an application for a revision should be made on time where this is required.

If an appeal is made and an application for a revision should have been made first, the CMS/CSA can treat the appeal as an application for a revision.[2] If the CMS/CSA does not do so, a revision should be sought as soon as possible, explaining why the application is late, if necessary. For '2003 rules' and '1993 rules' cases, there is an absolute time limit for seeking an 'any grounds' revision. For all three types of cases, decisions can be revised at any time in certain circumstances (see p218).

If an appeal is sent directly to the First-tier Tribunal when an application for a revision should have been made first, the Tribunal should return the appeal and advise the person to apply for a revision.

If the mandatory reconsideration rule does not apply, an appeal can be made directly against the decision.

Mandatory reconsideration is now likely to apply in almost all cases. For details of the appeal process if it does not apply, see previous editions of this *Handbook*.

Who can appeal

Usually, any relevant person (ie, a person with care, a non-resident parent or a child applicant in Scotland) has the right to appeal.[3]

Regardless of who makes an appeal, all parties have the same rights, except that only the person making the appeal (the 'appellant') can ask to withdraw the appeal. Because an appeal can be withdrawn without the consent of any other party (see p248), it is best for each party who wishes to challenge the decision to bring her/his own appeal. The appeals can be heard together.

The CMS/CSA may also refer a variation application to the First-tier Tribunal in certain cases. The First-tier Tribunal can also consider departures in '1993 rules' cases.

Person with right of appeal dies

If a person with a right of appeal dies, the executor or administrator of her/his estate can exercise the right of appeal and can continue with any appeals that are already underway.[4]

Decisions that cannot be appealed

Only decisions and, in some cases, refusals to make decisions, can be appealed. It is not possible to appeal if no decision has been made – eg, because of a delay. Instead, a complaint (see Chapter 15) or an application for judicial review could be considered. Similarly, decisions about fees and some decisions about the method of collection or the enforcement of payment cannot be appealed. Parents who are uncertain whether they can appeal against a decision should seek advice straight away.

Parentage disputes

An appeal involving a dispute about parentage is made in exactly the same way as any other appeal.[5] If someone denies s/he is the parent of a child named in the child support application, the appeal is not dealt with by the First-tier Tribunal, but by a court.[6] If there are other grounds for appeal apart from the dispute about parentage, the First-tier Tribunal deals with those issues and the parentage issue is dealt with by the court. If the appeal is sent to the First-tier Tribunal and it involves a denial of parentage, the First-tier Tribunal should transfer that issue to the court.[7] For more information about parentage disputes see p63.

---

2. **Appealing to the First-tier Tribunal**

When the Child Maintenance Service (CMS) or Child Support Agency (CSA) makes a decision, each relevant person must be sent a notice of that decision and information on the right of appeal.[8]

If a person challenging a decision disagrees with the mandatory reconsideration decision, an appeal is started by sending a notice of appeal directly to the First-tier Tribunal. Form SSCS2 should be used, which is available from the gov.uk website.[9]

The notice of appeal must include:[10]

- the name and address of the person making the appeal;
- the name and address of that person's representative (if s/he has one);
- an address to which documents about the appeal may be sent or delivered to the person making the appeal;
- the grounds of the appeal.

The person appealing must also send a copy of:[11]

- the mandatory reconsideration notice (if applicable), otherwise the decision being appealed;
- any statement of reasons received for the decision being appealed; *and*
- any documents supporting the appeal that have not already been supplied to the CMS/CSA or the other party.

There are strict time limits for making an appeal (see below), which can only be extended in certain circumstances (see p238). If the notice of appeal does not include sufficient information or is not made on the approved form, see p239.

There are CMS/CSA leaflets that explain the appeal process.[12]

Time limits

The time limit for appealing is very strict. An appeal must normally be received by the First-tier Tribunal within one month of the person appealing ('the appellant') being sent the result of the application for revision (the 'mandatory reconsideration notice').[13] The First-tier Tribunal can extend the time limit, but there is an absolute time limit within which the appeal must be made (see below).

If the appellant is appealing against a refusal to revise a decision following a late application for a revision (see p219) where time was not extended, this one-month time limit runs from the date of notification of the original decision, not the date on which the CMS/CSA notified her/him of its refusal to revise. However, if the CMS/CSA refused to revise a decision following an application for a revision that was made within the time limit (see p218) or the extended time limit, the one-month time limit runs from the date on which the notice of refusal to revise was issued. Similarly, if a decision is revised, the time for appealing runs from the date on which the revised decision is sent to the appellant.[14]

For the '2012 rules', a notice of a decision counts as having been sent on the second day after the day it was posted.[15]

For the '1993 rules' and '2003 rules', a notice of a decision counts as having been sent to the person on the day it is issued by the CSA.[16]

'Month' means a complete calendar month from the day of notification.[17] When calculating time, if something has to be done by a certain day, it must be done by 5pm that day. If a time limit ends on a day other than a working day, it must be done by the next working day to meet the time limit.[18]

Late appeals

If an appeal is not made within the time limit, in certain circumstances it can still be treated as made in time. However, the time limit can never be extended by more than 12 months from the normal time limit (ie, normally 13 months from the date of the mandatory reconsideration notice being sent to the person appealing).[19] This is an absolute legal time limit and cannot be extended further in any circumstances.

A late appeal will be admitted if it is within the absolute time limit, neither the CMS/CSA nor any other party objects and the First-tier Tribunal does not direct otherwise.[20]

If the CMS/CSA or any other party does object, the First-tier Tribunal decides whether the appeal should be admitted. This is a discretionary decision for the First-tier Tribunal, not for the CMS/CSA. The First-tier Tribunal should bear in mind the overriding objective that appeals should be dealt with fairly and justly (see p241). It should not limit its discretion by assuming, for example, that it has to be satisfied that there are special reasons.[21] However, there is no guarantee that the First-tier Tribunal will admit the appeal, so appeals should be made in time wherever possible.

If a notice of appeal is submitted outside the time limit, in addition to the information listed above, it must also include the reasons why it is late and a request for it to be accepted.[22] It is best to include as much detail as possible about why there may be special reasons for the appeal being late and why it would be fair for it still to be admitted.

If the First-tier Tribunal decides that an appeal cannot be admitted because it was made outside the absolute time limit for appealing, an appeal can be made to the Upper Tribunal (see p256) against this decision.[23]

The appeal form or letter has insufficient information

The First-tier Tribunal may use its general case management powers to allow the appellant to provide further information or amend a document.[24] This is a discretionary power and there is no guarantee that it will be used this way.

The appropriate form should be used if possible and care taken to provide all the required information.

After an appeal is made

When the First-tier Tribunal receives the appeal, the regional office of HM Courts and Tribunals Service (HMCTS) sends the appellant an acknowledgement. This advises the appellant that HMCTS has also sent a copy of the appeal and any accompanying documents to the CMS/CSA and any other party.[25]

HMCTS informs the appellant that the appeal can be arranged for a hearing at the nearest appeals venue. This is based on the appellant's postcode and, in some cases, may not be the most convenient venue for her/him. An appellant can request that the venue is changed to a different one. This should be done promptly as the later the request is left the more likely it is to be refused. In general, a request for a change of venue made in good time is likely to be agreed by HMCTS.

When the CMS/CSA receives a copy of the appeal, it may revise the decision when it considers the appeal. See p221 for further information about what may happen if the decision under appeal is revised.

The CMS/CSA should prepare a 'response' to the appeal. This should be sent to the First-tier Tribunal, and copied to the other parties to the appeal as soon as reasonably practical after receiving the notice of appeal. Since 1 October 2014, the CMS/CSA must send the response to the First-tier Tribunal within 42 days of the date on which the CMS/CSA received the copy of the notice of appeal.[26] The response should state:[27]

- the name and address of the official who made the decision;
- the name and address of that official's representative (if any), known as a 'presenting officer';
- an address where documents for the CMS/CSA can be sent or delivered;
- the name and addresses of any other respondents and their representatives (if any).

The response should explain what parts of the grounds put forward for the appeal the CMS/CSA disagrees with, and why.[28]

The response may also indicate whether the CMS/CSA thinks the case requires a hearing or could be decided by just considering the papers.[29]

The response must have attached to it:[30]

- a copy of any written record of the decision being appealed, and any statement of reasons for it, if they were not already sent with the appeal;
- copies of all documents relevant to the case that the CMS/CSA has;[31]
- if the appeal was one that was originally sent to the CMS/CSA rather than the First-tier Tribunal, a copy of the notice of appeal, and any documents submitted by the appellant.

If any delay in the CMS/CSA sending the response to the First-tier Tribunal is causing hardship, the appellant can apply to the Tribunal for a direction telling the CMS/CSA to provide the papers.

Once the appellant, and any other respondent, receives the copy of the response from the CMS/CSA, s/he can make a written submission and supply any further documents in reply to the CMS/CSA's response. This should be sent to the First-tier Tribunal within one month of receiving the response, and the Tribunal then sends a copy to the CMS/CSA and other parties.[32]

Although this one-month time limit is provided in the rules, it is likely that a refusal to accept further evidence and submissions after one month would be disproportionate, especially if there is to be an oral hearing (see p249) at which submissions and further evidence may be expected to be presented anyway. It is more helpful to the First-tier Tribunal to send evidence ahead of the hearing, even if later than one month after the response from the CMS/CSA was sent, than to present it on the day of the hearing, especially if there is a large quantity of evidence (which is likely to lead to an adjournment of the hearing and further delay).

If the person with care or non-resident parent has told the CMS/CSA or First-tier Tribunal that s/he would like her/his address, or the address of the child, to be kept confidential, they must take appropriate steps to ensure that this, or any information that would help identify this, is not revealed to other parties. The parties should make this request to the CMS/CSA or First-tier Tribunal on the notice of appeal or within 14 days of receiving an appeal enquiry form.[33]

3. **The appeal procedure**

Both the First-tier and Upper Tribunal have procedural rules setting out their powers and how they should deal with cases. There are also practice directions and practice statements, which set out how they should conduct themselves. The rules are similar for both the First-tier and Upper Tribunal and so this section applies to both (and explains where there are differences). The rules about hearings and decisions are also part of the procedural rules (see p249 and p252). See p254 for challenging and p256 for appealing against a First-tier Tribunal decision. Caselaw has also established a number of principles on how appeals should be conducted.

If the Tribunal fails to follow correct procedure, this may be grounds for appealing against a decision it reaches, as a breach of the procedural rules can mean that the decision is based on an error of law.[34] A complaint can also be made to HM Courts and Tribunals Service (HMCTS). For details of how to complain to HMCTS, see CPAG's *Welfare Benefits and Tax Credits Handbook*. A failure to follow procedure could also be challenged by judicial review (see p215).

The overriding objective: fair and just

The overriding objective of the rules is to enable the Tribunal to deal with cases 'fairly and justly'.[35] Whenever the Tribunal exercises a power under the rules (eg, to admit or not admit a late appeal, or to strike out an appeal), it must consider whether it would be fair and just. Similarly, when the Tribunal interprets what the rules mean or what the practice directions say, it must try to come to the interpretation which meets the overriding objective – ie, to enable a case to be dealt with in a way which is fair and just.[36]

It is therefore important to bear in mind the overriding objective in any dealings about the conduct of the proceedings – eg, directions that should be given, witnesses to be summonsed, a child giving evidence, asking for an adjournment or more time to give submissions or get evidence, and objecting to the CMS/CSA being given more time to get evidence. It may be worth explaining to the Tribunal why doing so would be fair and just.

The rules set out some of the things that must be taken into account when deciding whether a particular interpretation of the rules is fair and just, or in deciding whether it would be fair and just to exercise a power conferred by the rules in a particular way.[37] The Tribunal should:

- deal with the case in a way which is proportionate to its importance, the complexity of the issues, the anticipated costs and the resources of the parties;
- avoid unnecessary formality and be flexible in the proceedings;
- ensure, so far as practicable, that the parties are able to participate fully in the proceedings;
- use any special expertise of the Tribunal effectively; *and*
- avoid delay, so far as it is compatible with the proper consideration of the issues.

Note: this list is not exhaustive. Other matters can still be taken into account when considering what is fair and just in a particular case.[38]

The parties to an appeal have a duty to assist the Tribunal in dealing with cases fairly and justly.[39]

Applying for directions

Tribunals can give a wide range of directions in order to manage cases. Any such action must be consistent with the overriding objective (see p241).

A direction can be given at any time, either on the initiative of the Tribunal or following an application by a party to the proceedings.[40]

An application for a direction can be made either orally at a hearing or by writing to the Tribunal, and must include the reason for seeking the direction.

The Tribunal must, unless it considers there is a good reason not to do so, send a written notice of the direction to every party and to anyone else affected by it.

If a party is unhappy with a direction, s/he can apply for another direction which amends, suspends or sets aside the earlier direction.

If a party fails to comply with a direction, the case could be struck out (see p244) or the party barred from any hearing (see p245).

It may be possible to appeal to the Upper Tribunal about the content of a particular direction – eg, to exclude or include certain evidence.[41]

General case management powers

The Tribunal can give directions to:

- extend or shorten the time for complying with any rule, practice direction or direction. This is the only rule on extending time. It applies to any late application – eg, to appeal, for a statement of reasons or to set aside a decision. It does not contain any upper limit (although there is an upper limit of a 12-month extension for late appeals);
- consolidate or hear together two or more sets of proceedings (or parts of proceedings) raising common issues, or treat a case as a lead case;
- permit or require a party to amend a document;
- permit or require a party or another person to provide documents, information, evidence or submissions to the Tribunal or a party. There are more specific powers to obtain evidence (see p243);
- deal with an issue in the proceedings as a preliminary issue – eg, to decide precisely what decision is under appeal or whether the Tribunal has jurisdiction;
- hold a hearing to consider any matter, including a case management issue. This could include, for example, a preliminary hearing to decide what further evidence is needed and who should provide it, how much time the final hearing needs or whether the appeal should be struck out because of a failure to comply with a direction;
- decide the form of any hearing – eg, the order in which parties speak or give evidence and who questions the appellant;

- postpone a hearing, or adjourn one – eg, to require that further evidence be produced;
- require a party to produce a 'bundle' (an indexed set of documents relating to the case) for a hearing. The Tribunal must take into account the resources of the parties when issuing a direction;
- 'stay' (or, in Scotland, 'sist') proceedings. This allows the Tribunal to put the case on hold pending the outcome of another case in which it is expected that legal issues will be decided that are relevant to the outcome of the case;
- transfer proceedings to another court or tribunal. For example, if a non-resident parent denies parentage for the first time in the proceedings, the Tribunal does not have jurisdiction to decide that issue. Similarly, if a denial of parentage had not been noted by the CMS/CSA and the Tribunal becomes aware of it, the Tribunal must transfer the case;
- suspend the effect of its decision pending an application for permission to appeal against (and any appeal or review of) that decision.

Evidence

The Tribunal can give directions about:[42]
- issues on which it requires evidence or submissions;
- the nature of the evidence or submissions it requires, and the manner in which, and time at which, they are to be provided;
- whether the parties are permitted or required to provide expert evidence;
- any limit on the number of witnesses whose evidence a party may put forward, whether in relation to a particular issue or generally.

The Tribunal can exclude evidence if:
- it was not provided within a time limit in a direction or practice direction;
- it does not comply with a direction or a practice direction in some other way;
- it would be unfair to admit the evidence.

In giving directions about evidence, the Tribunal must take care not to make any comment or decision that would appear to compromise its independence.[43]

Harmful evidence

If a person with care or non-resident parent has told the First-tier Tribunal or CMS/CSA that s/he would like her/his address, or the address of a child, to be kept confidential, the Tribunal and CMS/CSA must take appropriate steps to ensure that it (or information that could be used to identify it) is not revealed to other parties. This also applies to the Upper Tribunal where it is considering an appeal against a First-tier Tribunal decision in which confidentiality was sought or where a party has told the Upper Tribunal that s/he wants the information to be kept confidential. The request should be made to the Upper Tribunal when appealing or seeking permission to appeal, within one month of receiving an enquiry form from the Upper Tribunal or when notifying it of a change of address.[44] The Tribunal can also order that documents or information relating to the proceedings are not to be disclosed, or that any matter which could allow the public to identify the people involved should not be disclosed.[45]

The Tribunal can also direct that a particular person does not get a document or information if:[46]

- disclosure would be likely to cause her/him or another person serious harm; *and*
- weighing up that potential harm against the interests of justice, it is proportionate not to disclose the information.

If a party thinks the Tribunal should direct that a particular document or piece of information should be withheld from another party, s/he must not give it to that party. Instead, s/he must send a copy of it to the Tribunal and explain why it should not be disclosed.[47]

The Tribunal can, however, disclose the document or information to the party's representative if it is satisfied that s/he will not disclose the document to another person without the consent of the Tribunal and that such disclosure is in the interests of justice.[48] If any evidence is withheld, the Tribunal must still ensure that there is a fair hearing and that each party has sufficient information to conduct the case. Evidence should not be withheld from the Tribunal itself.[49]

Witnesses

The Tribunal has power to summon (in Scotland, cite) witnesses and to order other documents to be produced.[50] The Tribunal may require any person to:

- attend as a witness at a hearing at the time and place specified;
- to answer any questions which relate to the proceedings;
- to provide any documents in her/his possession or control which relate to the proceedings.

The Tribunal must give the person summoned at least 14 days' notice of the hearing (or a shorter period if the Tribunal directs this). If the person summoned is not a party to the proceedings, her/his expenses are paid.

Note: the Tribunal cannot summon a child if this would be detrimental to her/his welfare.

Costs

Neither the First-tier Tribunal nor the Upper Tribunal can award costs (except in a judicial review).[51]

Failure to comply with the rules

If there has been a failure to comply with the rules, a practice direction or a direction, the Tribunal may take any action which it considers just, including:[52]

- waiving the requirement;
- requiring the failure to be remedied;
- striking out the appeal;
- referring the matter to the Upper Tribunal;
- restricting a party's participation in the proceedings;
- fining or committing someone to prison (Upper Tribunal only).

The Upper Tribunal has the same powers as the High Court (the Court of Session in Scotland) concerning the attendance and examination of witnesses and the production and inspection of documents.[53] It can therefore commit to prison someone who does not comply with its rules or impose a fine.

The First-tier Tribunal does not have this power, but can refer a person to the Upper Tribunal for it to deal with as if s/he had failed to comply with one of its own rules or directions.[54] The First-tier Tribunal can only refer someone if s/he has failed to:

- attend at any place to give evidence;
- otherwise make her/himself available to give evidence;
- swear an oath in connection with giving evidence;
- produce a document;
- facilitate the inspection of a document or any other thing (including premises).

Striking out an appeal and barring

In certain circumstances, the Tribunal can 'strike out' (ie, dismiss without considering the decision under appeal) an appeal, or part of an appeal.

The Tribunal *must* strike out an appeal, or part of an appeal, if:

- the appellant has failed to comply with a direction which stated that the appeal, or that part of the appeal, *would* be struck out for failure to comply;[55] *or*
- it does not have jurisdiction to decide the appeal (or that part of it) and has not transferred the appeal (or part of the appeal) to another tribunal or court.[56]

The Tribunal *may* strike out an appeal, or part of an appeal, if:

- the appellant has failed to comply with a direction which stated that the appeal, or that part of the appeal, *could* be struck out for failure to comply; *or*
- the appellant has failed to co-operate with the Tribunal to such an extent that the Tribunal cannot deal with the proceedings fairly and justly;[57] *or*
- it considers that the appeal has no reasonable prospects of success.[58]

The power to strike out an appeal because the appellant has failed to comply with a direction should be used in exceptional cases as a last resort.[59] If an appeal, or part of an appeal, is struck out for this reason, the appellant may apply in writing for the appeal, or that part of it, to be reinstated.[60] This should be received by the Tribunal within one month of its sending the appellant notice of the striking out.[61] This one-month time limit can be extended if the Tribunal considers it to be fair and just to do so.[62] If an application to reinstate an appeal has been rejected, a further application can be made if the appellant has further evidence or circumstances have changed.[63]

It is not possible for an appeal, or part of it, to be reinstated if it is struck out for a reason other than a failure to comply with a direction. However, the Tribunal cannot strike out an appeal for one of these reasons unless it has first invited the appellant to make representations about whether or not it should do so.[64] To ensure that the appellant has an effective opportunity to do this, it may be appropriate to request that all the documents relevant to the appeal should be provided to the parties.

The Tribunal must consider whether it would be fair and just to strike out the appeal. If the case is one where the key facts are in dispute between the parties, striking out an appeal on the grounds that it has no reasonable prospects of success is only likely to be appropriate in exceptional circumstances.[65]

The Tribunal must give a written notice of its decision to strike out an appeal, or part of an appeal, and should explain why it is doing so.[66] A party to the appeal can ask for a written statement of reasons for the decision and can seek permission to appeal to the Upper Tribunal against a striking-out decision by the First-tier Tribunal.[67]

The rules for striking out an appeal apply to the CMS/CSA in exactly the same way as they apply to the appellant, except that references to 'striking out' are to 'barring'. When the Tribunal 'bars' the respondent, it need not consider any response or other submission made by that respondent, and can determine any or all issues against that respondent.

Sending and receiving documents

If there is a time limit to provide a document, this starts to run from when the Tribunal sends the request. The time limit is met when the Tribunal receives the response.

Anything that must be done by a particular day must be done by 5pm on that day.[68]

If a time limit ends on a day other than a working day, the act is treated as being in time if it is done on the next working day.[69]

Documents can be sent to the Tribunal by pre-paid post (or fax) to the address (or number) specified for the proceedings. The Tribunal may give directions permitting documents to be sent by other methods.[70]

If a party provides a fax, email address or other method for receiving documents electronically, s/he must accept delivery of documents by that method unless s/he has explicitly stated that this is not acceptable.[71]

If a document is sent electronically, the recipient can request a hard copy and the sender must supply it (this also applies to appellants and their representatives).

The request for a hard copy should be made as soon as reasonably practicable after receiving the document electronically.[72]

Each party should assume that the address provided by another party remains valid unless s/he has received written notice to the contrary.[73]

Representatives

A party can appoint a representative (whether legally qualified or not) to represent her/him in the proceedings. Once appointed, a representative can do anything permitted or required to be done by the party (except sign a witness statement).[74]

The Tribunal should notify all other parties when a representative has been appointed. When a person (including the Tribunal itself) receives the notice of the appointment of a representative, s/he must provide her/him with any documents required to be issued to the represented party and need not send the documents to that party.[75] The enquiry form (see p240), however, is not a document that has to be issued to all parties and is generally sent by HMCTS only to the appellant.[76]

It should be assumed that the representative continues to act unless notice to the contrary from either the representative or the represented party is received.

Even if a party has not appointed a representative, s/he can still be accompanied at the hearing. Her/his companion may, with the permission of the Tribunal, act as a representative or otherwise assist in presenting the case at the hearing.[77]

Withdrawing an appeal

A party can withdraw all or part of her/his case.[78]

In the First-tier Tribunal, a case may be withdrawn by writing to the Tribunal before the hearing, or orally at a hearing. If a party waits until a hearing to withdraw, s/he can only do so with the Tribunal's consent.[79] If the notice of appeal was sent to the CMS/CSA and an appellant or her/his representative wishes to stop an appeal proceeding before it has been referred to the First-tier Tribunal, s/he can simply write to the CMS/CSA, which discontinues the action.[80] In the Upper Tribunal, consent is always needed to withdraw an appeal (even if the request is made in writing), unless the case is still at the stage of awaiting permission to appeal.[81]

Once a case has been withdrawn, it can be reinstated if the party writes to the Tribunal requesting this within one month of the notice of withdrawal being received by the Tribunal, or within a month of the date of the hearing at which the case was withdrawn.

When a case is withdrawn, the Tribunal must notify each party.

4. **Preparing a case**

The First-tier Tribunal may be the first chance for an independent evaluation of the decision under appeal. It may also be the last chance because there can only be an appeal to the Upper Tribunal on a point of law. Therefore, each party should make sure that the First-tier Tribunal knows the facts and arguments about the case.

Considering the facts and law

- Read the response from the Child Maintenance Service (CMS) or Child Support Agency (CSA) and any other documents to see whether it now accepts some of the arguments previously rejected or ignored. Just because the CMS/CSA accepts part of a person's case does not mean that the Tribunal will, especially if the other party disputes it.
- Check the law using this *Handbook* and other sources. If the CMS/CSA quotes a decision of the Upper Tribunal or of the commissioners, consider getting a copy. HM Courts and Tribunals Service (HMCTS) does not have copies of unreported decisions. If an unreported decision is to be relied on by the CMS/CSA, a copy should be supplied to the parties and to the First-tier Tribunal. If a party wishes to quote an unreported decision, s/he should supply copies to everyone, preferably by sending a copy to the Tribunal clerk in advance of the hearing. A party (including the CMS/CSA) can quote the CMS/CSA's internal procedural guidance, but it is important to remember that this guidance is not legally binding.
- Check the documents attached to the response. If anything relevant is missing, write to the First-tier Tribunal asking it to direct the CMS/CSA to provide it.

If the CMS/CSA delays producing its response to an appeal, the appellant can write to the First-tier Tribunal and ask for a direction that the appeal be heard. This may mean that the First-tier Tribunal will not have all the evidence the CMS/CSA has. However, a party can ask the First-tier Tribunal to direct the CMS/CSA (see p242) to provide copies of all the papers, explaining why these are needed. **Note:** from 1 October 2014, the CMS/CSA must provide a response to an appeal within 42 days (see p239).

Further evidence

Each party should consider:
- whether s/he has (or can get) any further relevant written evidence. This can be sent to the First-tier Tribunal at any stage, but it is best to do this soon after the response is sent out, so papers can be copied to the other parties. If evidence or unreported caselaw decisions are produced at the hearing or sent in shortly before, this may cause a postponement or an adjournment;

- how to explain the facts and law at the hearing. A party can 'give evidence' – ie, explain her/his situation. For example, 'I look after the child from Friday night to Monday night' may be the best evidence of those facts;
- whether to call any witnesses at the hearing (see p244).

Information relating to court proceedings concerning children heard in private or ancillary relief proceedings (ie, dealing with money and property) can be disclosed to the First-tier Tribunal by any party without permission being sought, provided the court does not direct otherwise.[82] This means that one parent can supply information about the finances of the other parent, to which s/he admitted in the course of divorce proceedings.

Obtaining information and evidence

A party may want another person to provide further information or documents. The party can write to the First-tier Tribunal requesting that the other person be directed to provide these. It is best for the party to send a prepared list to HMCTS, which is as precise as possible and explains why the documents are needed. For example, if a parent with care believes that a non-resident parent has received a pay increase, s/he could ask for 'pay slips from February to May 2014 (inclusive)'. A person who is not a party (eg, an employer) cannot be directed to provide evidence, but can be ordered to attend as a witness and produce documents (see p244). This should be done before the full hearing so the parties can consider that evidence.

If a person fails to comply without a good explanation, the First-tier Tribunal may decide that s/he has something to hide and so may not believe that person's evidence.[83] If the person is the appellant, the appeal can be struck out (see p245).

5. Hearings

'Hearing' in this section means an oral hearing (including one conducted by video link, telephone or other instant two-way electronic communication).[84]

When must a hearing be held

The rules about when a hearing must be held are different for the First-tier and Upper Tribunal.

The **First-tier Tribunal** must hold a hearing before making a final decision in a case unless:[85]

- it is exercising its powers to strike out the proceedings (see p245);
- each party has consented, or has not objected, to the matter being decided without a hearing and the First-tier Tribunal considers that it can decide the appeal fairly and justly without it. If it proceeds without a hearing, the First-

tier Tribunal must show that it has considered the matter and give reasons for concluding that it could decide the appeal that way;[86]
- it is deciding whether to admit an application for permission to appeal, set aside a decision or correct a decision;
- it is disposing of the proceedings by a consent order (see p254).

The **Upper Tribunal** may decide any case without a hearing, but must consider any views expressed by a party when deciding whether to hold a hearing.[87]

If there is not a hearing, the Tribunal makes its decision by considering what has been said on the appeal form, any other evidence provided by the parties, and the response from the Child Maintenance Service (CMS) or Child Support Agency (CSA). This is known as a 'paper hearing'.

Notice

The Tribunal must give reasonable notice of the time and place of the hearing and of any changes to the arrangements.[88] This must be at least 14 days, although shorter notice can be given with the parties' consent or in urgent or exceptional circumstances (if shorter notice is given, it must still be reasonable).[89] Papers, including evidence sent to the Tribunal by any party, should be sent (subject to the rules about withholding harmful information) to all parties in good time before the hearing.[90]

Attending a hearing

Generally, all hearings must be held in public and a party has a right to attend. However, the Tribunal may direct that all or part of a hearing is to be held in private and may determine who is allowed to attend.

Even in a public hearing, the Tribunal may exclude from all or part of it:[91]
- anyone whose conduct is disrupting, or is likely to disrupt, the hearing;
- anyone whose presence is likely to prevent another person from giving evidence or making submissions freely;
- anyone who should be excluded in order to prevent her/him hearing information that is likely to cause harm;
- anyone whose attendance would defeat the purpose of the hearing;
- a witness in the proceedings.

If a party fails to attend a hearing and the Tribunal is satisfied that s/he has been notified or that reasonable steps to notify her/him have been taken, it may proceed with the hearing if it is in the interests of justice.[92]

If a party chooses not to attend, s/he cannot then claim that the Tribunal has acted unfairly if it decides the case on evidence given at the hearing that s/he has not had a chance to contest.[93]

Composition of the Tribunal

When the First-tier Tribunal deals with a case involving a child support decision, it usually consists of a single member, called a 'tribunal judge'.[94] The judge is legally qualified.[95] If the appeal raises difficult issues about financial accounts, the First-tier Tribunal can include a financially qualified member (a 'tribunal member') – ie, a chartered or certified accountant.[96] If a First-tier Tribunal is composed of other members in addition to the tribunal judge, the judge is the 'presiding member', can regulate the proceedings and has the casting vote if there are an even number of members.[97]

The Upper Tribunal almost always consists of a single judge, who is legally qualified. If the case is particularly difficult or there is conflicting caselaw, there may be a panel of two or three judges.[98]

The venue

There should normally be separate waiting rooms available at the hearing venue for the non-resident parent, parent with care and presenting officer. A party who is worried about this should check with HM Courts and Tribunals Service (HMCTS) whether there are separate waiting areas available before the hearing and, if not, explain any problems this may cause. If another party or witness could become violent, the Tribunal clerk should be told as soon as possible and asked what steps will be taken.

The hearing is usually held in the appellant's area. Expenses, including travel expenses, subsistence and some compensation for loss of earnings, are paid to those who attend as a party, witness or unpaid representative. The clerk pays travel and subsistence on the day, unless these are high. Travel expenses can be paid in advance.

A party for whom it is difficult to attend the hearing (eg, because of disability) should inform the clerk. An alternative venue may be possible, but convenience to the other parties to the appeal are also considered.

Conduct of the hearing

The First-tier Tribunal attempts to be informal. Its member(s) usually sit on one side of a table. The clerk to the Tribunal (who does not take any part in making the decision) shows the parties into the room and they usually sit on the other side of the table, with the presenting officer between them. The judge introduces everyone and explains the Tribunal's role. If anyone's role is unclear, the judge should be asked for clarification.

Every party has the right to address the Tribunal, give evidence, call witnesses and put questions to any other party, the presenting officer or witnesses. The order in which the parties present their cases is up to the judge. The CMS/CSA is there to explain the decision, not to argue for the CMS/CSA. The presenting officer has a role, for example, to inform the Tribunal about CMS/CSA procedures.

It is rare for the presenting officer to call any witnesses. The Tribunal may require any witness, including a party, to take an oath or affirmation.

It is the policy of HMCTS to arrange an interpreter, if requested in good time. This should be requested on the pre-hearing enquiry form. The Tribunal should not place itself in the position of being seen to assist one of the parties make her/his case.[99]

The First-tier Tribunal can adjourn a hearing at any point – eg, if more documents are needed. If evidence has been taken, a new panel hearing the case must be made up of either exactly the same, or entirely different, members. Hearings can take one hour or longer.

6. **Decisions**

After the hearing, the First-tier Tribunal considers the case and makes its decision. If the appeal is allowed, the decision of the First-tier Tribunal replaces that of the Child Maintenance Service (CMS) or Child Support Agency (CSA). If the appeal is dismissed, the decision of the CMS/CSA remains in force. Similarly, the Upper Tribunal may replace the decision of the First-tier Tribunal (or can direct that the case be reconsidered by a new First-tier Tribunal).

Decisions of the First-tier Tribunal

In making its decision, the First-tier Tribunal looks afresh at the situation on the date of the CMS/CSA decision under appeal.[100]

It cannot take into account any change of circumstances that has occurred after the date of the decision under appeal.[101] If it decides to allow the appeal because the decision was wrong on the facts at the time it was made, it cannot go on to direct how the CMS/CSA should deal with a later change of circumstances. The whole appeal process can take some time, so if circumstances change while waiting for an appeal to be decided, a person with care or non-resident parent (or child applicant in Scotland) may wish to make a new application or request a supersession as well as pursuing the appeal.

The First-tier Tribunal can consider any evidence and arguments, including those rejected or overlooked by the CMS/CSA and those which have not been used before.[102] The First-tier Tribunal has no duty to consider any issue not raised in the appeal.[103] However, it is 'inquisitorial', which means that it can consider legal arguments and factual questions on its own initiative, if appropriate, and should not be unduly narrow in its approach.[104] The First-tier Tribunal must decide what it believes are the relevant facts by evaluating all the relevant available evidence.[105] The Tribunal can draw conclusions from the failure of a party to provide evidence.[106]

If the First-tier Tribunal reaches a different conclusion from that of the CMS/ CSA, it allows the appeal. **Note:** it may make a decision that is less advantageous to the appellant than the decision which has been appealed.[107]

If the appeal is against a refusal to revise/supersede, the First-tier Tribunal must decide whether a revision/supersession can be carried out. When considering this, it looks at the facts as they were when the CMS/CSA refused to supersede, or at the date of the original decision in the case of a refusal to revise, even if the CMS/CSA did not know those facts.[108] Unless there was a basis for a revision/ supersession at that time, a later change of circumstances is irrelevant.[109] A request for a supersession on the basis of the later change should be made instead.

The First-tier Tribunal can make a provisional decision, which will become final in specified circumstances. This may be done, for example, as a case management technique if the First-tier Tribunal wants to give one last chance to a non-compliant party to provide certain information within a specified time. The time limit for any further appeal runs from the date of the final decision.[110]

Decision notices

Usually, at the hearing the parties are invited to wait outside the hearing room and then asked to come back in to be told the decision. The First-tier Tribunal must also give a decision notice to the parties (unless it decides to withhold harmful information) as soon as reasonably practicable, stating:[111]
* its decision;
* any right to apply for reasons for the decision;
* any right of appeal against the decision, together with information about the time and manner in which such an appeal must be made.

The First-tier Tribunal can decide to issue a full statement of the reasons for its decision, either orally at the hearing or in writing to each party.[112] If it does not do this, a party can apply for a written statement of reasons, provided this is received by the Tribunal within a month of the party's being given or sent the decision notice.[113]

If a party has applied for a written statement of reasons (subject to the rules about withholding harmful information), the Tribunal must, unless the decision was a consent order (see p254), send them within one month of receiving the application, or as soon as reasonably practicable after that.[114]

Decisions of the Upper Tribunal

The Upper Tribunal may announce its final decision orally at a hearing (although this is far less common than at the First-tier Tribunal) and must then (unless it decides to withold harmful information) provide the parties with a notice stating its decision and details of any further rights of review and appeal. The Upper Tribunal must always give reasons for its decision, unless it was made with the consent of the parties or the parties have consented to a decision being given without reasons.[115]

Record of proceedings

The presiding member of the First-tier Tribunal must keep a record of proceedings. This should include any evidence taken, submissions made and any procedural issues – eg, if a party asked for an adjournment.[116]

The record can be in any form determined by the presiding member and must be kept by HM Courts and Tribunals Service for at least six months from either the date of the decision, the date the reasons for the decision were given, the date the decision was corrected, the date a refusal to set aside was made or the date of the determination of an application for permission to appeal (unless the documents are sent to the Upper Tribunal before the six months expire), whichever is the later. A party can request a copy of the record of proceedings within this six-month period and it must be provided.

In the Upper Tribunal, if the proceedings are recorded, this should be kept for six months. A party can apply for a transcript, but will have to pay for it unless s/he intends to or has challenged the decision, the transcript is necessary in order to bring that challenge, and the Upper Tribunal is satisfied that s/he cannot afford to pay.

Consent orders

If all the parties agree, they can request that the Tribunal makes an order disposing of (ie, cancelling) the proceedings with their consent. It only does so if it considers that it is appropriate.[117] It may simply make a decision on the appeal in the usual way.

If a consent order is made, there does not have to be a hearing and no reasons for the order need to be given. Independent advice should be sought *before* agreeing to request a consent order.

---

7. Changing a First-tier Tribunal decision

A First-tier Tribunal can change its decision by:[118]
- correcting an accidental error (see p255);
- setting aside the decision (see p255);
- reviewing the decision (see p255);
- allowing an appeal to the Upper Tribunal (see p256).

Note: an application for any of the above can be treated by the First-tier Tribunal as an application for any of the others.

Correcting an error

The First-tier Tribunal can, at any time, correct a clerical mistake or accidental slip or omission in a decision, direction or any document it produces by sending a notice of the amended decision or direction to all parties.[119] This only allows the First-tier Tribunal to correct inadvertent clerical errors, not to change the decision itself.[120]

Setting aside the decision

A decision, or part of a final decision, can be 'set aside' (ie, cancelled) by the First-tier Tribunal if it considers it to be in the interests of justice to do so. It can do this if:[121]

- a document relating to the proceedings was not sent to or received by the First-tier Tribunal, a party or representative at an appropriate time; *or*
- a party or representative was not present at the hearing; *or*
- there has been some other procedural irregularity.

An application for a set-aside must be received within one month of being sent the decision by the First-tier Tribunal. However, it appears that the Tribunal may exercise this power without receiving an application – ie, of its own volition.

On setting aside a decision, the First-tier Tribunal can then 'remake' the decision – ie, give a new final decision. Presumably, if the ground for a set-aside was that a party was not present, this would require the First-tier Tribunal to hold a hearing to avoid perpetuating the problem. It would also not be right to remake a decision if new documentary evidence or submissions were to be put before the First-tier Tribunal, unless the parties had been given an opportunity to comment on their significance.

In addition, if an application for permission to appeal has been made to the First-tier Tribunal and all the parties argue that the decision is an error of law, it will be set aside and referred to a differently constituted First-tier Tribunal to determine.[122]

Reviewing a decision

Since 3 November 2008, a First-tier Tribunal has the power to 'review' a decision.[123] It must consider whether to review its decision before considering whether to grant permission to appeal to the Upper Tribunal and so, in practice, every application for permission to appeal is effectively an application for a review.

The First-tier Tribunal may only review a decision if an application for permission to appeal has been made and it considers that there is an error of law.

If, on a review, the First-tier Tribunal considers that it is appropriate to amend the reasons for a decision, the parties should be given an opportunity to make suitable representations. The notice to the parties should identify the error of law and the course of action the Tribunal proposes to take.[124]

Note: a decision which has been reviewed can still be appealed to the Upper Tribunal. The First-tier Tribunal must notify the parties of the outcome of any review and of any right of appeal against it.

---

8. **Appealing to the Upper Tribunal**

Any party, including the Child Maintenance Service (CMS) or Child Support Agency (CSA), can appeal to the Upper Tribunal against a final decision of the First-tier Tribunal. An appeal will only succeed if there is an error of law in the First-tier Tribunal's decision. See p226 and CPAG's *Welfare Benefits and Tax Credits Handbook* for information about when a decision contains an error of law. It is not an error of law for the First-tier Tribunal simply not to have believed what one of the parties said, provided that decision is one which a reasonable tribunal could have arrived at, is properly explained and is based on all the evidence. What is an adequate statement of reasons for a decision depends on the facts of the case. It should include enough detail to allow all parties to understand how the main issues in the case were decided.[125]

The Upper Tribunal can give the decision it thinks the First-tier Tribunal should have given. Alternatively (particularly if it thinks the First-tier Tribunal did not find all the relevant facts or consider the evidence properly), it may refer the case back to the First-tier Tribunal for a new decision to be made. If a case is referred back, the new First-tier Tribunal must apply the law in the way that the Upper Tribunal has instructed.

Before the appeal can be dealt with by the Upper Tribunal, permission to appeal must be obtained from the First-tier Tribunal. If this is refused, an application for permission can be made direct to the Upper Tribunal. Permission should only be granted if it is arguable that there is an error of law in the First-tier Tribunal decision.

The procedural rules set out above also apply in the Upper Tribunal (except where stated).

Note: a decision of the First-tier Tribunal which is a procedural decision or ruling (against which there is normally no right of appeal) can be challenged by judicial review. The case is normally heard by the Upper Tribunal. See CPAG's *Welfare Benefits and Tax Credits Handbook* for details.

Applying for permission to appeal from the First-tier Tribunal

An application for permission to appeal against a final decision of the First-tier Tribunal must be in writing and be received by the Tribunal within one month of being sent the following, whichever is the latest:[126]

- a written statement of reasons for the decision;
- following a review, a notice that the reasons for the decision were amended or the decision corrected;
- a notice that an application for a set-aside made within the time limit was refused.

The application must state:[127]
- the decision of the First-tier Tribunal to which it relates;
- the alleged errors of law in the decision;
- the result sought.

If the application is made late, it must explain why and include a request for an extension of time.[128] The First-tier Tribunal can only consider a late application if it has agreed to use its general power to extend the time for applying.

Usually, it is necessary to have obtained the full statement of reasons for a decision before seeking permission to appeal. If no request for a statement of reasons has been made, the First-tier Tribunal must treat the application as an application for a statement of reasons rather than as an application for permission to appeal.[129] If reasons are issued, the party must then make a new application for permission to appeal. If a request for a statement of reasons has been refused because it was made late, the First-tier Tribunal can only grant permission to appeal if it is in the interests of justice to do so.[130]

When considering an application, the First-tier Tribunal must consider whether to review its decision.[131] If it has not changed the decision (or part of it) on review, it must consider whether to grant permission to appeal in respect of its decision, or the unchanged part of it.

The First-tier Tribunal must send a record of its decision on the application for permission to appeal to the parties.[132] If permission is refused in full or in part, the notice must include the reasons for this. It must also include notice of the right to apply directly to the Upper Tribunal for permission to appeal, the time within which this must be done and the method for making such an application.[133]

It is possible for the First-tier Tribunal to grant permission to appeal in respect of part of a decision. A party may then wish to file that appeal with the Upper Tribunal, and also to seek permission to appeal directly from the Upper Tribunal in respect of the parts of the decision for which permission has not been granted by the First-tier Tribunal.

Applying to the Upper Tribunal for permission to appeal

If permission to appeal has been refused (in whole or in part) by the First-tier Tribunal, an application can be made to the Upper Tribunal. An application can usually only be made to the Upper Tribunal if the First-tier Tribunal has refused permission to appeal or has refused to admit an application.[134]

The application to the Upper Tribunal must be made in writing and within one month of being sent the refusal of permission.[135] If made late, the application must include an explanation for why it is late, and it will not be considered unless the time limit is extended by the Upper Tribunal.[136] If the earlier application for a written statement of reasons to the First-tier Tribunal or the application for permission to appeal to the First-tier Tribunal was made late, an explanation must also be given and can only be considered if the Upper Tribunal considers it in the interests of justice to do so.[137]

The application must include details of:[138]

- the name and address of the appellant and any representative;
- an address for sending or delivering documents;
- details (including a full reference) of the decision challenged;
- the grounds on which the appellant is relying;
- whether the appellant wants a hearing of the application.

The application must include copies of:[139]

- the written record of the decision challenged;
- the written statement of reasons for the decision (if it exists);
- the First-tier Tribunal's notice of refusal of permission to appeal or refusal to admit the application.

Using Form UT1, *Application for Permission and Notice of Appeal from First-tier Tribunal (Social Entitlement Chamber)*, available from http://hmctsformfinder.justice.gov.uk, should ensure that applications are correctly made.[140]

The Upper Tribunal must send the appellant (but not the respondent) reasons for refusing an application.[141] There is no right of appeal against a decision of the Upper Tribunal to refuse permission to appeal.[142]

The Upper Tribunal must send notice of permission to appeal to all the parties.[143] If this happens, generally the application for permission will be treated as the notice of appeal. The Upper Tribunal sends a copy of this to all the parties and explains that it is treating the application for permission as the actual appeal.[144] If the parties agree, the Upper Tribunal can then determine the appeal without a need for any further response from them.[145]

Notice of appeal

If the First-tier Tribunal grants permission to appeal, the appellant should send a notice of appeal to the Upper Tribunal. If the appellant has received permission to appeal directly from the Upper Tribunal, this is usually treated as the notice of appeal, unless the Upper Tribunal directs otherwise.[146]

If needed, the notice of appeal must be received by the Upper Tribunal within one month of the party's being sent the notice of permission to appeal by the First-tier Tribunal.[147]

The same information and documents must be included with the notice of appeal as for an application for permission to appeal (except that the appellant will be sending the notice of grant and not refusal of permission).[148]

Late notices of appeal must include a request for an extension of time and the reasons why the notice was not provided in time, and cannot be admitted unless the time limit is extended by the Upper Tribunal.[149]

The Upper Tribunal must send a copy of the notice of appeal and accompanying documents to each respondent.[150]

Responses and replies

The other party can respond to the appeal, but does not have to unless the Upper Tribunal so directs.[151]

A response must be in writing and received by the Upper Tribunal within one month of being sent the notice of appeal (or the notice of a grant of permission to appeal, if this is treated as the notice of appeal). A late response must request an extension of the time limit and explain why it is late.[152]

The response must state:[153]
- the name and address of the respondent and any representative;
- an address for sending or delivering documents;
- whether the respondent opposes the appeal;
- the grounds on which the respondent intends to rely in the appeal;
- whether the respondent wants a hearing.

The Upper Tribunal must provide a copy of the response to the appellant and the other parties.[154]

The appellant may then reply to the response, but does not have to unless the Upper Tribunal so directs. The reply must be received within one month of being sent the response and is then copied to the other parties by the Upper Tribunal.[155]

Challenging decisions of the Upper Tribunal

Note: legal advice should always be sought when considering whether to challenge an Upper Tribunal decision.

Upper Tribunal decisions can be changed by:
- correcting an accidental error (see p255);[156]
- setting aside the decision (see p255);[157]
- appealing to the Court of Appeal (in Scotland, the Court of Session). Permission is needed for this, and the appeal must be on the grounds that the Upper Tribunal made an error of law. An application for permission must first be made to the Upper Tribunal.[158] This is similar to the procedure for applying for permission from the First-tier Tribunal, except that the time limit is three months. The Upper Tribunal must also consider a review (see p260) before deciding whether to grant permission. If the Upper Tribunal refuses permission,

the request can be made directly to the Court. The Upper Tribunal's refusal decision should include a statement of reasons, details of the relevant court and the time limit for applying.[159] Permission can only be granted if the Upper Tribunal or Court considers the appeal would raise an important point of principle or practice, or there is some other compelling reason to grant it;[160]

* reviewing the decision (see p255). The procedure is as for the First-tier Tribunal, except that the Upper Tribunal can only exercise this power if, when making its decision, it overlooked a legislative decision or binding authority which could have affected the decision or, since giving its decision, a court has made a decision which could have affected its decision.[161]

The Upper Tribunal may treat an application for a decision to be corrected, set aside or reviewed, or an application for permission to appeal against a decision, as an application for any one of these things.[162]

A decision of the Upper Tribunal that cannot be appealed against (eg, a refusal to grant leave to appeal from the First-tier Tribunal to the Upper Tribunal) can be challenged by applying for judicial review to the High Court (in England and Wales) or the Court of Session (in Scotland). This can only be done if the case would raise some important point of principle or practice, or if there is some other compelling reason.[163]

For further details about challenging decisions of the Upper Tribunal, see CPAG's *Welfare Benefits and Tax Credits Handbook*.

9. **Test case rules**

Special rules apply if a court or Upper Tribunal decision on a 'test case' is pending, or an Upper Tribunal or court decision on a test case has been made. A 'test case' is one in which a person is challenging the Child Maintenance Service's (CMS's) or Child Support Agency's (CSA's) interpretation of the law in a way that affects other cases more generally, even if it is the CMS/CSA's own appeal and even if the person does not consider the case to be a test case.

These rules apply to child support calculation decisions, revision and supersession decisions, and appeals to the First-tier or Upper Tribunal .

Test case pending

If a test case is decided against the CMS/CSA, it must usually follow the law in all other cases as decided in that case. However, if an appeal is pending before the Upper Tribunal or a court, the CMS/CSA can:[164]

* postpone making a decision on the application, revision or supersession in any other case which might be affected by the decision to be given in that appeal until the test case appeal has been decided; *or*

- in '2012 rules' cases, make a decision as if the test case had already been decided in a way that would result in the lowest possible amount of child support being payable in the case which might be affected by the decision. This only applies if there is no calculation in force in the case which might be affected by the test case decision;[165]
- in '1993 rules' and '2003 rules' cases, make a decision as if the test case appeal had already been decided against the person who applied for the decision (ie, the calculation, revision or supersession) if:[166]
  – before 12 April 2010, the CSA would otherwise have had to have made a calculation (including one on revision or supersession) leading to the parent with care becoming entitled to income support (IS) or a higher rate of IS; or
  – the non-resident parent is employed or self-employed.[167]

An appeal is 'pending' before a court if:[168]
- an appeal (including a judicial review) about child support has been made to the High Court, Court of Appeal, Court of Session or Supreme Court but has not been determined;
- an application for permission to make such an appeal (or judicial review) has been made, but has not been determined;
- the CMS/CSA has certified in writing that it is considering making such an appeal or application and the time for appealing or applying has not expired, and the CMS/CSA considers that the appeal might result in the non-resident parent's having no, or less, liability for child support.[169]

An appeal also counts as pending if a court (but not the Upper Tribunal) has referred a question to the European Court of Justice (ECJ) for a preliminary ruling.

If the CMS/CSA does not make an application or appeal in time, it can no longer postpone making a decision.

A decision to suspend or make a decision on the assumption that the CMS/CSA will win the test case is a discretionary one. The CMS/CSA must, therefore, take into account the welfare of the child when making it.

How a pending test case affects similar cases under appeal

If a test case pending (see above) before a court may affect a similar case awaiting a decision from the First-tier Tribunal or Upper Tribunal, or there is a possibility that the CMS/CSA may appeal, the CMS/CSA may:[170]
- direct the Tribunal to refer the similar case to the CMS/CSA. The CMS/CSA makes no decision until the test case is decided. It then revises the CMS/CSA decision under appeal or supersedes the Tribunal decision under appeal; or
- direct the Tribunal to deal with the case itself. The Tribunal must then either:
  – postpone its decision until the test case is decided; or
  – decide the appeal as if the test case appeal has already been decided against the person who appealed in the similar case. It should only do this if it

considers that it is in the appellant's interests. If the test case is later decided in that person's favour, the CMS/CSA supersedes the Tribunal decision in the similar case.

Test case decisions

If a decision of the Upper Tribunal or court interprets child support law, the CMS/CSA must usually apply that interpretation in the period before the decision was given. This usually requires the CMS/CSA to supersede all decisions which are affected.

However, if the Upper Tribunal/court rejected the CMS/CSA's interpretation of the law, that test case decision only has effect from the date it is made.[171] For the period before that date, the CMS/CSA (and either Tribunal) assumes that it was right in its interpretation of the law when making the original decision which led to the appeal.[172] This includes cases in which the test case appeal began with a First-tier Tribunal decision on a referral of an application for a variation. This rule applies:

- to calculations;[173]
- even if the application for a revision or supersession was made before the test case decision was given and regardless of whether the person applying raised that issue of law;[174]
- even if the Upper Tribunal/court decides that a regulation is *ultra vires*.[175] If this decision is made because the regulation is inconsistent with the European Convention on Human Rights, this rule may also breach that Convention;[176]
- even to decisions of the ECJ.[177] This rule is unlawful under European Union law, except in a case where the ECJ has itself decided that its decision only has effect from the date it is given.[178]

This rule does not apply to:

- an application for child support, or a reduced benefit decision, made before 1 June 1999;[179]
- a revision or supersession of any decision made before 1 June 1999;[180]
- a decision in a case where the CMS/CSA had suspended a decision under the test case pending rules (see p260);[181]
- a revision or supersession decision in a case where the CMS/CSA had required the First-tier or Upper Tribunal to refer the case to the CMS/CSA, or deal with it on the assumption that the test case had already been decided against the appellant.[182]

Notes

1. Decisions that can be appealed

1 s102 WRA 2012; s20(2A) and (2B) CSA 1991; reg 8(1) SS&CS(DA)(A) Regs 2013
   2012 rules Reg 14A CSMC Regs
   2003 rules Reg 3B SS&CS(D&A) Regs
   1993 rules Reg 17A CS(MAP) Regs
2 s20(4)(c) CSA 1991
   2012 rules Reg 14A(4) CSMC Regs
   2003 rules Reg 3B(4) SS&CS(D&A) Regs
   1993 rules Reg 17A(4) CS(MAP) Regs
3 s20 CSA 1991
4 Reg 12(1) CS(MPA) Regs
5 **EW** Art 5 CSA(JC)O 2002
   S Art 5 CSA(JC)(S)O
6 **EW** Arts 3 and 4 CSA(JC)O 2002
   S Arts 2, 3 and 4 CSA(JC)(S)O 2003
7 r5(3)(k) TP(FT) Rules

2. Appealing to the First-tier Tribunal

8 s20(3) CSA 1991
   2012 rules Regs 24-26 CSMC Regs
   2003 rules Reg 23 CS(MCP) Regs
   1993 rules Reg 10 CS(MAP) Regs
   1993 & 2003 rules Reg 15C SS&CS(DA) Regs
9 www.gov.uk/social-security-child-support-tribunal/overview
10 r22(3) TP(FT) Rules
11 r22(4) TP(FT) Rules
12 **2012 rules** *What To Do If You're Unhappy With the Child Maintenance Service*, CMSB011GB, October 2013
   2003 rules *How Can I Appeal Against a Child Maintenance Decision*, CSL 307, October 2013
   1993 rules *How to Appeal*, CSA 2006A, October 2013
13 r22(2)(d) and Sch 1 TP(FT) Rules
14 s16(5) CSA 1991
15 Reg 7(2) CSMC Regs
16 Reg 2(b) SS&CS(DA) Regs
17 R(IB) 4/02
18 r12 TP(FT) Rules
19 r22(8) TP(FT) Rules
20 r22(8) TP(FT) Rules

21 rr2(1), (2) and (3)(a) and 5(3)(a) TP(FT) Rules; *Information Commissioner v PS* [2011] UKUT 94 (AAC); *CD v First-tier Tribunal (CICA)* [2010] UKUT 181 (AAC), reported as [2011] AACR 1
22 r22(6) TP(FT) Rules
23 *LS v London Borough of Lambeth (HB)* [2010] UKUT 461 (AAC)
24 r5 TP(FT) Rules
25 r22(7) TP(FT) Rules
26 r24(1)(b)(ii) TP(FT) Rules
27 r24(2)(a)-(d) TP(FT) Rules
28 r24(2)(e) TP(FT) Rules
29 r24(3) TP(FT) Rules
30 r24(4) TP(FT) Rules
31 *TR v SSWP and PW(CSM)* [2013] UKUT 80 (AAC)
32 r24(6) and (7) TP(FT) Rules
33 r19(2) and (3) TP(FT) Rules

3. The appeal procedure

34 R(IS) 11/99; *KB v SSWP (DLA)* [2011] UKUT 388 (AAC)
35 r2 TP(FT) Rules; r2 TP(UT) Rules
36 r2(3) TP(FT) Rules; r2(3) TP(UT) Rules
37 r2(2) TP(FT) Rules; r2(2) TP(UT) Rules
38 *MS v SSWP* [2009] UKUT 211 (AAC)
39 r2(4) TP(FT) Rules; r2(4) TP(UT) Rules
40 r6(1) TP(FT) Rules; r6(1) TP(UT) Rules
41 *LM v London Borough of Lewisham* [2009] UKUT 204 (AAC)
42 r15 TP(FT) Rules; r15 TP(UT) Rules
43 *JD v SS for Defence (WP)* [2013] UKUT 119 (AAC)
44 r19(3) TP(FT) Rules; r19(2) and (4) TP(UT) Rules
45 r14(1) TP(FT) Rules; r14(1) TP(UT) Rules
46 r14(2) TP(FT) Rules; r14(2) TP(UT) Rules
47 r14(3) TP(FT) Rules; r14(3) TP(UT) Rules
48 r14(5) and (6) TP(FT) Rules; r14(5) and (6) TP(UT) Rules
49 R(CS) 3/06
50 r17 TP(FT) Rules; r17 TP(UT) Rules
51 r10 TP(FT) Rules; r10 TP(UT) Rules
52 r7 TP(FT) Rules; r7 TP(UT) Rules
53 s25 TCEA 2007
54 r7(3) and (4) TP(UT) Rules
55 r8(1) TP(FT) Rules; r8(1) TP(UT) Rules
56 r8(2) TP(FT) Rules; r8(2) TP(UT) Rules

57 r8(3)(b) TP(FT) Rules; r8(3)(b) TP(UT) Rules
58 r8(3)(c) TP(FT) Rules; r8(3)(c) TP(UT) Rules
59 *DTM v Kettering Borough Council (CTB)* [2013] UKUT 625 (AAC)
60 r8(5) TP(FT) Rules; r8(5) TP(UT) Rules
61 r8(6) TP(FT) Rules; r8(6) TP(UT) Rules
62 rr2(1) and (3)(a) and 5(3)(a) TP(FT) Rules ; rr2(1) and 3(a) and 5(3)(a) TP(UT) Rules
63 *R (BD) v First-tier Tribunal (CIC)* [2013] UKUT 332 (AAC)
64 r8(4) TP(FT) Rules; r8(4) TP(UT) Rules
65 *Ezsias v North Glamorgan NHS Trust* [2007] EWCA Civ 330
66 *RN v SSWP (RP)* [2013] UKUT 461 (AAC)
67 *Synergy Child Services Ltd v Ofsted* [2009] UKUT 125 (AAC); *LS v London Borough of Lambeth (HB)* [2010] UKUT 461 (AAC)
68 r12(1) TP(FT) Rules; r12(1) TP(UT) Rules
69 r12(2) and (3) TP(FT) Rules; r12(2) and (3) TP(UT) Rules
70 r13(1) TP(FT) Rules; r13(1) TP(UT) Rules
71 r13(2) and (3) TP(FT) Rules; r13(2) and (3) TP(UT) Rules
72 r13(4) TP(FT) Rules; r13(4) TP(UT) Rules
73 r13(5) TP(FT) Rules; r13(5) TP(UT) Rules
74 r11(5) TP(FT) Rules; r11(3) TP(UT) Rules
75 r11(6) TP(FT) Rules; r11(4) TP(UT) Rules
76 *MP v SSWP (DLA)* [2010] UKUT 103 (AAC)
77 r11(7) and (8) TP(FT) Rules; r11(5) and (6) TP(UT) Rules
78 r17 TP(FT) Rules; r17 TP(UT) Rules
79 r17(1)(b), (2) and (3)(b) TP(FT) Rules
80 **2012 rules** Sch para 3(10) CSMC Regs **1993 & 2003 rules** Reg 33(10) SS&CS(DA) Regs
81 r17(1) and (2) TP(UT) Rules

4. Preparing a case
82 r5 Family Proceedings Courts (CSA 1991) Rules 1993, No.627; r10.21A Family Proceedings Rules 1991, No.1247
83 CCS/3757/2004

5. Hearings
84 r1(3) TP(FT) Rules; r1(3) TP(UT) Rules
85 r27 TP(FT) Rules
86 *MM v SSWP (ESA)* [2011] UKUT 334 (AAC); *JP v SSWP (IB)* [2011] UKUT 459 (AAC)
87 r34 TP(UT) Rules
88 r29(1) TP(FT) Rules; r36(1) TP(UT) Rules

89 r29(2) TP(FT) Rules; r36(2)(b) TP(UT) Rules. The only other exception to this is when the Upper Tribunal is conducting a hearing of an application for permission to bring judicial review, in which at least two working days' notice must be given. Such proceedings are outside the scope of this *Handbook*.
90 CCS/1925/2002
91 r30 TP(FT) Rules; r37 TP(UT) Rules
92 r31 TP(FT) Rules; r38 TP(UT) Rules
93 CCS/1689/2007; CCS/2901/2001; CCS/2676/2001
94 Art 2 FT&UT(CT)O and Tribunals Judiciary Practice Statement, *Composition of Tribunals in Social Security and Child Support Cases in the Social Entitlement Chamber on or after 1 August 2013*, July 2013, para 6
95 Sch 2 para 1(2) TCEA 2007
96 Tribunals Judiciary Practice Statement, *Composition of Tribunals in Social Security and Child Support Cases in the Social Entitlement Chamber on or after 1 August 2013*, July 2013, para 7
97 Tribunals Judiciary Practice Statement, *Composition of Tribunals in Social Security and Child Support Cases in the Social Entitlement Chamber on or after 1 August 2013*, July 2013, para 12; Art 8 FT&UT(CT)O
98 Tribunals Judiciary Practice Statement, *Composition of Tribunals in Relation to Matters that Fall to be Decided by the Administrative Appeals Chamber of the Upper Tribunal on or after 26 March 2014*, March 2014, para 3a; Arts 3 and 4 FT&UT(CT)O
99 CSCS/16/2007

6. Decisions
100 s20(7) CSA 1991
101 s20(7)(b) CSA 1991
102 CCS/16351/1996; *MB v CMEC* [2009] UKUT 29 (AAC), para 16
103 s20(7)(a) CSA 1991
104 R(IB) 2/04; *A P-H v SSWP (DLA)* [2010] UKUT 183 (AAC); *JW v SSWP & MC & JC (CSM)* [2013] UKUT 407 (AAC)
105 CCS/2861/2001
106 CCS/3757/2004
107 R(IB) 2/04
108 CSCS/2/1994; CSCS/3/1994
109 CCS/511/1995
110 *AB v CMEC (CSM)* [2010] UKUT 385 (AAC)
111 r33 TP(FT) Rules
112 r34(2)(b) TP(FT) Rules

113 r34(3) and (4) TP(FT) Rules
114 r34(5) TP(FT) Rules
115 r40 TP(UT) Rules
116 Tribunals Judiciary Practice Statement, *Record of Proceedings in Social Security and Child Support Cases in the Social Entitlement Chamber on or after 3 November 2008,* November 2008
117 r32 TP(FT) Rules; r39 TP(UT) Rules

7. **Changing a First-tier Tribunal decision**

118 Not including judicial review of non-appealable decisions.
119 r42 TP(FT) Rules
120 *AS v SSWP (ESA)* [2011] UKUT 159 (AAC); *CG v SSWP (DLA)* [2011] UKUT 453 (AAC)
121 r37 TP(FT) Rules
122 s23A CSA 1991
123 Introduced by s9 TCEA 2007; see also r40 TP(FT) Rules
124 *JS v SSWP (DLA)* [2013] UKUT 100 (AAC), reported as [2013] AACR 30

8. **Appealing to the Upper Tribunal**

125 *MW v SSWP (II)* [2011] UKUT 465 (AAC)
126 r38(2) and (3) TP(FT) Rules
127 r38(6) TP(FT) Rules
128 r38(5) TP(FT) Rules
129 r38(7) TP(FT) Rules
130 r38(7)(c) TP(FT) Rules
131 r39(1) TP(FT) Rules
132 r39(3) TP(FT) Rules
133 r39(4) TP(FT) Rules
134 r21(2) TP(UT) Rules; *MA v SSD* [2009] UKUT 57 (AAC) stated that, under r7 TP(UT) Rules, the Upper Tribunal could waive this requirement.
135 r21(3)(b) TP(UT) Rules
136 r21(6) TP(UT) Rules
137 r21(7) TP(UT) Rules
138 r21(4) TP(UT) Rules
139 r21(5) TP(UT) Rules
140 Form UT1 is available from www.justice.gov.uk/forms
141 r22(1) TP(UT) Rules
142 *Cart and Others, R (on the application of) v The Upper Tribunal and Others* [2009] EWHC 3052 (Admin), 1 December 2009
143 r22(2)(a) TP(UT) Rules
144 r22(2)(b) TP(UT) Rules
145 r22(2)(c) TP(UT) Rules
146 r23(1) TP(UT) Rules
147 r23(2) TP(UT) Rules
148 r23(3) and (4) TP(UT) Rules
149 r23(5) TP(UT) Rules
150 r23(6) TP(UT) Rules
151 r24(1) TP(UT) Rules

152 r24(2) and (4) TP(UT) Rules
153 r24(3) TP(UT) Rules
154 r24(5) TP(UT) Rules
155 r25 TP(UT) Rules
156 r42 TP(UT) Rules
157 r43 TP(UT) Rules
158 s13 TCEA 2007; rr44 and 45 TP(UT) Rules
159 r45(4) TP(UT) Rules
160 s13(6) and (6A) TCEA 2007; AUTCAO; r41.57(2) Rules of the Court of Session
161 r46 TP(UT) Rules
162 r48 TP(UT) Rules
163 *R (Cart) v The Upper Tribunal* [2011] UKSC 28, 22 June 2011; *Eba v Advocate General for Scotland* [2011] UKSC 29, 22 June 2011

9. **Test case rules**

164 s28ZA(1) and (2) CSA 1991
165 Reg 28(1) CSMC Regs
166 Reg 23(3) and (5) SS&CS(DA) Regs
167 As defined in s2(1) SSCBA 1992
168 s28ZA(4) and (5) CSA 1991
169 s28ZA(4)(c) CSA 1991
     2012 rules Reg 28(2) CSMC Regs
     1993 & 2003 rules Reg 23(4) SS&CS(DA) Regs
170 s28ZB CSA 1991
171 s28ZC(1) and (3) CSA 1991
     2012 rules Regs 30-32 CSMC Regs
     1993 & 2003 rules Reg 7B and Sch 3D(12) SS&CS(DA) Regs
172 s28ZC(1) and (3) CSA 1991
173 s28ZC(1)(b) CSA 1991
174 s28ZC(5) CSA 1991
175 s28ZC(4) CSA 1991
176 Art 13 ECHR requires an effective remedy for violations.
177 s28ZC(6) CSA 1991
178 *Commission v France,* C-35/97 [1998] ECR I-5325
179 s28ZC(1)(b)(i) CSA 1991
180 s28ZC(1)(b)(ii) and (iii) CSA 1991
181 s28ZC(2)(a) CSA 1991
182 s28ZC(2)(b) CSA 1991

Chapter 14

Collection and enforcement

This chapter covers:
1. Introduction (below)
2. Payment of child support (p267)
3. Collection of other payments (p278)
4. Arrears (p279)
5. Enforcement (p292)
6. Fees for enforcement action (p312)
7. Delays in collection and enforcement (p313)
8. '1993 rules' and conversion cases (p315)

1. Introduction

Once decisions on liability for child support and the calculation have been made, payment can be made in different ways. The non-resident parent can pay directly to the person with care without the payment going through the Child Maintenance Service (CMS) or Child Support Agency (CSA). Alternatively, the CMS/CSA can arrange the collection and enforcement of child support[1] and certain other maintenance payments (see p278).[2]

For '2012 rules' cases, fees for using the CMS's collection service (see p270) were introduced on 11 August 2014 and fees for some types of enforcement action (see p312) were introduced on 30 June 2014.[3] The collection service has been free of charge to all CSA clients since April 1995,[4] and will remain free for those with cases under the '2003 rules' and '1993 rules' until these are closed (see p83).

If the collection service is being used, a collection schedule is set up. If the payment schedule breaks down and arrears accrue, debt management procedures may be put in place, or the CMS/CSA may decide to take enforcement action. If child support is being paid directly and payments are missed, the person with care can inform the CMS/CSA, and debt management and enforcement action can also be taken.

The CMS/CSA does not have discretion in decisions about liability for child support and the calculation decision.[5] The amount of child support calculated cannot be altered, except by revision, supersession, appeal or variation (departure under the '1993 rules'). The CMS/CSA does not suspend current collection just because the non-resident parent states that s/he cannot afford to pay. However, it may agree to lower payments if a decision on a revision, supersession, appeal or variation/departure is pending (see p284).

However, decisions on applying the law on how payment is enforced are discretionary, and should take into account all the circumstances of the individual case and the welfare of any child likely to be affected. This should allow scope for negotiation between the CMS/CSA and the individuals involved. The CMS/CSA should be asked to investigate the circumstances fully in order to allow it to exercise its discretion appropriately.

There is no right to challenge (ie, by seeking a revision and then an appeal to the First-tier Tribunal) a decision concerning collection and enforcement.[6] A deduction from earnings order (see p293) can, in limited circumstances, be appealed to a magistrates' court (England or Wales) or the sheriff court (Scotland) (see p293), and orders to deduct amounts from bank accounts (see p301) can be appealed in the county court (England and Wales) or the sheriff court (Scotland). It may be possible to challenge other decisions by judicial review (see p215). A complaint can also be made about the way the CMS/CSA has used its discretion (see Chapter 15).

2. **Payment of child support**

The Child Maintenance Service (CMS) or Child Support Agency (CSA) can require the non-resident parent to pay child support:[7]
- directly to the person with care;
- directly to a child applicant in Scotland;
- to, or via, the CMS/CSA (the CMS/CSA can only provide the collection service at the request of one of the parties to the calculation); *or*
- to, or via, another person.

The CMS/CSA has broad discretion to decide how payment is to be arranged. This includes the payment of any collection or enforcement fees.[8] Before making these decisions, the CMS/CSA must, as far as possible, give the non-resident parent and the person with care an opportunity to make representations and must take these into account.[9]

The CMS/CSA prefers the parties to agree that child support should be paid by the non-resident parent directly to the person with care, although there is no requirement to do this. If direct payments are agreed, once the CMS/CSA has calculated the amount owed, the parties make their own arrangement about when and how payments will be made. This is known as 'direct pay' (under the '2012 rules') or 'maintenance direct' (under the '1993 rules' and '2003 rules').

If direct payment is agreed, the CMS/CSA informs each parent about the amount of initial arrears and the date regular payments should start. It is up to the parties to decide how and when payments will be made. The CMS/CSA recommends payment by standing order or a money transfer service (such as PayPal or MoneyGram) if the person with care does not want to disclose financial details to the non-resident parent. The CSA/CMS can also advise the person with care about setting up a 'non-geographic' bank account (an account with a central or national sort code rather than one linked to a local branch) and can then pass the account details securely to the non-resident parent. This type of sort code does not give any information about the area in which the person with care lives.[11]

Direct payments are not monitored by the CMS/CSA. If the payment arrangement breaks down, the person with care can ask to use the collection service (see p269). Both parties should keep careful records of the payments made.

The CMS/CSA can only provide the collection service (ie, whereby the non-resident parent pays child support to the CMS/CSA, which then passes it on to the person with care) at the request of one of the parties to the calculation.[12] The collection service is known as 'collect and pay' for '2012 rules' cases.

From 30 June 2014, the CMS can only set up 'collect and pay' arrangements for '2012 rules' cases if the non-resident parent agrees, or if the CMS thinks that s/he is unlikely to pay otherwise. The CMS can allow the non-resident parent to apply to switch to 'direct pay' without the agreement of the person with care.[10] If the non-resident parent in an existing case that is due to close or transfer to the '2012 rules' (see Chapter 5) is subject to enforced methods of payment (such as a deduction from earnings order), the CMS offers her/him the opportunity to comply voluntarily (eg, by paying by direct debit) for a period before the case closes. S/he is only offered the option of 'direct pay' under the '2012 rules' if s/he proves s/he can comply. If s/he refuses or fails to comply, enforced methods of payment continue.[13]

If a child support calculation has been made and the CMS/CSA is collecting and enforcing the payment, it has discretion to decide:
- the method by which the non-resident parent pays;[14]
- the person to whom it is paid;[15]
- if payments are made through the CMS/CSA or someone else, the method by which payment is made to the person with care;[16]
- the timing of payments;[17] *and*
- the amount of payments towards arrears.[18]

The CMS/CSA must notify the non-resident parent in writing of the amounts and timing of payments due, to whom and how s/he must make payment and details of any amount that is overdue and remains outstanding.[19] This notice is sent as soon as possible after the calculation is made and again after any change in the details in the notice.[20] A copy is sent to the person with care.

The CMS/CSA can treat certain payments made to a third party (eg, a mortgage lender) as payments of child support. This can include voluntary payments made between the effective date and the date of the calculation (used to offset any initial arrears – see p275) and payments made after the effective date.[21]

The collection service

When child support payments are to be made to or via the CMS/CSA, this is referred to as the collection service (or 'collect and pay' for '2012 rules' cases). Any party to a case can request that payment be via the CMS/CSA[22] and the CSA usually provides the collection service if a party requests it, even if the other party does not.

From 30 June 2014, the CMS can only set up 'collect and pay' arrangements for '2012 rules' cases if the non-resident parent agrees or the CMS thinks that the non-resident parent is unlikely to pay otherwise (see p268).[23]

If the non-resident parent is on benefit, the person with care may use the collection service to obtain direct deductions from the benefit. This is particularly useful if a voluntary arrangement cannot be reached.

The collection service can be requested at a later date – eg, if payments become irregular. The request can be made verbally or in writing.

If payments are made to the CMS/CSA, only those actually received by the CMS/CSA can be passed on. The CMS/CSA aims to make the first payment to the person with care within six weeks of making initial payment arrangements with the non-resident parent. It also aims to transfer payments as soon as it receives them and within one week of receiving them from the non-resident parent.[24]

Using the collection service removes the need for direct contact between the non-resident parent and person with care (although using a non-geographic bank account and having the CMS/CSA pass the details to the non-resident parent can also remove the need for direct contact. It is also supposed to ensure regular payments by starting enforcement action (see p292) as soon as payments are missed, although this does not always happen.

Even if the collection service is used, the parties should always keep their own records and evidence of payments. Many accounts are in arrears and many persons with care and some non-resident parents have been unhappy with the level of service in the past. A payment statement is only issued periodically or on request (see p275) and, in the past, these have often been considered to be inaccurate. The CMS/CSA negotiates collection and arrears schedules with the parents and may agree to an arrears arrangement, despite any objections from the person with care.

Fees for using the collection service

Fees were introduced on 11 August 2014 for '2012 rules' cases where the 'collect and pay' service is used.[25] These are intended to encourage parties to make direct payments rather than use 'collect and pay'.[26] The CSA has written to the parties in '2012 rules' cases to explain the fees and how they can be avoided.

If the parties use the CMS to collect and pay the child support due, regular ongoing fees are charged on both the non-resident parent and the person with care:[27]

- a fee of 20 per cent in addition to the amount of child support liability the non-resident parent must pay; *and*
- a deduction of 4 per cent of the amount of child support due to the person with care.

For the non-resident parent, the fee is 20 per cent of the child support liability for each day that falls after the introduction of fees and for which 'collect and pay' arrangements are in place. If the non-resident parent is paying child support to more than one person with care and not all are paid by 'collect and pay', the fee is charged only on those payments for which 'collect and pay' has been arranged.[28]

For the person with care, the fee is deducted by the CMS before making the payment of child support to the person with care.[29] If the amount actually paid by the non-resident parent is lower than the amount due, the CMS still deducts a fee of 4 per cent of the amount paid before making the payment of child support to the person with care.[30]

Example 14.1

Joe is the non-resident parent of four children who live with his former partner, Susan. Joe has been assessed under the '2012 rules' as due to pay £35 a week in child support to Susan. If the collection service is used, Joe is, in fact, liable to pay £42 a week (£35 + (20% x £35)) to the CMS.

The CMS also deducts £1.40 (4% x £35) from the child support due to Susan, so she receives £33.60 a week. The balance of £8.40 a week is retained by the CMS.

Where the calculation of fees results in a fraction of a penny, this is disregarded if less than a half. If a half or over, it is rounded up to the next penny.[31]

If someone is both a person with care and a non-resident parent

In some child support calculations, a person might be both a person with care and a non-resident parent at the same time. This may arise where the qualifying children from a relationship live with different parents after the relationship has ended. In this situation, both parents may be liable to pay child support to each other and a separate calculation is made for each. If the collection service is being used, the CMS/CSA can offset their liabilities.[32]

Example 14.2

Ali and Nazia have two children, Mohammed and Faisal. When they separate, Mohammed lives with Ali and Faisal lives with Nazia. Both parents apply to use the collection service. Ali works full time and is liable to pay child support of £60 a week. Nazia works part time and is liable to pay child support of £20 a week.

Instead of the CMS/CSA collecting and distributing two sets of payments, it deducts Nazia's liability from Ali's:

£60 – £20 = £40

Ali pays Nazia £40 per week. Nazia does not pay anything.

Payments can only be offset if the collection service is being used.[33] However, for '1993 rules' and '2003 rules' cases, the current computer system is unable to process the arrangement. If parties to a calculation insist on offsetting payments, it is likely to mean that their case is dealt with manually ('clerical cases'). This can cause considerable delay at all stages, including the use of enforcement measures if these are required in the future. Parents whose cases are already treated as clerical should be able to request that offsetting is applied.

Note: if liabilities are being offset where the 'collect and pay' service is being used in a '2012 rules' case, collection fees are only calculated on the net amount paid rather than on the actual liabilities – ie, in *Example 14.2* above, Ali will pay £48 per week (£40 + 20 per cent) and Nazia will receive £38.40 per week (£40 – 4 per cent).

If both parties to a child support calculation are non-resident parents and persons with care and both fall into arrears, any arrears can also be offset so that the CMS/CSA only has to pursue the party with the largest debt (see p285).[34]

Person with care on benefits

Arrears of child support may be retained by the CSA if they are in respect of a period during which the person with care (or her/his partner) was in receipt of income support (IS), income-based jobseeker's allowance (JSA), income-related employment and support allowance (ESA) or pension credit (PC) and child support was not fully disregarded for these benefits.[35]

Note: from 12 April 2010, all child support is fully disregarded when working out these benefits, so the CSA should not retain any child support in respect of periods on or after this date.

The amount retained is equal to the difference between the amount of benefit paid to the person with care and the amount that would have been paid if the non-resident parent had made the required payments during the relevant period.

Before 27 October 2008, if payments were made via the CSA, the person with care received one credit transfer from Jobcentre Plus that included both IS/ income-based JSA/PC and child support. If the non-resident parent did not make a payment to the CSA, the person with care's benefit was still paid, but without child support. From this date, the CSA has paid all child support collected directly to the person with care. This is paid into the same account as the one into which benefits are paid, unless the CSA is notified otherwise.

The person with care must notify Jobcentre Plus of any child support received. Although child support is now fully disregarded for all means-tested benefits, Jobcentre Plus still requests that claimants inform it if they receive child support. This is to allow Jobcentre Plus to disregard child support income where appropriate and to check whether any of it would come under the capital rules. It is possible (although unusual) for child support payments to build up and exceed the capital rules for these benefits. If Jobcentre Plus is not notified promptly, the person with care could be accused of causing an overpayment by failing to disclose a material fact, particularly if s/he is found to have unexplained income in a bank account. The reason why child support must be declared in this way is not always fully explained to claimants.

Method of payment

The CMS/CSA can specify that the non-resident parent make payments by whichever of the following methods it considers appropriate:[36]
- standing order;
- direct debit;
- automated credit transfer;
- credit card;
- debit card;
- cheque;
- postal order;
- banker's draft;
- voluntary deductions from earnings order (see p293); *or*
- cash.

If the collection service is being used, the CMS/CSA asks for payment to be made by direct debit or by deductions from earnings.[37] The CMS/CSA can direct a non-resident parent to take all reasonable steps to open a bank or building society account for the purposes of paying child support and any collection fees.[38] However, there is no penalty for failing to do so. Non-resident parents who wish to pay by another method may have to persuade the CMS/CSA to discuss alternative payment arrangements.

When deciding the method of payment, the CMS/CSA should give the parties the opportunity to make respresentations and must take these into account.[39]

If the non-resident parent is receiving certain benefits, the CMS/CSA normally deducts the amount for child support directly from the benefit before s/he receives it (see below).[40]

If payment is made via the CMS/CSA, the person with care is usually paid by automated credit transfer, unless the CMS/CSA considers that it is necessary in the circumstances of the case to use another method.[41] The person with care is asked to provide details of a bank, building society or Post Office account. If s/he does not have an account, or experiences difficulty opening one, s/he should contact the CMS/CSA.

Deductions from benefit: '2012 rules' and '2003 rules'

If a non-resident parent on benefit is required to pay child support at the flat rate (see Chapter 6 for '2012 rules' cases and Chapter 8 for '2003 rules' cases), the CMS/CSA may request Jobcentre Plus to make a deduction for child support.[42] Deductions can be made from the benefits that qualify a non-resident parent for the flat rate (see p133).[43]

If someone should pay at the flat rate but a variation has been made which results in the reduced or basic rate being payable, deductions can be made towards the new amount of child support calculated.

If a non-resident parent and her/his partner are:[44]

- on IS, income-based JSA, income-related ESA, universal credit (UC) calculated on the basis that s/he has no earned income, or PC; *and*
- each is a non-resident parent,

the flat-rate deduction (£7 for '2012 rules' cases and £5 for '2003 rules' cases) is split between them so that each contributes half the amount to their respective persons with care.[45] (For the '2003 rules', in polygamous relationships where there is more than one new partner who is also a non-resident parent, the £5 is apportioned between all the non-resident parents.[46])

The CMS/CSA requests the deduction and Jobcentre Plus must make it in full wherever possible. The parent must be left with at least 10 pence a week (one pence for UC).[47] Partial deductions are not made. Under the '2012 rules' and '2003 rules', the deduction for child support is always made, whatever other deductions are due.

Note: from 11 August 2014 for '2012 rules' cases where the 'collect and pay' service is used, deductions from benefit also cover any fee due. Any amount of the deduction that is for fees is retained by the CMS.[48]

Both the person with care and the non-resident parent are notified that deductions are to be made.

If there are arrears of child support, a £1 per week deduction towards these may be made from benefits, except IS, income-based JSA, income-related ESA, UC and PC (see p285).

Deductions from benefit: '1993 rules'

When an application is received by the CSA and the non-resident parent is on IS/income-based JSA/income-related ESA/PC/UC, both parties are notified about whether or not deductions from benefit are possible. If the non-resident parent is not exempt from deductions, the Department for Work and Pensions is sent a notification requesting that a deduction be made. This is binding on the DWP, unless there are other deductions being made from the benefit that take precedence.[49]

Direct deductions for contributions of child support cannot be made from any benefit other than IS/income-based JSA/income-related ESA/PC/UC, unless contribution-based JSA, incapacity benefit, severe disablement allowance or retirement pension are paid together with those benefits.[50] After the deductions are made, a claimant must be left with at least 10 pence a week (one pence for UC).[51]

There is a maximum amount that can be deducted from IS/income-based JSA/income-related ESA/PC/UC for various payments.[52] The contribution for child support has a lower priority than some other possible deductions – eg, council tax arrears.[53] Therefore, in some cases where a non-resident parent has other deductions, it is not possible to deduct the full contribution to child support. For more information about deductions from benefits, see CPAG's *Welfare Benefits and Tax Credits Handbook*.

If full deductions from these benefits are not possible, arrears of child support contributions do *not* accrue.

The DWP tells the CSA whether deductions are possible. The CSA then notifies the non-resident parent and the person with care if deductions are going to begin. The deducted amount is paid to the person with care via the CSA.[54] The CSA notifies her/him of the way in which the payments will be made.

If there are arrears of child support, these can be deducted from contribution-based JSA or contributory ESA only (see p285).

Timing of payments

In **'2012 rules' cases**, the CMS calculates the total amount of child support and any collection fees due to be paid over a 'reference period' of 52 weeks, beginning on the initial effective date or on the annual review date.[55] This total amount due is based on the assumption that the amount of child support will remain unchanged for the 52-week period. The non-resident parent is then required to pay child support in equal instalments. The frequency of payments (usually weekly or monthly) is agreed with the non-resident parent, and is usually at the same frequency as her/his earnings are paid if s/he is employed. The non-resident parent is sent a 'payment plan', showing how much is due to be paid, the start and end dates of the reference period and the frequency of payments.[56] The person with care is sent an 'expected payment plan' showing the same information.[57] If payments are to be made by deductions from the non-resident parent's benefits, payments are usually at the same frequency as the benefits are paid. New payment plans are issued if the amount due changes.

In '1993 rules' and '2003 rules' cases, the CSA decides the day and frequency of payments,[58] but asks for the non-resident parent's preference. When deciding, the CSA must also take into account:[59]

- the day on which, and the interval at which, the non-resident parent receives her/his income;
- any other relevant circumstances of the non-resident parent;
- time for cheques to clear, if applicable, and for payments to be transferred to the person with care; *and*
- any representations by the parties.

Unless undue hardship would be caused to any of the parties, the frequency of payments to the person with care is the same as the frequency set for the non-resident parent's payments (but see p294 for deduction from earnings orders).[60]

Unless payments are to be by direct debit or standing order, the non-resident parent is advised to make each payment three to four days before the due date in order to ensure that payments are received on time and to avoid arrears. Clearance times are allowed for each method of payment, but the CMS/CSA aims to make payments to the person with care within a week of receiving them from the non-resident parent.[61] If a delay in payments is caused by maladministration on the part of the CMS/CSA, the person with care may be entitled to compensation. S/he must make a complaint first (see Chapter 15).

Records and evidence of payments

It is important that all parties keep records of the payments made and received, particularly given the high level of errors on child support accounts in the past. Records can be in the form of bank statements or receipts if payments are made in cash. If any party disputes the amount that the CMS/CSA says is owed, the CMS/CSA can be asked to provide a statement of transactions and a breakdown of its calculations.

Overpayments

An overpayment can arise because:

- a calculation has been changed and the amount of the child support due for a past period has been reduced;
- the non-resident parent has paid more than the regular payment due for some other reason (including making voluntary payments in the initial payment period); *or*
- there has been a CMS/CSA error.

If the CMS/CSA receives an unexpected payment from the non-resident parent, it should check to determine the reason for this – eg, it could be for an overdue collection to offset arrears or an amount towards a future collection.

If there is an overpayment, the CMS/CSA has discretion about how it deals with it.[62] The amount may be allocated to reduce arrears due under a previous calculation or, if there are no arrears, it can be used to reduce the amount payable under the current calculation.[63] Adjustments may also be made where there are overpayments of voluntary payments in the initial payment period.[64] The CMS/CSA seeks to make adjustments first to balance out the overpayment.

If all or some of an overpayment made by the non-resident parent remains after offsetting it against regular child support, arrears and other liability, the CMS/CSA can make a refund to the non-resident parent.[65] Refunds are only usually made if there are no overdue collections or arrears on the case. The CMS/CSA should refund overpayments made because of CMS/CSA error – eg, if a person was told to pay more than the calculation required. In such cases, the non-resident parent may also wish to complain and seek compensation (see Chapter 15).

When making all these discretionary decisions about dealing with overpayments, the CMS/CSA must consider the welfare of any children likely to be affected by the decision. Before allocating overpayments against arrears or regular child support payments it must also consider, in particular:[66]

- the circumstances of the non-resident parent and person with care;
- the amount of the overpayment in relation to the amount of the current calculation; *and*
- the period over which it would be reasonable to recoup the overpayment.

An adjustment of the amount due under the current child support calculation may reduce the amount to nil.[67] If it does, the parent with care would not receive any more child support until the overpayment had been recovered.

Recovery of overpayments from the person with care

The CMS/CSA may decide to allocate an overpayment against previous arrears or, if there are no outstanding arrears, against regular child support payments, reducing the amount to be paid to the person with care.[68] This could result in all arrears owed being paid off and/or in regular child support payments being reduced to nil until the overpayment is recovered.[69] Allocating overpayments in this way is a discretionary decision, and so the person with care may wish to negotiate with the CMS/CSA about the rate at which the amount is to be recovered or for repayment to be made in a different way.

If it is not possible to reduce previous arrears or regular child support payments (perhaps because there is no current calculation and no arrears owed), or if the CMS/CSA decides that recovering arrears in this way is not appropriate, it can decide to reimburse all or part of an overpayment directly to a non-resident parent.[70] If the CMS/CSA makes a reimbursement to the non-resident parent, it has the power to recover all or part of it from the person with care if s/he has benefitted from the overpayment.[71] This also applies to reimbursement of overpayments caused by voluntary payments made by the non-resident parent.[72]

The CMS/CSA seeks to recover overpayments in all cases, and contacts the person with care to ask for repayment and discuss options for how payment will be made. However, CMS/CSA guidance states that recovery of an overpayment from the person with care is not enforceable if there is no current child support calculation in force.[73] If the person with care does not agree to make the repayment, the debt is suspended. A reimbursement of an overpayment cannot be recovered from the person with care if s/he was on IS, income-based JSA, income-related ESA or PC at any time during the period in which the overpayment occurred or on the date the reimbursement was made to the non-resident parent.[74] CMS/CSA guidance also states that recovery of an overpayment becomes temporarily unenforceable when a person with care starts to receive benefits such as IS or income-based JSA, and will be suspended. It may be reconsidered for recovery at a future date. In addition, the guidance states that the CMS/CSA cannot enforce the recovery of overpayments caused by its own administrative error, but the person with care will be asked whether s/he is prepared to repay them.

All decisions relating to recovery of overpayments are discretionary. When making them, the CMS/CSA must consider the welfare of any children likely to be affected by the decision.

Before allocating overpayments against arrears or regular child support payments, the CMS/CSA must also consider, in particular:[75]

* the circumstances of the non-resident parent and person with care;
* the amount of the overpayment in relation to the amount of the current calculation; *and*
* the period over which it would be reasonable to recoup the overpayment.

If the person with care disputes whether an overpayment should be recovered from her/him, or if it appears to have been caused by an administrative error by the CMS/CSA, s/he should seek advice. S/he may wish to complain about any maladministration, taking into account all loss and inconvenience caused. S/he should argue that a past overpayment caused by an error by the CMS/CSA should not have an impact on her/him and the qualifying children now. See Chapter 15 for details on how to make a complaint.

Payments made to a third party

If the person with care agrees to receive payments from the non-resident parent outside the usual child support collection service, these may be offset against the amount of child support owed by the non-resident parent – eg, if a non-resident parent agrees to pay an urgent utility bill on behalf of the person with care.[76] The amount can be offset against any arrears owed, or from her/his ongoing liability if there are no arrears.

For the offsetting rule to apply, the payment must have been agreed by the person with care and must be for one of the following in relation to the home in which the qualifying child lives:[77]

- a mortgage or loan either to purchase the property or to pay for essential repairs to it;
- rent on the property;
- mains-supplied gas, water or electricity charges;
- council tax payable by the person with care;
- essential repairs to the heating system; *or*
- essential repairs to 'maintain the fabric' of the home.

Offsetting can only be used if child support is collected by the CMS/CSA's collection service, rather than paid by the non-resident parent directly to the person with care. Those who pay directly can reach their own offsetting agreement, but the CMS/CSA does not monitor it.[78]

If the CMS/CSA intends to reduce ongoing payments of child support to the person with care, it should take into account the circumstances of all parties and the period over which it would be reasonable to adjust the payments.[79] An adjustment of the current calculation may reduce the amount payable to nil.[80]

The decision to apply offsetting is discretionary and there is no right of appeal against it. Problems may therefore occur if the person with care denies having agreed to payments being made to third parties. The CMS/CSA's intention is to keep decisions out of the appeals system that are not concerned with the actual child support calculation or the underlying liability to pay child support.[81] However, a party could complain about how the CMS/CSA has exercised its discretion.

The above provisions apply to cases under all three sets of rules. For '1993 rules' cases, the CSA also has further discretion to accept certain payments made by the non-resident parent as voluntary payments to be set against the child support assessment. These payments do not have to come within the types of payments listed above. In exercising this discretion, the CSA must consider the view of the person with care, but must take into account all the circumstances of the individual case.[82]

3. **Collection of other payments**

The Child Maintenance Service (CMS) and Child Support Agency (CSA) can collect and enforce other forms of maintenance if child support is being collected.[83]

The CMS/CSA's power to collect other maintenance is discretionary. The CMS/CSA can only collect other maintenance that falls due after it gives the non-resident parent written notice that it will do so.[84]

The following payments under a court order can be collected by the CMS/CSA:[85]

- additional child maintenance in excess of the CMS/CSA maximum;
- maintenance for a child's education or training;
- maintenance paid to meet the expenses of a child with a disability;
- maintenance paid for a stepchild – ie, a child living with the person with care who used to live with the non-resident parent as an accepted member of her/his family;
- spousal or civil partner maintenance for a person with care of a child for whom child support is being collected.

The methods used by the CMS/CSA for collecting and enforcing other types of maintenance are the same as for child support.[86] If a non-resident parent is paying more than one type of maintenance and pays less than the total amount required, s/he should stipulate how the amounts are to be allocated. The CMS/CSA allocates as requested, except that where arrears of child support are specified, current child support is paid before arrears. If the non-resident parent does not stipulate, the CMS/CSA makes the payment of child support a priority.[87]

Collection of court costs

If a court decides, on the application of the CMS/CSA, that a person is a parent, it can order that person to pay the CMS/CSA's costs in bringing the case, including the cost of any DNA tests (see p67). Also, a non-resident parent may have agreed to pay DNA test fees to the CMS/CSA without a court order (see p67).

The CMS/CSA negotiates with the liable person about payment of these other liabilities. It initially requests the full amount due, but payments by instalment may be agreed.

Payment of fees and costs can only be enforced through court action. The rules for enforcement of child support (see p292) do not apply. The relevant court is the county court in England and Wales or the sheriff court in Scotland. If the case is contested, a hearing is arranged in the court with jurisdiction for the area in which the parent lives. A money judgment can be enforced by the usual debt enforcement procedures.

4. **Arrears**

The Child Maintenance Service (CMS) and Child Support Agency (CSA) act on arrears only if child support is arranged through them.[88] If the collection service is being used, the CMS/CSA can take action immediately when payments are missed. If the parties made an application to the CMS/CSA but the non-resident parent pays child support direct to the person with care ('direct pay' or 'maintenance direct'), the person with care must notify the CMS/CSA that payments have stopped. The CMS/CSA will otherwise not be aware of this. The CMS/CSA may then decide to enforce the agreement. If it does, it also starts managing ongoing payments in the future through the collection service.

If 'direct pay' or 'maintenance direct' is being used, the CMS/CSA does not continue to pursue action on arrears, even if arrears arise from a past period when the collection service was being used.

The CMS/CSA cannot take action on non-payment of maintenance in a private agreement. If a private agreement breaks down, the person with care can apply to the CMS/CSA for child support instead. The CMS/CSA can pursue all arrears from the date the child support calculation is requested.[89]

The priority of the CMS and CSA is to collect arrears in cases where child support is still in payment, so that children for whom child support is still paid can benefit from the arrears recovered. Historic arrears in cases where child support is no longer in payment are a lower priority, although the CMS/CSA still aims to collect them.[90]

If the non-resident parent now resides in another European Union country, the CMS/CSA can enquire about assets and enforce certain arrears that accrued while both parents were resident in the UK (see p35).

If '1993 rules' and '2003 rules' cases close as part of the case closure process and an application is made under the '2012 rules', any outstanding arrears from the closed cases are verified at that point and further action considered (see Chapter 5).

Initial arrears

As the first calculation is usually made after its effective date, there are almost always initial arrears. The CMS has said that it is seeking to improve the application process in order to reduce the potential for initial arrears.[91]

If a court order made on or after 3 March 2003 has been in force for more than a year and there is an application to the CMS, any payments due under it made by the non-resident parent beyond the effective date are treated as payments of child support.[92] This helps to avoid additional liability for child support accumulating if there is a gap between the effective date (and, therefore, the date the court order ceases to have effect) and the date the calculation is actually made. (**Note:** the effective date in a '2003 rules' case where such a court order has been in force for more than a year is two months and two days after the date of the application.) If the payments made under the court order are at a higher rate than those due under the calculation, this is treated as an overpayment of child support and the calculation can be adjusted accordingly.

The CMS/CSA draws up a collection schedule (known as a 'payment plan' for '2012 rules' cases), which shows payments for the following 12 months, including initial arrears. The proposed schedule is discussed and agreed with the non-resident parent. Written confirmation of the collection schedule is issued once the non-resident parent has agreed to it.[93]

The written notification states:[94]
- the amount due and to whom it is to be paid;
- how it is to be paid – ie, method, day and interval between payments;
- any amounts that are overdue and outstanding.

The CMS/CSA may request payment of the initial arrears as a lump sum. If a non-resident parent cannot pay this all at once, s/he may negotiate an agreement to pay in instalments or a collection schedule to cover both the initial payment and ongoing liability (see p283).

A parent who fails to make payment of the outstanding arrears within seven days of written notification of the amount due may face financial penalties and further enforcement action.

A parent who thinks the calculation is wrong may be able to challenge the decision (see Chapters 12 and 13). If s/he objects to the way the CMS/CSA is dealing with collections, s/he can make a complaint (see Chapter 15).

Voluntary payments made in the initial period

Voluntary payments made by the non-resident parent through the CMS/CSA (or, if the CMS/CSA agrees, directly to the person with care or a third party) after the effective date, but before the calculation is made and notified, may be offset against arrears of child support.[95] The CMS/CSA may seek the views of the parties when considering whether a payment is to be classed as a voluntary payment.[96] By accepting a payment as a voluntary payment, the CMS/CSA can be deemed to have agreed to its being made directly to the person with care or a third party.[97] As these are discretionary decisions, the CMS/CSA must consider the welfare of any child likely to be affected. There is no right of appeal against these decisions.

Only the following types of payment can be offset: [98]
- in lieu of child support;
- in respect of a mortgage or loan on the child's home, or for repairs or improvements to the property;
- rent on the child's home;
- mains gas, water or electricity at the child's home;
- council tax payable at the child's home;
- repairs to the heating system at the child's home; *or*
- repairs to the child's home.

Payments can be made by cash, standing order, cheque, postal order, debit card or other method or arrangement from an account of the non-resident parent or on her/his behalf – eg, credit card.[99]

If the payments are made to the CMS/CSA, they are passed on to the person with care. Once the calculation has been made, the voluntary payments are offset against the initial arrears.

If the payments are made directly to the person with care or a third party, the CMS/CSA checks with the person with care whether payments have been made.[100] This is normally done by phone. If the person with care confirms the payments were made, this is usually accepted without any further need for proof. If there is a dispute about whether a payment has been made, the CMS/CSA asks the non-resident parent to provide proof. Payment can be verified by bank statements, duplicates of cashed cheques, receipts, paid bills or invoices, or a written or oral statement from the person with care.[101] It is in the interests of both parties to ensure payments are recorded, and the CMS/CSA should explain to the non-resident parent the importance of keeping a record and provide a form on which to do so.

If either party disagrees with a decision about offsetting, a complaint can be made (see Chapter 15).

If offsetting means that there is an overpayment, the calculation may be adjusted to compensate the non-resident parent or a refund may be made.[102]

If payments are made by the non-resident parent outside the usual collection service after the calculation is made (eg, if s/he pays an urgent bill on behalf of the parent with care), see p277.

Arrears notice

If the non-resident parent has missed one or more child support payments, the CMS/CSA must send her/him an arrears notice stating the amount of all outstanding arrears owed. The notice also explains the rules about arrears and requests payment of the outstanding amount.[103] The CMS/CSA then contacts the non-resident parent to discuss the issue.

The arrears notice shows only the total amount of outstanding arrears, but the government has said that the CMS/CSA will provide an itemised list of payments due but not received if the non-resident parent requests this at any time.[104]

Non-resident parents should check that the amount owed is correct and tell the CMS/CSA of any mistakes. There have been high levels of mistakes on accounts in the past. Therefore, if there is a concern that the balance is incorrect, the non-resident parent should ask for a payment statement (see p275) and compare this with her/his own records. It is important that s/he keeps the CMS/CSA informed so that enforcement action is not started in the meantime.

The non-resident parent can contact the CMS/CSA to negotiate payment by instalments (see p283). Once an arrears notice has been served, another does not have to be sent if arrears remain uncleared, unless the non-resident parent has paid all arranged payments for a 12-week period.[105]

The above rules for arrears notices do not apply if:[106]

- direct pay ('maintenance direct') arrangements are in place, or the collection service is being used but no enforcement action is being taken; *and*
- the CMS/CSA has notified the non-resident parent during the previous 12 months that the CMS/CSA would consider taking collection and enforcement action if payments are missed.

In this case, the CMS/CSA can take enforcement action and start managing ongoing payments if the non-resident parent has missed one or more payments. A separate arrears notice is not required.

Negotiating an arrears agreement

If the non-resident parent receives an arrears notice, s/he should contact the CMS/CSA to negotiate an agreement to deal with the arrears.

Negotiations with the CMS/CSA may begin on notification of the collection schedule, or at a later date if the non-resident parent has difficulty making ongoing payments. However, the CMS/CSA does not normally agree to defer payment of current liability, although it may do so if a revision, supersession or appeal is pending.

There are no set rules on the level of payments or how quickly the arrears must be cleared. Although CMS/CSA staff always begin by requesting full payment of the outstanding arrears, an arrears agreement may be reached to pay the amount in instalments. The CMS/CSA aims to agree repayment plans that are affordable and that will be kept to.

In making this discretionary decision, the CMS/CSA must take into account the welfare of any child likely to be affected and should consider the:
- needs of the non-resident parent or any new family;
- representations of the non-resident parent about hardship;
- needs of the person with care and the qualifying child.

If a non-resident parent has other priorities (eg, fuel) or other large debts, s/he should seek independent money advice. Preparing a financial statement and sending it to the CMS/CSA may assist in reaching an agreement. However, existing arrangements with other creditors may have to be renegotiated to take into account the child support calculation. It is important to keep the CMS/CSA informed so that it does not assume that the non-resident parent is refusing to come to an agreement.

As the CMS/CSA can use other methods of recovery, it is unlikely to agree to a non-resident parent making low payments over a very long period. It is in the parent's interests to come to an agreement in order to avoid further enforcement action.

The CMS/CSA aims to collect arrears within two years, at a rate of up to 40 per cent of a non-resident parent's net income. It can use its discretion and take into account the non-resident parent's particular circumstances, if appropriate to do so.[107]

A plan to pay arrears by instalments over more than two years may be accepted, but the CMS/CSA is likely to obtain a liability order (see p306) if there will be more than £1,000 outstanding at the end of two years. A liability order gives the CMS/CSA discretion to use a wider range of methods to enforce payment, should the plan not be completed. The CMS/CSA may also consider other methods of recovery.

Repayments spread over several years may help non-resident parents who are in financial hardship, but this means that the person with care will receive payments very late and may want to make representations to the CMS/CSA. No interest is paid to the person with care in respect of arrears. If arrears have accrued because of CMS/CSA delay or error, the person with care (or a child applicant in Scotland) may, however, wish to consider making a complaint and requesting compensation (see Chapter 15).

The person with care and qualifying children are not consulted about the level at which arrears are collected, but are informed when the decision has been made. This practice may be contrary to the European Convention on Human Rights' protection of private property,[108] but there has been no reported caselaw on this point (see also p315 on the fact that a person with care cannot directly enforce the payment of child support).

Revision, supersession or appeal pending

The CMS/CSA can suspend collection of arrears if a decision on a revision, supersession, variation or appeal is pending. If the calculation is likely to be reduced, the CMS/CSA may agree to suspend collection of some of the ongoing payments. However, this does not happen often; the CMS/CSA prefers to speed up its consideration of the case and aims to supersede calculations to reflect changes quickly in order to minimise arrears.[109]

A non-resident parent who requests a revision, supersession or appeal and is having problems paying current child support or any arrears should make representations to the CMS/CSA for lower regular payments.

Payment of arrears

Arrears do not have to be paid by the same method as ongoing child support payments. For example, arrears could be collected via the CMS/CSA, while ongoing payments are made directly to the person with care. However, in practice the CMS/CSA prefers to use the same method of payment for both.

Arrears of child support may be retained by the CMS/CSA if they are in respect of a period before 12 April 2010 during which the person with care (or her/his partner) was in receipt of income support (IS), income-based jobseeker's allowance (JSA), income-related employment and support allowance (ESA) or pension credit

(PC). From this date, all child support is fully disregarded when working out the amount of benefit.[110]

The CMS/CSA can keep any arrears payments that would not have been passed to the person with care had the child support been paid when due[111] – ie, the CMS/CSA can retain an amount equal to the difference between the amount of benefit that was paid to the person with care and the amount that would have been paid had the non-resident parent not been in arrears.[112] Payments of arrears are allocated between the CMS/CSA and the person with care in the same way as overpayments (see p275).

Collection of arrears from a non-resident parent on benefit

In '2012 rules' and '2003 rules' cases, if the non-resident parent is in receipt of one of the benefits that would qualify her/him for the flat rate (see p133), a deduction of £1.20 may be made towards arrears. However, it is understood that no deduction from benefit for arrears will be made in '2012 rules' cases. Any amount of the deduction that is in respect of fees is retained by the CMS.[113]

This deduction is in addition to a deduction for flat rate child support. These deductions are separate to other deductions made from benefit and are not affected by priority rules on which deductions should be made first. The deduction cannot be made if IS, income-based JSA, income-related ESA, universal credit (UC) or PC are also being paid to the non-resident parent or her/his partner.[114]

This means that arrears action in '2012 rules' and '2003 rules' cases is suspended against non-resident parents on IS/income-based JSA/income-related ESA/UC/PC. If a person with care believes that the arrears action should be pursued in some other way, s/he should contact the CMS/CSA to explain her/his reasons. If the CMS/CSA is unwilling to take action, a complaint may be made (see Chapter 15).

In '1993 rules' cases, a deduction for arrears can only be made from contribution-based JSA or contributory ESA at a maximum of one-third of the age-related amount payable – eg, £24.36 a week in 2015/16 for a non-resident parent aged 25 or over.[115] In '1993 rules' cases, the priority rules on deductions from benefit apply and, therefore, the deduction may not be made if certain other deductions take priority – eg, for arrears of council tax.

For more information on the priority rules on deductions from benefit, see CPAG's *Welfare Benefits and Tax Credits Handbook*.

Offsetting arrears

'Offsetting' is a way of balancing payments or arrears that are owed by a person with care and a non-resident parent to each other, so that the CMS/CSA only has to pursue arrears from one party. Similarly, the amount of child support a non-resident parent is required to pay can be reduced to take account of arrears owed to her/him by the other party for a period when s/he was a person with care.

Offsetting therefore reduces any arrears due under any current or previous child support calculation made in respect of the same relevant persons – ie, a person with care, non-resident parent and child applicant in Scotland.[116]

Arrears may be offset if:

- a non-resident parent becomes a parent with care (see below); *or*
- arrears are owed by both parties to a calculation (see below).

A non-resident parent becomes a parent with care

From 25 January 2010, when a qualifying child for whom child support is payable moves households, so that the non-resident parent becomes the parent with care and vice versa, the CMS/CSA can offset the new non-resident parent's liability to pay child support against arrears owed to her/him by the other parent.[117] The amount payable in relation to the current calculation by the new non-resident parent can be reduced to nil.[118]

Before 25 January 2010, a new non-resident parent may have found that s/he had to pay child support to someone who still owed her/him arrears.

Example 14.3

Stephen and Zoe divorced five years ago. They have one child, Luke, who has lived with Zoe since the divorce. Zoe applied for child support and used the collection service. However, Stephen has not paid child support regularly for the past few years. Luke decides that he wants to live with Stephen, who becomes the parent with care. Zoe is now the non-resident parent. If Stephen applies for child support, the amount that Zoe must pay to Stephen each week can be reduced as a way of recovering the arrears still owed to her.

Arrears are owed by both parties to a calculation

From 25 January 2010, offsetting can also be used if the parties to a calculation owe each other arrears.[119]

Example 14.4

Luke has now lived with his father, Stephen, for two years. Zoe makes regular child support payments for the first year, but when Stephen moves in to live with his new partner, she starts to miss payments. Luke then decides to return to live with Zoe, who becomes the parent with care again. At this time, Zoe owes Stephen £1,000 in arrears. However, there are still £500 arrears that are yet to be recovered from when Stephen was the non-resident parent and did not make regular payments. Rather than both sets of arrears being pursued, Stephen's arrears are deducted from Zoe's.

Zoe pays Stephen £500 in arrears. Only Zoe is pursued for arrears. Stephen's liability under the current calculation could be reduced to recover these.

Offsetting of arrears may also apply if the qualifying children from a relationship live with different parents. In this situation, both are parents with care and non-resident parents in relation to different children.

If both are liable to pay child support, but one falls into arrears, the ongoing payments of the other parent can be reduced.[120]

Example 14.5

Tariq and Ann are separated. They have two children, Dina and Noreen. Dina lives with Tariq and Noreen lives with Ann. Both Tariq and Ann are liable to pay child support to each other and use the collection service. Tariq fails to make regular payments to Ann. As a result, the amount Ann has to pay each week is reduced to take account of the arrears owed to her by Tariq.

If Ann and Tariq fail to make regular child support payments to each other and Ann owes Tariq £300 in arrears and Tariq owes Ann £1,000, instead of both Ann and Tariq being pursued for arrears, the amount owed by Ann is deducted from what she is owed by Tariq.

When offsetting can be applied

Offsetting can only be applied when the collection service is being used. Those with an arrangement to pay child support directly can reach their own offsetting agreements, but the CMS/CSA does not monitor them.[121]

Offsetting is a discretionary power. The decision to offset does not require the agreement of either parent, but the CMS/CSA should notify all relevant parties to the calculation when it is considering offsetting and ask for their views. Parties have 14 days in which to respond. The CMS/CSA should take into account parents' wishes and should also have regard to the welfare of any child likely to be affected by the decision.[122]

If there are no arrears of child support due, or an amount remains to be offset after any arrears have been taken into account, the CMS/CSA can reduce the amount payable under the current calculation. When reducing ongoing payments to the person with care, the CMS/CSA should take into account the circumstances of all the parties and the period over which it would be reasonable to adjust payments. Payments can be reduced to nil.[123]

If the current child support calculation is reduced, either the person with care or the non-resident parent can contact the CMS/CSA at any time to ask that it be reviewed. The CMS/CSA should then discuss with both parties alternative ways of collecting any outstanding arrears.[124]

Starting recovery action

The CMS/CSA may begin to consider recovery action when:
- a payment from the non-resident parent to the CMS/CSA is not received; *or*

- in a case where child support is being paid by 'direct pay' or 'maintenance direct', the person with care notifies the CMS/CSA that a payment due has not been received.

The CMS/CSA aims to begin action within three days of a payment being missed.[125] The CMS/CSA contacts the non-resident parent to investigate, normally by telephone at first and followed up in writing if no response is received. The non-resident parent may request an appointment at a local office to discuss payment face to face with CMS/CSA staff.

If the non-resident parent intends to pay the amount, the CMS/CSA may:
- accept a delayed payment, setting a time limit by when payment must be received; *or*
- reschedule the amount to include it within the arrears.

If the parent indicates that a change of circumstances is causing difficulty in making payments, the CMS/CSA may investigate whether there should be a supersession.

If the parent refuses to pay, the CMS/CSA informs her/him of its powers to collect and enforce child support. The CMS/CSA can impose a penalty payment (see p289) to encourage her/him to pay. A parent can also be fined up to £1,000 for failing to provide required information or providing false information.[126]

To avoid other methods of recovery, the non-resident parent should come to an agreement (see p283) as soon as possible and comply with it. The CMS/CSA has discretion on agreements with parents about debt recovery. However, if the parent fails to come to a voluntary arrangement or breaks it, the CMS/CSA may enforce a deduction from earnings order (DEO) at up to 40 per cent of net income and/or take further enforcement action.

The CMS/CSA aims to take prompt action on new debts to reach an agreement with the non-resident parent or to obtain payment via non-legal means – eg, a DEO. If an arrangement is not reached, legal enforcement should begin. There is no set timescale in the legislation for how quickly action should begin if no arrangement has been agreed. The government has said that action will begin as quickly as possible.[127]

When the non-resident parent defaults

If the non-resident parent fails to keep to an arrears agreement:
- a penalty payment may be imposed (see p289); *and*
- a DEO or other method of enforcement may be considered (see p292).

In all cases, a parent who wants to co-operate should try to renegotiate an agreement in good time before any anticipated change in circumstances – eg, redundancy. If s/he has paid regularly and the change would reduce the amount due, the CMS/CSA may accept a lower amount. The parent could also try to negotiate a suspension in payments if personal circumstances make it difficult or insensitive to enforce recovery – eg, if s/he is unemployed, sick or in prison.

Penalty payments

In '2012 rules' and '2003 rules' cases, the power exists to impose a penalty payment on a non-resident parent who is in arrears with child support payments.[128] In practice, this power does not appear to be used at present. CMS/CSA leaflets and letters do not refer to penalty payments.

Interest

From 5 August 2008, interest is no longer added to child support arrears and any outstanding liability for interest has been removed.[129]

Accepting part payment in full and final settlement

Since 10 December 2012 the CMS/CSA has had the power, in certain circumstances, to treat a part payment of arrears of child support owed by a non-resident parent as full and final legal settlement of all arrears owed.[130] This flexibility is intended to act as an incentive for the non-resident parent to pay at least something, where s/he may not otherwise have done so.

At present, the CMS/CSA does not actively seek offers of part payment of arrears from non-resident parents. It is only likely to consider using the power if an offer is received from the non-resident parent or suggested by the person with care (or child applicant in Scotland).[131] In the future, the CMS/CSA may use the power more actively to try to reach agreements between parties.

The power to accept an offer of part payment is discretionary. If an offer of part payment is made, the CMS/CSA investigates the circumstances of the non-resident parent, and also considers the likely success of continued enforcement action in recovering the full arrears.[132] The CMS/CSA must also consider the welfare of any child likely to be affected by its use of this power.

If the CMS/CSA proposes to accept the offer, it prepares a written agreement. This agreement sets out:[133]

- the name of the non-resident parent;
- the name of the person with care (or child applicant in Scotland) if her/his consent is required (see below);
- the amount of arrears and the period to which they relate;
- the amount that the CMS/CSA proposes to accept as settlement of those arrears;
- who the amount will be paid to and by what method; *and*
- the date by which the payment must be made.

A copy of the agreement is sent to the non-resident parent and to each person with care (or child applicant in Scotland) affected by the proposed agreement.[134]

The CMS/CSA may decide not to contact the person with care with a proposed agreement if it considers the offer to be unreasonable. In some circumstances, it may insist on the full amount of the arrears being paid – eg, if it thinks that the non-resident parent has the ability to pay and there is a reasonable prospect of recovering the arrears.[135] Before accepting a part payment offer from the non-resident parent, the CMS/CSA must get the written consent of the person with care (or child applicant in Scotland, and person with care of that child).[136]

If there are arrears due both to a person with care and to the Department for Work and Pensions (DWP) (ie, because, for a period prior to 12 April 2010, the person with care would have received less benefit if the child support due had been paid), any part payment agreed is allocated to pay the person with care first. If it is only the DWP that will not be paid in full if the offer is accepted, the CMS/CSA does not need the consent of the person with care (or child applicant in Scotland) before accepting the offer.[137] In such a case, the CMS/CSA has discretion to decide whether the amount offered is reasonable in the non-resident parent's current financial circumstances.

If the non-resident parent has arrears that are due to more than one person with care, these are treated as separate amounts.[138] The CMS/CSA does not actively invite the non-resident parent to state a preference regarding which person with care should receive the part payment.[139] If the non-resident parent does not state a preference, the CMS/CSA apportions the payment between the persons with care. Each person with care is notified of how much of the part payment s/he will receive if s/he agrees to accept this as a full and final payment. If one or more persons with care reject(s) the offer, the CMS/CSA may apportion the amount between those who have accepted it. Arrears due to those who have rejected the offer remain outstanding and are pursued by the CMS/CSA.

If the offer of part payment is accepted and the agreed payment made, the person with care cannot then change her/his mind and ask the CMS/CSA to reinstate and pursue the arrears. If the non-resident parent complies with the agreement and pays all of the agreed amount, the liability on any outstanding arrears ceases and the CMS/CSA cannot take further action on the arrears.[140] If the non-resident parent does not comply with the terms of the agreement or fails to make all of the agreed part payment, s/he remains liable for the full amount of the outstanding arrears and the CMS/CSA pursues recovery.[141] The CMS/CSA can make a further proposed agreement for part payment in the future, even if the non-resident parent has failed to keep to the terms of a previous agreement. The new agreement replaces any previous one.[142]

At present, the part payment offered must be paid in one lump sum. It is expected that, at some point in the future, part payments will be able to be made by instalments in appropriate circumstances.[143]

Writing off arrears

Since 10 December 2012, the CMS/CSA has had the power to write off certain arrears if it considers that it would be unfair or inappropriate for it to enforce the liability.[144] Before this date, a decision not to pursue recovery resulted in the arrears being suspended, but the liability still remained. Suspended arrears can be revived by the CMS/CSA in certain circumstances, but many arrears remained on record even though there was no prospect of their ever being collected. This is a limited power, and the CMS/CSA does not intend to undertake a large-scale write-off of arrears. The CMS/CSA has various initiatives to pursue arrears in historic cases where a child support liability is no longer in force, although this action is a lower priority.[145] A person with care may be asked if s/he wishes arrears to be written off as part of the process of closing a '2003 rules' or '1993 rules' case (see Chapter 5).

The CMS/CSA can write off arrears only if it considers that it would be unfair or inappropriate for it to enforce the liability and:[146]

- the person with care (or child applicant, in Scotland) has requested the CMS/CSA to cease taking action on the arrears; *or*
- the person with care (or, in Scotland, the child applicant) has died; *or*
- the non-resident parent died before 25 January 2010 and there is no further action possible to recover the arrears from her/his estate; *or*
- the arrears have accrued from an 'interim maintenance assessment' (IMA – see previous editions of this *Handbook* for details of IMAs) in force between 5 April 1993 and 18 April 1995. These arrears (known as 'IMA gap debt') are not legally recoverable;[147] *or*
- the CMS/CSA has advised the non-resident parent that the arrears have been permanently suspended and that no further action will ever be taken to recover them. This may happen if, for example, the arrears resulted from a delay (which was not the non-resident parent's fault) in establishing child support liability.

The CMS/CSA has discretion whether to use this power to write off arrears. This means that, before doing so, it must consider all the circumstances of an individual case, the principles of child support law and the welfare of any child affected by the decision.

In cases where the non-resident parent has arrears that are due to more than one person with care, these are treated as separate amounts and separate decisions are made.[148] If it is considering writing off arrears, the CMS/CSA must give written notice to the person with care and non-resident parent (and a child applicant, in Scotland). The notice must set out:[149]

- the person with care (or child applicant, in Scotland) who is owed the arrears;
- the amount of arrears and the period to which they relate;

- the reasons why the CMS/CSA believes that it would be unfair or inappropriate to enforce the arrears;
- the effect of writing off the arrears; *and*
- an explanation of the right to make representations to the CMS/CSA about the proposal to write off the arrears within 30 days of receiving the notice.

The notice is treated as being received two days after it was sent by the CMS/CSA to the person's last known or notified address.[150]

When making its decision, the CMS/CSA must consider any representations made by any relevant party.[151] If no representations are made within 30 days, the CMS/CSA can decide to write off the arrears.[152] It must give written notice of its decision to the person with care and non-resident parent (and a child applicant, in Scotland). If the CMS/CSA does not write off the arrears, it may continue to pursue recovery. There is no right of appeal against its decision.

The duties on the CMS/CSA to give written notice do not apply in relation to any party who cannot be traced or who has died.[153]

5. **Enforcement**

A case should usually be considered for enforcement action as soon as it is clear that the non-resident parent has failed to keep to the agreed payment arrangements for child support and any fees due and has not responded to warnings.[154]

Court action may also be taken for criminal offences relating to the supply of information (see Chapter 4).[155]

In many cases, in order to pursue enforcement, the Child Maintenance Service (CMS) or Child Support Agency (CSA) must first obtain a **liability order** from the county court or, in Scotland, sheriff court (see p306). However, for an increasing number of enforcement options, the CMS/CSA does not need a liability order and no court action is required.

A liability order is not required for:
- a deduction from earnings order (DEO). This is usually appropriate when the non-resident parent is employed (see p293);
- deductions to be made from bank or building society accounts. This is likely to be used if the non-resident parent is not an employee (see p301);
- collecting arrears from a deceased person's estate (see p305).

However, the CMS/CSA must first obtain a liability order if it wants to:
- use bailiffs (see p308);
- disqualify the non-resident parent from driving (see p310);
- imprison the non-resident parent (see p310).

Note: fees for some enforcement actions were introduced on 30 June 2014 for '2012 rules' cases (see p312). The rules on collecting and enforcing payments of child support also apply to payment of any fees due, except that the CMS cannot seek disqualification from driving or imprisonment when enforcement action is being taken against the non-resident parent solely to recover fees.[156]

Deduction from earnings orders

The CMS/CSA may make a DEO. This is an order to the non-resident parent's employer to make deductions from her/his earnings and pay them to the CMS/CSA.[157] The CMS/CSA does not need to go to court to make a DEO. A DEO is the principal enforcement tool used against non-resident parents who are employed and cannot provide a good reason for the arrears, or who have failed to agree a method of payment with the CMS/CSA. It is the first option that is likely to be used in the case of an employed non-resident parent.[158]

A non-resident parent can choose a voluntary DEO as the method for making regular child support payments, even if s/he is not in arrears (see p272).

A DEO may not be made if there is good reason not to use that method of payment.[159] For what is considered 'good reason', see p299.

The best way for a non-resident parent to avoid a DEO is to negotiate an arrears agreement (see p283) and keep to it wherever possible. However, making ongoing payments in full may be enough to prevent a DEO from being made. Any objection to a DEO by a non-resident parent is likely to be rejected if it is unlikely that regular payments would be made using a different method.

The decision to make a DEO is discretionary and the welfare of any children must be considered (see p27).[160] If warned of a DEO, the non-resident parent should tell the CMS/CSA, preferably in writing, how any children would be affected. If a DEO is made, the non-resident parent can appeal to the magistrates' court in England and Wales, or sheriff court in Scotland (see p299).

A DEO can be made while the non-resident parent is waiting for a decision on a revision, supersession or appeal. The CMS/CSA should consider the grounds of the revision, supersession or appeal before making a DEO. A non-resident parent can also make representations about the amount and method of payments (see p272 and p279). The CMS/CSA may accept lower payments, but may still impose a DEO.

A DEO cannot be made if the employer is based outside the UK and has no place of business in the UK, but a DEO can be made in Great Britain against an employer in Northern Ireland and vice versa.[161]

A DEO cannot be made if the non-resident parent is in the armed forces. Instead, the CMS/CSA can request the armed forces to make deductions for child support under armed forces law, known as a deduction from earnings request, which sets limits on the amounts that can be deducted.[162]

If the full amount requested by the CMS/CSA cannot be deducted from earnings, the CMS/CSA uses other methods to collect and enforce the remainder.

If a deduction from earnings order is made

A copy of the DEO must be served on the employer and the non-resident parent.[163] The employer has to comply with the DEO within seven days of receiving it.[164] An employer can be fined up to £1,000 for providing false or misleading information, or deliberately withholding information from the CMS/CSA.[165]

The DEO must state:[166]

- the name and address of the non-resident parent;
- the name of the employer;
- the non-resident parent's place of work, employee number and national insurance (NI) number (if known by the CMS/CSA), and the nature of her/his work;
- the normal deduction rate(s) (see p296) and the date on which each takes effect;
- the protected earnings proportion;
- the address to which the deductions are to be sent.

The CMS/CSA and the child maintenance section of the gov.uk website provide further information for employers. Employers can manage DEOs for employees who are liable to pay child support under a '2012 rules' case through a self-service website.[167]

If an employer is implementing a DEO incorrectly and the non-resident parent disputes this, the parent should ask the CMS/CSA to intervene.

Date of payment

The employer must pay the CMS/CSA monthly by the 19th of the month following the month in which the deduction is made.[168] This means that there is always a delay before the person with care receives the first payment from the CMS/CSA. The person with care receives monthly payments, even if the non-resident parent is having weekly deductions made. These monthly payments may not always be for the same amount (see p298 and p317).

The payment by the employer may be made by credit transfer, cheque or any other method to which the CMS/CSA agrees.[169] The DEO reference number must be given so that the CMS/CSA can identify the person with care.

It is an offence punishable by a fine of up to £500 for an employer to fail to take all reasonable steps to pay the CMS/CSA on time.[170]

Providing information

For these purposes, information sent to the CMS/CSA is treated as having been given or sent on the day that it is received.[171]

Any notice sent from the CMS/CSA is treated as though it was given or sent on the day that it was posted.[172]

The non-resident parent

The non-resident parent must provide the name and address of her/his employer, the amount of earnings and anticipated earnings, place of work and the nature of work within seven days of being asked to do so in writing by the CMS/CSA.[173] Once a DEO is in force, s/he must inform the CMS/CSA within seven days of leaving employment or becoming employed or re-employed.[174] Failure to take all reasonable steps to comply with any of these requirements is an offence punishable by a fine of up to £500.[175]

The employer

An employer must inform the CMS/CSA in writing within 10 days of being served with a DEO if it does not, in fact, employ the non-resident parent.[176] If a parent who is subject to a DEO leaves her/his job, the employer must notify the CMS/CSA within 10 days.[177] If an employer finds out that a DEO is in force against an employee (eg, on becoming her/his employer), it must notify the CMS/CSA within seven days of becoming aware of this information.[178] Failure to take all reasonable steps to comply with any of these requirements is also an offence punishable by a fine of up to £500.[179]

The employer must inform the non-resident parent in writing of the amount of each deduction no later than the date of the deduction or, if not practicable, by the following payday.[180] Although child support law imposes no penalty on an employer who fails to do this, employment protection law requires the employer to give the non-resident parent a written statement of deductions on or before the payday.[181] If the deduction will always be the same amount, this can be done by a standing statement given at least annually.[182] If the employer does not give notice of the deduction, the non-resident parent can complain to an employment tribunal, which can order the employer to pay the non-resident parent a fine up to the total amount of the unnotified deductions, even if paid to the CMS/CSA.[183] This fine does not affect deductions already paid to the CMS/CSA.

For other duties about providing information, see p56. Employers can manage DEOs for employees who are liable to pay child support under a '2012 rules' case through a self-service website.[184]

Earnings

Earnings include wages, salary, fees, bonus, commission, overtime pay, occupational pension or statutory sick pay, any other payment made under an employment contract and a regular payment made in compensation for loss of wages.[185] Earnings do not include a payment by a foreign government or the government of Northern Ireland,[186] or a payment to a special member of a British reserved armed force.[187] Net earnings means, in this context, the amount remaining after tax, NI and contributions towards a pension scheme have been deducted.[188]

How much is deducted

The DEO states a **'normal deduction rate'** and a **'protected earnings proportion'**.[189] For **'1993 rules'** and **'2003 rules'** cases, these rates should usually correspond to the pay periods of the non-resident parent – ie, at a weekly rate if paid weekly, and a monthly rate if paid monthly.[190]

In **'2012 rules'** cases, the CMS does not know the non-resident parent's net income or pay frequency, as it receives only gross income information from HM Revenue and Customs. In these cases, the employer is responsible for calculating the protected earnings proportion. The CMS provides employers with pay frequency options for weekly, fortnightly, four-weekly and monthly pay, from which the employer selects the normal deduction rate corresponding to the parent's pay frequency.[191] If the parent is paid at a different frequency, the CMS must cancel the DEO (see p298).[192]

These rules may also apply to any DEO imposed after 10 December 2012 in an 'arrears only' case under the '1993 rules' and '2003 rules' – ie, cases where there are arrears outstanding but no regular ongoing child support liability. The rules only apply to such cases if the CMS/CSA gives written notice to the non-resident parent that they apply. Any DEO made before this date continues under the previous rules until it is cancelled or lapses.[193]

More than one normal deduction rate can be set, each applying to a different period.[194]

Normal deduction rate

The normal deduction rate is the amount that will be deducted each payday, provided it does not bring net earnings below the protected earnings proportion. The normal deduction rate can include the current child support liability and an amount for any arrears, penalty payments and any fees due. There are no special rules on how quickly the CMS/CSA should seek to clear the liability, although often the maximum deduction rate of 40 per cent of net income is applied (see p283). Non-resident parents may wish to discuss with the CMS/CSA how it has chosen to apply its discretion.

Protected earnings proportion

The protected earnings proportion is 60 per cent of net earnings.[195] Deductions must not reduce earnings below this level.

Administering a deduction from earnings order

An employer can deduct a charge for administrative costs each time a deduction is made under the DEO.[196] This means that employees paid weekly can be charged more for administrative costs. The charge must not exceed £1 per deduction and can be made even if this would bring earnings below the protected earnings proportion.

Each payday, the employer should make a deduction from net earnings at the normal deduction rate plus any administration charge. If deducting the normal deduction rate would reduce net earnings below the protected earnings proportion, the amount of the deduction is the excess of net earnings over the protected earnings proportion. In addition, an administration charge may be deducted.[197]

If the employer fails to make a deduction, or it is less than the normal deduction rate, arrears build up and are deducted at the next payday in addition to the normal deduction, applying the same rules for protected earnings.[198]

If, on a payday, the non-resident parent is paid for a period longer than that for which the normal deduction rate is set, the deduction is increased in proportion to the length of the pay period.[199]

Such fluctuations in deductions may mean that the person with care receives irregular payments.

Example 14.6

The non-resident parent is due to pay child support of £48 a week and has net earnings of £240 a week. When a DEO is considered, there are arrears of £458.40. The DEO shows a normal deduction rate of £60 (child support due plus £12 towards arrears) and a protected earnings proportion of £144. The employer can deduct £1 administrative costs for weeks in which a deduction is made.

Payday	Net pay	Child support due	Deduction	Pay	DEO unpaid
	£	£	£	£	£
5/7	240	60	61	179	
12/7	250	60	61	189	
19/7	160	60	17	143	44
26/7	160	104	17	143	88
2/8	240	148	97	143	52
9/8	250	112	107	143	6
16/8	250	66	67	183	
23/8	240	60	61	179	
30/8	120	60	Nil	120	60
6/9	240	120	97	143	24
13/9	240	84	85	155	
20/9	250	60	61	189	
27/9	240	60	61	179	

In the week of 19/7, the full deduction cannot be made, as this would take income below the protected earnings proportion. A deduction is made of £16 plus a £1 administration fee. The amount of the DEO outstanding is added to the next amount due on 26/7. As earnings are again low, the full deduction cannot be taken and is carried forward.

In the week of 30/8, earnings are too low for a deduction to be made and, therefore, there is no deduction and no administrative charge.

Payment to the person with care

An employer must pass the month's payments to the CMS/CSA by the 19th of the following month.[200] When these have reached the CMS/CSA, they should be passed on to the person with care within approximately 10 days. If s/he was on income support, income-based jobseeker's allowance, income-related employment and support allowance or pension credit in the period to which the arrears relate, some of the payments may be retained in lieu of benefit paid.[201] This only applies to arrears of child support payments that were due to be made before 12 April 2010. The person with care should receive all arrears relating to the period on or after 12 April 2010, when child support became fully disregarded for all means-tested benefits.

Example 14.7

Following on from the previous example where there are arrears of £432, the parent with care would receive the following payments.

Month	Payment by the 19th of the month £	Current liability paid (£48 a week due) £	Arrears paid (assigned to oldest debt) £
July		Nil	Nil
August	156	156	Nil
September	328	192	136
October	300	192	108

By the time the parent with care gets the first payment from the DEO in August, s/he is owed £624 (£432 + £192 (July)), but because of the fluctuating earnings of the non-resident parent, s/he receives less than the amount due. It is only in September that s/he begins to obtain arrears of child support, even though the DEO was put in place in July.

Priority of orders

A DEO takes priority over an attachment of earnings order for a judgment or administration debt (non-priority debts), and any arrestment of earnings under Scottish law.[202] In England and Wales, when a DEO is served on an employee who is already subject to an attachment of earnings order for a priority debt (eg, council tax or a fine), the earliest order has priority.[203]

Any deductions under a lower priority order are taken from the net earnings left after deductions under the first order have been made.[204]

Reviews, cancellations and lapsed orders

The CMS/CSA must review a DEO if there is a change in the amount of the calculation, or if any arrears, penalty payments and collection or enforcement fees included have been paid off.[205] This does not apply if a normal deduction rate that takes into account the change has already been specified (see p316). A DEO can be changed on this review.[206] An employer must comply with the change within seven days of the new DEO being served on it.[207] The usual penalties for failing to comply apply.

If the non-resident parent is paid at a frequency other than weekly, fortnightly, four-weekly or monthly, the CMS/CSA *must* cancel the DEO:[208]

- in a '2012 rules' case; *or*
- in an existing '1993 rules' or '2003 rules' case where there are only arrears and no ongoing liability, and the non-resident parent has been notified in writing that this rule applies.

The CMS/CSA *can* cancel the DEO if:[209]

- no further payments are due under it;
- the DEO is ineffective or there appears to be a more effective way of collecting the payments;
- the DEO is defective (see p300) or does not comply with a procedural requirement;
- the CMS/CSA did not have, or has ceased to have, jurisdiction to make a DEO; *or*
- a DEO being used to enforce a default maintenance decision or interim maintenance decision is no longer appropriate, given the compliance or attempted compliance of the non-resident parent.

The CMS/CSA can also cancel the DEO if:[210]

- it has agreed with the non-resident parent an alternative method for payment of the child support and any fees due; *and*
- it considers it is reasonable to cancel the order.

The CMS/CSA must send written notice of cancellation to the non-resident parent and employer.[211]

A DEO lapses when a non-resident parent leaves the employment.[212] The CMS/CSA can revive it if s/he finds a new job with the same or a different employer.[213] If it is revived, copies of the notice must be served on the parent and new employer.[214] Any shortfall under the DEO prior to the revival cannot be carried over to the revived DEO.[215]

Appeals

A non-resident parent can appeal against a DEO to the magistrates' court in England and Wales or sheriff court in Scotland.[216] The appeal must be made within 28 days of the DEO's being made (56 days if the parent is not resident in the UK).[217] An appeal can only be made on the grounds that the order is defective (see p300), that the payments made to the parent are not earnings (see p295)[218] or that there is 'good reason' not to use a DEO.[219]

When determining whether there is a good reason not to use a DEO, the CMS/CSA must consider whether making the order is likely to result in the disclosure of the parentage of a child and the likely impact of that disclosure on the non-resident parent's employment or on any relationship between the non-resident parent and a third party.[220] The impact of a third party becoming aware of the non-resident parent's DEO is not considered to be a good reason in any circumstances other than in connection with the disclosure of the parentage of a child.[221]

A good reason for not imposing a DEO may also exist if a family member of the non-resident parent or parent with care is employed by the same employer as the non-resident parent and that family member's employment is such that s/he is likely to acquire knowledge of the DEO. If the consequence of this is that the non-resident parent's employment status or family relationships may be adversely affected, there should be good reason not to impose a DEO.[222]

The fact that a non-resident parent may prefer a different method of payment or would prefer the employer not to be informed about her/his child support liability are not considered good reasons to refrain from using a DEO.[223]

If the CMS/CSA has not properly exercised its discretion in making a DEO, a complaint can be made (see Chapter 15) and/or judicial review can be sought (see p215).

A DEO is **defective** if it is impracticable for an employer to comply with it because it does not include the correct information required.[224] Many DEOs have included incorrect information (such as errors in names, addresses and dates), but an appeal will not succeed on this basis if the employer can still comply with the DEO. Although some early appeals were upheld because the DEO was unsigned, a signature is not legally required.

In Scotland, the form of the application for an appeal is laid out in the sheriff court child support rules.[225] In England and Wales, a complaint is made against the Secretary of State for Work and Pensions (who acts through the CMS/CSA). As there is no specific form given, the Scottish wording can be followed as an example, but including: 'This complaint is made under section 32(5) of the Child Support Act 1991 and regulation 22 of the Child Support (Collection and Enforcement) Regulations 1992.'

Once the complaint or application is made, the court notifies the CMS/CSA. The CMS/CSA checks the DEO and contacts the employer to check the earnings. If the DEO is based on the wrong amounts, the CMS/CSA varies and reissues it. If the case does get as far as a court hearing, the magistrates/sheriff may quash the DEO or specify which payments, if any, constitute earnings.[226] The court cannot question the child support calculation itself.[227]

Even if the court quashes the DEO, it cannot order the CMS/CSA to repay deductions to the non-resident parent.[228] For this reason, if deductions are being made from payments that are not earnings, or on the basis of an incorrect normal deduction rate or protected earnings proportion, it may be better to challenge the DEO by judicial review.

Either party can be represented by a lawyer. The CMS/CSA can (and does) instead appoint its own staff to conduct DEO appeals and appear at related court hearings.[229] The non-resident parent can also be represented by a lay person, if the magistrate or sheriff accepts that s/he is suitable. An authorised lay representative does not have the full rights of a legal representative, but may be entitled to expenses.

Deductions from bank accounts

The CMS/CSA has the power to make deduction orders to deduct money from a non-resident parent's current or savings accounts without her/his consent, and without applying to court or obtaining a liability order.[230] This includes accounts with banks, building societies and credit unions. The deductions can be either regular (see below) or made as a lump-sum payment (see p303).[231] As soon as a non-resident parent is in arrears, a deduction order becomes possible as a method of enforcement.

The use of deduction orders is intended to be considered as an option for all appropriate cases where there are arrears.[232] A deduction order may be sought if a non-resident parent is self-employed and a DEO is not possible.

If a non-resident parent has failed to pay child support, the CMS/CSA can make an order requiring a bank or building society with which s/he has an account to make deductions from that account and pay the CMS/CSA. The CMS/CSA has discretion to choose the most suitable account from which to make deductions. Generally, regular deduction orders are directed at current accounts and lump-sum deduction orders at savings accounts. The use of deduction orders on more complex accounts, such as notice accounts or stocks and shares accounts, may now also be considered.[233]

A lump-sum or regular deduction order cannot be made in respect of an account which is used wholly or partly for business purposes. This does not apply if a regular deduction order is made in respect of an account that relates to a non-resident parent who is a sole trader.[234] Powers to make deduction orders in respect of joint accounts have not yet been brought fully into effect, and it is understood that there are no immediate plans to do so.[235]

The bank or building society can take an amount from the non-resident parent's account to cover the administrative costs of setting up and paying a deduction order. The maximum amounts that can be charged are:[236]
- £10, in the case of each deduction made under a regular deduction order;
- £55, in the case of each deduction made under a lump-sum deduction order.

Regular deduction orders

A regular deduction order can be used to collect both arrears and ongoing child support payments that will become due under the calculation that is in place.[237]

When a regular deduction order is made, a copy is served on both the bank or building society and the non-resident parent. The order must specify the amount of the regular deduction and the dates on which deductions are due to be made.[238]

If there is a current child support calculation, or arrears are being collected for an arrangement which is no longer in force, the maximum that can be deducted is 40 per cent of the non-resident parent's gross weekly income in '2012 rules' cases (net weekly income in '1993 rules' and '2003 rules' cases). If a default maintenance decision has been made, the maximum that can be deducted is £80 a week.[239]

Before a regular deduction can be made from a joint account, each of the account holders should be given an opportunity to make representations on the making of the order and the amounts to be deducted.[240] **Note:** powers to make deductions from a joint account have not yet been brought fully into force.

A deduction cannot be made if the amount of credit in the relevant account is below a certain level on the date a deduction is due to be made. The minimum amounts are:

- £40, if deductions are made monthly;
- £10, if deductions are made weekly;
- if deductions are made for any other period, £10 for each whole week in that period, plus £1 for each additional day in that period.

In addition to these amounts, there must be sufficient funds in the account to pay the administrative costs charged.[241]

If the non-resident parent's account is subject to other deduction orders, such as third-party debt orders and garnishee orders, these are generally paid first before a regular deduction order is dealt with. The exception to this is where a third-party debt order or garnishee order is served on the bank or building society after the regular deduction order, but on or before the date a payment is due to be made under the deduction order. In this case, the deduction order is paid first on that occasion, unless the bank or building society has already taken steps to process the other orders. For future payments, it is assumed that the other orders take priority.[242]

It is an offence punishable by a fine of up to £500 for a person not to comply with the requirements of a regular deduction order, unless s/he can show that all reasonable steps were taken to comply.[243]

Reviews and variations of regular deduction orders

A non-resident parent or a bank or building society can apply to the CMS/CSA for a review of a regular deduction order if:[244]

- the non-resident parent or bank or building society can satisfy the CMS/CSA that the parent does not have a beneficial interest in some or all of the amount of money in the account that is subject to the order; *or*
- there has been a change in the amount of the child support calculation; *or*

- any amounts payable under the order have been paid; *or*
- there has been a change in the non-resident parent's current income in '2012 rules' cases (net weekly income in '1993 rules' and '2003 rules' cases);[245] *or*
- because of an official error, an incorrect amount has been specified in the order.

A regular deduction order can be varied to change the amount that is deducted if:[246]

- the CMS/CSA accepts that the non-resident parent has made a payment of child support and no alternative method of payment is in place; *or*
- there has been a successful appeal against a child support calculation; *or*
- the order has been changed following a successful review.

Lump-sum deduction orders

If it is established that the non-resident parent owes arrears of child support, the CMS/CSA considers whether a lump-sum deduction order is the most appropriate method of recovering them.

Once the CMS/CSA has decided to make a lump-sum deduction order, it serves an interim order on a 'deposit taker' (the non-resident parent's bank or building society, or other third party). This order acts as an instruction to secure funds up to the amount of the order in a specified account until further notice. The bank or building society is expected to prevent the funds from being moved or reduced below the amount that is ordered or, if funds are already below this amount, not to allow them to decrease further.

Once funds have been secured, a copy of the order is served on the non-resident parent. Both the deposit taker and the parent have 14 days from the date the order was served in which to make representations to the CMS/CSA. The order is treated as having been served on the parent at the end of the day on which the copy is posted to her/his last known address.[247]

When issuing the order and instructing the bank or building society to secure funds, the CMS/CSA should take into account:[248]

- any hardship that may be caused to the non-resident parent's partner or a relevant child;
- any written, contractual obligations regarding the money that were made before the order was made;
- any other circumstances that the CMS/CSA considers appropriate in the particular case.

The CMS/CSA should also ensure that the amount deducted from a joint account does not exceed an amount that is fair, given all the circumstances, especially the amounts contributed to the account by each of the account holders.[249] **Note:** the powers to make deductions from a joint account have not yet been brought fully into force.

In addition to this 14-day period, a non-resident parent or deposit taker can ask the CMS/CSA to use its discretion to vary the order in certain circumstances. These include if:[250]

- the CMS/CSA accepts the parent's agreement to make a payment;
- there has been a revision or supersession of, or a successful appeal against, the child support calculation that is the subject of the order;
- there has been an appeal to the county court (sheriff court in Scotland) against the making of an order, or against a refusal by the CMS/CSA to consent to funds being moved or reduced;
- the CMS/CSA agrees that hardship may be caused to the parent's partner or to a relevant child;
- the parent is under a written contractual obligation, made before the lump-sum deduction order was made.

Priority of payments

In **England and Wales**, if there is a final lump-sum deduction order and other interim third-party debt orders or garnishee orders *nisi*, a bank or building society must comply with them in the order in which they were served on it. If an interim lump-sum deduction order is served after an interim third-party debt order or garnishee order *nisi*, the final versions of these other orders take priority.[251]

In **Scotland**, a bank or building society must give priority to the lump-sum deduction order and any other orders, according to the order in which they were served on it.[252]

Minimum amounts

A deduction should not be made if the amount of credit in the relevant bank account is below a minimum level. The current minimum level is £55 plus the amount of administrative costs charged by the bank or building society.[253] The administrative costs must not be more than £55 for a lump-sum deduction order.[254]

Appeals

A non-resident parent has the right to appeal against a lump-sum deduction order or a regular deduction order and related decisions made by the CMS/CSA. The appeal is made to the county court in England and Wales or the sheriff court in Scotland.

The parent can appeal against:[255]

- the making of a regular deduction order;
- any decision by the CMS/CSA on a request to review a regular deduction order;
- a refusal to waive the requirement to freeze or protect funds which are the subject of an interim lump-sum deduction order;
- the making of a final lump-sum deduction order.

There is a time limit of 21 days from the date the final lump-sum deduction order is received in which to appeal against its being made. A non-resident parent is considered to have received the final lump-sum deduction order two days after it was posted. If, after 21 days have expired, no appeals have been made, the CMS/CSA instructs the deposit taker to pay the funds to the CMS/CSA.

Recovery of arrears from an estate

From 25 January 2010, the CMS/CSA has had powers to request the payment of arrears of child support (and, from 11 August 2014, any collection fees) from a deceased person's estate without having to apply to court or obtain a liability order. The decision to recover arrears is a discretionary one. The person must have died on or after 25 January 2010. Any arrears for which the deceased was liable immediately before death become a debt payable to the CMS/CSA from her/his estate.[256] The CMS/CSA can contact the administrator or executor of the estate to request payment.

The CMS/CSA aims to avoid legal action where possible when using this power and to avoid delaying or obstructing the administration of an estate.[257]

It is understood that the CMS/CSA is notified electronically when other government departments are informed of the death of a non-resident parent. However, the person with care may also wish to inform the CMS/CSA of the death of a non-resident parent who owes arrears of child support.

The administrator or executor has the same rights of appeal, following the same procedures and time limits, as the deceased person had before death. (If 'mandatory reconsideration' does not apply before there is a right of appeal (see p235), the CMS/CSA must appoint the administrator or executor to proceed with any appeal or, if there is no such person, the CMS/CSA can appoint someone it thinks fit.[258])

The CMS/CSA must disclose relevant information to enable the administrator or executor to make a decision about whether to pay or appeal the arrears. The CMS/CSA has discretion to decide whether the information requested is essential and, therefore, whether it should be disclosed.[259] Any application for information should be in writing and give reasons. The CMS/CSA should not disclose the address of any person involved in the case unless s/he has given written consent, and should also prevent the disclosure of any information that could lead to the person with care, or any other relevant person, being located.[260]

It is intended that child support arrears will be treated in the same way as other debts – eg, unpaid utility or council tax bills. It does not appear that they take priority over other payments.

Concerns have been raised about possible inaccuracies in calculating the correct amount of child support that may be owed by a deceased non-resident parent. Before making a claim on an estate, the CMS/CSA should thoroughly check the amount of outstanding debt, including completing any outstanding reassessments relating to periods before the death.[261] Administrators of the estate should check that the CMS/CSA has carried out this process and that the amount of debt to be recovered is accurate.

When arrears should not be recovered

The CMS/CSA should not pursue arrears from a deceased person's estate without seeking the consent of the person with care. If s/he does not wish to pursue the arrears, the CMS/CSA should not take any further action.[262] For further details on when arrears may be written off, see p291. The CMS/CSA also has a duty to take into account the welfare of any child likely to be affected by its decision.[263] This includes children of the deceased person who may not have been the subject of the child support calculation, or other dependent children who would otherwise benefit from the estate. When the CMS/CSA registers its claim against the estate, it may not be aware of other children or the potential implications for them. If the CMS/CSA later becomes aware of any potentially adverse impact on other children, it should reconsider whether to pursue the arrears.[264] The CMS/CSA also takes into account the administrative cost of recovering arrears in this way.[265]

If the arrears recovered from an estate would be retained by the CMS/CSA in lieu of any benefit paid, they should not be pursued if this would have a detrimental effect on a person with care or a qualifying child. This only applies to arrears relating to a period before 12 April 2010, when child support became fully disregarded for all means-tested benefits. The CMS/CSA should contact the person with care to establish what impact the recovery would have before approaching the administrators of the estate.[266]

Obtaining a liability order

If a DEO is inappropriate (eg, because the non-resident parent is not employed) or one has been made but proved ineffective, the CMS/CSA may apply to the magistrates' court in England and Wales, or sheriff court in Scotland, for a liability order.[267]

A liability order provides legal recognition of the debt, and allows the CMS/CSA to take further enforcement measures.

The CMS/CSA must give the non-resident parent seven days' notice of its intention to seek a liability order (28 days if s/he is not resident in the UK).[268] The notice must state the amount of child support outstanding, including any collection or enforcement fees or penalty payments.

If the court decides that the payments are due but have not been made, it must make the order.[269] The court cannot question the child support calculation itself.[270] When making a liability order, the court is, however, entitled to take into account payments made by the non-resident person by a method other than that specified by the CMS/CSA.[271]

An order (including one made in Northern Ireland) can be enforced anywhere in the UK.[272]

As with an appeal against a DEO (see p304), either party can be represented by a lawyer or by another person.

If the court makes the liability order, it can (and usually will) order the non-resident parent to pay the CMS/CSA's legal expenses.

Time limits for obtaining and using a liability order

Since 12 July 2006, there has been no time limit for applying for a liability order. Debts that were older than six years on 12 July 2006 (ie, that became due on or before 12 July 2000) and were not subject to a liability order cannot be enforced and will be recovered by other methods, such as a DEO.[273] The six years do not begin to run until the non-resident parent is notified of the assessment or calculation. Although an assessment/calculation can be backdated, liability does not exist until it is made.[274]

The CMS/CSA does not need to act on a liability order immediately after it is granted. If an order is made in time, there may be a long delay before the CMS/CSA takes any further action. Actions that directly aim to recover money (eg, levying distress) must be taken within six years from the date of the order.[275] The six-year time limit does not apply to actions that do not themselves recover money, such as imprisonment or disqualification from driving, and the CMS/CSA may be able to take action after this date.[276]

England and Wales

The non-resident parent is sent a summons giving 14 days' notice of the hearing. The magistrates decide whether or not to issue the liability order, but cannot consider whether the parent is liable or the assessment/calculation has been properly made.[277] If an appeal against a decision of the CMS/CSA on those issues is pending, however, the court may decide to adjourn.

The court may decide not to issue an order if the non-resident parent appears to be co-operating. However, the CMS/CSA may still ask for the order to be granted on the understanding that it will not be enforced if the parent continues to co-operate. If the parent does not attend the court, the CMS/CSA may still obtain the order, unless the application has not been properly made. It is unusual for a non-resident parent to attend a liability order hearing. If s/he does attend, the court may adjourn and arrange another hearing to ensure that there is sufficient time for her/him to speak.

There is a set form for the court order. It must specify the outstanding amounts of child support, penalty payments, fees and other forms of maintenance.[278]

Scotland

A CMS/CSA litigation officer can sign the liability order application instead of a solicitor.[279] Court officials serve notice of the application on the non-resident parent.[280] The parent has 21 days to object to the liability order's being made. This should be done in writing by returning the notice stating the grounds of the objection and enclosing evidence. If objections are received, a hearing is held. Even if the parent does not attend, the sheriff must still consider her/his objections.[281] As in England and Wales, the court cannot question the non-resident parent's liability for child support, or the calculation itself. An extract of the liability order may be issued 14 days after the order is actually made. All the forms used in this procedure are included in the sheriff court child support rules.[282]

Enforcing a liability order

In England and Wales, the CMS/CSA can decide to take control of goods (see below) or take action in the county court (see below). **In Scotland**, a liability order can be enforced by 'diligence' (the term for various processes of debt enforcement in Scottish law).[283]

The CMS/CSA aims to use the full range of sanctions available, including driving licence removal, imprisonment or seizure of assets, where appropriate.[284]

Taking control of goods

If a liability order has been made, the amount on the order can be enforced in England and Wales by taking control of and selling the person's goods (previously known as 'distress').[285] The enforcement agent carrying this out must give the person written notice at least seven clear days before taking action. The notice must include details of the liability order and the debt.[286] It must also explain how payment of the debt in full can be made to avoid the taking and subsequent sale of goods.[287]

Certain items cannot be taken. These include:[288]

- tools, books, vehicles and other items necessary for work, up to an aggregate value of £1,350; *and*
- clothing, bedding, furniture, household equipment and provisions reasonably required to meet the basic domestic needs of the non-resident parent and every member of her/his household.

Fees can be charged at each of the stages involved in the process.[289]

The non-resident parent can bring proceedings about the action in the county court or High Court. If the court finds that an enforcement agent has breached the rules, it may order the goods to be returned if they have been taken, or order the payment of damages in respect of any loss suffered because of the breach.[290]

County court action

Once a liability order has been made, the CMS/CSA can arrange for the county court to record the order as if it were a judgment debt.[291] This record is publicly available and damages the non-resident parent's credit rating (see also p75 for when the CMS/CSA can disclose information directly to credit reference agencies). The CMS/CSA can also use the county court to recover any amount that remains unpaid.[292]

A **charging order** allows a debt to be registered against certain assets, such as land, stocks, shares and any interest the non-resident parent may have in a trust. If a charge is registered and the assets are sold, the debt due under the liability order can be recovered from the proceeds of the sale. In some cases, it may not be possible to register a charge, in which case a caution against dealings may be obtained to prevent the property from being sold without the CMS/CSA's knowledge. Once a charge or caution has been registered, the CMS/CSA can consider applying to the court for an order of sale.

A **third-party debt order** can be obtained by the CMS/CSA if it is aware that the non-resident parent has a bank account or is owed money by a third party. The order freezes funds in the account and requires that person to release funds to the CMS/CSA up to the amount of the liability order.

Orders preventing the disposal of assets

From 6 April 2010, the CMS/CSA has had powers to take action to prevent a non-resident parent disposing of assets from which it could recover arrears.[293] The CMS/CSA may apply to the High Court (England and Wales) or the Court of Session or sheriff court (Scotland) if a non-resident parent has:

- arrears of child support; *and*
- on or after 6 April 2010, has disposed of, or is about to dispose of, assets with the intention of avoiding paying child support.

Disposing of assets includes any conveyance, assurance or gift of property of any description. It does not include assets transferred under a will or codicil.[294]

If the asset has already been disposed of, the court can make an order to 'set the transaction aside' or, in Scotland, to 'reduce the disposition' – ie, to reverse the disposal.[295] If the parent is about to dispose of an asset, the court can make a restraining order (England and Wales) or an interdicting order (Scotland) to prevent this.[296]

The court can review any disposal of assets by the non-resident parent, except if the asset was given as part of a contract with an innocent party who acted in good faith.[297] For example, if the parent disposes of a sum of money to purchase goods from an individual who had no knowledge of her/his intention to avoid paying child support, the transaction cannot be reversed. An asset transferred to another as part of a marriage agreement can, however, be reviewed by the court.[298]

If the court is satisfied that the CMS/CSA would be able to take action to recover arrears from the asset in question, the burden of proof is on the non-resident parent to show that s/he did not dispose of, or was not about to dispose of, the asset with the intention of avoiding paying child support.[299] If an order is made in Scotland, the parent can apply to the court to have it reviewed, varied or recalled at any time.[300]

Disqualification from driving or imprisonment

If all other methods of recovery have failed, the CMS/CSA may take action to disqualify the non-resident parent from driving or to imprison her/him (but not both).[301]

Before taking action, every attempt must be made to contact the parent. If no phone contact has been successful during the enforcement action, a face-to-face visit may be appropriate. These powers are only used as a last resort.[302] Suspended prison sentences and suspended disqualifications from driving are significantly more common than actual committals and disqualifications.[303]

As with the exercise of all discretionary powers, when deciding whether to take this action, the CMS/CSA should consider the welfare of any child likely to be affected.

Action for imprisonment or disqualification from driving

In England and Wales, if distress and/or county court proceedings have been tried (or, in Scotland, diligence via arrestments or inhibitions on sale), but an amount is still due under the liability order, the CMS/CSA can apply to the magistrates' court (or sheriff court) to issue either a warrant committing the non-resident parent to prison or an order disqualifying her/him from driving.[304] The CMS/CSA can only do this if the other proceedings have been tried unsuccessfully. It is not enough that they have been considered but not pursued.[305]

The hearing must take place in the presence of the parent.[306] The court can summon her/him to appear in court and produce her/his driving licence.[307] If s/he does not appear, the court may issue a warrant (citation in Scotland) for arrest.[308] The CMS/CSA should explain why it considers disqualification or imprisonment appropriate in the circumstances.

The court must enquire into the parent's means, whether s/he needs a driving licence to make a living and whether there has been 'wilful refusal or culpable neglect' on her/his part.[309] Only if there has been can the court commit the parent to prison or disqualify her/him from driving;[310] the decision whether to do so is at the court's discretion. The CMS/CSA must prove beyond reasonable doubt that the non-resident parent has the ability to pay and has wilfully refused.[311] As a result of caselaw establishing this point, the CMS/CSA has reviewed the forms and procedures it uses when taking action for imprisonment, in order to provide the required information about the non-resident parent's financial circumstances.

A written statement from an employer will be accepted as proof of earnings.[312]

Imprisonment

If the court decides that there has been wilful refusal or culpable neglect and committal is appropriate, a warrant for imprisonment is issued.[313] If the court decides on committal rather than disqualification from driving, it should explain the reasons why this was preferred.

A warrant cannot be issued against a non-resident parent who is under 18.[314]

Instead of immediate committal to prison, the court usually fixes a term of imprisonment and postpones it on conditions, usually of regular payments.[315] A warrant of commitment is issued, stating the total amount outstanding, including child support, penalty payments, fees, court costs and any other charges.[316] If the amount is paid in full, the non-resident parent will not be imprisoned.

The maximum period of imprisonment is six weeks.[317] If, after the warrant has been issued, part payment is made, the period of imprisonment is reduced by the same proportion as that by which the debt has been reduced.[318]

If the parent is imprisoned, s/he can be released immediately if the liability order debt is paid in full. If part of the debt is paid, the prison sentence can be reduced.[319] Advisers should check whether the payment needs to be made to the prison or to the CMS/CSA.

The court cannot write off the arrears, so if full payment is not made, arrears still exist following the period of imprisonment. If a warrant is not issued or the court does not fix a term of imprisonment, the CMS/CSA can renew the application at a later date on the grounds that the non-resident parent's circumstances have changed.

The ability to apply to court for a warrant for imprisonment is not a one-off power. If the non-resident parent builds up a new debt (eg, by not keeping up with current child support payments), the CMS/CSA can go back to court to request a warrant in respect of each new debt.[320]

Disqualification from driving

If the court decides that there has been wilful refusal or culpable neglect and disqualification from driving is appropriate, an order is issued.[321] The order may be issued but its implementation suspended on conditions – eg, regular payments. The order states the amount outstanding, including child support, court costs and any other charges.[322] If the amount is paid in full, the order is revoked.

The maximum period of disqualification is two years.[323] If, after the order has been issued, part payment is made, the period of disqualification may be reduced.[324] If the amount is paid in full, the order must be revoked. If, at the end of the period of disqualification, the arrears have not been paid in full, the CMS/CSA may apply again for imprisonment or disqualification.[325]

Bankruptcy

The CMS/CSA does not pursue bankruptcy (sequestration in Scotland), but a non-resident parent may have child support arrears when s/he is made bankrupt. The

CMS/CSA is not a creditor that can be bound by an individual voluntary arrangement (ie, in England and Wales, a binding compromise agreement with creditors to avoid the consequences of bankruptcy) made by a non-resident parent who has failed to pay child support. Any liability for arrears of child support cannot, therefore, be reduced by means of an individual voluntary arrangement.[326]

The CMS/CSA is unable to take enforcement action while a non-resident parent is being made bankrupt. Therefore, if the CMS/CSA is notified of bankruptcy, any ongoing enforcement action must cease until the bankruptcy order has been made.

In this case, the CMS/CSA may decide not to enforce the order because it may not be practical – eg, a charging order/inhibition of sale may not be effective, as any property may already have been sold to pay creditors. The CMS/CSA may secure a liability order to remind the non-resident parent that responsibility for child support cannot be avoided.

As part of bankruptcy proceedings, the non-resident parent can inform the court of her/his child support liabilities. The administrator of the bankruptcy should take this liability into account when deciding how much money the parent needs to meet basic living expenses. This decision is made before any available funds are distributed among creditors.

Bankruptcy in England and Wales may not prevent the CMS/CSA considering further enforcement measures, such as imprisonment or disqualification from driving – eg, further action may be pursued if the non-resident parent has a steady income. In these circumstances, the parent must show that s/he cannot afford to meet her/his child support liability. This may be more difficult if the administrator of the bankruptcy has already made provision for the current child support payments when deciding how much money the parent needs to meet basic living expenses. However, in the vast majority of cases, the CMS/CSA still pursues child support.[327]

If a non-resident parent is sequestrated in Scotland, any child support debt is wiped out and is no longer recoverable.[328]

---

6. **Fees for enforcement action**

Fees for enforcement action in '2012 rules' cases were introduced on 30 June 2014. If the Child Maintenance Service (CMS) undertakes certain enforcement action, fees will be imposed on the non-resident parent as follows:[329]

- £50 for making a deduction from earnings order (DEO) (see p293);
- £50 for making a regular deduction order (see p301);
- £200 for making a lump-sum deduction order (see p303);
- £300 for applying for a liability order (see p306).

Enforcement fees may be waived by the CMS if:[330]
- an additional fee would otherwise be due because:
  - more than one DEO is sought by the CMS because the non-resident parent has more than one employer or has recently changed jobs;
  - more than one regular deduction order or lump-sum order is sought because the non-resident parent holds more than one bank or building society account, or has recently changed accounts;
  - the amount being collected under a DEO or regular deduction order has changed;
- the CMS has sought a liability order but it was not granted;
- the CMS's action to impose a DEO, regular deduction order or lump-sum deduction order has been successfully challenged by the non-resident parent by appeal or judicial review;
- due to error or maladministration by the CMS, the DEO, regular deduction order or lump-sum deduction order has lapsed or been discharged;
- a DEO is made because the non-resident parent has chosen to use this as the method of paying her/his child support liability;
- a deduction from earnings request (see p293) is made for a non-resident parent in the armed forces when that parent is deployed on operational duty.

An enforcement fee is payable to the CMS, not the person with care. It is recovered by the CMS from any arrears owed by the non-resident parent before the balance is paid to the person with care.[331] If an enforcement fee is imposed, the CMS must send the non-resident parent a notice as soon as possible stating the amount of the fee and the enforcement action in respect of which it has been imposed.[332]

The rules on collecting and enforcing payments of child support also apply to payment of fees, except that the CMS cannot seek to disqualify a non-resident parent from driving or imprison her/him where enforcement action is being taken against her/him solely to recover fees.[333]

Note: fees were previously charged for Child Support Agency services before April 1995. From 5 August 2008, the requirement to pay any outstanding fees from the years before April 1995 was removed.[334]

7. **Delays in collection and enforcement**

Many cases may accumulate arrears. In recent years, the Child Maintenance Service (CMS)/Child Support Agency (CSA) has said that it has been pursuing a more vigorous and effective approach to enforcement and taking enforcement action more quickly in response to a non-resident parent's failure to pay. Performance on enforcement for '1993 rules' and '2003 rules' cases has been hindered by the substantial number of cases which have to be processed outside the main computer system. The arrangements and IT system for the '2012 rules' scheme are intended to avoid these difficulties.

A person with care who is concerned about the speed of pursuit should contact the CMS/CSA and explain the effects of this on the welfare of the child(ren). In particular, a person with care may want to request that a deduction from earnings order (DEO) be issued. If a DEO or another form of enforcement is refused, the reasons for this should be explained.

Note: enforcing the obligation to pay child support is at the discretion of the CMS/CSA.[335] This means that the person with care cannot decide which method of enforcement is used. If s/he believes that there has been undue delay by the CMS/CSA, or that it has not used its discretion reasonably or rationally, s/he can make a complaint (see Chapter 15). It is possible that judicial review (see p215) could also be considered. Specialist advice should be sought before considering an application for judicial review.

If arrears of over £100 have built up because of CMS/CSA maladministration, the person with care may be eligible for an advance payment (see below). This may be in addition to any payment of compensation (see p325).

Advance payments

An advance payment of child support is not compensation. The payment is to ensure the person with care is not worse off as a result of maladministration by the CMS/CSA. Essentially, it is advance payment of arrears that the CMS/CSA is collecting from the non-resident parent. The decision on whether or not to make an advance payment is discretionary and there are no guidelines laid down in legislation. Some details of when the CMS/CSA considers making an advance payment are available on the child maintenance section of the gov.uk website.

For an advance payment to be considered, there must be clear evidence of maladministration by the CMS/CSA. Maladministration may include:[336]

- rudeness;
- delay;
- refusal to answer reasonable questions;
- knowingly giving advice which is misleading or inadequate;
- incompetence;
- bias – eg, because of gender or ethnicity; *or*
- disregard of guidance that should be followed.

A request for an advance payment could also be considered even if the CMS/CSA is not able to recover arrears from the non-resident parent. This could apply if arrears of child support have become unenforceable – eg, because enforcement action was not taken within the time limits, or the non-resident parent has subsequently moved abroad and is outside the CMS/CSA's jurisdiction. If the arrears could have been collected had the CMS/CSA taken timely action, a request for an advance payment can be made. Although the power is discretionary, the Independent Case Examiner (ICE – see p327) has recommended payment in such cases.[337]

The CMS/CSA may consider an advance payment on its own initiative or at the request of the person with care. If an advance payment is to be made, the amount is the arrears that would have been due but for the maladministration. Allowances are made for normal processing time, so only delay over and above this is considered.

If a decision is made not to make a payment, there is no right of appeal. The person with care may provide further information to support the case, complain (see Chapter 15), contact her/his MP or possibly seek judicial review (see p215). If a complaint is made, the CMS/CSA may still refuse to make an advance payment. However, both the ICE and the Ombudsman have the power to recommend advance payments, so it may be worthwhile moving to the next stage of the complaints procedure if the person with care has reasonable grounds.

Where maladministration has occurred, there is also provision for the CMS/CSA to pay compensation or a consolatory special payment (see p325).

Enforcement by the person with care

Although there is no provision in child support legislation for the parent with care to bring her/his own court action against the non-resident parent for the child support due, it may be possible to do so. In practice, however, such action may be difficult. The European Court of Human Rights has confirmed that only the CMS/CSA has the legal standing to enforce child support, and that a lack of direct access to the courts by a person with care to enforce child support payments from a non-resident parent does not breach the right to a fair hearing under the European Convention on Human Rights.[338]

If the person with care has lost out because of CMS/CSA delay or maladministration, it may be possible to sue the CMS/CSA for negligence. Anyone considering doing either of the above should seek legal advice. Using the complaints procedure is more likely to be an effective means of obtaining redress within a reasonable timescale (see Chapter 15).

8. '1993 rules' and conversion cases

Existing '1993 rules' child support assessments are collected and enforced in much the same way as '2003 rules' and '2012 rules' calculations – involving negotiations, deduction from earnings orders (DEOs), liability orders and action for committal to prison or disqualification from driving. However, there are some important differences, which are outlined here.

Penalty payments do not apply to '1993 rules' cases. If a case has converted to the '2003 rules' (see Chapter 10 of the 2013/14 edition of this *Handbook* for details on conversions), the '2003 rules' penalty payments may be applied. This means that penalty payments can only be made in respect of missed or late payments after the date of conversion (see p289).

Voluntary payments are dealt with in the same way as for '2003 rules' cases.[339]

DEOs are calculated and applied in a slightly different way. At conversion, any old arrears not collected under the previous order may be included in a new one issued under the '2003 rules'.

Deduction from earnings orders

Deductions made are based on the '**normal deduction rate**' and the '**protected earnings rate**'.

Normal deduction rate

The normal deduction rate is the amount that will be deducted each payday, provided net earnings are not brought below the protected earnings rate. The normal deduction rate can include current child support liability and amounts for arrears due. No arrears can be included if they would have brought the non-resident parent's disposable income, on the date the current assessment was made, below the protected income level (not the protected earnings rate) *minus* the minimum payment (see p194).[340] This does not apply if the current assessment is an interim maintenance assessment (IMA – see previous editions of this *Handbook* for details of IMAs). Also see previous editions of this *Handbook* for details of the protected income level and disposable income.

Protected earnings rate

The protected earnings rate is the level below which earnings must not be reduced by the deductions. Unless a Category A or D IMA is in force, it is set at the exempt income level. See previous editions of this *Handbook* for details.[341] If a Category A or D IMA is in force, the protected earnings rate is either:[342]

- if the Child Support Agency (CSA) knows something of the non-resident parent's circumstances:
  - the income support (IS) single or couple personal allowance;
  - the IS personal allowance for any children under 16 living with her/him;
  - any relevant IS premiums; *plus*
  - £30; *or*
- otherwise, the IS adult personal allowance plus £30.

If there is no assessment in force, the protected earnings rate is the exempt income level for the last assessment. If the non-resident parent satisfies the CSA that her/his circumstances have since changed, the protected earnings rate is the exempt income level s/he would have if the assessment were superseded.[343] If the last assessment was a Category A or C IMA, the protected earnings rate is still worked out as for IMAs.

If the non-resident parent has more than one employer and a deduction order is made in respect of more than one of them, the protected earnings rate for each order is divided proportionally between the parent's earnings with each employer.[344]

Administering a deduction from earnings order

The rules on what an employer can deduct are almost identical to those described earlier in this chapter (see p296).

In addition to these rules, if on any payday net earnings are below the protected earnings rate, no deduction or charge can be made. When this occurs, the difference between net earnings and protected earnings is carried over and treated as additional protected earnings on the next payday.[345] For an illustration of how this operates in practice, see *Example 18.1* in the 2001/02 edition of this *Handbook*.

If two or more DEOs have been issued, the employer should deal with the earliest first.[346]

Notes

1. Introduction
1 s29(1) CSA 1991
2 s30(1) CSA 1991
3 *Supporting Separated Families: securing children's futures*, Cm 8399, DWP, July 2012; CS(F) Regs
4 Reg 3(3A) CSF Regs, as revoked by reg 4 CS(CEMA) Regs
5 R(CS) 9/98
6 *KA v CMEC* [2009] UKUT 99 (AAC)

2. Payment of child support
7 s29 CSA 1991; reg 2 CS(C&E) Regs
8 Reg 1(2A) CS(C&E) Regs
9 Reg 6 CS(C&E) Regs
10 ss4(2) and (2A) and 7(3) and (3A) CSA 1991; *Supporting Separated Families: securing children's futures*, Cm 8399, DWP, July 2012
11 *Managing Your Payments With Direct Pay*, CMS factsheet, October 2013, available at www.gov.uk
12 s29(1)(b) CSA 1991

13 Written ministerial statement by the Minister for State, DWP, 20 May 2013, House of Commons *Hansard*, col 58WS
14 Reg 3 CS(C&E) Regs
15 Reg 2 CS(C&E) Regs
16 Reg 5 CS(C&E) Regs
17 Reg 4 CS(C&E) Regs
18 Reg 4 CS(MPA) Regs
19 Reg 7(1) CS(C&E) Regs
20 Reg 7(2) CS(C&E) Regs
21 Regs 6 and 7 CS(MPA) Regs
22 s29(1)(b) CSA 1991
23 ss4(2) and (2A) and 7(3) and (3A) CSA 1991
24 **2012 rules** *Receiving Child Maintenance*, CMSB013GB, October 2013
   1993 & 2003 rules *What is Child Maintenance and How Does it Affect Me?* CLS301, October 2013
25 s6 CMOPA 2008; CSF Regs 2014

26 *Supporting Separated Families: securing children's futures,* Cm 8399, DWP, July 2012
27 *Supporting Separated Families: securing children's futures,* Cm 8399, DWP, July 2012
28 Reg 7(2) CSF Regs 2014
29 Reg 7(3) CSF Regs 2014
30 *Government Response to the Consultation Supporting Separated Families: securing children's futures,* Cm 8742, DWP, November 2013; reg 7(3) CSF Regs 2014
31 Reg 7(5) CSF Regs 2014
32 Reg 5 CS(MPA) Regs
33 s41C(3) CSA 1991
34 Reg 7 CS(MPA) Regs
35 Reg 8 CS(AIAMA) Regs
36 Reg 3(1) CS(C&E) Regs
37 **2012 rules** *Paying Child Maintenance,* CMSB009GB, October 2013
   1993 & 2003 rules *What is Child Maintenance and How Does it Affect Me?* CLS301, October 2013
38 Reg 3(2) CS(C&E) Regs
39 Reg 6 CS(C&E) Regs
40 **2012 rules** *Paying Child Maintenance,* CMSB009GB, October 2013
   1993 & 2003 rules *How Do I Pay Child Maintenance?* CSL305, October 2012
41 Reg 5(1) CS(C&E) Regs
42 s43 CSA 1991
43 s43 CSA 1991; Sch 9B SS(C&P) Regs
44 Sch 1 para 4(2) CSA 1991
   2012 rules Reg 44(2) CSMC Regs
   2003 rules Reg 4(2) CS(MCSC) Regs
45 **2012 rules** Reg 44(3) CSMC Regs
   2003 rules Reg 4(3)(a) CS(MCSC) Regs
46 Reg 4(3)(b) CS(MCSC) Regs
47 Reg 35(l) SS(C&P) Regs; Sch 9B SS(C&P) Regs; Sch 7 para 2(4) UC,PIP,JSA&ESA(C&P) Regs
48 Regs 14 and 15 CSF Regs 2014
49 Sch 9 para 7A(1) SS(C&P) Regs
50 Sch 9 paras 1 and 2(1)(f) SS(C&P) Regs
51 Sch 9 para 2(2) SS(C&P) Regs; Sch 7 para 2(4) UC,PIP,JSA&ESA(C&P) Regs
52 Sch 9 para 8 SS(C&P) Regs; Sch 6, paras 3 and 4 UC,PIP,JSA&ESA(C&P) Regs
53 Sch 9 para 9 SS(C&P) Regs; Sch 6 para 5 UC,PIP,JSA&ESA(C&P) Regs
54 Sch 5 para 9 CS(MASC) Regs
55 s29(3)(ca) and (3A) CSA 1991; reg 4 CS(C&E) Regs, as substituted by reg 4(1) CS(MOC&NCR)Regs
56 *Paying Child Maintenance,* CMSB009GB, October 2013

57 *Receiving Child Maintenance,* CMSB013GB, October 2013
58 Reg 4(1) CS(C&E) Regs
59 Regs 4(2) and 6 CS(C&E) Regs
60 Reg 5(3) CS(C&E) Regs
61 CMEC Business Plan 2008/09
   1993 & 2003 rules *How Will I Receive Child Maintenance?* CSL314, October 2012
   2012 rules *Paying Child Maintenance,* CMSB009GB, October 2013
62 Regs 8 and 9 CS(MPA) Regs
63 Reg 8 CS(MPA) Regs
64 Reg 9 CS(MPA) Regs
65 s41B(2) CSA 1991
66 Regs 8(2) and 9(2) CS(MPA) Regs
67 Regs 8(3) and 9(3) CS(MPA) Regs
68 Reg 8 CS(MPA) Regs
69 Reg 8(3) CS(MPA) Regs
70 s41B(2) CSA 1991
71 s41B(3) and (4) CSA 1991
72 s41B(7) CSA 1991
73 CSA online procedures, release No.153, December 2012
74 Regs 10A and 10B CS(AIAMA) Regs
75 Regs 8(2) and 9(2) CS(MPA) Regs
76 Reg 6 (1) CS(MPA) Regs
77 Reg 6(3)(a)-(f) CS(MPA) Regs
78 s41C(3) CSA 1991
79 Reg 7(2) CS(MPA) Regs
80 Reg 7(3) CS(MPA) Regs
81 CS(MPA) Regs, Explanatory Memorandum, para 7.11
82 *Green v SSWP* [2010] EWHC 1278, 16 July 2010

3. **Collection of other payments**
83 s30 CSA 1991; CS(CEOFM) Regs
84 Reg 5 CS(CEOFM) Regs
85 Reg 2 CS(CEOFM) Regs
86 Regs 3 and 4 CS(CEOFM) Regs
87 s30(3) CSA 1991

4. **Arrears**
88 ss4(2)(b) and 7(3)(b) CSA 1991
89 **2012 rules** *What Happens if a Paying Parent Doesn't Pay Child Maintenance?* CMB006GB, November 2013
   1993 & 2003 rules *What Action Can the CSA Take if Parents Don't Pay?* CSL306, October 2012
90 *Preparing for the Future, Tackling the Past: child maintenance – arrears and compliance strategy 2012–2017,* DWP, January 2013

91 *Preparing for the Future, Tackling the Past: child maintenance – arrears and compliance strategy 2012–2017*, DWP, January 2013
92 Reg 8A CS(MAJ) Regs 1992
93 **2012 rules** *Paying Child Maintenance*, CMSB009GB, October 20132
1993 & 2003 rules *How Do I Pay Child Maintenance?* CSL305, October 2012
94 Reg 7 CS(C&E) Regs
95 s28J CSA 1991
96 Reg 2(2) CS(VP) Regs
97 *DP v CMEC (CSM)* [2012] UKUT 63 (AAC)
98 Reg 3(b) CS(VP) Regs
99 Reg 3(a) CS(VP) Regs
100 Regs 2(2) and 4(b) CS(VP) Regs
101 Reg 4(a) CS(VP) Regs
102 s41B(1A) and (2) CSA 1991; reg 9 CS(MPA) Regs
103 Reg 3(3) CS(MPA) Regs
104 Reg 3(3)(a) CS(MPA) Regs; *Child Support (Miscellaneous Amendments) Regulations 2012: government response to consultation*, March 2012
105 Reg 3(4) CS(MPA) Regs
106 Reg 3A CS(MPA) Regs
107 *Child Maintenance Frequently Asked Questions*, DWP, August 2012
108 First protocol, Art 1 ECHR
109 *Preparing for the Future, Tackling the Past: child maintenance – arrears and compliance strategy 2012–2017*, DWP, January 2013
110 s41(2) CSA 1991
111 s41(2) and (2A) CSA 1991; reg 8 CS(AIAMA) Regs
112 Reg 8 CS(AIAMA) Regs
113 Sch 9B para 3(1) SS(C&P) Regs
114 s43 CSA 1991; Sch 9B SS(C&P) Regs
115 Sch 9 para 7B SS(C&P) Regs
116 Reg 7(1) CS(MPA) Regs
117 Reg 5 CS(MPA) Regs
118 Reg 7(3)(2) CS(MPA) Regs
119 Reg 5(2) CS(MPA) Regs
120 Reg 5(2) CS(MPA) Regs
121 *Child Maintenance and Other Payments Act Summary of Responses to the Consultation on Draft Regulations*, CMEC, November 2009, para 3
122 *Child Maintenance and Other Payments Act Summary of Responses to the Consultation on Draft Regulations*, CMEC, November 2009, para 3
123 Reg 7(3) CS(MPA) Regs
124 *Child Maintenance and Other Payments Act Summary of Responses to the Consultation on Draft Regulations*, CMEC, November 2009, para 3.5
125 *Preparing for the Future, Tackling the Past: child maintenance – arrears and compliance strategy 2012–2017*, DWP, January 2013
126 s14A CSA 1991
2012 rules *What Happens if a Paying Parent Doesn't Pay Child Maintenance?* CSMB006GB, November 2013
1993 & 2003 rules *What Action Can the CSA Take if Parents Don't Pay?* CSL306, October 2012
127 *Preparing for the Future, Tackling the Past: child maintenance – arrears and compliance strategy 2012–2017*, DWP, January 2013
128 s41A CSA 1991 and reg 7A CS(C&E) Regs; Sch 7, para 3(1) UC,PIP,JSA&ESA(C&P) Regs
129 s43 CMOPA 2008
130 s41D CSA 1991
131 *Government Response to Consultation on the Draft Child Support Management of Payments and Arrears (Amendment) Regulations 2012*, DWP, October 2012
132 *Government Response to Consultation on the Draft Child Support Management of Payments and Arrears (Amendment) Regulations 2012*, DWP, October 2012
133 Reg 13D(1) and (2) CS(MPA) Regs
134 Reg 13D(3) CS(MPA) Regs
135 *Government Response to Consultation on the Draft Child Support Management of Payments and Arrears (Amendment) Regulations 2012*, DWP, October 2012
136 s41D(3) and (5)-(7) CSA 1991
137 Reg 13C(1) CS(MPA) Regs
138 Reg 13B CS(MPA) Regs
139 *Government Response to Consultation on the Draft Child Support Management of Payments and Arrears (Amendment) Regulations 2012*, DWP, October 2012
140 Reg 13E(1) and (2) CS(MPA) Regs
141 Reg 13E(3) CS(MPA) Regs
142 Reg 13E(4) and (5) CS(MPA) Regs
143 *Government Response to Consultation on the Draft Child Support Management of Payments and Arrears (Amendment) Regulations 2012*, DWP, October 2012
144 s41E CSA 1991
145 *Preparing for the Future, Tackling the Past: child maintenance – arrears and compliance strategy 2012–2017*, DWP, January 2013
146 s41E(1) CSA 1991 and reg 13G CS(MPA) Regs

147 *Preparing for the Future, Tackling the Past: child maintenance – arrears and compliance strategy 2012–2017*, DWP, January 2013
148 Reg 13F CS(MPA) Regs
149 Reg 13H CS(MPA) Regs
150 Reg 13H(5) CS(MPA) Regs
151 Reg 13I CS(MPA) Regs
152 Reg 13H(4) CS(MPA) Regs
153 Regs 13(2) and 13H(2) CS(MPA) Regs

5. Enforcement
154 **2012 rules** *What Happens if a Paying Parent Doesn't Pay Child Maintenance?* CMSB006GB, November 2013
   1993 & 2003 rules *What Action Can the CSA Take if Parents Don't Pay?* CSL306, October 2012
155 s14A CSA 1991
156 Reg 13 CSF Regs
157 s31 CSA 1991
158 **2012 rules** *What Happens if a Paying Parent Doesn't Pay Child Maintenance?* CMSB006GB, November 2013
   1993 & 2003 rules *What Action Can the CSA Take if Parents Don't Pay?* CSL 306, October 2012
159 s29(4)(a) CSA 1991
160 *R v Secretary of State for Social Security ex parte Biggin* [1995] 2 FCR 595, [1995] 1 FLR 851
161 Sch 1 para 10 CS(NIRA) Regs
162 CSA(CA)O; Army Act 1955; Air Force Act 1955; Naval Forces (Enforcement of Maintenance Liabilities) Act 1947; Merchant Shipping Act 1970
163 s31(6) CSA 1991
164 s31(7) CSA 1991
165 s14 CSA 1991; reg 4(2)(b) CSI Regs
166 Reg 9 CS(C&E) Regs
167 https:// childmaintenanceservice.direct.gov.uk/ site/public/organisation
168 Reg 14(1) CS(C&E) Regs
169 Reg 14(2) CS(C&E) Regs
170 s32(8) and (11) CSA 1991; reg 25(aa) CS(C&E) Regs
171 Reg 1(3)(a) CS(C&E) Regs
172 Reg 1(3)(b) CS(C&E) Regs
173 Reg 15 CS(C&E) Regs
174 Reg 15(1) CS(C&E) Regs
175 s32(8) and (11) CSA 1991; reg 25(ab) and (b) CS(C&E) Regs
176 Reg 16(1) CS(C&E) Regs
177 Reg 16(2) CS(C&E) Regs
178 Reg 16(3) CS(C&E) Regs
179 s32(8) and (11) CSA 1991; reg 25(ab) and (b) CS(C&E) Regs

180 Reg 13 CS(C&E) Regs
181 s8(2)(b) ERA 1996
182 s9 ERA 1996
183 s12(3)-(5) ERA 1996
184 https:// childmaintenanceservice.direct.gov.uk/ site/public/organisation
185 Reg 8(3) and (4) CS(C&E) Regs
186 Reg 8(4)(a) CS(C&E) Regs
187 Reg 8(4)(b) CS(C&E) Regs
188 Reg 8(5) CS(C&E) Regs
189 Reg 9 CS(C&E) Regs
190 Regs 10(1) and 11(1) CS(C&E) Regs
191 Regs 10(1) and (2) and 11 CS(C&E) Regs, as substituted for '2012 rules' cases and other 'arrears only' cases by reg 4(4) CS(MOC&NCR) Regs
192 Reg 10(3) CS(C&E) Regs, as substituted for '2012 rules' cases by reg 4(4) CS(MOC&NCR) Regs
193 Regs 1(4), 11 and 12 CS(MOC&NCR) Regs
194 Reg 9(d) CS(C&E) Regs
195 Reg 11(2) CS(C&E) Regs
196 Reg 12(6) CS(C&E) Regs
197 Reg 12(2) CS(C&E) Regs
198 Reg 12(4) CS(C&E) Regs
199 Reg 12(3A) CS(C&E) Regs
200 Reg 14(1) CS(C&E) Regs
201 Reg 8 CS(AIAMA) Regs
202 Reg 24(2)(a) CS(C&E) Regs
203 Reg 24(2)(b) CS(C&E) Regs
204 Reg 24(2)(a) and (3) CS(C&E) Regs
205 Reg 17 CS(C&E) Regs
206 Reg 18 CS(C&E) Regs
207 Reg 19 CS(C&E) Regs
208 Regs 10(3) and 20(1)(g) CS(C&E) Regs, as substituted for '2012 rules' cases and other 'arrears only' cases by regs 4(4) and (6) and 11 CS(MOC&NCR) Regs
209 Reg 20(1) CS(C&E) Regs
210 Reg 20(1A) CS(C&E) Regs
211 Reg 20(2) CS(C&E) Regs
212 Reg 21(1) CS(C&E) Regs
213 Reg 21(4) CS(C&E) Regs
214 Reg 21(5) CS(C&E) Regs
215 Reg 21(6) CS(C&E) Regs
216 Reg 22(1) CS(C&E) Regs
217 Reg 22(2) CS(C&E) Regs
218 Reg 22(3) CS(C&E) Regs
219 Reg 22(3A) CS(C&E) Regs
220 Reg 3(4) CS(C&E) Regs
221 Reg 3(6)(c) CS(C&E) Regs
222 Reg 3(5) CS(C&E) Regs
223 Reg 3(6) CS(C&E) Regs
224 Reg 8(1) CS(C&E) Regs
225 r5 and Form 6 AS(CSR)
226 Reg 22(4) CS(C&E) Regs

227 s32(6) CSA 1991
228 *Secretary of State for Social Security v Shotton* [1996] 2 FLR 241
229 ss48 and 49 CSA 1991; r6 AS(CSR)
230 ss32A and 32F CSA 1991
231 Reg 25A CS(C&E) Regs
232 CMEC Research Report No.2, *Deduction Order Review*, March 2011, pp2 and 4
233 CMEC Research Report No.2, *Deduction Order Review*, March 2011, p16
234 Reg 25X CS(C&E) Regs
235 CMEC Research Report No.2, *Deduction Order Review*, March 2011, p15
236 Reg 25Z CS(C&E) Regs
237 s32A CSA 1991
238 Reg 25B(1) CS(C&E) Regs
239 Reg 25C CS(C&E) Regs, as amended by reg 4(7) CS(MOC&NCR) Regs for '2012 rules' cases
240 s32B CSA 1991
241 Reg 25D CS(C&E) Regs
242 Reg 25H CS(C&E) Regs
243 s32D CSA 1991
244 Reg 25G CS(C&E) Regs, as amended by reg 4(7) CS(MOC&NCR) Regs for '2012 rules' cases
245 Reg 25G(2)(d) CS(C&E) Regs, as amended by reg 4(5) CS(MA) Regs for '2012 rules' cases
246 Reg 25I CS(C&E) Regs
247 Reg 25A(3)(b) CS(C&E) Regs
248 Reg 25N(1) CS(C&E) Regs
249 s32F(3)(b) and (4) CSA 1991
250 Regs 25R and 25N CS(C&E) Regs
251 Reg 25P(1) and (2) CS(C&E) Regs
252 Reg 25P(6) CS(C&E) Regs
253 Reg 25Q CS(C&E) Regs
254 Reg 25Z(b) CS(C&E) Regs
255 Reg 25AB CS(C&E) Regs
256 s43A CSA 1991; reg 11 CS(MPA) Regs
257 *CMOPA 2008: Summary of Responses to the Consultation on the Draft Regulations*, CMEC, November 2009, para 4.9
258 Reg 12 CS(MPA) Regs
259 Reg 13 CS(MPA) Regs
260 Reg 13(3) CS(MPA) Regs
261 *CMOPA 2008: Summary of Responses to the Consultation on the Draft Regulations*, CMEC, November 2009, para 4.11
262 *CMOPA 2008: Summary of Responses to the Consultation on the Draft Regulations*, CMEC, November 2009, para 4.6
263 *CMOPA 2008: Summary of Responses to the Consultation on the Draft Regulations*, CMEC, November 2009, para 4.8
264 *CMOPA 2008: Summary of Responses to the Consultation on the Draft Regulations*, CMEC, November 2009, para 4.8
265 *Preparing for the Future, Tackling the Past: child maintenance – arrears and compliance strategy 2012–2017*, DWP, January 2013
266 *CMOPA 2008: Summary of Responses to the Consultation on the Draft Regulations*, CMEC, November 2009, para 4.7
267 s33 CSA 1991
268 Reg 27 CS(C&E) Regs
269 s33(3) CSA 1991
270 s33(4) CSA 1991
271 *Bird v SSWP* [2008] EWHC 3159 (Admin)
272 Reg 29 CS(C&E) Regs; r3 AS(CSR)
273 Reg 28(2) and (2A) CS(C&E) Regs; *Preparing for the Future, Tackling the Past: child maintenance – arrears and compliance strategy 2012–2017*, DWP, January 2013
274 *R Sutherland (on the application of) v SSWP* [2004] EWHC 800 (Admin)
275 s9 Limitation Act 1980
276 *CMEC v Mitchell* [2010] EWCA Civ 333
277 *Farley v CSA and Another* [2006] UKHL 31
278 Reg 29(1) and Sch 1 CS(C&E) Regs
279 *Secretary of State for Social Security v Love* [1996] SLT 78
280 r2 AS(CSR)
281 *Secretary of State for Social Security v Nicol* [1996] SLT 34
282 Forms 1-4 AS(CSR)
283 ss38(1)(a) and 58(9) CSA 1991
284 *Preparing for the Future, Tackling the Past: child maintenance – arrears and compliance strategy 2012–2017*, DWP, January 2013
285 s35 CSA 1991; Part 3 TCEA 2007
286 Regs 6–8 Taking Control of Goods Regulations 2013, No.1894
287 Sch 12 para 58 TCEA 2007
288 Reg 4 Taking Control of Goods Regulations 2013, No.1894
289 Taking Control of Goods (Fees) Regulations 2014, No.1
290 Sch 12 para 66 TCEA 2007
291 s33(5) CSA 1991
292 s36 CSA 1991
293 s32L CSA 1991
294 s32L(8) CSA 1991
295 s32L(2) CSA 1991
296 s32L(1) CSA 1991
297 s32L(5) CSA 1991
298 s32L(5) CSA 1991
299 s32L (7) CSA 1991
300 s32L(11)(b) CSA 1991
301 s39A CSA 1991

302 *Preparing for the Future, Tackling the Past: child maintenance – arrears and compliance strategy 2012–2017*, DWP, January 2013
303 DWP/National Statistics, *CSA Quarterly Summary Statistics*, December 2013
304 ss39A(2) and 40(1)-(11) CSA 1991
305 s39A(1) CSA 1991; *Karoonian v CMEC and Gibbons v CMEC* [2012] EWCA Civ 1379
306 s39A(3) CSA 1991
307 Reg 35(1) CS(C&E) Regs
308 s40(11) CSA 1991
309 s39A(3) CSA 1991
310 ss40(3) and 40A(1) CSA 1991
311 *Karoonian v CMEC and Gibbons v CMEC* [2012] EWCA Civ 1379
312 ss40(11) and 40A(8) CSA 1991; reg 35(2) CS(C&E) Regs
313 ss40 and 40B CSA 1991
314 ss40(5) and 40A(3) CSA 1991
315 ss40(3) and 40B(1) CSA 1991
316 Sch 3 CS(C&E) Regs
317 ss40(7) and 40A(5) CSA 1991
318 Reg 34(5) and (6) CS(C&E) Regs
319 **2012 rules** *What Happens if a Paying Parent Doesn't Pay Child Maintenance*, CMB006GB, November 2013
1993 & 2003 rules *What Action Can the CSA Take if Parents Don't Pay?* CSL306, October 2012
320 **2012 rules** *What Happens if a Paying Parent Doesn't Pay Child Maintenance*, CMB006GB, November 2013
1993 & 2003 rules *What Action Can the CSA Take if Parents Don't Pay?* CSL306, October 2012
321 s40B CSA 1991
322 Reg 35(4)-(5) and Sch 4 CS(C&E) Regs
323 s40B(1) CSA 1991
324 s40B(5) CSA 1991
325 s40B(7) CSA 1991
326 *CMEC v Beesley* [2010] EWCA Civ 1344; s382(5) Insolvency Act 1986, as to be amended by s142 WRA 2012
327 *Preparing for the Future, Tackling the Past: child maintenance – arrears and compliance strategy 2012–2017*, DWP, January 2013
328 *Independent Case Examiner's Annual Report 2011/12*

6. Fees for enforcement action
329 Reg 10 CSF Regs 2014
330 Reg 12 CSF Regs 2014
331 Reg 11 CSF Regs 2014
332 Reg 7(1B) and (4) CS(C&E) Regs
333 Reg 13 CSF Regs 2014

334 s43 CMOPA 2008

7. Delays in collection and enforcement
335 *Kehoe v UK* [2009] 48 EHRR, [2008] 2 FLR 1014
336 *How Do I Complain About the Service I Get From the Child Support Agency?* CSL308, October 2013
337 *Independent Case Examiner's Annual Report 2008/09*
338 *Kehoe v UK* [2009] 48 EHRR, [2008] 2 FLR 1014

8. '1993 rules' and conversion cases
339 Reg 2(2) CS(MPA) Regs
340 Reg 10 CS(C&E) Regs
341 Reg 11(2) CS(C&E) Regs
342 Reg 11(3) CS(C&E) Regs
343 Reg 11(4) CS(C&E) Regs
344 Reg 11(6) CS(C&E) Regs
345 Reg 12(5) CS(C&E) Regs
346 Reg 24(1) CS(C&E) Regs

Chapter 15

Complaints

This chapter covers:

1. Introduction

A complaint can be made about any aspect of the administration of the statutory child support schemes.

A complaint is a separate process to an appeal or revision and does not necessarily lead to a decision being changed. However, a complaint may be appropriate if the decision is one with no right of appeal. In some of these cases, judicial review may also be possible (instead of, or as well as, making a complaint). Legal advice should be sought if a judicial review is being considered (see also p215). In some cases, an appeal may be appropriate as well as a complaint – eg, if a person thinks that child support has been wrongly calculated and appeals against the decision but also wishes to complain about a delay in making the calculation. **Note:** a revision (a 'mandatory reconsideration') must be sought before an appeal can be made to the First-tier Tribunal.

It is important to be clear which organisation has caused the problem. In most cases, this will be the Child Maintenance Service/Child Support Agency. However, problems concerning the deduction of payments from benefits may be caused by Jobcentre Plus. Complaints about any Jobcentre Plus function should be made to Jobcentre Plus. If there are delays or poor administration of an appeal by HM Courts and Tribunals Service (HMCTS), the complaint should be made to HMCTS. For information about making complaints to HMCTS, see CPAG's *Welfare Benefits and Tax Credits Handbook*.

2. **Complaining to the Child Maintenance Service or Child Support Agency**

Most complaints involving child support are made to the Child Maintenance Service (CMS) or Child Support Agency (CSA). Complaints are likely to be about:

- standards of service, including delays, staff communications, poor administration and lost papers; *or*
- how discretionary decisions are made – eg, failure to follow guidance, following it too strictly or failing to take all the relevant circumstances into account. It may be appropriate to seek advice on whether judicial review is also possible.

A complaint should be started by contacting the person who has been dealing with the case, or her/his manager. This information should be in letters sent by the CMS/CSA. The complaint can be made either by telephone, in writing, or by using the online contact form on the www.gov.uk/child-maintenance website. Records of all communications should be kept in case the complaint is taken further. A complaint made by email should be headed 'Complaint'.

If the CMS/CSA officer or manager cannot resolve the complaint, it can be taken further by contacting the complaints resolution team at the office handling the case. Contact details should be given in any letters sent.

If someone is still not satisfied with the outcome or if there has been an unreasonable delay, s/he can ask for a review. The complaints review team can check whether the complaint was dealt with properly and if anything else can be done. Contact details for the complaints review team should be given in the letter received from the complaints resolution team.

At each of these stages of the complaints procedure, the CMS/CSA should acknowledge the complaint within two days and should normally resolve it within 15 working days. If it is expected to take longer, the CMS/CSA should keep the person who complained informed and agree a timescale with her/him.

More information about the complaints procedure is given in CMS/CSA leaflets[1] or on the www.gov.uk/child-maintenance website.

If someone is not satisfied that the complaint has been resolved, s/he can contact the Independent Case Examiner (see p327).

The final option in the complaints procedure is the Parliamentary and Health Service Ombudsman (see p329).

Standards of service

When considering whether, or at what point, to make a complaint, it may be useful to be aware of the standards of service that the CMS/CSA says it will meet.

The CMS/CSA no longer publishes detailed information about its service standards, although some information is published in various documents.

Standards that should be expected include the following. The CMS/CSA aims to:
- start gathering information from the non-resident parent within four weeks of a child support application, if it has contact details;
- make an accurate decision on an application within 12 weeks (but in some cases, a decision may take up to 26 weeks);
- make payments to the person with care within a week of receiving the money from the non-resident parent, if the collection service is being used;
- take action to use a deduction from earnings order, where appropriate, within four months of a non-resident parent's first being informed of her/his liability;
- answer telephone calls within one minute;
- respond to letters, and either resolve complaints or agree on the next course of action, within three weeks of receiving them.

Compensation

If anyone has lost out because of CMS/CSA error, delay or standard of service, it may be appropriate to request compensation or a consolatory payment (see below) when making a complaint. *Ex gratia* payments can be made if someone has experienced a financial loss or significant delay or has been caused severe distress or inconvenience.

The *Special Payments Guide* explains the rules on whether financial compensation should be paid and, if so, how much is appropriate. It is available on the gov.uk website[2] or on request from the CMS/CSA.

There is no legal right to these payments, but it can sometimes be useful to make it clear that financial compensation would help to resolve the complaint. No duty of care can be imposed on the CSA in order to recover damages in negligence. The complaints system (together with the ability to seek judicial review if the CSA acts unreasonably) has been held to be sufficient redress for parties unhappy with the way the CSA has dealt with their case. The CSA cannot be pursued for any breach of duty of care in order to recover damages in negligence.[3] These principles also apply to the CMS.

Compensation payments may be appropriate if there has been:
- significant delay – eg, in making calculations or reviewing liability. It is useful to refer to the service standards when assessing how severe the delay has been;
- delays or errors in enforcement;
- delays in passing child support payments to the person with care;
- wrong identification of non-resident parents;
- financial loss because of CMS/CSA error – eg, in bank or telephone charges;
- other examples of gross inconvenience, embarrassment, breach of confidentiality or severe distress.

If someone is not offered compensation and believes that it should have been offered, or is not offered as much as s/he thinks is appropriate, s/he can consider taking the complaint further – ie, to the Independent Case Examiner or the Ombudsman.

Consolatory payments

Consolatory payments are smaller payments that can be made if action by the CMS/CSA has caused serious inconvenience because the same mistakes were made more than once, or they caused severe embarrassment or humiliation.[4] Evidence of the person's (or a family member's) health being affected as a result may also be considered if it can be shown to be a direct result of errors made by the CMS/CSA.[5] Consolatory payments are made in recognition of the effect of an error on someone's life and, therefore, it is possible to claim them even if there is no financial loss.

Many users of the CMS/CSA experience inconvenience and frustration, and this alone is not enough to secure a consolatory payment.

The CMS/CSA makes separate decisions on whether to award compensation or a consolatory payment, based on the facts of each case. In some cases, it may pay both.[6] The *Special Payments Guide* covers both compensation and consolatory payments.

3. Complaining to the Child Maintenance Options service

The complaints process for the Child Maintenance Options service is similar to that for the Child Maintenance Service and the Child Support Agency (see p324). A complaint should be started by talking to the person dealing with the enquiry, or to her/his manager. If the matter cannot be resolved, a complaint can be made by phone, in writing or by email via www.cmoptions.org. If made by email or letter, it should be clearly headed 'complaint'. Child maintenance Options confirms that complaints made by email or letter have been received.[7]

If someone is not satisfied after following this procedure, s/he can ask for a review. The complaints review team should look at the complaint again to see whether there is more that can be done. The review team aims to resolve complaints within 15 days.[8]

Further details of the complaints process can be found in *How to Complain About Child Maintenance Options*, available from the above website or by telephoning 0800 988 0988 (in Northern Ireland, 0800 028 7439).

If someone has gone through every stage of the complaints procedure and is still not satisfied, s/he can complain to the Independent Case Examiner (see p327), or, via her/his MP, to the Parliamentary and Health Service Ombudsman (see p329).

4. **Complaining to Jobcentre Plus**

As part of the Department for Work and Pensions (DWP), Jobcentre Plus has a similar complaints procedure to the Child Maintenance Service (CMS)/Child Support Agency (CSA). A non-resident parent may want to complain about the way in which child support payments have (or have not) been deducted from her/his benefit. However, a non-resident parent receiving benefits who disagrees with the rate of child support s/he should be paying (and therefore with the deduction being made from benefit) should challenge the decision of the CMS/CSA, not complain to Jobcentre Plus. A complaint to Jobcentre Plus can be made if it is about the administration of the deductions. Jobcentre Plus can make compensatory payments if appropriate.

Note: the CMS/CSA may not automatically know if a non-resident parent or a parent with care is in receipt of benefits. Although the Secretary of State for Work and Pensions is ultimately responsible for administering both Jobcentre Plus and the CMS/CSA, knowledge gained by her/him in one role should not be attributed to her/his other area of responsibility.[9]

See CPAG's *Welfare Benefits and Tax Credits Handbook* for more information about how to complain about Jobcentre Plus.

If someone has gone through every stage of the Jobcentre Plus complaints procedure and is still not satisfied, s/he can complain to the Independent Case Examiner (see below) or, via her/his MP, to the Parliamentary and Health Service Ombudsman (see p329).

Note: remember that some decisions about benefits carry the right of appeal and an individual can challenge them. It may be necessary to do this as well as, or instead of, complaining.

5. **Complaining to the Independent Case Examiner**

The Independent Case Examiner's (ICE) office helps resolve the situation where people believe that certain government agencies have not dealt with them fairly or resolved complaints to their satisfaction. ICE is an independent referee, completely separate from the Child Maintenance Service (CMS), Child Support Agency (CSA), Child Maintenance Options service or any other government department.

A complaint can only go to ICE after the CMS/CSA's (or other agency's) complaints procedure has been used and a final response received – ie, a decision on a review of the complaint, which advises that the complaint can be made to ICE. The complaint to ICE should be made within six months of the final response. ICE cannot look at complaints made after this date.

ICE cannot consider a complaint which is being investigated, or which has been investigated, by the Parliamentary and Health Service Ombudsman (see p329). There may be a choice of complaining directly to the Ombudsman via an MP, but the Ombudsman's office usually encourages people to use ICE first.

Complaints can be made in writing or by telephone on 0345 606 0777. Contact details can be found on the ICE website.[10] A complaint form can be obtained from the helpline number above. All the relevant facts, including the CMS/CSA office being complained about, should be included, together with details of the complaint and the response. ICE can give further advice on making a complaint, or appoint a representative to act on someone's behalf, if required.

ICE investigates and decide whether or not it can accept the complaint. If it can, it attempts to settle the complaint by suggesting ways in which the CMS/CSA and the person affected can come to an agreement. If this fails, ICE prepares a formal report setting out how the complaint arose and how it believes it should be settled. In 2013/14, ICE upheld some aspects of nearly two-thirds of the child support complaints on which it reached findings and conclusions.[11] If it makes a recommendation of action to the CMS/CSA, this is almost always followed. Details of ICE's standards of service are available on its website.[12]

6. **Using an MP**

It may be appropriate to consult an MP at any stage of the complaints process. An MP may be able to provide advocacy or other support to get the matter resolved more quickly. However, consulting an MP is particularly important if someone has been through the complaints process of the Child Maintenance Service/Child Support Agency (or Child Maintenance Options or Jobcentre Plus) without a satisfactory resolution, and even more so if s/he has used the Independent Case Examiner but still wants to take matters further.

An MP may be able to advise on whether taking the complaint further is worthwhile. It may be that someone is unhappy about an aspect of child support law, in which case a complaint is not appropriate. Whether the issue concerns law or procedure, an MP may be willing to take matters further to try to get legislation changed or practice improved. An MP may also refer the complaint to the Parliamentary and Health Service Ombudsman (see p329).

Anyone can find out who her/his MP is by using a constituency locator on the House of Commons Information Office website, or by ringing it on 020 7219 4272 or emailing info@parliament.uk. Most MPs have local surgeries where they meet constituents. Alternatively, a complaint can be passed to the MP in writing. Contact details, including email addresses, for MPs are available on the UK Parliament website.[13]

---

7. Complaining to the Ombudsman

The Parliamentary and Health Service Ombudsman investigates complaints about a range of government departments and other public bodies.

Before using the Ombudsman, the organisation should have a full chance to respond to the complaint and put things right. For complaints about the Child Maintenance Service/Child Support Agency, Child Maintenance Options and Jobcentre Plus, the Independent Case Examiner (ICE) (see p327) can be used. This does not need a referral from an MP, and the Ombudsman's office encourages people to use ICE first.

The first stage of using the Ombudsman is to send the complaint to the relevant MP, who decides whether or not to pass it on to the Ombudsman. Normally, the Ombudsman does not investigate if the complaint is passed to an MP more than 12 months after the complainant became aware that s/he had a good reason to complain – ie, that there was a need to take the complaint further.

If the complaint is investigated, the MP is sent a full report. The Ombudsman may recommend an apology and possibly compensation. Ombudsman reports can also lead to changed practices and procedures in the agencies under investigation.

More information about the Ombudsman is available at www.ombudsman.org.uk, or from the helpline on 0345 015 4033.

Notes

2. **Complaining to the Child Maintenance Service or Child Support Agency**
   1 **2012 rules** *What to Do if You're Unhappy With the Child Maintenance Service,* CMSB011GB, October 2013
      1993 & 2003 rules *How Do I Complain About the Service I Get From the Child Support Agency?* CSL308, October 2013
   2 www.gov.uk/government/publications/special-payments-guide
   3 *Rowley and Others v SSWP* [2007] EWCA Civ 598, 19 June 2007
   4 *How Do I Complain About the Service I Get From the Child Support Agency?* CSL308, October 2013

   5 *How Do I Complain About the Service I Get From the Child Support Agency?* CSL308, October 2013
   6 *How Do I Complain About the Service I Get From the Child Support Agency?* CSL308, October 2013

3. **Complaining to the Child Maintenance Options service**
   7 *How to Complain About Child Maintenance Options,* November 2013
   8 *How to Complain About Child Maintenance Options ,* November 2013

4. **Complaining to Jobcentre Plus**
   9 *R (Rew) v SSWP* [2008] EWHC 2120
      (Admin)

5. **Complaining to the Independent Case
   Examiner**
   10 www.gov.uk/government/
       organisations/independent-case-
       examiner
   11 *Independent Case Examiner for the
       Department for Work and Pensions:
       Annual Report: 1st April 2013 – 31st
       March 2014*, DWP, August 2014
   12 www.gov.uk/government/
       organisations/independent-case-
       examiner

6. **Using an MP**
   13 www.parliament.uk/mps-lords-and-
       offices/mps

Appendices

Appendix 1

Useful addresses

Department for Work and Pensions
www.gov.uk/government/
organisations/department-for-work-
pensions

Child Maintenance Options
(England, Wales and Scotland)
PO Box 578
Rotherham S63 3FP
Tel: 0800 988 0988
www.cmoptions.org

Child Maintenance Choices
(Northern Ireland)
Tel: 0800 028 7439
Textphone: 08001/0800 028 7439
www.nidirect.gov.uk/choices-2

Child Support Agency
Tel: 0345 713 3133
Textphone: 0345 713 8924
www.gov.uk/child-maintenance/
contact

Child Maintenance Service
www.gov.uk/child-maintenance/
contact

Child Support Agency/Child Maintenance Service local rate telephone lines
Further contact details, including
full postal details for Child Support
Agency offices dealing with '2003
rules' and '1993 rules' cases for the
different regions, are available
at: www.gov.uk/child-maintenance/
contact.

National enquiry line   0345 713 3133

(for general enquiries and enquiries
about '1993 rules' cases from every
region)

Welsh language enquiry line
0345 713 8091

Enquiries for '2003 rules' cases:
Hastings
(South East England)   0345 609 0052
Plymouth
(South West England) 0345 609 0072
Dudley
(The Midlands)   0345 609 0062
Birkenhead
(North West England) 0345 609 0082
Belfast
(Great Britain –
Eastern England)   0345 609 0092
Falkirk
(Scotland and North
East England)   0345 609 0042

Enquiries for '2012 rules' cases and new applications:
National enquiry line   0345 266 8792

New applicants must telephone Child Maintenance Options first. People with existing '2012 rules' cases will have been given contact details on any letters received.

Northern Ireland
'2012 rules' cases and new applications:
Child Maintenance Service
PO Box 252
Mitcheldean GL17 1AP

'2003 rules' and '1993 rules' cases:
Freepost RTGR-ACYG-XXLE
Mail Handling Site A
Wolverhampton WV98 1SX
General enquiries: 0845 608 0022 or
0345 6028 0022
Textphone: 0845 713 9704
'2012 rules': 0845 266 8978 or
0345 266 8978
'2003 rules': 0845 608 0022 or
0345 308 0022
'1993 rules': 0845 713 9896 or
0345 713 9896
www.dsdni.gov.uk/index/cmed.htm

HM Courts and Tribunals Service
Appeals should be sent to:
England and Wales:
HMCTS SSCS Appeal Centre
PO Box 1203
Bradford BD1 9WP

Scotland:
HMCTS SSCS Appeal Centre
PO Box 27080
Glasgow G2 9HQ

The offices below are the regional offices for social security and child support appeals. They will advise about your nearest tribunal venue.

Epsom
Epsom Point
84–90 East Street
Epsom KT17 1HF
Tel: 0300 123 1142
Textphone: 0300 123 1264
SSCSA-Epsom@hmcts.gsi.gov.uk

Leeds
York House
31 York Place
Leeds LS1 2ED
Tel: 0300 123 1142
Textphone: 0300 123 1264
SSCSA-Leeds@hmcts.gsi.gov.uk

Liverpool
36 Dale Street
Liverpool L2 5UZ
Tel: 0300 123 1142
Textphone: 0300 123 1264
SSCSA-Liverpool@hmcts.gsi.gov.uk

Newcastle
Manorview House
Kings Manor
Newcastle upon Tyne NE1 6PA
Tel: 0300 123 1142
Textphone: 0300 123 1264
SSCSA-Newcastle@hmcts.gsi.gov.uk

Sutton

Copthall House
9 The Pavement
Grove Road
Sutton SM1 1DA
Tel: 0300 123 1142
Textphone: 0300 123 1264
SSCSA-Sutton@hmcts.gsi.gov.uk

Birmingham

Administrative Support Centre
PO Box 14620
Birmingham B16 6FR
Tel: 0300 123 1142
ASCBirmingham@hmcts.gsi.gov.uk

Cardiff

Eastgate House
Newport Road
Cardiff CF24 0YP
Tel: 0300 123 1142
Textphone: 0300 123 1264
cardiff-sscsa@hmcts.gsi.gov.uk

Glasgow

Wellington House
134–136 Wellington Street
Glasgow G2 2XL
Tel: 0141 354 8400
Textphone: 0141 354 8413
SSCSA-Glasgow@hmcts.gsi.gov.uk

Offices of Adminstrative Appeals Chamber of the Upper Tribunal

www.gov.uk/administrative-appeals-tribunal/overview

England and Wales

5th Floor Rolls Building
7 Rolls Buildings
Fetter Lane
London EC4A 1NL

Tel: 020 7071 5662
TypeTalk: 18001 020 7071 5662
adminappeals@hmcts.gsi.gov.uk

Scotland

George House
126 George Street
Edinburgh EH2 4HH
Tel: 0131 271 4310
adminappeals@hmcts.gsi.gov.uk

Northern Ireland

Tribunal Hearing Centre
2nd Floor
Royal Courts of Justice
Chichester Street
Belfast BT1 3JT
Tel: 028 9072 4848
adminappeals@hmcts.gsi.gov.uk
www.courtsni.gov.uk/en-GB/
tribunals/ossc

Independent Case Examiner

PO Box 209
Bootle L20 7WA
Tel: 0345 606 0777
Textphone: 18001 0345 606 0777
www.gov.uk/government/
organisations/independent-case-
examiner
ice@dwp.gsi.gov.uk

The Parliamentary and Health Service Ombudsman

Millbank Tower
Millbank
London SW1P 4QP
Tel: 0345 015 4033
Textphone: 0300 061 4298
www.ombudsman.org.uk
phso.enquiries@ombudsman.org.uk

Appendix 2

Statutes

A man is assumed to be the father of a child for child support purposes if he is found to be the father by a court in England or Wales in proceedings under one of the following statutes.

s42 National Assistance Act 1948
Affiliation Proceedings Act 1957
s6 Family Law Reform Act 1969
Guardianship of Minors Act 1971
Children Act 1975
Child Care Act 1980
Children Act 1989
s26 Social Security Act 1986
s4 Family Law Reform Act 1987
s105 Social Security Administration Act 1992

A maintenance order only prevents an application to the Child Maintenance Service under section 4 or 7 of the Child Support Act 1991 if it was made in proceedings under one of the following statutes.

Conjugal Rights (Scotland) Amendment Act 1861
Court of Session Act 1868
Sheriff Courts (Scotland) Act 1907
Guardianship of Infants Act 1925
Illegitimate Children (Scotland) Act 1930
Children and Young Persons (Scotland) Act 1932
Children and Young Persons (Scotland) Act 1937
Custody of Children (Scotland) Act 1939
National Assistance Act 1948
Affiliation Orders Act 1952
Affiliation Proceedings Act 1957
Matrimonial Proceedings (Children) Act 1958
Guardianship of Minors Act 1971

Part II Matrimonial Causes Act 1973

Guardianship Act 1973

Children Act 1975

Supplementary Benefits Act 1976

Domestic Proceedings and Magistrates' Courts Act 1978

Part III Matrimonial and Family Proceedings Act 1984

Family Law (Scotland) Act 1985

Social Security Act 1986

Schedule 1 Children Act 1989

Social Security Administration Act 1992

Schedule 5, 6 or 7 Civil Partnership Act 2004

The court order usually states the legal provisions under which it was made.

Appendix 3

Information and advice

It may be easier to get a positive response from the Child Support Agency or Child Maintenance Service if you have taken advice about your rights or have an adviser assisting you. The following agencies may be able to help.

- Citizens Advice Bureaux (CAB) and other local advice centres provide information, and may be able to represent you. You can find your nearest CAB from www.citizensadvice.org.uk.
- Law centres can help with advice and representation, but may not cover child support problems and may limit their help to people who live and work in certain areas. You can check whether you are near a law centre from www.lawcentres.org.uk.
- Solicitors can give free legal advice to people on low incomes under the 'legal help' scheme (advice and assistance scheme in Scotland). This does not cover the cost of representation at an appeal hearing, but can cover the cost of preparing written submissions and obtaining evidence such as medical reports. However, solicitors do not always have a good working knowledge of the child support rules and you may need to shop around until you find one who does.
- http://find-legal-advice.justice.gov.uk can be used to find high quality legal advisers in England and Wales, including advice agencies and solicitors.
- Local authority welfare rights workers provide an advice and representation service for benefit claimants in many areas.
- Lone-parent organisations may offer help and advice about child support, or it may help to talk to other parents about their experiences. For details of your local group and for helpline advice, contact: Single Parent Action Network (0117 951 4231; www.spanuk.org.uk); Gingerbread (single-parent helpline 0808 802 0925; www.gingerbread.org.uk); One Parent Families Scotland (helpline 0808 801 0323; www.opfs.org.uk).
- There are some groups supporting parents who may be able to provide advice. These include the National Association for Child Support Action, Loverock House, Brettell Lane, Brierley Hill, West Midlands DY5 3JS (www.nacsa.co.uk). For general enquiry support, you can write, telephone (01384 572525) or email (admin@nacsa.co.uk). A telephone advice line for advice on individual cases is available to subscribers.
- Many trade unions provide advice to members on child support.

- Local organisations for particular groups may offer help – eg, unemployed centres, claimants' unions and centres for people with disabilities.

Representation at the First-tier Tribunal

Some parents may find it difficult to obtain representation at appeal hearings. Although many parents, especially with the help of Chapter 13, will be able to present their own case, it can be invaluable to obtain objective independent advice which draws on the legislation. An advice centre which has a copy of the legislation (see Appendix 4) and experience of representing at tribunals in other sorts of cases (eg, social security) may be able to provide a representative for a child support appeal.

Child Poverty Action Group

Unfortunately, CPAG is unable to deal with enquiries, either from advisers or members of the public, on child support issues.

Appendix 4

Useful publications

Stationery Office books are available from Stationery Office bookshops or can be ordered from The Stationery Office, Post Cash Department, PO Box 29, Norwich NR3 1GN (tel: 0333 200 2425; email: esupport@tso.co.uk; web: www.tsoshop.co.uk). Many publications listed are available from CPAG. See below for order details, or order from www.cpag.org.uk/bookshop/.

1. Caselaw and legislation

Child Support: the legislation
E Jacobs (CPAG) Legislation with detailed commentary. 12th edition main volume (September 2015): £99

The Law Relating to Social Security
All the legislation but without any comment. Available at http://lawvolumes.dwp.gov.uk.

The Law Relating to Child Support
Consolidated legislation without any commentary. Shows the law as it applies both before and after the rule changes come into force for a particular case. Also known as the 'Orange Volumes'. Available at http://lawvolumes.dwp.gov.uk.

Social Security Legislation, Volume I:
Non-Means-Tested Benefits and
Employment and Support Allowance
D Bonner, I Hooker and R White (Sweet & Maxwell) Legislation with commentary. 2015/16 edition (September 2015): £107 for the main volume.

Social Security Legislation, Volume II:
Income Support, Jobseeker's Allowance,
State Pension Credit and the Social
Fund
P Wood, R Poynter, N Wikeley and D Bonner (Sweet & Maxwell) Legislation with commentary. 2015/16 edition (September 2015): £107 for the main volume.

Social Security Legislation, Volume III:
Administration, Adjudication and the
European Dimension
M Rowland and R White (Sweet & Maxwell) Legislation with commentary. 2015/16 edition (September 2015): £107 for the main volume.

Social Security Legislation, Volume IV:
Tax Credits and HMRC-administered
Social Security Benefits
N Wikeley and D Williams (Sweet & Maxwell) Legislation with commentary. 2015/16 edition (September 2015): £107 for the main volume.

Social Security Legislation, Volume V: Universal Credit
P Wood, R Poynter and N Wikeley (Sweet & Maxwell) Legislation with commentary. 2014/15 edition (September 2014): £104 for the main volume.

Social Security Legislation – updating supplement
(Sweet & Maxwell) The spring 2015 update to the 2014/15 main volumes: £66.

CPAG's Housing Benefit and Council Tax Reduction Legislation
L Findlay, R Poynter, S Wright, C George, M Williams (CPAG) Legislation with detailed commentary. 2015/16 (28th) edition (December 2015): £119 including updating Supplement.

2. Periodicals
Welfare Rights Bulletin
(CPAG, bimonthly). Covers developments in social security law, including decisions of the courts and the Upper Tribunal, and updates CPAG's *Welfare Benefits and Tax Credits Handbook*. The annual subscription is £37 but it is sent automatically to CPAG Rights members (contact CPAG or see www.cpag.org.uk/membership for details).

Articles on social security can also be found in *Legal Action* (Legal Action Group, monthly magazine), *Adviser* (Citizens Advice, bi-monthly magazine) and the *Journal of Social Security Law* (Sweet & Maxwell, three issues a year).

3. Department for Work and Pensions publications
Many leaflets and factsheets explaining the statutory child support schemes are available through the gov.uk website (www.gov.uk/child-maintenance). Other leaflets on child maintenance issues are available from Child Maintenance Options on 0800 988 0988 (www.cmoptions.org).

Leaflets and most other Child Support Agency publications can also be obtained from the national enquiry line: 0345 713 3133. Leaflets relating to the '2012 rules' scheme can be obtained from the Child Maintenance Service enquiry line: 0345 266 8792. Most leaflets are also available in Welsh language versions.

Bulk copies of leaflets (more than 50 copies) can be ordered by advice agencies from iON on 0845 850 0475. An order form is available on the Department for Work and Pensions website (www.gov.uk/government/publications/dwp-leaflets-order-form).

Leaflets cover a wide range of subjects, including:
- how to apply;
- how child support is worked out and paid;
- how shared care and split care affect child support;
- what happens if someone denies s/he is a parent of a child;
- how the statutory child support services use personal information;
- what happens if the non-resident parent does not pay child support;

- information for a non-resident parent's employer;
- disputing decisions, making a complaint and appealing;
- changes that must be reported.

Where rules differ for each of the three statutory child support schemes, there are specific versions of the leaflets for each scheme.

4. Other publications: general

Welfare Benefits and Tax Credits Handbook (CPAG)
£59/£12 for claimants (2015/16, April 2015).

CPAG's Welfare Benefits and Tax Credits Online
(CPAG) Includes the full text of the *Welfare Benefits and Tax Credits Handbook* updated throughout the year. £69 + VAT per user (bulk discounts available). More information at http://onlineservices.cpag.org.uk

Council Tax Handbook (CPAG)
£22 (11th edition, autumn 2015)

Debt Advice Handbook (CPAG)
£26 (11th edition, July 2015)

Fuel Rights Handbook (CPAG)
£25 (17th edition, 2014)

Benefits for Migrants Handbook (CPAG)
£35 (7th edition, autumn 2015)

Student Support and Benefits Handbook (CPAG)
£20 (12th edition, autumn 2015)

Benefits for Students in Scotland Handbook (CPAG)
£20 (13th edition, autumn 2015)

Children's Handbook Scotland: a benefits guide for children living away from their parents (CPAG)
£18 (8th edition, autumn 2015)

Universal Credit: what you need to know (CPAG)
£15 (3rd edition, autumn 2015)

Personal Independence Payment: what you need to know (CPAG)
£12 (1st edition, 2013)

Winning Your Benefit Appeal: what you need to know (CPAG)
£12 (1st edition, 2013)

Help with Housing Costs: Guide to Universal Credit and Council Tax Rebates 2015/16 (Shelter/CIH)
£39.99 (June 2015)

Help with Housing Costs: Guide to Housing Benefit 2015–2017 (Shelter/CIH)
£39.99 (June 2015)

Disability Rights Handbook (Disability Rights UK)
£33.50 (40th edition, May 2015)

Disabled Children: a legal handbook (Legal Action Group)
£45 (2nd edition, autumn 2015)

Tribunal Practice and Procedure (Legal Action Group)
£55 (3rd edition, autumn 2014)

*Children in Need: local authority
support for children and families* (Legal
Action Group)
£50 (2nd edition, November 2013)

*Big Book of Benefits and Mental
Health* (Big Book of Benefits)
£23 (15th edition, April 2015)

**For CPAG publications and most of
those in Sections 1 and 4 contact:**
CPAG, 30 Micawber Street, London
N1 7TB, tel: 020 7837 7979. Online
shop at
www.onlineservices.cpag.org.uk/
shop. Postage and packing: free for
orders up to £10 in value; for order
value £10.01–£100 add a flat rate
charge of £3.99; for order value
£100.01–£400 add £6.99; for order
value £400+ add £10.99.

Appendix 5:

Abbreviations used in the notes

AAC	Administrative Appeals Chamber	FLR	Family Law Reports
AACR	Administrative Appeals Chamber Reports	GWD	Greens Weekly Digest
		HL	House of Lords
AC	Appeal Cases	para(s)	paragraph(s)
All ER	All England Reports	r(r)	rule(s)
Art(s)	Article(s)	Reg(s)	Regulation(s)
CA	Court of Appeal	s(s)	section(s)
Ch	Chapter	SC	Supreme Court
CMLR	Common Market Law Reports	SCLR	Scottish Civil Law Reports
		Sch(s)	Schedule(s)
col	column	SLT	Scots Law Times
ECR	European Court Reports	UKHL	United Kingdom House of Lords
EHRR	European Human Rights Reports	UKSC	United Kingdom Supreme Court
EWCA	England and Wales Court of Appeal	UKUT	United Kingdom Upper Tribunal
EWHC	England and Wales High Court	Vol	Volume
FCR	Family Court Reports	WLR	Weekly Law Reports

Acts of Parliament

Unless information in this *Handbook* specifically relates to '1993 rules' cases, legislative references are for '2003 rules' and '2012 rules' cases only. Provisions for '1993 rules' cases are as the law stood before the Child Support, Pensions and Social Security Act 2000 came into force. Full legislative referencing for '1993 rules' cases can be found in the 2001/02 and 2002/03 editions of this *Handbook*.

AA 1976	Adoption Act 1976
A(S)A 1978	Adoption (Scotland) Act 1978
A&CA 2002	Adoption and Children Act 2002
A&C(S)A 2007	Adoption and Children (Scotland) Act 2007
CA 1989	Children Act 1989
C(S)A 1995	Children (Scotland) Act 1995
CMOPA 2008	Child Maintenance and Other Payments Act 2008
CPA 2004	Civil Partnership Act 2004
CSA 1991	Child Support Act 1991
CSA 1995	Child Support Act 1995
CSPSSA 2000	Child Support, Pensions and Social Security Act 2000
DPMCA 1978	Domestic Proceedings and Magistrates' Courts Act 1978
ERA 1996	Employment Rights Act 1996
FLRA 1969	Family Law Reform Act 1969
HF&EA 1990	Human Fertilisation and Embryology Act 1990
HF&EA 2008	Human Fertilisation and Embryology Act 2008
HRA 1998	Human Rights Act 1998
ICTA 1988	Income and Corporation Taxes Act 1988
ITA 2007	Income Tax Act 2007
IT(EP)A 2003	Income Tax (Earnings and Pensions) Act 2003
IT(TOI)A 2005	Income Tax (Trading and Other Income) Act 2005
LR(PC)(S)A 1986	Law Reform (Parent and Child) (Scotland) Act 1986
MCA 1973	Matrimonial Causes Act 1973
MO(RE)A 1992	Maintenance Orders (Reciprocal Enforcement) Act 1992
SSA 1998	Social Security Act 1998
SSCBA 1992	Social Security Contributions and Benefits Act 1992
TCA 2002	Tax Credits Act 2002
TCEA 2007	Tribunals, Courts and Enforcement Act 2007
WRA 2012	Welfare Reform Act 2012

Regulations and other statutory instruments

Most provisions in regulations have equivalents for each of the three statutory child support schemes. For example, the CS(MASC) Regs contain the '1993 rules' equivalent of the '2003 rules' provisions in the CS(MCSC) Regs, and the CSMC Regs include equivalent provision where appropriate for the '2012 rules'. Unless information specifically relates to '1993 rules' cases, the legislative references in this *Handbook* do not generally relate to '1993 rules' cases. Full legislative referencing for '1993 rules' cases can be found in the 2001/02 and 2002/03 editions of this *Handbook*. If you are unsure of the correct '1993 rules' legislative reference, seek advice.

AS(CSA)(AOCSCR)	The Act of Sederunt (Child Support Act 1991) (Amendment of Ordinary Cause and Summary Cause Rules) 1993 No.919
AS(CSR)	The Act of Sederunt (Child Support Rules) 1993 No.920
AUTCAO	The Appeals from the Upper Tribunal to the Court of Appeal Order 2008 No.2834
C(AP)O	The Children (Allocation of Proceedings) Order 1991 No.1677
CB Regs	The Child Benefit (General) Regulations 2006 No.223
CCR 1981	The County Court Rules 1981 No.1687
CMOPA(Comm 10)O	The Child Maintenance and Other Payments Act 2008 (Commencement No.10 and Transitional Provisions) Order 2012 No.3042
CMOPA(Comm 11)O	The Child Maintenance and Other Payments Act 2008 (Commencement No.11 and Transitional Provisions) Order 2013 No. 1860
CMOPA(Comm 12)O	The Child Maintenance and Other Payments Act 2008 (Commencement No.12 and Savings Provisions) and the Welfare Reform Act 2012 (Commencement No.15) Order 2013 No.2947
CMOPA(Comm 14)O	The Child Maintenance and Other Payments Act 2008 (Commencement No.14 and Transitional Provisions) and Welfare Reform Act 2012 (Commencement No.18 and Transitional and Savings Provisions) Order 2014 No.1635
CP(PSS&CS)(CP)O	The Civil Partnership (Pensions, Social Security and Child Support) (Consequential, etc. Provisions) Order 2005 No.2877

CPA 2004(RACP)O	The Civil Partnership Act 2004 (Relationships Arising Through Civil Partnership) Order 2005 No.3137
CS(AIAMA) Regs	The Child Support (Arrears, Interest and Adjustment of Maintenance Assessments) Regulations 1992 No.1816
CS(APD) Regs	The Child Support (Applications: Prescribed Date) Regulations 2003 No.194
CS(C&E) Regs	The Child Support (Collection and Enforcement) Regulations 1992 No.1989
CS(CEMA) Regs	The Child Support (Collection and Enforcement and Miscellaneous Amendments) Regulations 2000 No.2001/162
CS(CEOFM) Regs	The Child Support (Collection and Enforcement of Other Forms of Maintenance) Regulations 1992 No.2643
CS(ELEC) Regs	The Child Support (Ending Liability in Existing Cases and Transition to New Calculation Rules) Regulations 2014 No.614
CS(MA) Regs	The Child Support (Miscellaneous Amendments) Regulations 2013 No.1517
CS(MAJ) Regs	The Child Support (Maintenance Arrangements and Jurisdiction) Regulations 1992 No.2645
CS(MAP) Regs	The Child Support (Maintenance Assessment Procedure) Regulations 1992 No.1813
CS(MASC) Regs	The Child Support (Maintenance Assessments and Special Cases) Regulations 1992 No.1815
CS(MCP) Regs	The Child Support (Maintenance Calculation Procedure) Regulations 2000 No.2001/157
CS(MCSC) Regs	The Child Support (Maintenance Calculations and Special Cases) Regulations 2000 No.2001/155
CS(MOC&NCR) Regs	The Child Support (Meaning of Child and New Calculation Rules) (Consequential and Miscellaneous Amendment) Regulations 2012 No.2785
CS(MPA) Regs	The Child Support (Management of Payments and Arrears) Regulations 2009 No.3151
CS(MPA)A Regs	The Child Support Management of Payments and Arrears (Amendment) Regulations 2012 No.3002
CS(NIRA) Regs	The Child Support (Northern Ireland Reciprocal Arrangements) Regulations 1993 No.584

CS(NIRA)(A) Regs 2014	The Child Support (Northern Ireland Reciprocal Arrangements) Amendment Regulations 2014 No.1423
CS(V) Regs	The Child Support (Variations) Regulations 2000 No.2001/156
CS(V)(MSP) Regs	The Child Support (Variations) (Modification of Statutory Provisions) Regulations 2000 No.3173
CS(VP) Regs	The Child Support (Voluntary Payments) Regulations 2000 No.3177
CSA(CA)O	The Child Support Act 1991 (Consequential Amendments) Order 1993 No.785
CSA(JC)O	The Child Support Appeals (Jurisdiction of Courts) Order 1993 No.961
CSA(JC)O 2002	The Child Support Appeals (Jurisdiction of Courts) Order 2002 No.1915
CSA(JC)(S)O	The Child Support Appeals (Jurisdiction of Courts) (Scotland) Order 2003 No.96
CSC(P) Regs	The Child Support Commissioners (Procedure) Regulations 1999 No.1305
CSDDCA Regs	The Child Support Departure Direction and Consequential Amendments Regulations 1996 No.2907
CSF Regs	The Child Support Fees Regulations 1992 No.3094
CSF Regs 2014	The Child Support Fees Regulations 2014 No.612
CSI Regs	The Child Support Information Regulations 2008 No.2551
CSM(CBR) Regs	The Child Support Maintenance (Changes to Basic Rate Calculation and Minimum Amount of Liability) Regulations 2012 No.2678
CSMC Regs	The Child Support Maintenance Calculation Regulations 2012 No.2677
FT&UT(CT)O	The First-tier Tribunal and Upper Tribunal (Composition of Tribunal) Order 2008 No.2835
PB(CMEC)O	The Public Bodies (Child Maintenance and Enforcement Commission: Abolition and Transfer of Functions) Order 2012 No.2007
SS(C&P) Regs	The Social Security (Claims and Payments) Regulations 1987 No.1968
SS&CS(DA) Regs	The Social Security and Child Support (Decisions and Appeals) Regulations 1999 No.991

SS&CS(DA)(A) Regs 2013	The Social Security, Child Support, Vaccine Damage and Other Payments (Decisions and Appeals) (Amendment) Regulations 2013 No.2380
TP(A) Rules	The Tribunal Procedure (Amendment) Rules 2013 No.477
TP(FT) Rules	The Tribunal Procedure (First-tier Tribunal) (Social Entitlement Chamber) Rules 2008 No.2685
TP(UT) Rules	The Tribunal Procedure (Upper Tribunal) Rules 2008 No.2698
UC,PIP,JSA&ESA(C&P) Regs	The Universal Credit, Personal Independence Payment, Jobseeker's Allowance and Employment and Support Allowance (Claims and Payments) Regulations 2013 No.380

Index

· ·

How to use this Index

Entries against the bold headings direct you to the general information on the subject, or where the subject is covered most fully. Sub-entries are listed alphabetically and direct you to specific aspects of the subject.

CMS   Child Maintenance Service   CSA   Child Support Agency